# GREEK REALITIES

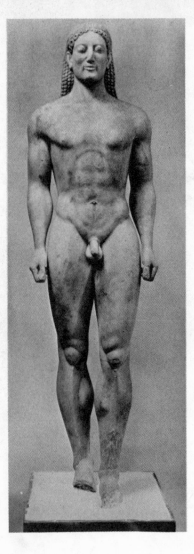

*Finley Hooper*

*Wayne State University*

GREEK

# REALITIES

## LIFE AND THOUGHT IN ANCIENT GREECE

*Wayne State University Press   Detroit, 1978*

*Waynebook 44*

Library of Congress Cataloging in Publication Data

Hooper, Finley Allison, 1922–
  Greek realities.

  Reprint of the 1967 ed. published by Scribner,
New York.
  Bibliography: p.
  Includes index.
  1.  Civilization, Greek.  2.  Greece—History.
I.  Title.
[DF77.H67  1978]      938      78-19547
  ISBN 0-8143-1596-8
  ISBN 0-8143-1597-6 pbk.

TO MOTHER

*Lola Allison Hooper*

# Foreword

Greece is a land of memories, a place for reminiscence. I remember how much I owe to my long-time associates at the Kelsey Museum of Archaeology in Ann Arbor: Enoch E. Peterson, Director Emeritus; Louise A. Shier, Curator of the Museum; and Elinor M. Husselman, recently retired as Curator. I recall too the recent good fortune to have J. G. E. Hopkins of Scribner's read this manuscript and give me the benefit of his experienced eye.

Finally, I remember, with deep appreciation, Goldwin Smith, my friend and colleague at Wayne State University, for his encouragement and his invaluable counsel.

F.H.

*Athens.*

# Contents

# List of Illustrations

## List of Maps

# Introduction

The story of the ancient Greeks has often been yoked unequally to the cause of entertainment. Magazine articles or books written from the romantic point of view effect the impression that Greek civilization was a miraculous occurrence somehow divorced from the ordinary course of human events. The casual reader finds himself in an unreal world he can perhaps enjoy, yet not recognize. To be sure, the dramatic episodes of long ago provide a colorful pageantry, but the greater significance of the ancient Greeks is that they first exposed the human condition in all its wisdom and foolishness for what it has been and what it is likely to remain. Their experience did not encompass all of man's problems, yet they were confronted by a large share of them.

For the most part, this history of the Greek people from the earliest times to the late fourth century B.C. is about a few men whose talents made all the others remembered. That would be true, in part, of any people. In ancient times, the sources of information about the average man and his life were very limited, yet one of the realities of Greek history is the wide disparity in outlook between the creative minority which held the spotlight and the far more numerous goatherders, beekeepers, olive growers, fishermen, seers, and sometimes charlatans, who along with other nameless folk made up the greater part of the population.

Romantic glorifications of Greece create the impression that the Greeks sought rational solutions and were imaginative and intellectually curious as a people. Actually, far from being devoted to the risks of rationality, the vast majority of the Greeks sought always the safe haven of superstition and the comfort of magic charms. Only a relatively few thinkers offered a wondrous variety of ideas in their tireless quest for truth. To study various opinions, each of which appears to have some element of truth, is not a risk everyone should take and by no means did all the ancient Greeks take it. Yet enough did, so as to enable a whole people to be associated with the beginnings of philosophy, including the objectivity of scientific inquiry.

The Greeks who belonged to the creative minority were no more like everybody else than such folk ever have been. More people today would recognize Leonardo da Vinci's *Last Supper* than could identify any given classical statue, yet few who hang a reproduction of that honored painting in their houses really know the artist. Leonardo was not a family man. His familiar painting may hang quietly on the wall but the artist himself—inquisitive, eccentric, even bizarre—would have proved rather disturbing. Nor could all of the Greek poets, artists and philosophers have been so tidily arranged as their works now seem to be. Some, like Leonardo, might not even be welcome to us. They were restless, talkative, critical and sometimes tiresome. Yet their lives as much as their works reveal Greece, for better or for worse, in the way it really was. After Homer, lyric poets went wandering from place to place, in exile from their native cities; before the time of Aristotle, Socrates was executed. If the Greeks invented intellectualism, they were also the first to suppress it. They were, in brief, a people who showed others both how to succeed and how to fail at the things which men might try.

As has often been said, the first democratic society known to man originated in Greece. For this expression of human freedom the Greeks have deservedly received everlasting credit. Yet it is also true that democratic governments were never adopted by a majority of Greek states, and those established were bitterly contested from within and without. In Athens where democracy had its best chance, the government was always threatened by the schemes of oligarchical clubs which sought by any means possible to subvert it. Ironically, Athenian democracy actually failed because of the mistakes of those whom it benefited most, rather than through the machinations of men waiting in the wings to take over. Then, as now, beneath the surface of events there persisted the tension between the material benefits to be obtained through state intervention and the more dynamic vitality which prevails where individuals are left more free to serve and, as it happens, to exploit one another.

A historian must be careful in drawing parallels. The number of individuals in a Greek democracy whose freedom was at stake would be considerably fewer than nowadays. The history of ancient Greece came before the time when all men were created equal. Even the brilliant Aristotle accepted at face value the evidence that certain individuals were endowed with superior qualities. He saw no reason why all men should be treated alike before the law. In fact, he allowed that certain extraordinary persons might be above the law altogether. Some men seemed born to rule and others to serve. There was no common ground between them.

The egalitarian concept that every human being has been endowed by his creator with certain inalienable rights was not a part of the Greek democratic tradition. Pericles, the great Athenian statesman, said that the Athenians considered debate a necessary prelude to any wise action. At the same time, he had a narrow view as to who should do the debating. At Athens, women, foreigners and slaves were all excluded from political life. The actual citizenry was therefore a distinct minority of those living in the city.

In other Greek cities, political power continued to be vested in a small clique (an oligarchy) or in the hands of one man, and often with beneficial results. Various answers to the same political and social problems were proposed and because there were differences there were conflicts. Those who sought to reduce the conflicts also sought to curb the differences, the very same which gave Greek society its exciting vitality. Here we have one of the ironies of human history. Amid bitter often arrogant quarrelsomeness, the Greeks created a civilization which has been much admired. Yet, the price of it has been largely ignored. Hard choices are rarely popular. The Greeks provide the agonizing lesson that men do struggle with one another and in doing so are actually better off than when they live in collective submission to a single idea.

The realities of the whole story should serve to restore a sense of balance. By no means are the Greeks to be left in a sordid and pitiable state, a condition which appears to be the current connotation of the term "realistic." Greek thinkers may have suffered through unsettling self-doubt yet most of them considered this condition to be the starting point for philosophy, not the end of it. Nor were the poets, historians, and philosophers who gave expression to the Greek spirit pitiable men peddling their own personal weaknesses. Their ken was larger than that. The ancient painful dilemmas of human life which they considered still confront us.

*Greek Realities* has an anti-romantic bias but it is not altogether so. While romanticism may tend to overlook the less pleasing aspects of Greek society and to stress only the brighter side, the idealistic view of life is not to be dismissed. Because high ideals are not exactly attainable does not mean that they are not worth pursuing. Courageous action has often been taken by men who believed in more than the facts allowed. Actually, men may at times be so determined to prove themselves worthy of the "ideals" of their ancestors that they act with an honor and justice their antecedents never exhibited. As one man may think more highly of himself than another and so behave in a more assured manner, so too a people who conceive of themselves in the familiar "god-fearing" and "freedom-loving" terms will suffer if this self-image is undermined by those who emphasize only hypocrisy and despair.

The Greek poets and thinkers helped to mold a conception of life which has ever since been hailed as inspirational. Moreover, if anything is to be said in favor of the aristocratic tone in much of their society, it is that men did not cease to strive toward high purposes simply because so few could reach their mark.

Nobility is not a word well-suited to our times. Present-day *literati* search for truth by sifting the selfish, usually hidden, motives (economic or sexual) which presumably account for any and all actions. This bloodless realism ignores the potential qualities of men motivated by faith.

Looking at history is akin to looking at a painting. A man sees mostly what he already knows. The romanticists have loved the Greeks too much. Others tend to slight their intangible qualities. This book argues that reality is a balance between the two. It is not a novel idea.

## The Evidence

In striking contrast to much of modern history, often a *pasticcio* of newspaper and magazine quotations, letters, memoirs and official memoranda, a history of the ancient Greeks is in large part supplied by the best in their literature, including some of the masterpieces of all time. There is no denying that the impression received from the writers of these works has contributed to an unbalanced picture of Greek life. These authors were primarily from the upper ranks of society. They had wealth and education, and so, with a few notable exceptions, lent a refinement to Greek history which has accounted for its enviable reputation as a cultural experience.

The literary tradition in Greece began about the eighth century B.C. with the Homeric epics, the *Iliad* and the *Odyssey*. Before that time, the historian must depend on what archaeologists have discovered, including the ruins of walled cities, palaces, graves, fine jewelry and an abundance of pottery. The pottery has been especially useful for tracing the movements of early peoples and their relative advancements in skill and taste. The clay tablets which date to this earliest period are inscribed in a rudimentary Greek which was adequate for record keeping, but not sufficiently developed to explain what all the records meant, much less to provide a literary account of the times.

Homer's epics preserved old stories which could be sifted for clues to the social and political mores of the earlier "heroic" age. The more mundane poetical works of Hesiod offered actual descriptions of contemporary life. The scarcity of other extant works for the eighth and seventh centuries has meant that almost any chance fragment of lyric or choral poetry may provide a historical note. There are also available certain fragments of law codes dated to the seventh century. The coins which began to be used about that time add a story of their own. Lists of the athletic victors at Olympia date back to 776 B.C. and the names of the magistrates at Athens to 683 B.C. Any continuous narrative of events for the period in which the Greeks were slowly developing the pattern to be known in full bloom as Hellenism is altogether lacking.

History for history's sake was not written until the sixth century. By that time, at least a few men were willing to wonder if the myths which gave each city an equally marvelous origin should not be supplemented by a serious attempt to learn what really happened. Hecataeus of Miletus was the most famous of the pioneer historians but only fragments of his work remain. Solid ground is not reached before the middle of the fifth century when Herodotus wrote *The Persian Wars*. This work together with Thucydides' *History of the Peloponnesian War,* composed toward the end of the century, and Xenophon's *Hellenica* which began where Thucydides left off and continued to 362 B.C., make up the core of Greek history. Together, these three works, which include references to earlier times, allow for a general sketch of events during the sixth, fifth and early fourth centuries. However, they provide a continuous year-to-year chronicle only for certain limited periods within that time span. For instance, while Athens plays a pre-eminent role in these histories, the political history of that city for the years at the end of the sixth century and the beginning of the fifth century is given only in rough outline. There would be less to say about the middle years of the century were it not that democratic leaders, at Athens and elsewhere, began about that time to have laws and treaties inscribed on stone for public inspection. This documentary evidence is spotty, however, and while the surviving inscriptions offer details about important matters, other equally significant questions remain unanswered.

The dramatists of the fifth century were interested in entertaining their contemporary audiences, not in educating future readers, but their extant plays do provide certain insights into the political life of the times. The topical comedies of Aristophanes, which name names and air accusations, are especially intriguing.

In the fourth century, when dramatists began to be more discreet in their references, the orations of Isocrates, Lysias and Demosthenes and the writings of the philosophers, especially Plato and Aristotle, supplement the historical commentaries of Ephorus and Theopompus. However, unlike Herodotus and Thucydides, whose literary talents guaranteed their works a place in the "great books" tradition, these two latterday historians did not have staying power beyond ancient times. Like so much else that was eventually lost, however, their histories lasted long enough to be used by later writers and so were in part transmitted secondhand. Thus, the writings of the Roman Cornelius Nepos, and the Sicilian Diodorus, who wrote in the first century B.C., and of the Greeks, Arrian and especially Plutarch who were writing in the second century A.D., are extremely valuable even though they discuss events which occurred centuries before their own times. Plutarch (*circa* 46–*circa* 120 A.D.), a native of Chaeronea in Boeotia, has been particularly noted for his *Parallel Lives,* in which he matches famous Greeks and Romans in short biographies which reveal his divided interest between history and character study. After the works of Herodotus, Thucydides and Xenophon, the *Lives* are perhaps the most useful source material available for Greek history. Obviously, what Plutarch chose to preserve of materials now lost leaves the present-day historian at the mercy of his judgment. Yet, in a facile style which has stood the test of time, he put flesh on bare bones and without him the record would be no better and certainly much barer than it is.

Another writer of the second century A.D., Pausanias, was an inveterate traveler whose encyclopedic *Description of Greece* was based on the notes he took about the places he visited and the people he talked to. This work is a mine of information about topography, local traditions and religious cults. Pausanias also bridges seventeen hundred years in presenting ancient sites as they looked in his own day. His descriptions of statuary and buildings still standing at that time have been invaluable to the historians of Greek art. He has also supplied clues to archaeologists about where to search for monuments subsequently buried by chance or hidden on purpose.

In addition to the works of these significant writers, a collection of bits and pieces—mostly quotations from works of lesser known authors—has contributed to the building of the Greek historical tradition, a record which in places may be as mythical as the legendary lore it tries to forget and replace.

It is convenient for an historian writing about ancient times occasionally to use the phrase "the tradition says" without citing specific sources. The reader is thereby warned that what follows is information passed down from generation to generation without any positive means of checking the truthfulness of the original source. It is obviously a device by which an historian may salve his conscience while keeping the story going. Moreover, the method is as old as Herodotus who occasionally admitted that what he was about to relate was not based on what he had seen, only what he had heard.

## *Fertile Plains, Mountains and Coast*

Greece has magnificent ruins, beautiful scenery and (most of the time) good weather. It has never been the land of opportunity.

The mainland and the islands have a surface area which is only upwards of 50,000 square miles. This may not have seemed as small in the ancient world as it does on a modern scale, yet it makes little difference; there was never much of this space that was useable. In contrast with the monotonous, but productive flatlands of the American plains states—Kansas with its 82,000 square miles for instance—Greece offers extraordinary contrasts of terrain within short distances. Mountain ranges, mostly of limestone with some marble (especially in east Greece), cut the land in all directions leaving numerous fertile, but relatively small, plains in the valleys and along the coast.

On a map the sea never looks far away. However, for those living in central Greece, cut off by the mountains, it may be a long way around—especially on a donkey with a makeshift saddle, which is still the standard means of transportation in rural Greece.

The inland plains are also cut off from the comfortable winds which in the coastal regions help to assuage the dry and hot summers and so account for the salubrious weather for which the Mediterranean is famous. In general, the winters in Greece are mild except in the mountains. There is ample rainfall, especially on the western side, but it is the sunshine, to be expected nearly everywhere at almost anytime, which has given the people of this land their reputation for outdoor living.

In ancient times, government, business and the arts were practiced under the sky. Moreover, the climate which made this possible has also been used to explain the robustness of life among the Greeks, especially their talkativeness. Suffice it to say that they have always had more practice than peoples in northerly lands who have less chance to talk to neighbors from late autumn to early spring. The truth about the weather anywhere is that it may occasionally be surprising. Nevertheless reputation means a lot to "good weather" people. A downpour in May on the idyllic and "always sunny" island of Cos prompts the natives to express shock and dismay. They will tell you that the oldest man alive on the island cannot remember rain so late in the year. It is a good story and it stands up well, unless it rains for three days in a row.

In many parts of the world today industrialization and rapid transportation have shaded the old geographical boundaries between mountain, plain and shore. In Greece that process is only now beginning to take place. Certainly in ancient times geography largely determined how a man earned his living. In the highlands, which remained grassy during the summer droughts, the villagers lived a pastoral existence tending sheep, goats and pigs. Because the mountains were more heavily forested with cedar, cypress and pine than they are now, timber was a natural product. There was also some beekeeping. That was about all.

Life in this sparsely settled region was uncomplicated except that chances for a livelihood were limited. Consequently, there was a tendency for extra sons to move down into the lowlands where they were not always welcome. In the more densely settled plains the land was carefully parcelled out for grain, vineyards, and for orchards of figs and especially olives, one of the necessities of Greek life. It has always been a familiar measure of the simple economy of the times that the Greeks used olive oil for cooking, for soap, and for the fuel in their lamps.

Fishing was another possibility of employment and, here and there, some mining. Yet metals, except silver and copper, were scarce and coal non-existent. This shortage of minerals was not as crucial a matter in ancient times as it has proved to be in the modern age of industry; still, it helps to account for the fact that Greece always was, and has remained, primarily agricultural. There are productive bauxite mines in operation today, but only tobacco has managed to top olives and wine in the list of Greek exports.

Beginning about the eighth century B.C., the indigent from the rural areas could seek a new start in the centers of commerce which began to grow up near the sea as outlets for the export of domestic goods. But these cities were never large by modern standards, nor was "manufacturing" advanced enough to absorb all the unemployed. Then as now, the final answer was emigration.

This description of highland, lowland and coast does not mean that the history of Greece is a story of three regions. In the north, Thessaly is largely a land of plains surrounded by mountains. In the Peloponnesus, Arcadia is mostly mountainous. Many sections of Greece, the peninsula of Attica among them, include a balance of all three of the main features: fertile plains, mountains and coast. The same variety is true of the islands. Corcyra (modern Corfu), off the west coast, and Euboea, a larger island stretching along the eastern coast, have arable land, wooded highlands, and harbors through which to trade with the mainland. On the other hand, certain islands like Salamis, little more than the peaks of submerged mountain ranges, are too small and too rocky to support more than a sparse population of fishermen and other seafarers. The Aegean islands to the east of Attica have marble deposits and small plains, but if they produce anything it is usually olives and wine. The largest group is the Cyclades, arranged around small and rocky Delos which because of its good harbor acted in ancient times as a trading post for goods traveling east or west. That advantage gave this otherwise barren island an amazing prosperity even when the rest of Greece was in the throes of a slow decline.

Neither on the Greek mainland nor in the islands was there in antiquity a geographical interdependence which might have encouraged unification and a central government, as the Nile required in Egypt. Settlers in places like Attica or Euboea could be relatively self-sufficient. Moreover, communications in the early years were rudimentary and trade, even between various parts of the mainland, was better conducted by sea than overland. Local custom and local history encouraged the growth of a number of small states, each with parochial pride and a closely guarded citizenship. Where the political life of an area was centralized in a single dominant city—Athens in Attica, Corinth in Corinthia or Sparta in Laconia—the resulting government was a *polis*, or city-state. In other places, towns formed federal leagues and pooled their resources for joint defense. Nevertheless, they too were often dominated by a single city-state, as was shown by the long and often hectic association between Thebes and her neighbors in Boeotia. The smaller towns were determined to defend their local autonomy in most matters.

In brief, the story of ancient Greece is not the story of a nation. It is rather the story of a people who shared language, religion and literature, yet remained politically a family of small independent states, sometimes cooperating against an outsider but usually venting their tempers on one another. Taken singly, especially Athens, their contributions to Western art and thought were invaluable, yet taken together these little states with their petty jealousies and intrigues wore themselves down into a condition of disgrace and helplessness.

The firmest friendship survives a knowledge of faults as well as virtues. At some things worth doing, the Greeks excelled any human effort since, but (to be honest) we must admit that at other things worth doing they failed very badly. It is an irony, perhaps better implied in their story than stated here, that the reason they succeeded so well on the one hand was precisely why they failed on the other. To know this is perhaps to know something about life itself. Their successes and their failures go together. So do their shining ideals and their bewildering behavior.

# PART ONE

*Before the Fifth Century B.C.*

# Prehistory and the Bronze Age

I

History is a continuous story at both ends of the scale. A recorder of modern events revises his last chapter; the historian of ancient times worries about the first. His account begins in that hazy period before the invention of writing, and each time some village buried for thousands of years is suddenly uncovered he has an earlier dateline even if not much new data. Only when men succeeded in complicating their lives beyond hunting and fishing did they feel a need for written records. Their history prior to their use of writing must be sketched from whatever they left behind, including their own remains.

Recovering this evidence is the work of the archaeologist, a hardy professional who thrives on hard labor, painstaking research and a small budget. Or so it has seemed since the time of Heinrich Schliemann (1822–1890) who pioneered the work in classical lands beginning in 1871. Schliemann was not as careful a workman as his successors have learned to be, but he had money and it was his own.

Schliemann was the kind of man for whom a shipwreck could be a blessing. The son of a poor clergyman in a small town in northern Germany, he went to work as a grocery clerk when he was fourteen.

Later, as a cabin boy on an ill-fated ship bound for South America, he landed in a Dutch hospital owning only the clothes on his back. Amsterdam was his city of destiny. There he began an intensive study of languages and his amazing facility with seven tongues besides his own opened doors to him in the Dutch market place. It was the door to St. Petersburg which led to his success as an expert broker in Russian exports. At twenty-five, Schliemann was in business for himself. By the time he was forty he was a millionaire.

The amazing speed with which this self-made man accumulated money was matched by the unorthodox way he chose to spend it. While developing a shrewd capacity for business, he had never abandoned his childhood love of lost worlds. The age of heroes which Homer had described he found especially fascinating. Schliemann's contemporaries had good reason to suspect that such a time never existed. Some said Homer had not either.

Homer was as real to Schliemann as he was to the classical Greeks. Although men in the fifth century B.C. knew no more of their greatest poet than we do now, they did not doubt that he had lived some three or four centuries before their own time and that the stories he told were true. From his epics they learned how their distant ancestors had sailed across the Aegean Sea and sacked the rich city of Troy. The *Iliad* was a tale woven around one of these warriors, Achilles, whose strength and weaknesses had had a decisive impact on the lives of his companions. Among them was Odysseus, whose perilous trip home to Ithaca was described in the *Odyssey*.

Schliemann was convinced that the fabulous ruined city of Troy must still be buried somewhere in northwestern Asia Minor (modern Turkey) and he was willing to pay to prove that he was right. Nor was he a man for time-consuming speculation. He packed up and went in search of history and treasure. With him was his second wife, a young Greek girl whom he had married when he was forty-six and she was seventeen. It was another good investment. On the job she was a godsend.

Schliemann's fascination with gold was well known. He had become an American citizen because he happened to be on hand for the gold rush just before California was admitted as a state. Now, half a world away, he would find the city where King Priam's treasure lay. Earlier unsuccessful attempts by others had fed the suspicion that Priam and his reputed wealth were only a myth but Schliemann trusted Homer. While the poet had not said exactly where Troy was located, his description of the place offered valuable

BLACK
SEA

MACEDONIA

THRACE

EPIRUS

THESSALY

Agios
Georgios

AEGEAN

Troy

ASIA

EUBOEA

MINOR

Orchomenus

Thebes

SEA

Corinth

Athens

GULF OF CORINTH

Mycenae

ARGOLIS

Tiryns

CYCLADES

Miletus

PELOPONNESUS

Bodrum (Modern)

Pylos

Sparta

Vaphio

DELOS

RHODES

MELOS

CRETE

Knossos

Phaistos

Mallia

MEDITERRANEAN     SEA

MAP 1
THE BRONZE AGE

0          100          200 MILES

SAMᴸ H. BRYANT

clues. Schliemann guessed where it should be and there to be sure it was—just south of the Hellespont, buried beneath a hill called Hissarlik. The so-called "Trojan letters" which Schliemann wrote at this site show that although he is easily caricatured as a gold-seeker he was at the same time a man sincerely dedicated to discovery.

To his everlasting credit, this enthusiastic amateur had indeed found the lost city of Troy. Actually he had found nine Troys, one on top of the other, although their delineation had to await the more precise work of his young associate Wilhelm Dörpfeld. Through the centuries, from about 2600 B.C. onwards, ruined buildings of clay brick or stone, whether leveled by earthquake or victorious marauders, had supplied the base for a new city to follow. The analogy to a layer cake has often been used because it is a good one.

Schliemann had proved that Troy belonged to history, not fiction. His next move was less memorable. In his enthusiasm to find Priam's rich city he dug hurriedly to the level of Troy II and in the process destroyed, or at least disturbed, valuable evidence in the layers above.

Subsequent work at Troy revealed that the nine major levels could be subdivided into forty-six sections. In the nineteen-thirties the American archaeologist Carl Blegen showed that the lower section of the seventh level (Troy VII a) was the important one. It was not as rich a city as the great Troy VI or even Schliemann's Troy II, but nonetheless it was near the walls of this sacked city with its unburied corpses that Priam's son, noble Hector, tamer of horses, was slain by fleet-footed Achilles. So said Homer.

Achilles was only one of the well-known warriors who had come by sea to attack this strategic city, rich from tolls, a gateway to Asia Minor. What of his homeland? Where were the cities whence he and the others, Ajax, Nestor and Diomedes, had sailed? Surely their leader, the mighty Agamemnon, a king among kings, had been buried in some fabulous tomb. Schliemann believed that he knew where to look. Back in Greece the ruins of Mycenae stood in the plain of Argolis. They had been there in Homer's day and the poet had known from the old sagas that this city had once been richer and grander than Troy.

Atop the acropolis at Mycenae thick walls enclosed the citadel. Did the graves of long lost heroes lie somewhere within these ruins? For Schliemann there were no doubts to be removed, only centuries of debris. In December, 1876, he found what he was looking for. Within a grave circle formed by stone markers, he uncovered a series of royal burials containing fifteen skeletons (two more were found later). Around them all that glittered was gold. Not just pieces of gold, but finely wrought cups, daggers and jewelry, including funerary diadems (Pl. 1, 2). Most spectacular of all were the golden death masks

*Pl. 1 Gold diadem found during Schliemann's excavations, from Shaft Grave III at Mycenae*

*Pl. 2 Head of a stickpin, gold and silver, from the same grave as the diadem*

equipped with hooks that were used to attach them like spectacles to the ears of the corpses (Pl. 3, 4). While each face was distinguishable one from the other, they all had stylized beards, sharp noses and thin lips. A cautious researcher would have hesitated to identify them but Schliemann wired the king of Greece that he had found Agamemnon.

No one knows even yet the actual identity of the persons placed to rest in these tombs, but the riches they took with them (at least as far as the grave) left no doubt that they belonged to a ruling Mycenaean dynasty. Today, the gold mask of Schliemann's "Agamemnon" is simply labeled as that of "an 'Achaean' king," but it is prominently featured in its own small pedestal case in the National Archaeological Museum in Athens. The mask is back to back with a golden cup from the same grave. The other masks are in cases nearby in a central room off the main entrance hall of the museum. The profusion of the golden items which the visitor sees here recalls again Schliemann's near uncontrollable excitement as he lifted these articles from the earth.

In later years Schliemann continued his search for other heroes who had lived and died in neighboring kingdoms. Although he excavated at Orchomenus in 1880, it was not until 1884–85 that he made his next major find and his last one. In the Argolid plain, at Tiryns, just south of Mycenae, he uncovered the ruins of an impressive palace including pottery and paintings similar in style to the materials already discovered. These excavations and those since

LEFT: *Pl. 3 Gold-foil death mask from Shaft Grave V at Mycenae, circa 1550 B.C.* RIGHT: *Pl. 4 Mask of an "Achaean king," Schliemann's "Agamemnon," from Shaft Grave V at Mycenae, circa 1550 B.C.*

Schliemann's day, including Professor Blegen's skillful work at Pylos, have revealed a flourishing civilization built by the conquerors of Troy. It has been called Mycenaean after that premier city in an era of brilliance and prosperity of which we now know more than Homer did. And we will know even more tomorrow. In central and southern Greece, a recent study has pinpointed nearly 390 different sites where materials of the Mycenaean type have been found and others are likely buried.

The work which Schliemann began was carried on by men of greater competence and scholarship but no one has ever had as much help from the gods. Only the British archaeologist Sir Arthur Evans came close to approximating Schliemann's success in finding treasure-filled cities. Sir Arthur belonged to the new breed of professionals. Heinrich Schliemann had lived in an era of his own. The story was told, true or not, that he had actually invoked the Olympian deities. There has never been such a tale even imagined about his more scholarly successors.

In 1900, Evans went to Crete to pursue his interest in early forms of writing. While there he became curious about the upcroppings of ruins near the center of the northern coast of the island. The ancient Cretan city of Knossos was reported to have been located in this area. Schliemann, who had died in 1890, had been interested in these ruins but negotiations for the land collapsed over the price. The owner had lied about the number of olive trees he was losing. Schliemann, wearing his business hat, had counted them.

The olive grove was truly deceptive. Beneath this land Evans unearthed a great palace which covered five-and-a-half acres. It was the show place of a Cretan civilization even more magnificent than that of the mainland. Evans made a career of Knossos and worked there for over a quarter of a century. During that time he began the restoration of the palace which has made Knossos one of the outstanding tourist attractions in the Mediterranean area. Visitors familiar with the grandeur that was Rome nineteen hundred years ago might well be fascinated with the modernity and magnificence of a city twice as old again.

## A Long Prehistoric Period

The spectacular finds at Troy, Mycenae and Knossos belonged to an age which was "late" in terms of the earliest settlements in the Aegean region. Before the time of these Bronze Age cities, there was a long prehistoric period which Homer had never heard about. In this earlier shadowy epoch, a great variety of peoples had migrated into the Aegean area. Those who came first did not even have a bow and arrow, whereas men later on brought developed customs and skills. The last of the strangers to arrive were people from the north who only slowly made their way into the land which their descendants have called Hellas and we call Greece. With some mixing these Greek-speaking peoples have been there ever since. And yet, other men had lived in the land many thousands of years before they arrived.

From the earliest hammer to the atom bomb, the ages of man have been named for his tools and weapons. In the long Palaeolithic, or Old Stone Age, men were nomadic hunters ever on the move in search of game. The traces they left in Greece were not evidence of permanent settlements, but only of periodic sojourns which lasted long enough for them to leave behind deposits of crude axes and skin scrapers. Such finds anywhere are scarce, but in Greece especially so. Recently, however, in northern Greece, at a site near the village of Agios Georgios, British archaeologists have discovered a great quantity and variety of prehistoric implements. The accumulation of rhinoceros, bear and deer bones meant that, relatively speaking, the area was prosperous. The men who trapped these animals in pits or drove them over cliffs to slaughter about forty or fifty thousand years ago have been hailed as the earliest inhabitants of Greece. These hunters and their successors were "passing through" until about seven thousand years ago. Then came the transition to the Neolithic, or New Stone Age.

There are numerous sites in Crete, in the Aegean Islands and in mainland Greece especially Thessaly, where the rudimentary legacy of Neolithic settlers has revealed that they were settled down and were raising crops and tending animals. They had abandoned the nomadic gathering of food and were doing just a little better than staying alive. Moreover, somewhere along the way they had discovered a fertility goddess to thank for it.

She has also been helpful to archaeologists. Clay statuettes featuring outré buttocks and pendulous breasts have been found at widespread Neolithic sites around the Aegean shores. The same conspicuousness is a characteristic of the squat figurines discovered throughout the Near East where Mother Earth became all important in a crop-growing society. This coincidence, along with similar characteristic Eastern styles of pottery, offers evidence to show that the Aegean Neolithic settlers had migrated westward by sea from the general area now occupied by Turkey, Syria and Palestine. Apparently in the older area their ancestors had learned to produce a food surplus by means of domesticated plants and animals. That simple but revolutionary step allowed some men to pursue occupations other than hunting and fishing. They could be spared from the struggle for existence and with their "leisure" time began to make pottery and cloth, and presumably boats.

It would be pretentious to categorize the political, social and religious life of these Neolithic settlements. All activity was regulated by a tribal system in which custom ordered behavior. The few goods produced were mostly intended for local use. Commercial dealings, tax collecting systems and government inventories, all of which might require written records, were still a long way off.

For men using implements of stone and bone, the next revolutionary step was the gradual adoption of copper followed by the introduction of bronze, an alloy of copper and tin. These changes were momentous, but there is not enough known about them to be sure when or how they happened. For convenience sake, it may be said that the Aegean world passed from the Neolithic stage into the Bronze Age about 2600 B.C. Yet even this general statement must be qualified. The new metals meant the beginning of a new age only for those who had them. The advantages of using a bronze tool or weapon did not at first belong to all the Aegean peoples alike. Moreover, neighboring peoples might each possess bronze and yet have distinctly different cultural patterns, with one group actually advanced over the other in technique and standards of taste. Communications in the ancient world never challenged local custom the way they do today and the farther back we go, the more true that would be.

## Bronze Age Chronology

Archaeologists, noted for "camping out," actually spend most of their time indoors classifying objects. The result is history in the form of a chart. For the Bronze Age (*circa* 2600–*circa* 1125)* they have arranged in chronological order their findings from each of four major regions of the Aegean area: Crete, mainland Greece, the islands, and

---

* B.C. and A.D. will be eliminated where the designation of the date is obvious.

Troy. This information shatters the grand simplification of an Aegean civilization by showing that it is a picture puzzle of many pieces.

In Crete the name of the fabulous, and maybe fabled, King Minos was put to practical use when Evans decided to divide the Bronze Age for the island into three time periods. The approximate dates currently being quoted are: Early Minoan (2600–2000); Middle Minoan (2000–1600); and Late Minoan (1600–1125). According to Evans' findings, each of these divisions could in turn be subdivided. The result was Early Minoan I, Early Minoan II and Early Minoan III, and the same for the Middle and Late periods. This arrangement was based on archaeological data, not on lists of kings or eyewitness reports.

The physical remains at various sites are like bank accounts in that they reflect the ebb and flow of fortune which is the stuff of history. For instance, between Early Minoan II (*circa* 2300–2100) and Early Minoan III (*circa* 2100–2000) there was an apparent shift in power from east Crete to central Crete where "cities" like Knossos and Phaistos developed. These were not really modern cities, but places where houses and shops clustered nearby a complex series of buildings which we call a palace. This development foreshadowed the more significant break between all of Early Minoan times and the Middle Minoan age to follow. A relatively simple life of many small villages gave way to a more sophisticated society in which a few centers dominated the land and enhanced their wealth by means of "international" trade. These later times of elaborate palaces, up-to-date fashions, and skillful works of art may deserve a more imaginative title, but archaeologists have been true to their science and Middle Minoan it is.

In order to arrange this timetable so as to agree with our own dating system there had to be a common reference. For this purpose the exchange of goods carried on between the Aegean centers and Egypt has proved invaluable. The Egyptians left elaborate records of the reigns of their Pharaohs and by using these as a frame of reference their history has been recast according to our dates. The Aegean kingdoms were not so accommodating. Nevertheless easily datable Egyptian objects discovered at Aegean sites or Aegean articles found in Egyptian tombs supply clues by which their time may reasonably be established. Of course the clues may sometimes be false. Articles discovered together need not be any more contemporaneous than are for instance the rejected treasures in your attic.

## Cretan Prosperity

During the Bronze Age, the island of Crete achieved a bountiful economic and artistic life earlier than the other parts of the Aegean world. The exchange of goods with Egypt began sooner in Crete and this communication with an established center of civilization has always supplied a ready explanation for an early blossoming. The Cretans may also have learned about the usefulness of metals before their neighbors. Certainly they had advanced techniques of seamanship. Whatever the advantages of these islanders, they made the most of them. The distribution of their pottery and the widespread influence of Minoan motifs have shown how extensively they traveled in all parts of the surrounding waters.

The wealth and power accruing to Crete from its own resources and from overseas ventures have prompted the tag "little England" as a likely analogy. In a romantic sense this may have been true but, to be realistic, how far can commerce develop without a coinage? Cretan prosperity must have depended on the successful barter of items then current in international trade. Presumably their ships carried special items like ivory and obsidian as well as cargoes of skins, olive oil, wine and timber. Archaeologists have found ingots of copper stored on the island. In the absence of any evidence to the contrary, it has been assumed that these slabs of metal weighing sixty pounds or more were used for balance of trade payments. At least the guess seems logical.

Ingots of this type are on display in the Archaeological Museum of Heraclion, the modern city near the ancient site of Knossos. This spacious museum houses the lion's share of the materials which have been recovered in Crete. Currency ingots are also exhibited at Bodrum, the Turkish town situated where ancient Halicarnassus once stood. The small, but up-to-date museum at this place has a special interest because it displays some of the finds from the recent underwater archaeological expeditions conducted off the coast of Turkey. Apparently not all of the payments reached their destination.

The memory of Cretan power in the eastern Mediterranean has been preserved in the story of the Athenian hero Theseus defeating the Minotaur (half man, half bull). According to the legend, the Athenians had been required each year to send a payment of seven

youths and seven maidens to Crete. Theseus with the help of Minos'
daughter Ariadne finally ended this disgraceful subservience. Were
there any historical clues hidden amid the romance of this myth? It
has been suggested that Theseus was actually seeking to end the
impressment of Athenian youths into the Cretan navy. If so, the myth
bore witness to a naval power which at one time or another dominated the Aegean Sea. Archaeologists have been more exact. Their
evidence shows that Crete was enjoying her greatest days during the
period designated as Middle Minoan III and Late Minoan I—roughly
the three hundred years between 1750 and 1450.

The excavations of Cretan palaces have supplied the best evidence of the life and times of this period. Attention usually centers
on the principal city Knossos and the second city Phaistos, but there
have also been informative finds in less pretentious palaces such as
the one at Mallia. At these sites the problem has not been merely to
recover a single structure which had been built and later buried;
archaeologists have found remains of buildings reconstructed at various times along with the evidence of changes made in between.

Earthquakes during the Bronze Age were hard on Cretan architecture. They still are. In examining the effects of an earthquake on
a Minoan palace in the sixteenth century B.C. or on a house shattered
as recently as A.D. 1935, the cracks in partly demolished walls are
seen to run the same way, diagonally upward toward the south.

Atop the primary Neolithic material at Knossos was evidence of
a palace which had been damaged by an earthquake about 1700 B.C.
Studies showed that this building and others at Phaistos and Mallia
were later repaired and enlarged and then toppled by another catastrophe in the sixteenth century. At Knossos, there followed a much
grander palace which extended over and included the previously used
space. The rapidity with which this residence was rebuilt attests to
the continuing prosperity of the Cretans at the time.

The time of building of this last great palace of the Cretan
civilization has served archaeologists as a dividing point between the
Middle Minoan III period and Late Minoan I. But the construction
was not so much a peak as it was a significant point in the plateau
from 1750 to 1450. Before this prosperous period there was a slow
development; not long afterwards, a decline.

Although the king at Knossos needed and could afford a larger
establishment than was necessary at Phaistos, the palaces at these
major centers were much alike. Both were multi-level complexes with
rooms of all sizes, including an unusual variety of large and small

*Pl. 5 Light well and grand staircase in the east wing of the Palace at Knossos*

halls for state meetings and receptions. At Knossos, in the rebuilding after 1700, the grand staircase which so often appears in photographs of the palace (Pl. 5) was added. It began at the Hall of Colonnades and led up to the second and third floors, where most of the space was given over to living quarters with some rooms apparently grouped together as apartments. Among the other facilities of the palace were a variety of "service" rooms including workshops where furniture might be made or repaired. Storerooms were everywhere and the containers once used for storing wine and grain are still to be seen.

For all its surprising complexity, the palace at Knossos was still not in a class with Louis XIV's Versailles although the idea was similar. The king kept an eye on his relatives and nobles by having them live on the premises. Because of the many internal rooms it was necessary to build light wells here and there, just as in modern apartment structures. But the real surprise of the living quarters were the bathrooms served by drains and an extensive sewerage system. A small room in the palace at Knossos, which has been dubbed the Queen's Lavatory, was equipped with a flush toilet, an extraordinarily refined accommodation for so early a date. The use of metals had indeed revolutionized society. In the earlier Neolithic period there were of course houses, at least for tribal leaders, but many families were still living in caves. Zeus, so says the myth, was born in one.

Gaily colored plants and animals were the chief subjects in the imaginative frescoes which decorated the rooms and hallways at Knossos. The paintings now seen *in situ* at the palace are copies. The fragments of the originals which have survived are exhibited in splendid fashion in Room K, the Hall of the Minoan Frescoes, in the Archaeological Museum of Heraclion. Among them are the remarkable *La Parisienne* (Pl. 6) and the *Cup-bearer* (Pl. 7) which bring to mind Picasso and an ancient Egyptian stylist both at once.

The Cretan artists who hurriedly but skillfully dashed paint on the wet plaster at Knossos remain nameless, even though their naturalism and *joie de vivre* delight us so today. Their interest in nature for its own sake was strikingly secular. Missing were the usual foreboding solemnities so typical of other early societies.

The popularity of exported Minoan pottery is understandable in view of its attractiveness. Surviving examples exhibit flowers in pastel

LEFT: *Pl. 6 Priestess, the so-called* La Parisienne, *circa 1500–1450 B.C., fragment of fresco from the Palace at Knossos.* RIGHT: *Pl. 7 Fragment of fresco from the Palace at Knossos.* Cup-bearer, *circa 1500–1450 B.C.*

LEFT: *Pl. 8 Three-handled jar (helmet design) from a tomb at Katsamba, harbor town of Knossos, circa 1400 B.C.* RIGHT: *Pl. 9 Three-handled* pithos *(fish design) from Old Palace of Phaistos, Middle Minoan II*

shades of pink and blue and orange. There was also a willingness to borrow ideas from abroad, as seen in the frequent ingenuous displays of the papyrus plant indigenous to Egypt. This was part of a continuing search for novelty evident in fresh designs combining rocks, seaweed and fish. Lively spirals were everywhere a useful decoration in the ancient world, and the Cretan artists used them too, but they also delighted to think of variations. Why not, for example, substitute the curling tentacles of octopuses? (Pl. 8, 9, 10, 16.)

*Pl. 10 Lentoid flask (octopus design) from Palaikastro, east Crete, circa 1500 B.C.*

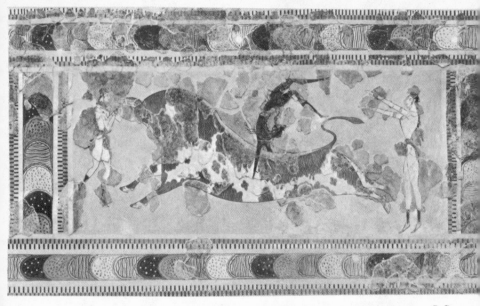

*Pl. 11 Bull-ring fresco from the Palace at Knossos,* circa *1500 B.C.*

Cretan artists showed an extraordinary boldness in the use of colors. In their frescoes, if they wanted to paint a monkey blue they did, and so added brightness of accent to match the agility of the animals which enlivened the wall of some dimly lit room.

The occasional frescoes which show dancers, soldiers or athletes are among the best-known works by these Cretan painters. Especially famous is a bull-leaping scene in which trim young men and girls are engaged in gymnastic exercises over the backs of bulls (Pl. 11). This so-called "Toreador" fresco and the frequent scenes of boxers show the Cretans to have been forerunners of the Greeks in their stress on athletics.

The colorful art and its display of a lively sociability between men and women in Crete gives an impression of modernity. In religion, although the dominance of the female had not changed since the Neolithic period, the Cretan conception of their chief deity had been updated. At the height of the Bronze Age she was still a nature goddess, but her appearance had been radically altered (Pl. 12). In contrast with the earlier fetish-like appearance, she had become a graceful figure dressed in the fashion of the day. The extant statuettes from the Middle Minoan period display full skirts touching the ground. The short-sleeved blouses are tightly bodiced at the waist, but open at the front with the breasts entirely exposed. The costume was typical of the times and only the symbols of divinity marked the goddess. She was frequently adorned with snakes. One might be placed around her neck and then entwined around her arms. In another example she is shown with arms outstretched holding a snake in each hand.

The snake was a familiar symbol in ancient times and there could scarcely have been a more ambivalent one. The Cretans, however, seem to have regarded serpents more with reverence than with fear. On the household level, the snake was popularly considered a "good luck" charm. As an attribute of the goddess the snake appeared as a symbol of her protective care for the community. The deity also had her special bird and was frequently shown with a dove perched on her head.

If the stream of Cretan religious life ran back in time to the East, in the future it was to extend its influence northward to the mainland. The Athenians as late as the seventh century B.C. sent to Crete for a purifier when their city became "polluted" from blood shed on holy ground. A plausible conclusion would be that the arts

*Pl. 12 Faience goddess with snakes and dove from the Palace at Knossos, circa 1600–1580 B.C.*

of divination had spread from Crete northward and that in time of serious trouble the mainlanders sought an expert at the source.

No temples were built during the Bronze Age as in later classical times. State rites were conducted in the palace. Archaeologists have designated certain rooms as shrines wherein Cretan kings, like the rulers in earlier Near Eastern kingdoms, served as chief priests and conducted rites for the welfare of all. On the walls at Knossos were prominent drawings of the double axe sacred to the chief goddess. Interestingly enough, the Greeks who borrowed the term *labrys* for double axe from the Lydians later referred to the palace in their myths as the labyrinth.

Ordinary men worshipped at small household altars or perhaps more frequently out-of-doors. In Crete, the adoration of pillars and the worship of trees and streams foreshadowed a day when the olive tree became sacred to Athena and it was said that a brook at Delphi carried the voice of Apollo.

At Knossos, a simple, straight-back, armless stone throne identifies the Throne Room. The stone benches around the wall suggest the sitting of a council or perhaps a court. A sunken area, called a lustral basin, partially partitioned off at one side, was undoubtedly used for

*Pl. 13 Throne Room (restored) of the Palace at Knossos*

ritual bathing. In view of the civil and religious powers held by the king, there can be little argument against the notion that proceedings of an official character began with sacred ceremonials (Pl. 13).

When visiting this low-pitched and small, somewhat mysterious chamber, a visitor's attention is easily diverted from the question of its possible uses by the colorful murals so generously added by modern restorers. The extant portions of the original frescoes served to inspire the present decoration of the room. Evans found the remains of a couchant wingless griffin on either side of a doorway in the west wall. During the subsequent restoration work, a similar pattern of matching griffins (with considerable elaboration) was painted on the wall behind the throne. The bright reds, yellows and blues in these paintings give the room a rather startling appearance but, as previously noted, there is ample evidence at Knossos and elsewhere to show that the Cretans overcame drabness in their palaces with brilliantly painted columns and walls. The degree of satisfaction which the modern work affords varies with the individual beholder. The tourist enjoys the spirit of the restoration. It means there is something to see. The specialist focuses a critical eye on the figures themselves. For instance, it has been suggested that bulls, symbolic of the king as the hero-consort of the Cretan goddess, might have been the original guardians of the throne. However, a crucial fragment from this wall supports the decision by Evans to place these griffins where they are. Does this mean that the throne actually belonged to a Priestess of the Mother Goddess and not to the king? Interested scholars continue to exchange opinions about such questions.

Either griffins or bulls in the Throne Room at Knossos add another link to the eastern Mediterranean where such designs were frequently represented in paint and stone. Nowhere, however, could they have guarded a throne so self-confidently secure as the one in Crete. The palace was not fortified, nor were there walls around the houses and shops grouped nearby. The absence of a citadel may be taken to mean that the rulers of this wealthy capital were sufficiently concerned about the welfare of all the Cretans so as to insure a tranquil loyalty. Communications over the connecting roads of the island must have been good and the allegiance of the ruler at Phaistos seems to have been assumed without force. Whether a king in his own right or a loyal baron, he would appear not to have felt abused. In brief, the king at Knossos guaranteed prosperity to the island and furnished a navy to guard its shores. These were the weapons of internal peace.

## Strange Appearing Tablets

It has already been mentioned that Sir Arthur Evans' original purpose in going to Crete was to look for evidence of prehistoric writing. He did not have far to search. Native women on the island were using as charms small seal-stones which had been found in the countryside, relics of the distant past. The signs on these stones were hieroglyphs—pictures used as words for the objects represented. In Egypt and elsewhere in the Near East, writing had begun in the same simple way.

In March, 1900, within a week after Evans began his excavations at Knossos, he discovered clay tablets bearing a more complex system of writing. The find was not unexpected. The rudimentary markings of the seal-stones were obviously not equal to the task of keeping records during the commercially advanced Bronze Age.

Storerooms in the palace at Knossos suggest that inventories had been kept—on *papyri* (paper) and on clay tablets. *Papyri,* however, have only rarely been preserved away from the dry and saving sands of Egypt. The records Evans found were written on clay and at that only kept by chance. Customarily, tablets were not baked; they were only dried, since the same clay was reused again and again. In later days, when consuming fires destroyed the palace, some tablets were by ill-fortune baked and so by good fortune preserved. They are, however, fragile "documents" and now and then a few have been lost when left absentmindedly in the rain.

The tablets found at Knossos and later at other sites in Crete range in size from one inch to one foot in width. They exhibit a variety of strange appearing symbols written from left to right, with some pictographs and obvious ciphers (e.g., $111 =$ three) mixed in. We know now that the symbols represent a shift from pictures to syllables. It was a momentous step. Assume, for example, that the writer had already a picture of a "bee" and a picture of a "leaf." He could combine the two pictures (now using the symbols phonetically) and so write the word "belief" for which there was no picture. The alternative would have been to invent pictures for words like "belief" arbitrarily and thus to write as the Chinese still do with a vast number of pictographs. The syllabic system is easier. And the later alphabetic device of using a limited number of letters to form syllables is even simpler.

To the non-specialist the tablets recovered in Crete look much alike. Close examination by Evans and his staff, however, revealed

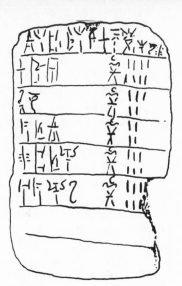

Pl. 14 The first Linear B tablet found on the mainland of Greece—at Pylos in 1939

Pl. 15 Drawing and translation of tablet shown in Plate 14:

Rowers to go to Pleuron:

| | | |
|---|---|---|
| from | Ro-o-wa | 8 Men, |
| from | Rhion | 5 Men, |
| from | Po-ra- | 4 Men, |
| from | Te-ta-ra-ne | 6 Men, |
| from | A-po-ne-we | 7 Men. |

that they were actually of two types and it was apparent that one script had been derived from the other. Since neither could be identified with any known system of writing, Evans, for convenience sake, called the earlier script Linear A and the later "derived script" Linear B (Pl. 14, 15). Linear A was found at various sites in Crete, but Linear B only at Knossos.

It was observed at the outset that the records written in these curious scripts were primarily inventories, probably accounts of royal wealth or payments due the palace. Obviously they were not literary pieces in which the scribes revealed either their own thoughts or those of the rulers whom they served. So, even if easily read, the tablets would not have provided an historical account to explain why Linear A was replaced at Knossos by Linear B.

Evans has been generously praised for recovering the evidence of three stages of writing in Crete: the early hieroglyphic type which yielded to Linear A about 1650 (although hieroglyphs continued to be used for sacred writings) and finally Linear B which came into use at Knossos about 1450. Unfortunately, for almost forty years this noted archaeologist's preoccupation with the architecture of the palace at Knossos and his unpraiseworthy reluctance to release the tablets to others hampered further investigation of the subject.

Nevertheless, since preliminary studies had shown that nearly half of the signs used in Linear B had been carried over from Linear A, it was assumed that both scripts were used for writing the same Minoan tongue (although what language the Minoans were speaking remained unknown). The fact that Linear B was found at Knossos and nowhere else in Crete was explained by the assumption that only in a busy capital would any variant be needed. This hypothesis held up until Professor Blegen discovered Linear B tablets at Pylos on the mainland in 1939. In 1952, Professor Alan B. Wace had similar good fortune at Mycenae. Tablets continue to be recovered. The most recent finds have been at Thebes.

The discovery by Blegen offered a better explanation for the mystery of the two scripts at Knossos. It seemed apparent that since Linear B belonged to the mainlanders they must have captured Knossos about 1450. Yet the invaders had not brought this script with them; rather they had first found a need for writing after they reached Crete. At Knossos they became the new owners of abundant and various kinds of property, including storerooms of chariot chassis and separate stores of wheels. They needed written inventories of their own. Linear B was therefore an adaptation of Linear A to a new language altogether. The mainlanders carried this method of writing home with them as a convenient device by which to record their mounting wealth. These later tablets are the ones now being recovered.

Ironically the new discovery created more darkness than light. If Linear B was not "Minoan" what was it? Schliemann had brought Homer's Achaeans into the light of day. Now these strange looking tablets made them a mystery people. Who in fact were the builders of Mycenae, Tiryns and Pylos?

It was not until 1952 that Linear B was deciphered. Michael Ventris, a young English architect, found these curious signs intriguing and unforgettable. This was fortunate for he kept working on the problem and finally made the tablets talk. More experienced scholars had busied themselves studying the tablets from the "outside" by looking for parallels elsewhere. The classical Cypriot script seemed particularly inviting. Ventris carefully considered the various possible affinities, but it was his decision to work from "inside" Linear B that lead to his eventual triumph.

Some of the symbols in Linear B looked alike, but about eighty-nine of them were sufficiently different to form a list. A publication of the Pylos tablets by Professor Emmett L. Bennett of the University of Wisconsin helped immeasurably with this count. Because the eighty-nine symbols were too few for a pictographic system of writing and too many for an alphabetic one, it was apparent that they were syllables. Ventris tried various approaches in his effort to learn how these syllables "behaved," and so to discover the pattern of the language which they represented. The usefulness of probability in breaking an enemy code was borrowed from cryptography. On a given page of English it is to be expected that words such as "and" or "the" will have a high rate of frequency. As it happened, Ventris discovered that in the Linear B script "and" was a syllable which occurred frequently at the end of one word as a connective with the next. Unfortunately the problem of decipherment involved many more difficulties than this simple illustration would indicate.

To determine what possible relationships the syllables held to one another, Ventris charted the history of each symbol (syllable). How many times did it appear at the beginning of a word, in the middle or at the end? Which symbols appeared together most often and what was their position when they did? He was aided in this direction by the work of the late Alice Kober, an American scholar who had concluded that the language of Linear B was inflected (i.e., word endings changed according to case, gender and number, as in Latin).

Ventris' "grids" on which he pictorially worked out the behavior of the symbols appear bewilderingly complex to the layman. Nor should we be surprised that much of this young Englishman's success has been attributed to his amazing powers of visual memory. In brief, the decipherment of Linear B was a game of many moves. Ventris had a good head for it. He eventually saw how the syllables were behaving. To his amazement he was not looking at a new pattern, but simply recognizing an old one. Linear B was an archaic form of Greek. Ventris had discovered that the Mycenaeans had borrowed Linear A which the Minoans used to write their language (whatever it may have been) and adapted it to suit the Greek tongue. Centuries later, the Greeks of Homer's day would represent their syllables with alphabetic letters rather than those odd signs, but they would be saying the same thing.

By a series of brilliant deductions a "dead" language had been brought to life in one of the major coups of modern scholarship. A triumph all the more astounding for having crowned so brief a career. In 1956 Michael Ventris was killed in an automobile accident at the age of thirty-four.

An account of the complexities involved in the decipherment of Linear B has been written by John Chadwick who was among the first to accept Ventris' hypothesis. He later became his collaborator and then in a sense his heir. His discussion of linguistic problems, while lucid, may have a limited appeal. On the other hand even a non-specialist can appreciate the difficulty of reading obscure signs in various hands. The scribes were not writing for later researchers but for each other. They found it easier to recognize a carelessly written symbol than a modern reader who must stop and ask himself if a peculiar looking sign is something new. Even mistakes may at times be helpful. Chadwick points out the usefulness of erasures. Here and there a symbol on a tablet had been partially rubbed out and a new one put in its place. Since men usually confuse signs or sounds which are much alike, these careless mistakes became valuable clues, contributions to modern scholarship from scribes dead for three thousand years.

The news that the Mycenaeans were Greeks was welcomed in the scholarly world which had long awaited a solution to this perplexing problem. Heinrich Schliemann would not have been so surprised. He knew the Mycenaeans spoke Greek. Homer said so.

Almost everybody now accepts the Ventris decipherment of Linear B. There are only variant expert opinions about Linear A. The use of syllables and ciphers is plain. The language which the Minoans may have been using is not. The best known of the proposals about Linear A is the suggestion of Semitic (Akkadian) affinities advanced in 1957 by Professor Cyrus Gordon of Brandeis University. Other scholars have found more comfort by working back from the Greek of Linear B with the expectation that the substitution of known values from the later script may provide valuable clues to the earlier one.

As Chadwick remarks, there is no evidence that Mycenaean scribes attempted complicated or even long sentences. As Evans had surmised, the deciphered Linear B tablets are primarily inventories and so provide no more of an explanation why the capital city of Crete was taken over by the Achaeans about 1450 than would the Linear A records.

Had success alone invited trouble? Perhaps Knossos became a decadent plum, ripe for picking by the more militant mainlanders. Nobody knows what happened. Nevertheless, according to the tradition which Evans established, the great days of the island were numbered. A scant fifty years later, about 1400, all of Crete was laid waste by some catastrophe. It has been postulated that the earlier Mycenaean attack had triggered a softening of Cretan defenses and morale. Then an invading coalition of old enemies successfully put this long-time sea power to rest. Other scholars have argued that a native rebellion accounted for the widespread destruction, and still others say the holocaust was ordered by the Mycenaean overlords grown impatient with the problems of the island. A more radical approach delays the end until 1200 and attributes it to the later Dorian invasions which also devastated the mainland.

Almost everybody seems to agree that the Greeks did invade Crete and rule at Knossos for a period of fifty or maybe two hundred and fifty years. Also, the greater number of Mycenaean wares than Cretan products found in Egypt for the period after about 1500 shows that the mainland had far outstripped Crete in exports. The historical embroidery which interested scholars have sewn around these two points has been torn with controversy. And it will continue to be. Recent geological studies have prompted the eminent Greek archaeologist Spyridon Marinatos to hypothesize that the great Minoan catastrophe actually occurred before 1450 B.C. and was caused by the effects of volcanic eruptions on the nearby island of Thera.

*Pl. 16 Three-handled jar (papyrus design) from the Palace at Knossos, circa 1425 B.C.*

# The Mycenaean Civilization; Homer

## II

The Greeks are so often remembered as hapless victims of the heavy-footed Romans that it seems strange to find them as seafaring invaders. They have been remembered best for their later cultural achievements and until the archaeological work of the past century there was little else to consider. The early history of the land was unknown. It is still by no means a complete and clear, or even continuous, story but a few points at least seem well established.

As in Crete, the Neolithic period on the mainland stretched back before 3000 B.C. Traces of the earliest settlements suggest (again as in Crete) that they were initiated by migrants from the East. During the shadowy period of the third millennium, 3000 to 2000 B.C., other peoples arrived, among them the carriers of copper and bronze. The arrival of these newcomers is also associated by archaeologists with the appearance of better-made pottery carrying novel designs. The earlier Neolithic arrivals and these later invaders spoke languages related to Minoan and were presumably part of the same migratory movements in which waves of settlers moved westward from Asia Minor and Syria.

It was also during the third millennium (about 2600) that Greek-speaking tribes began to move down from the north into the Balkan peninsula. They did not, however, continue all the way south, but settled in the northern reaches of Macedonia and Epirus where they then remained for several centuries. Their language tied them to a family of peoples who during this same period were moving in different directions from a common, albeit vast, homeland. Presumably they all came from somewhere north of the Danube, between the Baltic and Black Seas. Today, the similarities of basic words in the Germanic, Italic, Greek and Sanskrit languages argue that in the remote past the ancestors of these peoples, now scattered from England to India, were once neighbors. They were the possessors of Indo-European tongues to be distinguished, for instance, from the Semitic group.

No one knows why these people began to move or took the various directions they did. It is certain, however, that it was a very long time before they became settled where we now know them to be. Significantly, it was perhaps a thousand years or more after Greek-speaking tribes first arrived in the Balkans before their descendants fully possessed the southernmost region which became their historic homeland. Far from bringing new skills with them, they had actually less advanced techniques than those of the Neolithic folk settled in the northern regions where they first intruded. At the time the sounds of a different language would have easily identified the newcomers. Modern excavators must spot their presence at various sites by the sudden appearance of a new kind of dwelling, a rectangular building with a porch at the front supported by two posts. Apparently the classical temples were distantly descended from this rudimentary *megaron* structure.

The Greek-speaking tribes did not begin to move from the outlying regions of northern Macedonia and Epirus into the southernmost part of the Balkan peninsula until about 1900. Archaeological charts show that after that date (and at least one expert thinks that it should be set earlier at 2100), burials of taller "Nordic" skeletons began to appear more to the south than they had previously. Other skeletal remains show that these northerners were bringing horses with them, perhaps only as pack animals or for a Hun-style cavalry. The day of charioteering as a part of warfare and games was a long way off. Yet the future was foreshadowed in other ways. The votive deities found among the remains of their settlements indicate a shift toward the masculine side of religion. Wherever these new people settled, phallic figures rivaled the established fertility goddesses. At a later day, to be sure, the Father Zeus would reign on Olympus. Did classical myth sanctify the succession by ascribing his birth to an older nature goddess of Crete?

The historical distribution of place names in Greece supports the archaeological thesis of a southerly migration. Among names older than memory, those with pre-Greek endings dominate in the south where they are expected. Town names with Greek endings are concentrated in the north.

The arrival of the Greek-speaking tribes in central Greece and the Peloponnesus was not a peaceful operation. At various sites a level of burnt brick offers wordless testimony of a violent attack. The frequency of this evidence in the years following 1900 shows the scope and seriousness of the new invasions. Yet the cultural evolution of Helladic civilization was not interrupted in the sense that there was a Dark Age. On the contrary, the invaders whose descendants became Homer's "fair-haired Achaeans" assimilated the advanced agricultural skills and craftsmanship of the "pre-Greek" population. Furthermore, fair-haired or not, these descendants would be a mixture of both Nordic and Mediterranean physical types although in the long run the short, dark characteristics of the south became predominant. In brief, the Mycenaeans were Greeks in the same way that the Angles and Saxons who conquered the Britons were Englishmen.

Again, as with the Angles and Saxons, the speech of the Greek-speaking invaders tended to absorb and drown out other sounds. Yet not altogether. In classical times the survival of isolated pockets of non-Greek languages, such as Pelasgian, offered the last echoes of the pre-Greek peoples who had once dominated the land.

During the long period in which the Greeks remained settled in the northern regions, Macedonia, Thessaly, and Epirus, they had developed different dialects. When members of each of these regions moved into Greece they stayed with their own. Those speaking the Ionic dialect eventually settled in Attica and were the forefathers of the Athenians. The Aeolic dialect prevailed in central and north-eastern Greece while the Arcadian became predominant in the Peloponnesus.

Historians have borrowed the term Achaean from Homer and the term Mycenaean from archaeologists. Both names have been used more or less interchangeably to refer to all the Greeks of the Bronze Age. To be more exact, however, they pertain to the Arcadian and

Aeolian Greeks rather than to the Ionians. The main centers of the Mycenaean civilization which flourished from about 1600 to about 1150 were in the Peloponnesus and central Greece. "Mycenaean" materials have been found in Ionian Attica and in outposts in the eastern Aegean, but they are secondary to the finds in the heartland which stretched from Pylos through the Argolid to Thebes. The *Iliad* offers corroborative evidence. The host assembled for the attack on Troy was gathered primarily from that heartland region. Moreover, Homer used the term Danaan as well as Achaean to refer to the Mycenaeans, and both names have been recognized as the sea-raiders who are mentioned in surviving inscriptions of the Hittites and Egyptians. Only the citadels built by the Arcadians and Aeolians show either the wealth or strength which could have won such international attention.

*The Way They Find Them*

It is not known exactly when Mycenae began its career as the major center of the earliest Greek civilization. Obviously its acropolis offered an excellent defensive position which enabled those who held it to command respect in the Argolid plain. Today, the visitor to this lofty citadel looks out across the countryside for miles around. It is apparent that no one could approach unnoticed (Pl. 17).

The acropolis at Mycenae, like the more famous site at Athens, was occupied from Neolithic times onward. The first clear evidence of power and prosperity at this place has been found in twenty-four graves which have been dated to about 1700, or maybe somewhat later. Men who have possessed exalted power and wealth have frequently used a large share of both to provide themselves with impressive entombments. The pyramids of Egypt are the best example. Never for a moment have those Pharaonic monuments allowed the memory of their builders to lapse. The rulers of Mycenae were not so fortunate. Until Schliemann began their restoration to history they had slipped back into myth. In lieu of other evidence, the types of burials which these rulers provided for themselves have become important. Archaeologists, prosaically but honestly, label the Mycenaean kings the way they find them. The earliest, those found in the graves dated to about 1700, have been called the First Shaft Dynasty. The later burials which Schliemann found have been designated as those of the Second Shaft Dynasty. There followed under different arrangements a Tholos Tomb Dynasty.

*Pl. 17 Citadel at Mycenae as seen from Mt. Zara. At right, the palace; at left, the grave circle*

Shaft graves were cut vertically into ground composed of more rock than earth. They were marked by sculptured *stelae,* corresponding to modern tombstones. In the earliest graves, the skeletons (some singly, but in one instance four together) belonged to descendants of tall people from the north, not the short Mediterranean men. Very likely they were the first Greek-speaking rulers of Mycenae. In any event they seem to have been too busy establishing their power locally to have had any "international" relations. The weaponry and jewelry in their tombs cannot easily be equated to Minoan objects of the same time. Nor at this early date need there have been any contact with Crete.

The shaft graves which Schliemann discovered offer a different story. They belonged to a line of rulers who reigned from about

1600 to 1500. In this later era, the golden articles deposited in the burials show Cretan influence in both technique and motif. Of special interest are the many pieces of jewelry shaped like octopuses (Pl. 18).

How much of a spell Crete cast over the budding Mycenaean civilization has become a controversial question. At one time the arts of the mainland were considered to be little more than an off-shoot of the more advanced Minoan culture. Because Evans had placed the evolution of the Cretan civilization well in advance of the Mycenaean achievement, that viewpoint seemed plausible. Furthermore, critics observed that the Mycenaean possessions appeared less tasteful than those of the Minoan kings. There seemed to be too much gold added, a gaudiness which was to be expected from late-comers.

In spite of these arguments, there has always been some specu-lation about the traditional chronology which Evans established. However, it has only come under heavy attack in recent years. The ever increasing fund of information about the Mycenaean civilization has encouraged certain observers like L. R. Palmer, Professor of Comparative Philology in Oxford University, to suggest revisions in

*Pl. 18 Thin gold-sheet ornaments in form of octopuses from Shaft Grave IV at Mycenae, often sewn on hems of garments*

chronology which would tend to downgrade Cretan precedence and by the same process give more credit to native initiative on the mainland.

The painters at Mycenae, Pylos and Tiryns served local patrons whose tastes and interest inspired a tradition different from that of Crete. Thus, scenes of war and hunting at Mycenae offer a contrast to the idyllic flora and fauna of Knossos. Nor should the emphasis on warfare be unexpected. The Mycenaeans were settled in independent kingdoms and apparently spent their time battling each other when not united against an outsider. Under these conditions their presumed lack of taste has been happily described as the warrior's love of splendor.

Even accepting the arguments for greater Mycenaean independence, a consensus remains that the Bronze Age reached a climax earlier in Crete than elsewhere in the Aegean world. The excellence of Mycenaean works in the sixteenth century might still, in part, have been attributable to Cretan craftsmen who journeyed northward. Without question Minoan motifs were borrowed by mainlanders to decorate their palace walls. In fact, by good fortune, it has been possible to restore the so-called "shield fresco" in the palace at Knossos because a smaller copy of the original has survived on the mainland in the palace of Tiryns.

In Late Minoan times realistic Mycenaean scenes of hunting and warfare appeared with increasing frequency in Crete. Obviously the borrowing went both ways. Therefore it might be concluded that in the beginning the tide flowed mostly from Crete northward and afterwards there was a mixture of Minoan and Mycenaean styles. It is a simple statement. Yet on the subject of artistic dependency there is always room for argument since most answers are probably as good as the question.

The perpetuation of ancestral custom has always been a means to stability and continuity. In the custom-conscious ancient world it was unlikely that the members of a royal family would depart from the ways of their forefathers, especially in the matter of burials. Accordingly the introduction of a new type of tomb at Mycenae about 1500 has been used by scholars to mark the beginning of a new dynasty. The shaft grave gave way to the more elaborate *tholos* tomb made by cutting a beehive-type chamber in the side of a hill. A passageway was cut leading to the portal where the rise of the hill was sufficient to allow for the height of the tomb. When this

*Pl. 19 Entrance way to the Treasury of Atreus at Mycenae*

corridor was lined with large blocks of stone it offered a formal entrance way. The most famous of the beehive chambers measures over
forty-six feet in diameter and reaches a height in the center of better
than forty-three feet. It has been called the "Treasury of Atreus"
because it was assumed by excavators that such an elaborate facility
must have housed the wealth of the father of Agamemnon (Pl. 19).
Off the main chamber, a small, low-ceiling room seems to have been
designed expressly for that purpose. However, this was not common
and only one other tomb is known to have had one. What treasure
the largest of the *tholos* tombs actually contained must remain unknown for they were conspicuous on the landscape and a monumental
temptation to grave robbers. The size and finish of these tombs
marked them as belonging to royalty. As in life, so in death their
noble associates were nearby, resting in less elaborate rooms. These
smaller entombments had unlined entrance ways and were in fact

*Pl. 20 Lion Gate at Mycenae*

crude chambers cut out of the hillside with even the interior left unfinished. At Dendra, about seven miles southeast of Mycenae, a minor *tholos* tomb was discovered intact in 1926 and its gold and silver treasures, now in the National Museum in Athens, are a clue to the valuables which the widespread *tholoi* once contained.

During the time that the Tholos Tomb Dynasty ruled at Mycenae, Knossos was captured by the mainlanders. Included in the evidence of foreign domination at the Cretan capital is the introduction of beehive tombs. The eclipse of Cretan power was coincident with the rise of the ambitious mainland centers. Pylos, Tiryns, and especially Mycenae, saw their best days in the two centuries and a half between 1400 and 1150. At Mycenae two lions (to be exact, lionesses) carved on a triangular stone stood guard above the main entrance to the citadel. And they are still there, although now headless, to mark the "Lion Gate" (Pl. 20) through which rode the kings who lived in the palace and were buried in the great *tholos* tombs on the plain below. The palace itself was actually a group of buildings surrounding large and small courtyards. There were occasional ceremonial halls, shrines, bedrooms and bathrooms similar to those in the complex at Knossos, but on a much smaller scale.

The remains of other palaces and *tholos* tombs elsewhere in the Peloponnesus mark the location of rival dynasties. Everywhere there were riches. The golden cups discovered in a *tholos* tomb at little

*Pl. 21 Gold cup I (bull caught in a net) from* tholos *tomb at Vaphio,* circa *1500 B.C.*

*Pl. 22 Gold cup II (hunter, bulls and decoy-cow) from* tholos *tomb at Vaphio,* circa *1500 B.C.*

known Vaphio, near Sparta, are among the most publicized articles yet found in Greece (Pl. 21, 22). These matching cups, showing embossed scenes of a wild boar hunt, were perhaps the work of a craftsman who traveled from court to court, a busy restless Cellini of his time. Were the cups sent as a gift to a neighboring ruler? In Homer, the honor of receiving a precious artistic piece could be heightened by the announcement of the notables who had once possessed it.

### A Familiar Pyramid of Classes

The rulers of these Achaean kingdoms may have had wealth to rival that of the earlier kings at Knossos, but they do not seem to have known the same sense of security—except possibly at Pylos where neither Nestor nor his predecessors felt any need for walled fortifications. About 1350, a wall of huge stones to a width of twenty-three feet was built to guard the acropolis at Mycenae. At Tiryns, the walls of a later date were even more impressive. These stone fortresses may be taken as a fair measure of the anxiety which so often accompanies the accumulation of wealth. They also conjure up a thought of the Middle Ages. And with good reason for the earliest Greek society was similar in certain respects to that of Medieval Europe. Significantly, in each of these small Achaean kingdoms there was a familiar pyramid of classes. We have no eye-witness accounts, to be sure, but that is the picture supplied by archaeological finds, by the Linear B tablets and the writings of Homer.

Homer's epics were of course not contemporary writings, nor were they intended to describe or explain the Achaean world. Homer knew little enough about those times himself. In fact, he could not avoid some anachronisms. Here and there he mentions iron which had been introduced long before his own era, but was presumably missing in the Achaean Age. He also thought that cremation was as common a practice in Mycenaean times as in his own. The *tholos* tombs have yielded evidence of some cremations but they are exceptional. There are other difficulties—a sufficient number to allow some scholars to doubt that the Homeric epics retain a reliable memory of Mycenaean times. The Linear B records suggest a highly bureaucratical society akin to that of earlier Near Eastern states and out of tenor with Homer's stories. Yet the view from a great distance cannot be expected to be the same as one close-up. Nor are the interests of a poet the same as those of a scribe. Broadly speaking, the tales which Homer retold centuries later did correctly reflect a society of rank and custom.

At the apex of the pyramid stood the king and his well-born friends. These aristocrats, born and raised to predatory habits, occupied themselves in accumulating wealth and defending what they owned. In the *Iliad,* they talked much of honor and were known by their armor and weapons. Achaean warriors customarily wore leather helmets with metal pieces attached, but Homer mentions a helmet decorated with boars' teeth and a colorful fresco dated to the period shows a man wearing one (Pl. 23). Other Mycenaean paintings depict warriors with plated corselets and carrying shields shaped like figure "eights," large enough to cover them from head to toe (Pl. 24). In contrast, on a vase from Mycenae there are shown fighters who have only small round shields for protection (Pl. 25). These men carry the familiar bronze-tipped spears. Elsewhere warriors are seen armed with two-edged swords and short daggers similar to those which have been found in Mycenaean tombs. The Achaean warriors may not have been so attached to their weapons as was the medieval knight Roland, who named his sword Durendal, but they did live by them and they were buried with them.

*Pl. 23 Mycenaean carved ivory figure wearing a boar's-tusk helmet*

*Pl. 24 Bronze dagger with gold, silver and niello inlays, from Shaft Grave IV, Mycenae,* circa *1550 B.C. A lion hunt, showing figure-eight shields*

The son of an aristocrat was trained in his father's image. He grew up familiar with palace life and skilled in handling a chariot, the class symbol of those who rode to the hunt and to war (by this time chariots were being used in actual combat). As usual, even those who possessed the most felt the urge for something extra. While the detachable wheels of most chariots were made of wood, some have been found made partly of bronze or rimmed in bronze. Those with silver were surely used for ceremonial purposes and perhaps only by the king.

The dominant position of the aristocrats was secure. Artisans, bards, seers and scribes served them and were dependent on their good will. Even the making and trading of pottery seems to have been a royal monopoly. These clients did not constitute an independent bourgeoisie who might muster the support of the peasantry to challenge the political power of the well-born. Their power was not in fact political at all. By custom, men of every class accepted the fact that they should live the way their ancestors had lived. Status was fixed by the amount of land owned; and a given family remained on the same property, be it large or small, generation after generation. The internal peace and order of such societies have always seemed to sanctify them as being right. What always was, would always be. The danger to the king and his companions would not be from below but from each other and from outside forces.

In the *Iliad,* Agamemnon appears as a king among kings, the first among equals. Like the early Capetian monarchs in France, he ruled a strategic area of land and managed by his wealth and his position to dominate his neighbors. In turn, he won allegiance, even if it were grudging, from more distant rulers. Yet domination of the Argolid plain did not mean absolute power. The thickness of the walls at Tiryns testified to that. As in Medieval times, various kingdoms quarreled incessantly and yet joined together in the crusades, so too, in Homer's account of the Trojan War, there were contingents of only six ships allied with others up to one hundred. Agamemnon may have been the leader of this host which sailed for Troy, but the *Iliad* shows that he could not make Achilles obey him after they arrived. Moreover, the *Odyssey* makes it clear that a king could have trouble with his own native nobility. The spirited Odysseus, like a later lion-hearted Richard, might well have wondered what was happening during his absence from home.

In Homer's description of the local scene at Ithaca, the landholders seem less like romantic knights and more like patriarchal ranchers of our own Old West—ranchers who were not above rustling each other's cattle.

Family loyalty was all important. When a son married, he brought his wife into an established household ruled by his father. The produce of the estate was kept in common storerooms and the family treasure remained intact until the father died. The surviving sons then set up their own households. And so it went from generation

*Pl. 25 Crater known as "Warrior Vase," from citadel at Mycenae, circa 1200 B.C., showing small shields.*

to generation. A man's identity was not established by his own name, but by the names of his ancestors. Genealogies were often recited and family ties were rarely broken. Brothers fought together. Whoever offended one offended the other. So it was that Agamemnon brought more ships to Troy than any other king for the abducted Helen was his brother's wife.

The intensity of these blood ties led to great respect for those who were kinsmen and little regard for those who were not. There were vendettas, raids on neighboring estates, and the unwelcome intrusion of free-loaders if a master happened to be absent from his household. So it was that Odysseus returned to face the obstreperous suitors who had served themselves from his well-stocked storerooms and thrown fear into his wife and family. When these suitors arrived in Hades it was apparently not unexpected that Agamemnon would ask them if they had been slain stealing sheep or women.

If piracy was a pastime with the Achaeans, so was hospitality. Then, as now, the year of a vintage was important and the best wine was saved for an occasion. Homer also recounts how the nobles generously bestowed their captured booty on one another with all the aplomb of robber-barons. In the *Odyssey* there are frequent references to gifts exchanged between friends and strangers alike. No guest, invited or in passing, should leave empty-handed.

Tacitus (*circa* 55–*circa* 117 A.D.), a Roman historian, describes in the *Germania* the same contrasting roles of violence and generosity among the early Germans. According to his account, the Germans too found a quiet life boring and lived in an uproarious routine of blood and plunder. Yet he calls these restless warriors the most hospitable of all men. Like Homer's Achaeans they seemed never to have been merely eating, much less dining, but always enjoying a feast.

The Mycenaeans were restless on land among themselves and a bane by sea to others, including the Hittites. These were an Indo-European people who moved into Asia Minor about the same time as the Greeks were arriving in the southern Balkans. Although their empire centered in the hinterland, it extended westward toward the Aegean Sea. Apparently they had contacts with the outposts which the Mycenaeans established in Melos, Rhodes, Cyprus, and at Miletus on the coast of Asia Minor. Hittite records which are dated between the fourteenth and twelfth centuries mention the kings and the land of Ahhiyava, which for the time and place could only mean the Achaeans. These documents describe the customary exchange of gifts, and also show how Achaean carelessness about other people's property put a severe strain on diplomatic relations. The same was true in Egypt where inscriptions of the thirteenth and twelfth centuries tell of the defeat of marauders from the north including the Akaiwasha (Achaeans) and the Denyen (Danaans).

Against this historical background the epic assault on Troy has been put into better perspective. Helen's face may have launched a few ships but the rest were on a more practical mission. The famed walls of Troy were a clue to the city's importance. This fortress city guarded the approaches to the Hellespont (Dardanelles) and held sway over the other towns in the Hellespontine region which comprised the northwest sector of Asia Minor. Rich from tolls and tribute, Troy was also the place to be taken if raiders were to pass inland. The Trojan episode therefore appears to have been another campaign by which the Achaeans sought to enrich themselves at the expense of their affluent neighbors. The date for the fall of Troy has been much disputed. The traditional year is 1184. Modern authorities like 1260 better.

The warrior class of the Achaeans could afford the entertainment of bards who sang tales about their exploits and in the process lifted these piratical excursions out of the ordinary into the realm of heroic adventure. Ever since the time when Homer retold these same stories centuries later, Achilles and Odysseus have been the stout-hearted yet tender-hearted prototypes of folk heroes. Either of these warriors could have fought alongside Roland and his Frankish knights on that marvelous and bloody day at Roncesvalles. Such is the gift of poetry.

Since the reconstruction of Achaean society has been based on inferences it must be offered cautiously. If a detailed report of "how things really were" happened to be available, it might include some surprises.

Throughout ancient times the vast majority of men were busy in the production of food. The same is true in underdeveloped areas today. Call them peasants, serfs, or tenant farmers, they comprise the broad base of any pyramid. In the Classical Age, a thousand years after the Mycenaean period, there were fewer trees on the Greek horizon, but the herders of goats and sheep and the farmers gathering grain were everlastingly the same. In Achaean times, these men, along with those who grew olives or kept bees, lived in villages which dotted the countryside. For them life was local and routine. Few men knew how to keep records. Nor did they need to. Scribes of the king kept their accounts for them, and for tax purposes. The

Linear B tablets say that much. They also offer a sufficient variety of official titles to suggest that there was a hierarchy of bureaucrats although they do not say exactly what these persons might have been doing, if anything.

Neither does the available evidence offer a clear picture of the intricacies of landholding. Still, enough is known to avoid the temptation of filling in the story by borrowing too much from the better documented Middle Ages. The comparison cannot be stretched to include all the complexities of feudalism. The *aristoi,* the noble companions who fought alongside the king, were to be sure large landowners and their wealth and privileges were held by hereditary right. But they do not seem to have been "dukes" and "counts" who stood between the sovereign and his subjects. Although there may have been some tenancy and even debt peonage, the majority of small herders and farmers appear to have been yeomen, free and responsible only to the king. Responsible, probably, for hard labor on his walls, roads and fortifications.

Archaeologists have found an amazing array of objects produced by men who belonged neither to the small warrior class which Homer described, nor to the peasantry whose pigs were so carefully listed on the Linear B tablets. Marble tables inlaid with gold, fancy footstools inlaid with ivory, and jewelry of sparkling originality represent an artisan class quite apart from the usual weavers and armor makers. If specialization offers a clue to the level of a civilization, then the Mycenaean society was well along. Here again, archaeological findings have shown that Homer was misinformed. Despite his knowledge about Mycenaean wealth, he did not realize what a brilliant artistic season this city had had. He assumed that fine jewelry and articles of rare craftsmanship were brought to Greece by the Phoenicians, just as in his own day. Subsequent to Schliemann's time, archaeological discoveries from Sicily to Palestine, and at sites far up the Nile in Egypt, have shown that the Mycenaeans were exporters of an extra fine pottery which appears as a luxury item alongside the native wares of the overseas buyers.

Below the skilled craftsmen who served the king and his court was a large group of personal attendants. They included the usual palace contingent of valets, maids, nurses, and cooks. Furthermore, according to Homer, it was customary for the king and his friends to be accompanied by a retinue of servants on their campaigns. Remaining at home were the hired hands who worked the fields and tended the flocks of their wealthy employers.

Off the social scale altogether were the slaves. They were mostly women, for men were killed as they expected to be if they lost a battle. The women, however, were carted off as booty to become the cleaning women of the wives of the conquerors. Or, if young and attractive, to serve the pleasure of the warriors themselves. Maybe. Homer mentions at least one wife who refused to tolerate it.

## Inside the Old Stories

The *Iliad* and the *Odyssey* have been relied upon to patch together the history of Achaean Greece. The survival of these epics has made them valuable source material; and yet using them for this purpose is akin to writing a history of the American Civil War from the works of Walt Whitman. Events and places are incidental to a poet, even if he notes them correctly. The poet is not after facts; he searches for the mystery of life. And he often finds it locked inside old stories, for they are the best stories and never really old at all. True, they may describe how particular men behaved according to the customs of their times, but more importantly they speak of emotions which have always been the same. The historical value of Homer's epics have not accounted for their survival. They meant much more than mere history to the Greeks of classical times, and to those who have read them since.

Despite all that Heinrich Schliemann proved, there is still a Homeric question. It concerns what he wrote, not whether he ever lived or where. Today it is generally accepted that the seven Aegean cities which claimed Homer as a native were quarreling over a real person. There was a poet by that name who was born in Smyrna and later lived in Chios. Or was it the other way around? Certainly classical artists of the fifth century never doubted that there had been a Homer about three or four centuries before their time. They no more knew what he looked like than medieval artists knew the lineaments of St. Paul; they simply made busts of a man in keeping with their conception of a poet. And yet they may have had one feature correct. Tradition said that Homer was blind, and in the few copies of Homer's graven image which have survived the artists gave his eyes the appearance of blindness.

The background of Homer's two famous epics is no less obscure than that of the poet himself. Homer, like Shakespeare, used oldtime tales as material. For centuries, since Mycenaean times, these stories had been memorized and sung by bards who altered and expanded them in the process. The state of this material when it reached Homer cannot be known. The works of earlier poets were either not written down or, if they were, have been lost. The *Iliad* and the *Odyssey* must therefore be judged by what they appear to be. In some respects they appear to be strikingly different. In the *Iliad,* valiant heroes fight well, suffer much, and are finally doomed. Achilles and Hector are exemplary men in a real-life struggle and their fateful dilemma is something for men to ponder. The *Odyssey* is a romance. Odysseus conquers all and in the end lives happily ever after. He is a hero to dream about.

Today, critics are generally agreed that the *Iliad* shows the hand of a single artist who borrowed selections from inherited lore, recast them, and created a work of art. A few alterations and additions may have been made by later editors, but taken as a whole this "best epic" speaks for a man of genius as author. The *Odyssey* is another matter. It may not have been Homer's work at all.

Unsettling opinions invite a reaction. In modern times the critical analysis of Homer's epics has undoubtedly been both fruitful and overdone. Critics study the texts, and by checking back and forth see contradictions and unevenness which would have been difficult to detect if they had been listening to these poems sung in the way the Greeks did. Epics were "performed" in ancient times by men who knew various stock epithets and phrases which they used to embroider their work. In singing the story they sometimes added a section here and left out something there. In brief, the oral tradition did not fix the material in a definitive pattern in the way a written text tends to do. The familiar division of each epic into twenty-four books, for example, was an invention of Hellenistic scholars living in Alexandria centuries after Homer's day.

In Homer's time, following a long dark age, the Greeks began to write again and the epics were written down. They were still intended to be sung, however, for few men could read. Homer must therefore be judged as a poet, not as a novelist—yet even as poetry, the *Iliad* and the *Odyssey* differ in their composition and level of thought.

The *Odyssey* assumes a knowledge of the events told in the *Iliad.* It would seem likely therefore that it was written later. Critics who would accept the idea of a single author for both epics argue that since the *Odyssey* is more tightly constructed than the *Iliad* it shows the hand of a mature technician who has learned from his previous mistakes. If the *Odyssey* does not soar and sing with the intensity of the earlier epic it is because the music of age happens to be mellower.

On the other hand, there are those who doubt that Homer would have lost so much artistic sophistication no matter how long he lived. The argument for two authors instead of one is based on what appear to be irreconcilable differences in outlook and tone between the two epics. The *Iliad* gains its intensity because the story is told in a single setting, is related to an historical event, and has the true-to-life tone of tragedy. Odysseus, however, roams over the wine-dark sea to never-never lands of pure imagination and even pays a brief visit to Hades. Although a wonderfully versatile man, this daring adventurer plays the role of a "dragon-killer," even akin to the Babylonian Gilgamesh. His encounter with the Cyclops is weird and melodramatic; it has nothing in common with the taut scene between Achilles and Hector in the *Iliad*. The *Odyssey* is a fantasy set in western lands. It accords with the beginning of the Greek colonization in the mid-eighth century. So that it would more likely have been composed after the *Iliad* and by some poet living later in a different part of Greece. The argument has merit. Yet, so long as we lack proof beyond a shadow of a doubt, the time-worn phrase "The *Iliad* and the *Odyssey* by Homer" will very likely endure. In this book it will simply be assumed that the unknown author of the *Odyssey* could have been Homer.

The human complexion which Homer describes is no more dated than that of Shakespeare. The *Iliad,* a long narrative poem, begins with a quarrel and ends with a funeral. Between these extremes, the deeds of men struggling in behalf of their own good causes are recounted. Is there anything unfamiliar here?

When the epic begins, the siege of Troy is in the background. The listener's attention is focused on a dispute in progress between two stalwart Greeks. Agamemnon has lost his maid servant, the prize of a previous raid, and has decided to appropriate a girl belonging to Achilles. Outraged, the younger man refuses to take any further part in the struggle with the Trojans. He is the kind of hero whose presence makes a difference, and so his comrades, bystanders in the quarrel, suffer dearly for his intransigence. Even when Agamemnon seeks to make amends Achilles remains aloof, frozen with wrath. Then a message arrives. Patroclus, Achilles' dearest friend, has been slain by Hector, son of Priam, the king of Troy.

Achilles' quarrel with Agamemnon is suddenly overshadowed by grief. His perspective has not been restored by death alone, there has been much of that, but by a single death which touches him so deeply that it divides his life. He must at any cost avenge his fallen comrade.

Achilles meets Hector before the walls of Troy and kills him there. He is at first pitiless toward Hector's corpse and insists that it be left exposed to be devoured by dogs. The pleas of Priam, the aged king, speaking now only as a bereaved father, cannot move him. Prompted by Apollo, however, he relents and allows the body to be recovered. The *Iliad* concludes with Hector's funeral.

The poetic narrative of the *Iliad* is frequently obscured by lengthy descriptions of bloody combat. During these long passages, episodes flash up as if a spotlight on a stage has settled on two people with a battle swirling around them. The din and dust is always present. So is black death, weaving back and forth from side to side. As Goethe says: "An inch beneath the *Iliad* is Hell." The warriors who met each other in single contests of skill and strength could not have shared his objectivity. They were born the sons of brave fighters. What else should they do but win honors in the only life they knew?

Honor was a matter of life and death in the society which Homer described. Unlike our own day, there was no success without it. Achilles, aroused to great passion over a slight in a small matter, was not just being petty. It was of the greatest consequence that Agamemnon had offended him as a man. His sensitivity about it was characteristic of an aristocratic society. The sorrow which his stubborn anger brought to his innocent comrades has a more universal message. So has the contest with Hector.

Duty was not to king and country—it was to a relative or a friend. Sunk in his loneliness and grief, Achilles felt stir in him the fire of revenge for the death of Patroclus. According to his code, it was right that he should kill Hector. By the same code, it was also right that Hector should defend himself, his home, his wife and his child. Moreover, Hector must fight because Achilles challenged him to fight. Then, Homer says, a man must stand up or be counted as a woman. Hector one day prayed for his son: "May he kill his enemy and bring home the bloodstained spoils, and give joy to his mother's heart." In other words let him be strong and courageous even as I and my father before me. Yet there was something else. Whether describing Achilles' bereavement for Patroclus or Hector's farewell to Andromache, Homer gave to his heroes a manly measure of tenderness.

What should be said of a contest between men of such courage and good hearts? Homer does not present the Greek Achilles as "our hero" and the Trojan Hector as "the enemy." The outcome of their conflict is not to be accounted for in terms of right against wrong. Achilles and Hector face each other equally as men, both possessing good and bad qualities. Each is doing what he must do. Yet one must die. Why one or the other? Homer does not have the answer. Nor do the gods. True, the machinations of the gods brought these warriors into mortal combat, but thereafter they became the instruments of dreary fate.

In popular imagination evil and ugliness go down to destruction before goodness and beauty. This is entertainment. It allows a momentary escape from the reality which we live. The *Iliad* is the reality. It asks the old, old question: Why does this happen to me?

The *Odyssey* is an epic of wild adventure. And yet it would be difficult to fault its neat arrangement. The story begins at Ithaca which along with smaller adjacent islands is ruled by Odysseus. Because of the king's lengthy absence at Troy his wife, Penelope, is greatly worried for his life. She is also distracted by importunate wooers eager to take his place. The succession of a ruler was an affair of the palace, not a public matter; the commoners would serve the man who managed to be king. Usually the greater wealth and good connections of a prince enabled him to take his father's place, but in this "heroic" age he had to also prove himself worthy of the seat. Telemachus, the princely heir, who was growing up while Odysseus was away, seemed a doubtful match for the persistent nobles who sought his mother's hand. The goddess Athena gave help to Penelope by urging Telemachus to go in search of his father.

The opening passages of the *Odyssey* foreshadow the story to follow. Although Odysseus does not appear, he is the topic of conversation and the listener is prepared for high adventure. Homer then relates the perilous escapes of Odysseus on his way home from Troy. Included are the familiar tales of the one-eyed Cyclops, the enchanting Circe, the Singing Sirens, the treacherous monster Scylla, and the whirlpool Charybdis. After which there are seven reposeful years in the company of the demi-goddess Calypso. Amid these circumstances, having incurred the ill-will of Poseidon, it often seems doubtful that Odysseus will ever reach Ithaca. Nor would he have made it without the help of the gods. His survival is impressive and singular. Twelve ships and nearly six hundred companions are lost along the way. Here and there, a variety of other tales are woven into the story. A flashback tells of the Trojan Horse incident. On another occasion, Odysseus descends into Hades and talks with heroes of the past.

Odysseus was absent from Ithaca for twenty years. The Trojan War had lasted ten and it took another ten for the trip home. The length of time elapsed made his homecoming difficult. In fact, the neighboring noblemen had become so well entrenched in his household that Athena found it necessary to disguise him as a beggar in order to plot and achieve his revenge. As usual, his varied talents gave him an advantage amid difficulties which seemed insurmountable. Athena was also there to help, and after the suitors were slain by Odysseus, she arranged for peace with their numerous revengeful relatives. So, the epic was concluded in the same setting in which it had begun. At the end, Odysseus was secure on his throne, the troubles described in the beginning were over, and his heart was glad.

## Conditions Which Men Cannot Change

The Homeric epics were as important to ancient Greek society as the Bible is to our own. Perhaps more so, for the *Iliad* and the *Odyssey* were the primers of Greek education. They still are. To the credit of the Greeks, their children have always learned to read and write by examples from the very best in native literature. A child may not go far with his schooling, but if he learns to read and write he knows Homer. When Socrates made his famous appeal to a large jury in Athens in 399 B.C. he quoted from the *Iliad*. Here at least was common ground.

Homer's writings did not comprise scripture in the sense that they were the "revealed word of God." Yet, as in the Bible, there were woven into these epics three persistent themes of human interest: the nature of the supernatural, the intervention of the supernatural in human events, and acute observations about the behavior of men toward one another.

The epics describe the province of each of the twelve Olympian gods. Nearly all of them were named in the Linear B tablets. Homer writes about the same deities as the Mycenaeans had actually worshipped. Yet the tablets mention other gods and not all of them have been clearly identified. Perhaps some of these represent the cruder aspects of religious practices, snake cults and fertility rites which Homer ignores. When the poet limited the number of gods to be given preference, he introduced order and a degree of sophistication into a highly confusing, often interchangeable, list of deities.

In the remote past, sticks and stones had been considered divine, but Homer spoke for an age when supernatural powers were personified as men and women, larger than life, living forever on special food. They acted according to the same passions and prejudices of

men, even as the Hebrew Yahweh who walked and talked in the cool
of the evening, and described himself as a jealous God.

The nature of God is not a matter which historians need to
decide for others, but the various ways in which men have conceived
of the divine is a matter of historical interest. It may be observed
that although a few Greek philosophers spoke of a single creative
principle, the overwhelming majority of the Greeks throughout ancient
times accounted for events according to the wishes of these anthropo-
morphic gods which Homer describes.

In the *Iliad,* Homer makes it plain how this happened. It is
Apollo who demands that Agamemnon return the captured maid
Chryseis to her father. When he refuses the god sends a plague to
show his displeasure. How else could the sudden deaths of so many
Achaeans be explained? Finally, Agamemnon is forced to accede to
the god's wishes. It is then that he takes Briseis from Achilles. In turn,
Achilles' mother, Thetis, appeals to Zeus for revenge and according
to the god's promise matters do appear to go hard for the Achaeans.
Later, when Hector goes out to meet Achilles, it is Athena who disguises herself and tricks him into believing that she is his brother
and will give him another spear if his first throw misses. It is Athena
too who grabs Hector's well-aimed missile and saves Achilles from
being struck. Why else would this most skilled of all Trojan warriors
have missed? Yet even these well-intended favors for Achilles do not
really decide the issue. There are matters beyond the gods themselves.
Homer tells how Zeus, the Father, held the scales. At first they were
balanced. Then they tipped against Hector. As he is dying, Hector
voices a plaint which would echo again and again in Greek literature:
"At last my fate has found me." Achilles says, "Let me too die as
nobly as this man when my time comes." Ancient man lived a shorter,
far less comfortable life than his modern counterpart. He was preoccupied with how best to face adversity. By contrast, modern man,
studying to improve himself, paddling his own canoe, seeks to make
his own fate and so avoid adversity altogether.

Only on one occasion does Zeus point a finger at man. In the
*Odyssey* he asks: "Why do men so often rage against the will of the
gods when it is the wickedness of their own hearts which brings them
woe?" This idea was not popularized before the time of the renowned
secularists Euripides and Thucydides in the late fifth century, yet
there was no reason why this notion should not appear in Homer.
He was telling stories. The explanations why things happened in the
way they did were not more contradictory than life itself. Each suited

a particular circumstance and a different way in which a man might look at destiny.

Homer's epics do not offer an evolutionary development toward a higher concept of God, nor any single set of answers to life's major questions. As such, these "teachings" gave the religion common to all the Greeks a totally undogmatic character. The gods of course aided men and they must be worshipped, flattered and obeyed. The welfare of the state could depend on this. To deny the gods was dangerous, even unpatriotic. But there was no creed or sets of tenets to which a man must subscribe. Although the Greeks often quarreled over the physical control of their shrines, they never fought a religious war over faith. Ironically, the adherents of the later higher religions have suffered the embarrassment of bloodshed in the name of sacred books. Homer's writings actually united the Greeks by reconciling them to the common dilemma of human existence.

Courage and honor were the unquestioned standards by which a warrior lived. The intransigence of Achilles about an offence to his honor followed from the kind of man he was. Agamemnon was a warrior too. The quarrel between them which brought grief to themselves and others was rooted in their pride. Yet Homer was concerned with more than a particular incident between these two men. He recognized the inevitability of human differences and therefore the inevitability of conflict and sorrow. Tragedy has to do with conditions which men cannot change. No matter how much individuals may alter their course, a diversity of personality and temperament persists. In short, parts of the human complexion may shift places, but the total complexion remains the same. There will always be conflicts in which both the innocent and the guilty suffer. Here is the essence of tragedy. Long afterwards the poet Aeschylus gave this message a dramatic setting. It has been expressed many times since. In the literature of the Western world, Homer said it first, beautifully, once and for all.

# The Dark Ages;
# Colonization

**III**

The Trojan War, which Homer made famous, has always been the best-known event of the Achaean period. It was also one of the last. Sometime after the victorious Achaeans returned from Troy, they were themselves besieged and their citadels taken and burned. Unlike their own forays, this was not an intrusion by marauders who might take what they wanted and leave. It was an invasion by whole tribes who moved down from the rough north country and came to stay. They did not all appear at once out of a cloud of dust. On the contrary, a variety of peoples arrived at different times and because their movements lacked the planning of civilized encroachments, there were areas like Attica which suffered less than others. All of Greece, however, was affected one way or another.

No one can say what propelled the invaders southward. It is always fair to guess that they were forced to move by other peoples less pleasant than themselves; and it is equally plausible that, for their own reasons, they were looking for more living space. In ancient times, overpopulation in one area was easily solved by migrating to another and there was not as yet any conscience about dispossessing those in the way. It was only later after the migrants had become settled that stories were advanced to put the conquest in a better light. For instance, certain of their descendants claimed that the invasion was actually only the return of the Heraclidae, the "sons of Heracles," who came to re-establish themselves in the land which had once been theirs. Thus, legends have helped to hide the real reasons for the invasions, but what actually happened has never been in doubt. The invaders who struck the Mycenaean area came in great numbers and overwhelmed a settled and stable society which was in every way superior to their own except possibly in the possession of iron and in the intensity of their warlike spirit. Actually, iron weapons were not intrinsically any better than those of bronze, but iron was more plentiful and on a percentage basis many more of the invaders were armed than were the defenders with their costly traditional weaponry.

The newcomers were not total strangers. In fact they spoke dialects of Greek and were distantly related to the Ionians and Achaeans who had preceded them into this region about eight hundred years before.

The hypothesis is as follows. Sometime in the past beyond recall, the ancestors of all these Greek-speaking peoples had lived together somewhere in the Danubian region of central Europe. For reasons we know nothing about, the various groups became separated and in the course of time they were even speaking different dialects. Moreover, because of their separate experiences and contacts, they eventually lived on vastly different cultural levels. The first Greek-speaking peoples who moved south came under the influence of the older Cretan and Egyptian civilizations and built the impressive Mycenaean civilization, but about the twelfth century B.C. their flourishing centers were put to the torch by other Greek-speaking peoples who, far from appreciating what they found, did not even save it for themselves.

The arrival of these rude relations has generally been treated as a single event and called the Dorian invasion. This was because those who spoke the Dorian dialect comprised the largest segment of the invaders and spread themselves over the widest area of the Aegean world. In the Peloponnesus in particular it was the Dorians who destroyed the major centers of Mycenaean civilization and so made the most dramatic, if not the best, impression. Apparently during the previous centuries these people had been living in southern Macedonia. From there they moved southward and stayed for a time in Doris, just north of the Corinthian Gulf, and it was from this area that they eventually invaded the Peloponnesus. For this reason the inhabitants of Argolis and Laconia, whose land they appropriated, called them the *Dorieis* or Dorians, and in classical times, among the descendants of these invaders, the age-old relationship with Doris was kept alive. In fact, the Spartans, the most famous of the Dorians, found it a useful concept and whenever it suited their interest to interfere in central Greece, they would march to Doris to protect the motherland.

At the same time as the Dorians were arriving, other tribes were making inroads from the north. They spoke a dialect which, though closely related to the Dorian, was distinctly different. While the Dorians were living in Macedonia these people were settled nearby to the west, in southern Epirus. From there some of them moved due south across the Corinthian Gulf and into Elis, the northwestern section of the Peloponnesus. Others, the Thessaloi and the Boiotoi moved east and southeast and gave their names to the lands where they finally settled.

It is not possible to fix exact dates for these invasions which resulted in a reshuffling of nearly all the peoples of the Aegean world. The various tribes traveled both by land and by sea and the earliest migrants were on the move even before the fall of Troy. Archaeological evidence shows that by the late thirteenth century the Dorians had already arrived in Crete and Rhodes. Yet as late as the mid-eleventh century still other Dorians were moving to these islands from their newly established position in the Peloponnesus. Thus, for a very long time, perhaps two centuries or more, there were continuous movements of peoples who only gradually settled into the areas where they were found in classical times. For the sake of chronology, however, it seems safe to say that by about 1150 outsiders were arriving in Greece in sufficient numbers to disrupt the settled conditions of the land.

The arrival of these invading tribes precipitated a series of migrations by the peoples they attacked and displaced. Some fled into the mountainous region of the central Peloponnesus, called Arcadia, where in classical times their descendants still lived. Most of the refugees fled across the Aegean Sea due east of where they were. The Aeolians crossed over from Thessaly to Lesbos and the northern coast of Asia Minor which came to be known as Aeolis. At the same time the Ionians in central Greece moved to the central and southern coastline of Asia Minor as well as to the islands nearby, and this whole region came to be known as Ionia.

By circumstance then, the refugees from the brilliant Mycenaean culture of Greece came into closer contact than ever before with the older, more advanced centers of civilization in the East. And unlike what was happening in the homeland, this was not a meeting of "bearskin and toga." It was rather an encounter of two different modes of civilized life. Manners of dress, habits of eating, religious conventions and political points of view met and interacted in the towns which grew up with connections both east and west. It was from these centers that the Greeks traveled along the caravan routes to the East and, like the famed Herodotus of a later day, they brought home news when they returned. In other words, unlike the homeland where much was being forgotten, in Ionia there was a chance for learning and progress. It was here in any event that the tempo of Greek civilization was first revived. Like Attica, which would later be the center of the high classical culture, so Ionia, already by the ninth century B.C., was the focus of the budding intellectual life of the post-invasion era. Miletus in particular was a city so favored by geography as to be easily defensible and therefore likely to grow and to afford progress. Yet it was only the most famous of the traditional twelve cities of this region which prospered as western terminals of the trade routes from the East. Here in this transplanted Greece, the old stories dating back to before the cataclysmic invasions were first set down by Homer and his contemporaries. It was in Ionia too that the future was foreshadowed, for at Miletus the first philosophers appeared and began a tradition of rational thinking which became a characteristic of Greek intellectual life.

It is fair to assume that the advanced cultural life of the eastern Aegean reflected the early revival of trade and urban life, for the arts are costly and are usually performed in cities. But this pleasant generalization does not rule out the possibility that certain areas in the homeland did keep pace, at least in an economic sense, with Ionia.

Turning back in our view to the homeland from which the Aeolians and Ionians fled, it is apparent that every place was not affected alike. The invading tribes did not move like glaciers. The archaeological record suggests that some areas were only taken by slow infiltration while others—centers of power and wealth like Pylos, Mycenae and Tiryns—were struck and destroyed as if by a whirlwind, although they were not exactly taken by surprise. Among the Linear B tablets found at Pylos are inscriptions which offer reports about precautionary movements of land and sea forces, plus an inventory of the available bronze being stockpiled in the face of imminent danger. Some of them give the impression that women and children were being moved to safety. If so, it was a false hope. These tablets were buried along with the rest of the city when the Dorians took the place and burned it.

During the invasions and their aftermath, from about 1200 to about 750, the tempo of life in Greece was neither what it had been nor what it would be again. Whether a place was taken by attrition or overrun by a shock attack, there was a lowering of standards to some degree and in many areas the common denominator became mere subsistence. Archaeologists have recovered pottery and other objects dated to this period which show that by comparison with pre-invasion times there was a decline in productivity as well as in technique and taste. Yet this was probably only true of the most advanced areas of Greece which were the hardest hit. It does not mean that stagnation and decline were everywhere. Actually in Attica, which had never been a major center of Mycenaean culture, there was an advance over previous times. There was of course a problem of overcrowding owing to refugees flooding in from nearby. Nor could the forays of marauders, who never took the Acropolis but ravaged the vicinity, have helped matters any. Nevertheless, the refugees appear to have brought new designs and skills which resulted in progressive improvements in Athenian pottery. The National Archaeological Museum in Athens has an especially fine display of vases which exhibit this gradual refinement. They are classified as proto-geometric and geometric types and feature patterns of concentric

*Pl. 26 Attic Protogeometric cup, tenth century B.C.*

*Pl. 27 Attic Geometric amphora, eighth century B.C. This amphora showing a few human figures, and others of the same style, are called Dipylon vases. Several of them were found near the Dipylon Gate of Athens.*

circles, parallel and zigzagging lines, meanders and chequered areas (Pl. 26, 27). In later examples, human and animal figures begin to be seen sparingly and are evidence of the continuing advances in local artistry. Attica aside, however, the deterioration of conditions in most of Greece is plain in the record.

Under the circumstances it is easier to borrow the term Dark Ages than it is to avoid it. Comparison with the more famous Dark Ages which followed the fall of Rome is obvious. Similar periods everywhere seem both to begin and end alike. In Western Europe, the Dark Ages followed a series of invasions which swamped the centers of Roman culture. Anyone who knows only a little about this later period of history is aware that there were also present in the Roman Empire economic and political troubles which were perhaps crucial in softening it up for the barbarian kill. It is pertinent therefore to ask if the Mycenaean civilization might not also have been suffering internal problems which made the invaders look better than they were. Unfortunately, information about such conditions in Achaean Greece is not even sufficient to allow a debate such as the one which persists about the Roman decline. The lamps did go out, however, and in Europe as in Greece, depression, illiteracy and disorganization marked the ensuing centuries. Again, both periods ended with a revival of trade and town life, but in the meantime the established patterns of an earlier society had broken down.

In the pre-invasion Greece which Homer described, the dominant group of men, the aristocracy, had roamed off on profitable sea-raids which entailed much fighting, but they eventually returned home and home was well fortified. In the *Odyssey*, Penelope was not a wife forever packing, but a patient queen waiting for Odysseus to return from the gods knew where. The substantial palaces, exquisite jewelry, elaborate weaponry, well-designed pottery, and sizeable tombs, described in the foregoing chapter attest a settled, somewhat specialized, society which had achieved in certain respects a sense of refinement. The kings and their noble companions, secure in their own wealth and privileges, provided for the protection and needs of the lower classes of artisans and farmers according to the familiar pattern of *noblesse oblige*. Everyone had his place and his obligation and as is customary under such conditions, the busy work of the many provided the good life for the few. Otherwise they lived different lives. The problems and goals of the man with the wooden plow were quite different from those of the warrior with the high-bossed shield.

The invasions brought the same misery to everyone. No longer did the kings gather together their warriors for some joint venture such as the attack on Troy. Now the fighting was at home and all classes suffered. Aristocrats who lost their palaces, their daggers inlaid with gold, and their many slaves must have felt that they suffered the most. As always under such circumstances local problems became paramount and interests were narrowed to the nearest horizon. The times encouraged everyone to be for himself and not all of those with the most to lose resisted the conquerors. Some turned against their own people and joined the enemy in order to salvage something for themselves.

Both at home and abroad, the nobility which emerged from this unsettling period were not the kind of men their ancestors had been in the Bronze Age. Whether the descendants of Dorian conquerors or of Ionian forebears who had fled across the seas, the new aristocrats were settled on the land and remained at home to guard their property and their privileges. Their inherited wealth and status gave them advantages which enabled them not only to defend their own interests but to infringe on those of others. With the passing of time there gradually evolved amongst noblemen of whatever origin a sense of selfish class unity which created a bond amongst the "better" people against all others. So it was that the new aristocracy, far from acting as the protectors of the common folk as in the old days, even preyed on them in order to maintain their own positions. Yet for all the significance of this change there is actually only one eyewitness account to support it, and the aristocracy stands indicted by a single complaint.

### Hesiod, A Farmer and Sometime Poet

For most of the Dark Ages there is no written description whatsoever. Nothing points more tellingly to the drastic disintegration of society during this time than the conclusion that writing had probably disappeared. Apparently it was not until during the ninth century that conditions had settled enough, at least in Ionia, for the art of writing to reappear. And when it did, instead of the earlier syllabic form of Linear B, an alphabet was used, probably as a result of contact with the Near East. Also, whereas the earlier tablets suggest that writing was used only for inventories and the like, the new material was poetic and preserved whole stories. This was the beginning of a true literary tradition, but even so, little was being written about everyday conditions. Homer and his contemporaries were mostly busy retelling stories from the distant past. These tales of bygone days were what the aristocrats wanted to hear, for it is evident that there was little in their present of which they could be proud. Only one writer mentions their vicious use of wealth and rank to defraud. As might be expected, he was among the victims. This is Hesiod, a farmer and sometime poet, who talks about life in the eighth century in his poem *Works and Days*. He is the eyewitness and what he tells us about himself and his times is still our best knowledge of Greece during the latter part of the Dark Ages.

Hesiod agreed with the nobility that the best of times were long ago and the worst of times were his own. He spoke from bitter experience. His brother Perses, he said, had cheated him out of a fair share of their father's estate by bribing one of the local well-born judges. Still he had not lost as much as some who were squeezed out entirely by these "swallowers of bribes" as he calls them. Other men were being coerced by violence and Hesiod is frank about this too, yet somehow he never actually becomes excited and under the circumstances, his manner seems naive or at least overly cautious. His expressed belief that all-seeing Zeus would punish these crimes surely helped to hold his temper down. It is possible too that he was a quiet man, or that he was afraid. Whatever the reason, his *Works and Days* reflects a kind of mentality which must always have been present, but never before had appeared in writing. The heroic figures drawn by Homer were active, bold and self-willed men. Hesiod is somebody in the neighborhood.

The setting for the *Works and Days* was a work-a-day world and not the far-off places of an odyssey. As was customary, Hesiod began by asking the muses for a gift of words. They were not as generous to him as they were to Homer, it would seem, but then they did not need to be. Hesiod was not writing about exciting adventurers who roamed the seas, but of men like himself who had spent their entire lives in one place. For Hesiod this was Ascra in Boeotia. His father may have brought him there as a child from Aeolis or perhaps he was born there. Exactly when is also indefinite. The historian Herodotus, writing in the fifth century B.C., loosely links Hesiod to Homer by saying that they both lived no earlier than four hundred years before his own time. It is generally conceded that Homer was writing no earlier than the late ninth century and was an older contemporary of Hesiod. A poem of unknown authorship entitled *The Contest Between Homer and Hesiod* has them meeting face to face, but all it actually shows is that the Greeks were fond of contests, real or imagined.

No one should be bothered by the difference in tone between the works of these two men or seek an elaborate explanation why Homer's more sophisticated view of the gods should give place to mere superstition in Hesiod. Men think on different levels in all ages. In the twelfth century, the farmers who worked the soil at home while Achilles and Hector fought before Troy, thought just about the way Hesiod would think in the eighth century. But there was no poet to speak for them then and they had no role in the sagas sung for, and about, the nobility. So too the aristocrats of Hesiod's day continued to enjoy hearing how their ancestors took Troy while all they were taking themselves were petty bribes. Homer registered the heroic mood which only occurs from time to time yet lingers on in memory. He describes extraordinary men, the kind who seem always to have lived a long time ago. Those whom Hesiod talks about are an ordinary sort, less talented perhaps, but more enduring.

Part of the *Works and Days* has the orderliness of an almanac, and all of it speaks for a man who finds the times risky enough without taking any chances. The cry of the crane is the signal for winter ploughing. When Orion is seen, then the chaff should be fanned from the grain. There is a time for this and a time for that, but not for everything. A ladle should never be crossed over a wine bowl; nor should a man bathe in water a woman has used. Hesiod's verse was new, but the material was familiar, for the stars and superstitions he mentions had been guides of conduct long before his own time. So perhaps were his maxims which, like all proverbial sayings, sound ageless. The blacksmith shop, he warned, was a place for idlers in winter. The talkative man who gossips about others will soon be the object of gossip himself. A man should always be busy with the chores at hand or in preparation for those to come. The time to build barns is midsummer, not when the harvest is near. Such are the works which will keep a man out of trouble, but Hesiod also lists the unlucky days when things may go wrong. The fifth day of the month, for instance, would be a bad day for anything, including marriage. And in taking a wife there are other precautions a man might consider. Choose a girl in the neighborhood, he advises, one young enough to be trained in prudent habits. It all added up—a good reputation, a good barn, a good wife, and especially hard work.

Hesiod is the prototype of the self-made man with all the simple virtues. Benjamin Franklin comes to mind and then remains for another reason. It will be recalled that during Franklin's later life while serving at the court in Paris, he was noted for his dalliance with the ladies. By coincidence there is a similar story about Hesiod and a more serious one for in this instance the byplay was fatal. The tradition says that in his old age two brothers whom he was visiting in Locris accused him of abusing their sister and murdered him for the deed then and there. If the story is true it is a curious turn of events, not only because Hesiod was a man of such good advice, but also because he apparently was reluctant to travel in the first place. Aside from this account of a final trip there is only one reference to his having left his farm in Boeotia. He mentions that he won first prize in a poetry contest on the island of Euboea. Everything else known about him suggests that his world was a small one, governed by the routine of the seasons and circumscribed by superstition. He was not a man to be optimistic about any changes. For him the present was a hard Age of Iron and his writings do not offer any prophecy of a better way of life or a Golden Age to come. In the light of this outlook it is ironical that his *Works and Days* survived to become the major literary source about events which radically altered the course of Greek history.

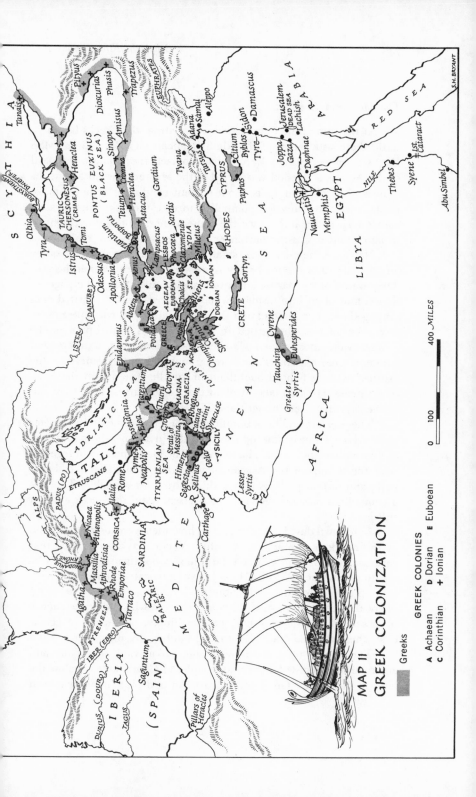

MAP II
GREEK COLONIZATION

Greeks

GREEK COLONIES
▲ Achaean    ▫ Dorian    ▪ Euboean
c Corinthian    + Ionian

0    100    400 MILES

S.H. BRYANT

## The Movement Overseas

At the same time that Hesiod was writing, the Greeks began to settle the coastal areas of the Mediterranean and Black Seas (Map II), as in modern times Europeans colonized the Atlantic seaboard of the Americas. Hesiod was afraid of the sea and warned against its dangers, but his comments about current conditions at home make it plain why so many felt compelled to take the risk. There was of course no way for him to see the consequences of this movement or to know that it was the harbinger of a great age.

Nor were the men whose small ships hugged the shore for safety any less afraid of the sea or any more aware of destiny than he was. They were not the daring adventurers who sail through the pages of fiction and often into history. Surely there were a few spirited ones among them, but imagination is not a quality you encounter every day. The Greeks who settled in small colonies from Spain to the Crimea were mostly men who left their homes for ordinary and common-sense reasons. They were no more adventuresome than the "Okies" who fled the droughtland of middle America in the nineteen thirties. Hesiod makes it plain that they went because they had to; he says they were hungry and in debt.

The pressure had been building up for a long time. In the quieter years which followed the upheaval of the invasions, the population had far outstripped the available land. The Greek peninsula together with the islands of the Aegean offered little enough land to begin with, and of that perhaps only a third or so was workable. This was a compelling reason for men to go overseas. And in Greece today it still is.

In his own day, Hesiod remarked how men were losing their land at the hands of a predatory nobility. Yet it may also be true that certain families owning large estates took a positive role in the colonization movement. While Hesiod never advocates taking land away from the wealthy and redistributing it among the poor, it seems likely that there were men without property who did make such a proposal. The aristocracy may have willingly, perhaps even generously, helped these "radicals" to find land in distant places.

The Greeks were not moving into unknown lands. Time and again, archaeologists have found samples of Greek pottery below the level of the earliest Greek settlements. An odd piece may have been carried by others, the Phoenicians perhaps, but there are sufficient examples to prove that Greek traders had preceded the settlers. References here and there in the poems of Homer and Hesiod suggest what the poets knew of the rest of the world, but it was less than the traders knew who left products behind them which tell us where they had traveled. A few traders may even have settled abroad, but most of them returned home carrying the news which prompted others to emigrate.

While some settlers took individual passage on trading ships, most of the immigrants joined groups sponsored by cities which began to make a business of organizing and outfitting expeditions. By the eighth century, Miletus, as has been mentioned, was already a flourishing trade center. Very likely she was the first to sponsor overseas settlements. Estimates vary on how many were sent out, but eighty is the minimum figure. The success of these early ventures enabled her to become a commercial and cultural center long before Athens, the city of the future, had founded even a single colony.

Phocaea, north of Miletus on the Ionian coast, Chalcis and Eretria on the island of Euboea, and Megara and Corinth on the mainland were prominent among the other cities which followed the example of Miletus and began to send out colonists. Some of the sites selected for settlement were so ideally chosen that they have been occupied ever since. In the western Mediterranean, modern Marseilles spreads out along the shore where the Phocaeans once established the colony of Massilia. In the East, Istanbul occupies the site of Byzantium, which was founded by colonists from Megara a thousand years before the Roman Emperor Constantine renamed the place for himself. In Sicily, Corinth's famous Syracuse has never changed its name. Among the settlers going to Italy were the *Graioi* from Boeotia, where Hesiod lived. The colony they helped to establish never became very famous, but they themselves did because the Romans talked about the *Graeci*—and so today we talk about the Greeks.

Massilia, Byzantium and Syracuse are perhaps the best known of the colonies, but there were hundreds of others founded during a period roughly from about 750 to about 550. In Greek history this two hundred years is arbitrarily but conveniently called the Age of Colonization. It was a time of expanding trade, growing cities, and an increasing literacy and artistic output. Each of these trends marked the end of the Dark Ages and foreshadowed the brighter times ahead.

Like the modern Europeans who came to the Americas in the seventeenth and eighteenth centuries, the ancient Greeks who went overseas changed both the lands to which they went and the home-land from which they came. Wherever they traveled they carried with them their old habits and needs. They fought the original in-habitants, took their land and introduced them to a higher way of life, although, like the American Indians, not all of the natives lived to enjoy it. Once established, the colonies (in reality independent communities) became markets for products from home and outlets for the exchange of goods with the hinterland. Among the chief neces-sities shipped from the mother cities were wine and olive oil which were sent in local pottery jars. The package itself was a product. Cities specializing in textiles, armaments, pottery or shipbuilding had a promising future and the grain, fish and slaves sent back from the colonies helped to sustain growing urban populations. By this process local self-sufficiency gave way to overseas involvements and with growth and prosperity came the problems of success. What happened is com-parable to the mercantile developments of early modern times. It was all on a smaller stage with fewer people involved, but in their ambi-tions and conflicts the Greek city-states behaved like miniature nations of Europe.

## A New Kind Of Wealth

None of this would have been possible without the convenience of money. Many early peoples, including the Greeks, had long used large weights of one metal or another as a medium of exchange in addition to the old system of barter. The Lydians, a neighboring people in Asia Minor, were apparently the first to stamp small pieces with a guaranteed value and it seems likely that their coins were the earliest to be seen in Greek markets. As would be expected, the first Greek cities to copy the practice and mint their own coins were those which had begun to produce cloth and pottery for export. As with colonies, so with coinage; Miletus, located near to Lydia, took the lead.

Coins speeded up the activities of man faster than any invention since the wheel. They were easy to carry, accumulate, bury or borrow. A man could get rich faster and he could go bankrupt faster. Wher-ever money was introduced, nothing could again be the same and everybody was affected in one way or another. Although literary men have given more space to the invention of the alphabet, there are still more people who can count money than can read or write.

Land and cattle would always be riches, but money was a new

kind of wealth and it is customarily said that it gave rise to a new class, the bourgeoisie. True, but just as important was the fact that money cut across class lines altogether. Some of the men who began to engage in the new ventures of trading and mining were members of the aristocracy, which as a rule was comfortably situated on the land and considered commerce a lowly occupation. They might be the young sons of old families interested in new possibilities, or perhaps disinherited or bankrupt relatives now interested in any possibility. Regardless of their reasons, these men and their descendants would in some respects have a different outlook from the majority of their class. Their experiences, interests and contacts tied them in new ways to common-born craftsmen and traders. So the use of money, while not actually breaking down the class barriers, did shade them, and for the simple reason that business is a practical matter. So is politics. Many of the leaders on the side of reform in the later political upheavals would come from this dissident faction of the nobility.

Even those noblemen who frowned on commercial activity encouraged its growth by constituting the best market for luxury items from abroad. In other ways too, their interests became involved with the new order of things. The increasing demands for the produce of their estates gave them more wealth than ever before and they used part of this capital to make profitable loans to their hard-pressed neighbors. One effect of this was the slow strangulation of marginal farmers who never had a future to borrow against in the first place. It is an old saw, but true, that the many fell deeper in debt to the few. The aristocracy did, in fact, by their own greed contribute to an intolerable situation which would one day be part of their own undoing. If this sounds like the familiar Marxist theme of the rich driving the poor to the wall and thereby sealing their own doom, it should be remembered that the Greeks offer little comfort to any kind of determinist; for they, if any people do, show man to be a multisided creature, never just this or that.

Most of the men who were making the wheels turn in the new economy were of common birth. In time, some of them became the familiar *nouveau riche,* who could afford land and cattle and in fact everything the aristocracy had except a proper birthright, the door to political power. While intermarriage was neither impossible nor unknown, it was too infrequent to be of much help. So, as matters stood, there was an ever increasing number of men who had enough experience, wealth and education to realize what they were also missing.

At the broad base of this society were the poor farmers, many of whom were losing what little they already had. Changes which promise a better future for all often in the short term hurt those least able to afford a loss. Money was an indispensable necessity for the growth of commerce yet it offered the small farmer the temptation to take greater risks by the availability of ready funds to borrow. From this circumstance came the worst abuse of the times, widespread debt slavery. By long-standing custom a man could offer himself and even his family as a surety for a loan. In the earlier days of barter, when dealings were less complicated, this practice did not involve the risk which it did with money.

The small investor was also hurt by the impact of cheap grain from the colonies. Large landowners with ready capital could easily shift acreage to grapes and olives, which were highly favored by the soil and climate. Vineyards and orchards required more land and a longer term investment, however, than the little man could afford. Some impoverished farmers went into the city and worked for wages in small shops and kilns and others served as rowers in an expanding merchant fleet. But both the birth rate and the use of slave labor worked against full employment and the final solution was, as it had always been, to pack up and leave in search of a better chance elsewhere.

## The Champions of the New Instead of the Old

The aristocrats enjoyed their greater profits from the increased demand for wine and olive oil and the new possibilities for the investment of capital, but that was all the change most of them cared to see. They had altered neither their habits nor their thinking and, except for a fraction of their members, were unwilling to abandon a position so well guarded by custom. Their exclusive rights meant that the men of common birth, who were actually responsible for the prosperity and growth of the new cities, were frozen out of any effective participation in their government. It should be noted, however, that these well-to-do commoners were not necessarily interested in justice for all, but were seeking it mainly for themselves. Their strength was in their money rather than in their principles. They could afford the arms with which to challenge the old guard.

In modern times, wherever constitutional processes have been available, social and political reforms have been effected without the widespread violence which has occurred in countries lacking democratic institutions. In seventh century Greece, democracy was still a long way off and in many places it never was to come at all. Therefore, in lieu of any constitutional means by which to bring about changes, inherited privilege was overthrown and reforms were sanctioned by force. Some of the nobility were killed and many more were exiled, for those who upset the old order often acted with no less cruelty than Hesiod had suggested it took to maintain it.

These uprisings were not for the purpose of establishing democracies. Wherever they occurred, aristocratic rule was replaced by that of a strong man whose policies were intended to favor the commercial classes who supported him with their money and the poor farmers who backed him with their clamoring. Here was the familiar "man on horseback" who, for better or for worse, by fair means or foul, sought to solve the problems of the times.

These champions of the common man were usually members of the highest class who abandoned the status they had inherited but not the money, and found a cause and an opportunity among the rank and file. In renouncing their favored ancestry they took advantage of circumstances which afforded another kind of power. At least one of them, Pheidon of Argos, may have been a king before he decided to shift with the times and become the champion of the new instead of the old. As might be expected, some of these men came to power by means of high military office, as if at the head of a Latin American *junta*. Others, without any official position to use as a springboard, employed money, influence and popularity.

Ironically, the aristocracy, which by custom and education had remained the school for leadership, produced the men who would undermine its power. The break was a sharp one. The aims and methods of these new leaders were practical and they acted without respect for class or custom. Except among his former friends such a man was considered a benefactor, and the fact that he was called a tyrant by no means meant that he was thought to be oppressive. It was not until the fourth century B.C. that this title took on the altogether ugly association it has today. In the beginning *tyrannos* meant "overseer" and was, in certain instances, used interchangeably with *basileus,* king. It is often said that our equivalent term today would be "benevolent despot," but this is too elaborate. His military backing aside, he was just a city boss.

The tyrants, as individuals, were as varied in their qualities as men are likely to be, but it can be said of them as a group that they were part opportunists thriving on the needs of the times and part conscientious "public servants." What mattered most, however, was that they claimed the power once held by the aristocrats and that they made better use of it.

The tyrant ruled not because he had a right to rule or because his family had always ruled. He was in power to satisfy the needs of the community which he served. It was therefore to his advantage to undermine as much as possible the old order and to create a united citizenry devoted to the city, to its patron deity, and, hopefully to himself who served both city and god so well.

A major obstacle which the reform-minded tyrants faced was the ancient tribal system, a legacy from a time beyond memory. Homer's *Iliad* mentions the brotherhoods of warriors, or phratries, which combined to make up a tribe, or *phyle*. These terms have been accepted by many scholars as being derived from the military organization of the primitive Greeks even before their migration south of the Danube. On the other hand, in Attica, where the population was distributed among the four Ionian tribes, each bearing the name of one of the legendary sons of Ion, it has been suggested that tribal names such as *Hopletes* and *Aigikoreis* referred to occupation—warriors and goatherders. In any event these ancient associations in time created strong social, political and religious ties. In simple societies where no more sophisticated means of identification were available, such ties of blood and religion gave the individual a sense of belonging and security within a larger "family" than modern societies normally supply.

A man inherited tribal membership from his father and was bound by blood to all his "brothers" whose lineage was traced back to a single progenitor. Similarly there were protecting deities for each tribe and phratry. Among the Ionians, a child born during the previous year was officially registered in his father's brotherhood with accompanying sacrifices during the autumnal festival of the Apaturia. This familiar custom was not bothersome to the tyrants. What did stand in their way was the fact that for a long time the phratries, and through them the tribes, had been under the domination of certain prominent families whose power was exemplified in their hereditary control of the major priesthoods. It followed that their position depended on the maintenance of the old ways in opposition to the leveling which might result from a new concept of community citizenship.

The tyrants argued that the welfare of all would be best served by the lowering of the old barriers. Thus, while a man continued to be rated as a member of a given family and class, increasingly his role as a citizen took on greater significance. The success of the tyrants in instilling loyalty and pride in the citizens of the various cities served to enliven contests both on and off the battlefield. Even so, time and again a city faltered because of class strife which disrupted the home scene. With distressing frequency parties of citizens betrayed their own city to outsiders who would promise support in return for a favor. It is true that the tyrants were the builders of civic loyalty, but the Greeks have a tendency toward excitability, quarrelsomeness and devious dealings with one another. Nothing has ever changed that.

The first item on a tyrant's agenda was the opening of public offices to men who qualified on the basis of wealth rather than birth alone. This move ended the political monopoly of the aristocracy. Men of noble birth, able to accommodate themselves to the new circumstances, were still active in the affairs of the city, but the opportunity was now open for any man to succeed in public life if he had already succeeded in making money. The tyrant thus assured himself of the support of the commercial interests by taking at least their wealthier members into partnership. In certain places this was the initial step toward democracy, while elsewhere it meant that the city would eventually fall into the hands of a wealthy clique.

The grip of the aristocracy was loosened in other ways. If old customs were abusive or unfair the tyrant was determined to correct them. He ordered traditional laws, hitherto known only to men of the highest class, to be written down for ready reference by all. The laws were as partial to property rights as they had ever been, but they were now available for everybody to read and no longer secreted in the memory of the aristocrats who monopolized the judicial powers. They were also subject to change. Alterations sanctioned by the tyrants were especially designed to free the individual from a maze of tribal restrictions over personal matters. It became possible, for instance, for a man without heirs to name a beneficiary rather than have his property revert to the control of the clan and its leaders. So, bit by bit, the power of the tribes was undermined and with it the special position of the old families which controlled them.

Such a trend was bound to benefit the poorer citizens in the long run, yet it would be a mistake to assume that all of them were anxious to upset the established lines of responsibility. As a rule, immediate material benefits are more popular with the needy than are subtle efforts to undermine the basic structure of society. The tyrants assured themselves of continued support therefore, when they freed men who had been enslaved for debt, abolished debt slavery altogether, and reduced or cancelled heavy liens on small plots of land. Furthermore, the construction of temples, theaters and aqueducts meant not only beautiful and useful new structures for the city, but jobs for the unemployed as well.

The tyrants were not merely shrewd; they were also brave, as any man must be who tries to reform a calendar. The early lunar calendars required that extra days be added occasionally in order to keep up with the seasons. Since the sun and the moon played prominent parts in Greek religious lore, it was inevitable that priests were the ones to make the additions. But sometimes they neglected this duty, and in areas where commercial interests became predominant, something had to be done. The priests were not only professionally committed to tradition, but, as aristocrats, took the dim view of that class toward any changes. Therefore the power of a tyrant was needed to sweep barriers aside and arrange for the necessary regularity. Similarly, alterations of coinage and of weights and measures were sometimes needed and were generally good for business.

When a tyrant took over a city, it was his to defend. The usual Greek community spread out from the base of some high ground—an acropolis—which was walled and served as a fortress. As the city prospered it might also come to include other hills nearby. It is not surprising, then, to find that as part of his building program a tyrant would order construction of a wall around the whole region in order to provide better security for more people. When this was done, the area atop the acropolis which had served as a citadel became a religious and civic center, which in ancient Greece were actually one and the same.

The tyrant was ever mindful of all the needs of the city. If there had been trains he would have made them run on time. It is easy to imagine a man who takes all power despotically to himself as mean and ugly, as he often is; it is more difficult to accept the evidence that a tyrant's success may have depended on the fact that he was a sincere and dedicated man who served the needs as well as the prejudices of those who supported him. This trust and the pressing needs of the moment helped postpone the simple question of how, if ever, the city might in the future be rid of him or his successor.

The tyrants were usually secure so long as their cities grew and prospered and the commercial and working class interests were satisfied. Some tyrants were strongly enough entrenched to provide for the succession of a son or other relative. Orthagoras founded a dynasty at Sicyon in 655 which lasted for nearly a hundred years. Such ruling

houses were similar to those of the despots who governed the autonomous Italian cities of early modern times, the Medici at Florence
for example. Yet a son was not always as worthy as his father and a
grandson or nephew might be worse. And so the question of how to
end a tyranny did sometimes arise. As resignations were hard to get,
a tyranny usually was finished the way it began, with violence.

## The Will of Apollo

Tyrants might come and go, political and economic power might
shift from one region of Greece to another, but through the years the
great pan-Hellenic shrines held their own. At these centers, the same
gods were worshipped by all and the troubled Greeks found common
ground. Those who came were suppliants offering gifts, not only
statuary and money, but athletic and dramatic talents too. They were
grateful for past favors and hopeful of continued guidance. Man could
know the past and the present. Only the gods knew the future.

Experience is a good teacher but a hard one. It is not strange
that men would gladly avoid its rigors if they could know in advance
what to do. In every age there are some who have had the secret. One
of the oldest forms of augury consisted of the search for special signs
on the livers of sacrificial animals. The Romans, like their predecessors, busily scanned the sky. Your horoscope for today is in the
morning paper.

If the Greeks had an important decision to make they visited an
oracle. The word has three uses. It may refer to a location of an
oracular shrine, the priestess in charge of the shrine, and also the
answers she gives. Thus, it may be said that an oracle was pronounced
by the oracle who presided at an oracle.

There were many places of this kind in Greece, including the
oracles of Zeus at Olympia and at Dodona in Epirus which was
probably the oldest of them all. The central figure in these oracles
was a priestess. Exactly how women came to hold a monopoly on the
mediumistic arts in Greece is no clearer than why they have managed to maintain their lead. There is no conclusive evidence as to
how they were chosen or what their qualifications had to be. Suffice
it to say that when one priestess died there was probably available a
young woman whose "otherness" made her a likely candidate for
the position.

According to tradition, the priestess at Dodona heard sounds in
the rustlings of an oak tree sacred to Zeus and when her enraptured

*Pl. 28 Sanctuary at Delphi. The theater is in the foreground and the ruins of the temple of Apollo in the center.*

utterances had been decoded by the priests of the shrine, the petitioner received an answer, usually in verse. At Delphi, seat of the most
famous of the oracles, the priestess (or *Pythia* as she was called) was
reputed to have listened to a brook sacred to Apollo and heard the
voice of the god. Others have attributed her powers to the inhaling of
vapors rising out of the earth and the guides at the site still tell this
story although it has not been verified by archaeologists. In his
enlightening work *The Greeks and the Irrational*, E. R. Dodds suggests
that the *Pythia* behaved like a modern medium who in a seance pre-
pares herself to be used by a voice from the beyond. In other words
Apollo was using her voice. Whatever her resources were, the responses
which the priestess gave required editing and, as at Dodona, they
were interpreted by the assisting priests. Even so, the final statement
was often couched in such ambiguous language that the petitioner
was left with the problem of reading his answer in at least one of two
ways. If he misjudged the advice it was his own fault. The god was
never wrong. Neither are the stars for those who follow them.

Certainly for a long period of time the Delphic oracle must have
supplied satisfactory guidance to many private persons as well as to
states, native and foreign, which sent ambassadors with questions of
political import. How otherwise could the fame, wealth and power of
this place have grown as it did? As Professor Dodds observes, the
continued faith in the oracle, even after the shrine's inscrutable
neutrality at the time of the Persian threat in the early fifth century,
indicates that the Greeks by that time had developed such an irrational dependence on the oracle that they could even overlook its
sometimes curious policies.

The dramatic and athletic festivals in honor of Apollo at Delphi
rivalled those held elsewhere on behalf of the Father Zeus and his
amazing daughter Athena. Representatives from all over the Greek
world brought to the shrine the official salutation of their respective
cities. Small temple-like structures were built to house these perennial
visitors. They also served as repositories for the gifts the envoys brought
with them and so were called treasuries: the Treasury of the Athenians,
for instance, and the Treasury of the Siphnians (Pl. 29).

Today, Delphi can be visited by means of a comfortable bus
which leaves Athens in the morning about seven and returns in the
evening around nine. The distance is a little over a hundred miles
and the route is a panorama of scenic views (Pl. 28). The ride on
winding mountain roads up to a height of about 1700 feet above sea
level also makes it apparent why the ancient Greeks considered the

*Pl. 29 Detail of north frieze from the Treasury of the Siphnians at Delphi,* circa
*525 B.C. Apollo and Artemis are shown in combat with three Giants.*

trip to Delphi a good journey and once there preferred to stay for
awhile. Ample temptation is offered today by the beautiful hotels
situated so as to capture the full glory of the view southward across
the valley toward the Corinthian Gulf and the picturesque setting
of the small port of Itea.

Part of the fascination of the trip to Delphi is seeing the sights of
the past which have not disappeared. The landscape includes countless shimmering, silvery olive trees and terraced plantings of vines.
Here and there too are seen men and women carrying packs of
brushwood on their backs or using long shepherd's crooks to guide
their belled and befuddled goats. Most striking of all is the sight of
women alongside men fixed in an age-old tableau as they lean low
in the fields working with small iron hoes.

At Delphi, there is ample evidence of the complex of buildings
which once stood in the vicinity including the theater and stadium.
The actual sanctuary sacred to Apollo, once surrounded by a wall,
was spread over five terraces in the southern foothills of Mount Par-
nassus which towers above the surrounding country 8,060 feet high.

The gymnasium and palaestra where athletes practiced for the games were located a short distance away from the sanctuary and a visitor from the south or east arrives at these sites before coming to the Castalian Spring. In ancient times the spring was where the "pilgrim" purified himself in anticipation of a visit to the holy places above. The water is still cool and drinkable, but the fountain house with spouting lion heads is now missing. From the spring a winding path leads upward toward the temple of Apollo which stands on the topmost level of the sanctuary. Enroute are the crumbled bases which once held statues and the ruined foundations of buildings including the various treasuries. Only the Treasury of the Athenians has been restored (Pl. 30).

Looking upward from the sanctuary, you can see the ancient theater at the left on a higher level. The stadium (Pl. 31) was built on a plateau farther away. These auxiliary facilities, which to the modern eye seem out of place in a religious setting, were nonetheless integral parts of the means by which the Greeks offered honor and gratitude to their gods. Today, along the road to Delphi, small wayside shrines testify to the continuing religiosity of the Greeks and in particular their devotion to Christian saints; but nowhere in modern

*Pl. 30 Treasury of the Athenians at Delphi*

*Pl. 31 Stadium at Delphi*

Greece is there so grandiose a shrine as the ancients built for Apollo. Delphi, by its own pronouncement, was the center of the universe.

The ingathering at Delphi of many ambassadors from domestic and foreign states was obviously an invitation to politics. The shrine became a kind of listening post, and the answers given by the oracle on major questions of war and peace could scarcely have been divorced from the knowledge of events which the priests acquired. Partisanship on behalf of one city against another could only be interpreted as the will of Apollo, but the Greeks were alert to the possibility of bribes. The historian Herodotus specifically named a priestess, Perialla, who was found guilty of this crime and dismissed from her office. At the same time, however, wealthy cities competed with one another in the size of their gifts and could hardly have felt that the god or his agents were unmindful of which city had contributed the most.

# Corinth and Sparta

**IV**

In general, in the span of years from Mycenaean times through the Dark Ages and into the Colonization Period, monarchies were replaced by aristocracies and the aristocracies in turn by tyrannies. What happened next depended on local conditions and experiences. At Corinth, the last tyrant was assassinated by order of a few wealthy men who then set up an oligarchy. Much later at Athens, under different circumstances, tyrants actually abetted the cause of democracy, although this was not their intention. Sparta, which never became a commercial city and never had a tyranny, is a story apart, typical of herself and with problems to match.

The contrasting experiences of the Greek cities provide their history with a special flavor; as among individuals, the differences account for much of the interest in each story, as well as for much of the trouble that arose. In the Colonization Age, Corinth and Sparta offer a sharp contrast. The first was a bustling trade center whose citizens were so occupied buying and selling that they sometimes hired others to fight for them. In Sparta, the citizens were forbidden to handle money at all and spent their time preparing for war. Yet, different as they were, Corinth and Sparta would one day join forces against Athens, whose growth in commerce and military power came later and threatened them both. In the meantime they were the most important cities in Greece, and of the two the heyday of Corinth came first.

Corinth is not where it used to be, but the site of the ancient city which the Romans destroyed is not far away. It was an ideal place for the early development of trade. The city was located in the Peloponnesus near the Isthmus of Corinth and was a likely crossroads. In addition, it was situated between the Corinthian Gulf and the Saronic Gulf, only a few miles from embarkation points, east and west. Wherever the archaeologists of today dig around the Mediterranean Sea, whether in Syria, Egypt or Sicily, they are likely as not to find a Corinthian vase.

As light falls upon the scene in the second half of the eighth century, Corinth is under the rule of a Dorian clan called the Bacchiadae, who claimed by birth what their ancestors had won by force. The leaders of this clan recognized the potentialities of Corinth's position in terms of overseas trade and are credited with the founding of her great colonies at Syracuse and Corcyra (modern Corfu). By encouraging trade, the Bacchiadae put Corinth on the course to her future strength and prosperity, and, ironically, in so doing contributed to their own downfall. As Corinth prospered, the Bacchiadae who were only a small segment of the nobility used their position to exploit the market and grew wealthy from the business of others. Not all new developments were in their favor. As the city grew, so did its commitments and it was soon faced with the problems which wealth and expansion often invite. It became necessary to maintain a new-style army in order to compete with the advanced type of warfare used elsewhere. During the Colonization Age, men who had gained wealth by craftsmanship or trading were able to afford the cost of armament and consequently there was a shift from dependency on the old Homeric style of warrior who fought in single combat, to the new middle-class *hoplite* who joined in a formation and fought as one of a group. And so at Corinth, as time went on, those whose industry gave prosperity to the city also furnished its protection. Sooner or later it was bound to be recognized that the Bacchiadae were representative of an expendable tradition. The names and the details of this story belong to Corinth, but this was a typical crisis of the kind which produced conflict and then tyranny.

That the leader of the ensuing rebellion would be a military figure would not be unexpected. Cypselus, the founder of the tyranny, may have been one, but of this there is no proof. Nor are we sure that the story which related him to the Bacchiadae was any truer than the other "hidden child" tales told in the lives of better-known notables, including Moses and Cyrus.

The story begins with the fact that the Bacchiadae only married within their own clan. There was a girl in the family, however, who was lame and, being unwanted by her relatives, sought a husband where she could. She married a man of another clan and became the mother of Cypselus. The Bacchiadae had been forewarned by oracles of danger in store for them at the hands of this son of an outsider and so were determined to kill him. The boy was hidden in what is variously described as a chest, or jug or grain bin (the root word for Cypselus suggests such a hiding place), and so was saved from those who sought his life. This exciting escape foreshadowed a charmed existence which made the downfall of his relatives a foregone conclusion. Tradition says that by 657 Cypselus had sufficient military and popular support to seize the city and establish a tyranny. He executed certain of the Bacchiadae, exiled others and then, by measures familiar to tyranny everywhere, repaid those who had supported his cause. The commercial interests were given a place in the government and the poor were relieved of their debts. The already established policy of sending out colonies was continued and a revision of the coinage helped to increase trade. As usual with tyrants it was Cypselus' success which secured his position and the continued prosperity of the city was seen in the generous gifts he offered at Delphi and Olympia. Certainly he had reason for gratitude at Delphi. There is a report that the oracle accepted him as the legitimate ruler of Corinth and even addressed him as a king. So that it was with Apollo's approval that he launched a thirty-year reign.

Historians writing long after Cypselus' day kept alive opposite traditions about his character. One version, while admitting that his reign was always prosperous, refers to him only as a self-seeking opportunist. The other portrays him as a man genuinely dedicated to good causes. There is less disagreement about his son and successor, Periander, who is customarily described as a cruel and vengeful man of iron. Nevertheless, his reign from 627 to 586 is usually conceded to have been even better materially than his father's and in fact the acme of Corinthian power and prestige—a time when her pottery was found in markets everywhere and was especially predominant in the western Mediterranean.

Because Cypselus managed to stay in power for so long does not mean that tyranny was as popular at his death as when he had first launched his crusade. Periander found it necessary to employ a strong bodyguard and his anxiety about his position may account for the harsh policies which he adopted. Another suggestion is offered by Herodotus, who tells a story about some advice which Periander had received from a fellow tyrant. Periander sent a messenger to Thrasybulus, the seasoned ruler of Miletus, to learn the formula for his success. The aging tyrant took the emissary for a walk through a grain field. While he said never a word, he kept breaking off the best samples of the crop and throwing them away. He then sent the man home with the obvious message that those who would safeguard their own position must rid themselves of any talented opposition and keep a sharp eye on budding talent lest it grow to competition. It seems strange that a man of Periander's capacity would have had to resort to such tactics and stranger yet that he had to be told about them, since petty men with less talent have been discovering these devices on their own ever since.

Periander had his problems abroad as well as at home. Corinth's power and prestige were dependent on her commerce, and her attempts to dictate to her colonies and hold them close in line brought her more and more trouble as time went on. The strategic colony at Corcyra was always a problem. It was there, in fact, that Periander's younger son was killed during an uprising. The tyrant himself had sent the boy into exile, still his murder is said to have prompted the tyrant to order three hundred Corcyrean boys sent to the king of Lydia to be mutilated and used as eunuchs at a foreign court. That they were saved on the way never abated the horror of future generations at the unbridled power which had allowed one man to attempt such a revenge.

Consistently the tradition insists that Periander lacked the good heart and decency of his father, yet he seems to have sought at least outwardly the favor of gods and men. His rich offerings to the chief shrines in Greece were like those of Cypselus, and at home he built a reputation as a patron of the arts on the basis of his friendship and support of the poet Arion. He was also responsible for making famous the Isthmian games which every fourth year attracted the best athletes in Greece to the region of Corinth. Furthermore, he began a building program aimed at enriching the city with fine temples. The famous seven columns of the temple to Apollo which still stand at the site of the ancient city are exceptional because each column is a monolith rather than a series of drums pegged together. This temple has customarily been dated to Periander's time, but recent work at the site suggests that it may actually have been built fifty years later.

Periander felt that his fellow citizens were best controlled by fear but his attitude was not incompatible with a concern for their welfare. He sought to protect the interest of the city workers by limiting the number of those allowed to come in from the country, and by prohibiting the import of slaves. At the same time, laws against loafing by some, or extravagant living by others, were intended to maintain a healthy morale amongst the citizens. Periander also had a sharp eye for practical improvements. A wooden roadway for hauling ships across the Isthmus was his most spectacular accomplishment but he must be credited with at least thinking of digging a canal. The French finally built one in A.D. 1896.

The collection of tolls for the use of her strategic harbors kept Corinth free from burdensome taxes and while this would have been true no matter who ruled, it was a circumstance which redounded to the tyrant's favor.

Altogether Periander was a captain who might be admired for running a tight ship, but was not a person to be loved into the bargain. According to Herodotus, the oracle of Delphi had declared that Cypselus and his children would rule, but not his children's children. And so it turned out although the story may have originated after the event. The fortunes of the children were tied to an unhappy home as well as to tyranny. Periander was accused of killing his wife. While the matter was much disputed, his only worthwhile son believed it and the breach between them never healed. This was the young Lycophron who had been sent to live in Corcyra where, as we have seen, he was subsequently killed. The aging and bitter Periander did not long survive him. He died in 586 and four years later a nephew who had succeeded to power was assassinated. The tyranny was then replaced by an oligarchy whereby the affairs of the city were conducted by a few of the wealthiest men. They had tired of hereditary rulers and decided to manage for themselves.

In Corinth, tyranny did not prepare the way for democracy as it did elsewhere. There is no simple answer to account for this. Discussion about the matter has added up to a conclusion that different geographical circumstances and the conditioning of local history promote different political solutions.

The course of events at Corinth is comparable to that at Carthage, another commercial city in the ancient world where, under similar conditions, stable rule was provided by an oligarchy of wealth.

It is significant that neither Carthage nor Corinth had much economic diversity, so that there was never in either place a need for accommodating various strong factions. While some farm land surrounded Corinth, it was not sufficient to allow the creation of a self-satisfied aristocracy interested only in land and forever trying to thwart those who sought to develop the commercial potentialities of the city. On the contrary, the aristocracy of Corinth was interested from the beginning in the growth of trade and commerce. Unlike the usual situation in which the aristocracy became divided in loyalties between the old ways and the new, all classes at Corinth were involved all along in the city's success as a port and an exporter of goods. In contrast with events at Athens, the inter-party struggles which might have led to that government by compromise which is democracy did not develop.

Corinth, like Carthage, was essentially a large corporation, seemingly best managed by a board of directors. The well-to-do managers of the city formulated policies designed to promote commercial prosperity. What was good for business was good for all. The emphasis was one-sided, so much so in fact that the Corinthians made a habit of hiring mercenary soldiers and sailors to defend them. Consequently Corinth never built a citizen army equal to that of either Sparta or Athens. She also failed to develop a united citizenry which lived, worked, voted and fought together. The management of the city was entrusted to a small council and the byword was efficiency. Like the tyrants, this group wisely recognized that a concern for the welfare of all was the best insurance for domestic peace.

The idea that the Greeks had democracy in their genes is rather widely held, yet Corinth was an important city in Greece until the time of its destruction by the Romans in the second century B.C. and it had a democracy (most likely imposed by outsiders from Argos) for only a five-year period in the early fourth century. Here was a city interested almost exclusively in business and managed well by businessmen, but there was an indefinite something missing in its corporate life, which may well have been the excitement of the conflicting factions of a democracy. Whatever it was, the intellectuals of the fifth century passed by and through Corinth on the way to Athens.

Not all of the Greeks shared in the experience of colonizing and commerce. Areas like Thessaly and Epirus in the north remained distinctly rural and pastoral. Arcadia, the mountainous region of the north-central Peloponnesus, was even less in touch with developments in the rest of Greece. These regions remained backward in the sense that they never developed the trade and industry necessary for the growth of cities wherein there would be a variety of occupations and an influx of traders with news and new ideas. In general it may be said that those people who did not take part in the colonization movement did not play a major role in Greek history. Sparta is the exception and an important one.

## For the Good of the State

There is not much to see at Sparta today, but then there never was. Not even in its heyday was it a city of beautiful buildings and fine statues. The historian Thucydides cited Sparta as an example of why no city should be judged by its outward appearance. He observed that while a visitor might find the place mean and shabby, it ruled outright two-thirds of the Peloponnesus and was one of the foremost powers in Greece.

In spite of their success, the Spartans lived a life as spare as the city and were noted for their rejection of soft and ostentatious living in favor of rugged simplicity. For anyone accustomed to equating power and prestige with material well-being, the Spartans offer a contradiction. But only for the outsider. Those inside the system were as consistent as another tough-minded people in history—the Puritans, who worked hard for money but never found any joy in spending it, much less in the things it could buy. It is true that the Spartans and the Puritans had radically different goals, but the single-mindedness of each system offers a close parallel between them. The Puritans were as determined on salvation as the Spartans were on military prowess. Significantly, each sought to avoid the snare of materialism.

Spartan austerity was only one result of a system of indoctrination which became a curiosity among fellow Greeks and whose sole aim was to create an irresistible military force. For this purpose the entire community became a school, or rather a training camp. The male citizenry was cut off as far as possible from the ties of home and family and trained and disciplined through life for the service of the state. Girls too were given gymnastic training and encouraged to prove themselves the mother heroes of the community.

Aside from certain monastic orders, Sparta is the best example available of the human capacity for discipline. No single part of the system was unusual in itself; it was the totality of the program which was unique and insured a spectacular success. From late in the seventh century through the forepart of the fourth century, Sparta remained the dominant land power in Greece and ruled over neighboring peoples who may at one time have outnumbered the Spartans twenty-five to one.

Exactly when and how the Spartans adopted their peculiar institutions is a matter of speculation. They apparently believed that their laws had been prescribed by a certain Lycurgus but nobody today knows who this man was (if anybody) or how his name came to carry such significance. Rather than being the result of a single master plan or blueprint, it seems more likely that the system was the culmination of a series of adopted practices which eventually settled into a fixed pattern.

As at Corinth, geography helped to decide the future of Sparta. Corinth's location committed her to be a market place destined for a great commercial future. Sparta's position in the center of Laconia, one of the most fertile plains in Greece, established her ties to the land.

By some process or event which we do not know, five Dorian villages combined to form the Spartan state which during the eighth century conquered all the other peoples of Laconia. Though the Spartans thus extended their territory, they did not extend their citizenship. The new subjects, *perioikoi* (literally, "the dwellers around"), were residents of Lacedaemonia but citizenship was limited to those native-born at Sparta. Some of the *perioikoi* were liable to taxation, others might be called up for military duty in time of emergency, but their over-all function was quietly to produce goods and services for the Spartans.

In the latter part of the eighth century, at about the same time as other city-states began their overseas expansion, the Spartans crossed over Mt. Taygetus and conquered Messenia, a plain as large and rich as Laconia. It was not an easy venture and later tradition says that it took twenty years or so. The conquered Messenians were not even given the token membership in the Lacedaemonian state which the Spartans had accorded their fellow Dorians. They became helots or, as we would say, serfs, bound to the land for the purpose of producing food for themselves and Lacedaemonia. During the next century or so, the arrangement remained an unhappy one for the Messenians and an uneasy one for the Spartans. Finally in the latter part of the seventh century, the Spartans definitely established dominion by suppressing a full-scale helot rebellion. But this was not done without setbacks, and the outcome of a series of bloody campaigns had been dubious enough to make the Spartans wary of ever again relaxing their preparedness. It is assumed that at about this time the reforms known as the Lycurgan laws were adopted as assurance against further trouble.

The new policy was based in part on the conclusion that the arts had had a weakening effect on Spartan military strength. Henceforth priority was to be given to those exercises of mind and body which might toughen a man and make him a better soldier. Prior to this time the cultural life of Sparta had apparently pursued a normal course. Both pottery and poetry of quality are dated to the early part of the seventh century. While Sparta could not claim Terpander, who had brought his lyre from Lesbos, or Alcmon, who had come from Sardis to stay and write his pleasant verse about love, she could boast of Tyrtaeus. In later times when poetry was foreign to Sparta, it was perhaps difficult for anyone to imagine that she had had so great a poet; and the Athenians went so far as to claim him as their own. Yet Tyrtaeus was very likely a native son, Sparta's one great master of elegy, first and last. His martial verse had inspired the men who went out to quell the Messenian revolt and he had himself served the cause as a general in the field, but there was not to be room for the likes of him again. It was the turn of the road for Sparta and the variety of life for which the Greeks are justly famous would no longer be found among Spartans.

Since Sparta had acquired land in her neighborhood and with it food, she did not find it necessary to engage in an overseas expansion program. Consequently, she never faced the familiar sequence of economic problems and solutions including tyranny which occurred elsewhere. Tarentum, however, situated on the southern Italian coast between the toe and the heel, was known as a Spartan settlement. Later generations seem to have viewed this as a strange occurrence and an interesting legend was fabricated to account for it. The story tells how the Spartans were once away from home for several years fighting the Messenians and in their absence their wives bore sons by helots who lived nearby. These offspring in later years caused trouble and, being driven out, went off to found Tarentum. Such was the fanciful story used to explain an event which we can only guess had some connection with the Messenian Wars. A modern suggestion has been made that before the Spartans supplied themselves with the whole land of Messenia, they lacked space for a growing population, and so the founding of Tarentum was owing to overcrowding at home. In other words, the Spartans were behaving like everybody else until the Messenian "solution" abruptly changed the course of their lives.

As they owned the helots and dominated the *perioikoi*, their entire economy was based on forced labor. At all costs they had to hold these subject people in their place. The training program of every young Spartan included time spent watching and spying, which served as a good conditioner for a lifetime spent on the alert.

The Spartans became committed to an extraordinary existence which was in many respects a brutal one. Every Spartan was born in doubt whether or not he would be allowed to live. His father brought him before a tribal board of elders who examined him to see if he were hardy enough for the rigors of the life before him. A baby found wanting would be abandoned to die of exposure for his own good and for the good of the state. Since the life of the society was geared to the performance of every man as a first-rate soldier, concern over the prospective health of newborn boys does not seem unusual.

At the age of seven, a young Spartan was inducted into the initial stage of training. He was assigned to the care of a guardian (*paidonomos*) appointed by the state. Under the general supervision of this magistrate, companies of boys were led each by an older youth already indoctrinated into the system. From the beginning, their training was characterized by competition both between groups and amongst boys of the same company. They competed for the praise of their superiors and were made to feel shame for not measuring up to required standards. Also, certain honorary units were given coveted standing. The desire to be distinguished was made all the more intense by the fact that no boy ever went home or found any other form of consolation. He lived with his peers and sought to be accepted and praised. This element of human psychology has long been a major asset to athletic coaches everywhere, but with the men who trained the Spartans it was only the beginning. The encouragement of boys to fight amongst themselves was considered a good means of discovering where a trace of cowardice might still remain. Various allurements were used to tempt boys to steal food and severe whippings were meted out to those who were caught. Such were the devices calculated to produce the toughness of mind so invaluable in time of war.

Young boys were taught to groom their bodies by exercise alone. Their hair was cut too short to need attention, bathing and oiling were discouraged, and after they were twelve years old one garment for all the year round was considered sufficient. Going barefoot at all times was good training for future footwork on rough terrain. Finally, their diet was such that an outsider was once moved to comment that Spartan courage in the face of death was not so surprising in view of the food in their mess halls.

The Spartan system was a logical extension of the axiom that men become soldiers by soldiering. A boy who, from the age of seven, has had constant competition, exercise, drill, and nothing else, may well be a soldier by the time he is twenty. Moreover, he thinks like one and feels more comfortable in the barracks or in the field than anywhere else. A disciplined fighter is useful, but a man happy to be one is the best you can get.

The Spartan expectation of what life could be was determined by what it was and had always been. A Spartan's thinking from the beginning was committed to militarism, which meant that he had the same answer for every problem. There is only one place safely to control a man and that is within his own mind. Those indoctrinated under this system were its staunchest defenders. What else did they have? To ask why the Spartans did not change their thinking and so challenge this one-sided life is to forget that this is precisely what indoctrination is designed to prevent.

Nothing changed much in Sparta. Long after monarchies had disappeared almost everywhere else, there were still kings in Sparta. In fact there were two at once, and each came from a family which traced its lineage back to Heracles. This claim agreed with the familiar Dorian rationalization for their invasion—that it was really only the return of the sons of Heracles who were reclaiming what had once been theirs. A good modern guess about the dual kingship is that it was the result of a compromise between two tribes in the region which decided to unite.

These kings had certain religious duties which was true of kingship everywhere, but, more significantly, at Sparta they retained their position at the head of the army. At times the kingship was weakened by competition between the two, but the capacities of individual kings was the important factor in determining their influence. In time it became customary for the citizenry to designate one or the other as the head of the army for a given campaign and there was often an obvious choice.

In spite of their prominence on military campaigns, the duties of the kings while at home became more and more formal. Except for rulers like the striking Cleomenes I whose reign began in the late sixth century, they were mere figureheads presiding over the adoption of children and the like. At the same time the actual direction of the affairs of the city fell increasingly to a board of five annually elected ephors. Because of this number five, it has been suggested that the ephorate was perhaps an extension of a group of commissioners who had originally represented each of the five villages from which Sparta was formed. But this is only guesswork. Others have speculated that the office was not established until the time of the Lycurgan reforms in the late seventh century. If this is true, then the origin of the ephors may represent an effort to balance the power of the kings and the nobility with that of the officers who represented the population at large. This would also accord with the idea that the major uprising in Messenia created such a serious threat to the security of the state that those citizens who had so ably served the common cause had now earned better representation at the highest level.

While their origin is disputed, there is little doubt that the ephors offer one example of evolutionary change in the Spartan government, for only gradually did they come to a commanding position in the state. However, by the sixth century certainly, they were the chief executive officers and had the power to investigate and bring to trial any and all officials. Even the kings were liable to be called to account for their conduct in a particular campaign. The average citizen was expected to be immediately obedient to their orders. Yet they were only the watchdogs of the state and not a law unto themselves. Over all stood the Lycurgan rules. The ephors frequently swore oaths of loyalty to the kings and these were matched with the kings' oaths to abide by the laws.

As old as the dual kingship was the Council or *gerousia*, which served as an advisory body of elders. True to the Spartan deference to tradition and age, this influential group included twenty-eight of the most respected citizens over sixty years old, plus the two kings. Those elected by the Assembly to this select circle held office for life. The small size of the Council, along with the age, experience and continuity of its membership, contributed to its prestige and the weight of its opinion. While the board of ephors sat as a civil court, the Council acted on all criminal matters. Furthermore, any business to be brought before the entire citizenry was first cleared by these few men.

The Assembly, or *apella*, made up of all Spartans over thirty years of age, gave the system a democratic appearance. However, one assembly is not equal to another and much depends on the character of the group. Because Spartan training was lopsided in favor of physical exercise and discipline, it was not likely to encourage interest in a discussion of issues. Nor did the elders of the state respect the decisions of the Assembly as final. In theory, of course, the voice of the entire citizenry was supposed to be final, but if the Council disapproved of the way the shouting went, they could dismiss a meeting and so avoid any formal proclamation of its decision. Thus, regardless of how it appeared on paper, the Spartan system was not a democracy. In practice, the policies and decisions were clearly in the hands of a few seasoned leaders.

The mechanism of this system was not as important as the fact that the Spartans were hedged in by inflexible rules which bound them to a fixed pattern of behavior. If they were a dominated people, it was by laws rather than by men. The regulation of society and the control of human behavior by means of unchanging laws has occurred with other peoples in varying degrees and with similar results. The orthodox Jew who lives today in strict observance to the letter of the Law and the devout Moslem who obeys every word of the Koran enjoy the stability and the strength which come to those who live their lives in accordance with decisions made long ago, and not subject to time.

Even in emergencies the Spartans rarely acted in haste. As we shall see, they often did not act at all. Their reputation for being cautious and slow was well deserved and easily understood.

It is true that the Spartans lived in a world of their own and that they were taught to be proud of their differences. Yet they were not really isolated and their leaders at least were well aware of what was happening elsewhere. Naturally they were interested in developments which might jeopardize the Spartan position *vis-à-vis* the rest of Greece, and so they followed a fairly consistent policy of undermining the rule of tyrants, who generally were ambitious and aggressive men interested in expanding the influence of their cities for commercial purposes. At the same time the Spartans shared the growing apprehension of other Greek states over the Persians who had begun their course of expansion about the middle of the sixth century and had in fifty years extended their control across Asia Minor to the Aegean Sea.

Toward her rivals, real or imagined, at home or abroad, Sparta took a defensive attitude. After the Messenian conquest she was not an aggressive power in the sense that she sought to win commercial advantages, or to increase her territory beyond the establishment of what she considered her rightful boundaries. Her moves were designed to prevent the enlargement of hostile power and her interest in any event could usually be calculated by an inverse ratio of the distance it occurred from Sparta. Her most pressing problems were naturally with nearby states. There were boundary disputes to consider, and also the Spartan insistence that no neighbor provide a refuge for runaway helots. As a result of victories over both Tegea and Argos she secured the northern boundary of her territory, largely at the expense of Argos who surrendered some long-disputed land. Time and again Sparta exerted her full effort against Argos, but she was not satisfied until 494 when she inflicted on this city a crushing and humiliating defeat.

No similar persistence marked her first venture into the Aegean area where, about 524, she led the effort to overthrow the tyrant Polycrates at Samos. Discouraged by the failure of the initial siege, she withdrew her help and returned home. At an earlier date, Croesus, king of the more distant Lydia, had sought Spartan help against the Persians. An alliance was actually concluded, but when the time came the Spartans did not arrive. No one doubted that they were great fighters, maybe the best anywhere, but if the battle was far from home, it was no sure thing that they would appear.

The Spartans could be counted on anywhere in the Peloponnesus, however. Determined to make neighboring states share in the defense of that area, they sought to achieve this by alliances rather than outright territorial expansion. These agreements were of course intended to benefit both parties, but, for obvious reasons, Sparta was always the senior partner. Only Argos remained permanently estranged.

Before the sixth century was over, Sparta had expanded her circle of friends by including states in central Greece. In 510, an agreement was made with Athens as a result of Spartan aid in the overthrow of tyranny there. When in the early years of the fifth century Greece was faced by two massive invasions by the Persians, these mutual assistance pacts between Sparta and her neighbors constituted the only unity that existed. During the first onslaught in 490, the system was not effective and Athens withstood the assault at Marathon practically alone. However, ten years later when the Persians returned with a greater force, Sparta supplied the rallying point for a cooperative effort which with a little luck finally turned the tide.

Following these wars, Sparta lost the initiative in Greek affairs and returned to her role as a self-sufficient state primarily interested in the *status quo*. Consequently the opportunity to organize and lead the Greek states fell to the daring and confident Athenians who, far from backing away from the task, actually succeeded too well.

One day, long after the Persian Wars, an ambassador from Corinth, when speaking to the Spartan Assembly, had occasion to compare the character of the Spartans with that of the Athenians. With typical Greek bluntness, he told the Spartans that while they had the strongest army in Greece, they were nevertheless slow to act, overly cautious and generally lacking in any excitement of the mind. On the other hand, he observed, the Athenians were ingenious and ever anxious to learn and practice new ideas. They had been educated to think and act as free men, each as an individual. Curiously enough, the ambassador had come to enlist the aid of the strong but cloddish Spartans in the defense of other Greek states against these same busy and thoughtful Athenians.

The spectacular achievements of Athens in the arts and in democracy were accompanied by Athenian failures in foreign policy which robbed the Greek world of the best leadership available. The equally spectacular success of Sparta as the foremost military power in Greece was unsupported by intellectual accomplishments in any way comparable to those of Athens. The contrasting history of these two states, exposing the strengths and weaknesses of each system, illustrates how each could succeed and how each could fail. The simple truth that two contrasting aims (though each be desirable) cannot be achieved together is one of the hard lessons of history.

Philosophers like Plato, who found much to praise in the orderliness of the Spartan system, were at the same time bothered by the absence at Sparta of any truly educated class. Time and again the Spartans, when given a chance to act as arbiters of Greek affairs, showed a shocking deficiency of imagination or originality. Indoctrination demands limits and it gets them. The Spartan was taught that his small world depended on the maintenance of an unchallengeable military force. He was not interested in making any changes which might upset or undermine the only truth that he knew. For this reason the Spartans, in spite of their militarism, were less feared in Greece than were the free Athenians. These dreamers and builders, as the Corinthian ambassador observed, never took any rest themselves and never gave any to others.

# The Arts

**V** At Sparta, the arts were stillborn in the barracks. Men whose minds were as disciplined as their well-trained bodies were not likely to be writing poetry on the side. While it is true that talent and imagination may appear anywhere, creativity is encouraged by an audience and certainly needs an opportunity. Both were missing under the Lycurgan laws. After the seventh century B.C., there was no more intellectual life in Sparta than among the goatherders of Thessaly.

Elsewhere during the seventh and sixth centuries, colonists and traders were creating a different scene and the future was to be decided by men who were busy making money. In time the new commerce would provide wider distribution of wealth and a better education for those who could afford it. The result was a middle-class audience with an ear for something besides the extraordinary deeds of Homer's warriors or the cautious routine of Hesiod's gentry. The earlier works continued to be read and recited, but shipbuilders and shopkeepers wanted to hear also about themselves. As a consequence, writers wrote less about the spectacular or the superstitious and more about the ordinary interests of people who might perhaps be called a "public." A poet of the day is remembered for a line which says that money is all that matters. There is nothing spectacular or superstitious about that.

The tyrants typified the new mood. These sometimes colorful, always ambitious, men cut across class lines and ignored tradition in their search for practical solutions to the problems of their time. Along with enterprising producers and traders who were moving ahead in the commercial field, the tyrants expressed the new individualism of men who were acting on their own initiative rather than following the code of their ancestors. Still, it was the poets, artists, and philosophers who supplied a better argument for self-expression and gave to Greek life a remarkable variety which has ever since been a defense against all its faults.

Other peoples of the ancient world may have had as much talent, genius if you like, but nowhere else was there a diversity akin to that of the Greeks. Especially noticeable were the personal opinions which began appearing in the works of poets who were speaking their minds on the drift of current events. Nor was this a momentary reaction to changing times. It was the beginning of a habit of controversy which lends to Greek literature a perennial modernity. In the early years, this conflict of opinions was not the result of some special native instinct as to the value of critical thinking. Actually, in the seventh and sixth centuries there was no single place in Greece where all points of view could be heard and encouraged. Certainly neither militaristic Sparta nor rural Thessaly offered any platform for new opinions; and even the tyrant who was willing to support artists in order to brighten the reputation of his city was in fact a promoter rather than a connoisseur. He may have been happy to have poets express their feelings about the beauties of nature and love and their city, but he was not interested in unfavorable comments about himself or his program, nor did he hesitate to send packing any poet whose verse took the wrong political turn. Elsewhere, in cities still under the rule of privileged aristocrats, there was no more encouragement or sympathy for fresh suggestions than there had ever been. Even the fledgling democracies, when they first appeared, were guided by men who were intolerant of those out of step with their ideas.

In the early centuries the circumstance of many separate governments, each supporting a different point of view, produced the variety of opinion. The numerous little city-states, each autonomous and proud, blocked the establishment of a single jurisdiction which might channel all available intellectual talent toward a single purpose. Freedom of expression, which Athena would one day protect at Athens, did not, like the goddess, spring suddenly full-born from the head of Zeus. It was nurtured by men and it grew slowly and with difficulty. Not until the fifth century could the great popular leader Pericles declare that the Athenians considered debate as a necessary prelude to any wise action. But the variety in ideas and in art so characteristic of the Greeks had its beginning long before that momentous declaration.

## The Absence of an All-Inclusive Commitment

In all earlier societies, the energies of the intellectual elite were commandeered for service to religious cults or to an absolute ruler. In a sacred monarchy the end was the same. Egypt is everybody's favorite example, and for good reason. Life in Egypt was absolutely dependent on a single river and the need for control of both irrigation and shipping led naturally to centralized power. History gives us no better example of how such a power can grow. In time the living god-king, who was the Pharaoh, dominated every area of thought and action. There were rare moments in Egyptian literature when an individual was found expressing his personal views, but, as might be expected, this occurred usually when the Pharaoh's position was weak or temporarily interrupted by rebellious princes. In any event the disturbances never lasted long enough to allow for much self-expression. Always, there was a return to the conformity peculiar to societies in which all men serve the same purpose. In Egypt there was not even a codification of the laws until late in dynastic times. The Pharaoh knew the law and his agents dispensed the will of this ever-present deity.

Among another early people, the Hebrews, although their God did not reside among them His law was there to direct and to dominate. Many secular subjects are discussed in the Old Testament, but the overwhelming interest of those who furnished the wisdom of this book was with the known God and man's relationship to Him. In this respect, the law was the way. The Hebrew intellectual tradition was neither artistic nor philosophical; it was concerned with a covenant, a peculiar history, and the recording of prophecy. Like the Pharaoh in Egypt, the law was a commitment and there was no escape from it.

Neither by circumstance nor by birth was the Greek intellectual beholden to a single patronage like that of the Pharaoh, or to a single destiny like that of the Hebrew. During the great period of Greek civilization there was never any central jurisdiction and because the Greeks had separate experiences there resulted differences of interest and opinion and an amazing variety of creative works. A poet driven from one city by a tyrant could find refuge in another where friendly aristocrats continued to rule. A poet sympathetic to tyranny and critical of the old aristocracy might pass him on the road going the other way. In short, Greece offered the artist and thinker the possibility of becoming a free agent, if he were willing to travel.

At a time when the Greeks imagined their gods as beautiful manlike beings, the philosopher Xenophanes was noted for his remark that if cattle could draw, they would picture their gods as cattle. There is little reason to question the report that a man such as this did indeed keep moving from place to place. The more famous Pythagoras left his native Samos during the reign of the tyrant Polycrates. As a refugee, he traveled to the Greek colony of Croton in southern Italy and was later expelled from there too. However, unlike an Egyptian or Hebrew, who would have had to live in exile amongst men of strange habits and speech, Xenophanes and Pythagoras went from place to place, writing as they pleased, always in the company of other Greeks.

Many artists and thinkers stayed put, however, and were devoted to their native city-state. Nor were they the less talented for having accepted whatever limits their immobility may have imposed. It cannot be denied that those remarkable craftsmen who, for millennia, served the Pharaohs of Egypt produced great art on a beautiful, if a single, theme. As in Egypt, so in Greece there were artists who practiced traditionalism; but in Greece there were others who showed the way to experimentation and variety. Limited to a single theme or bound by taboos as in Egypt or in medieval times, artists can still perform well within the range of what is ordered. Yet if left to do what they will, as in Greece, they have exciting ideas and exhibit all kinds of differences. This is not what all men can be, nor need to try to be, but it is a possibility for some.

Religion was never the inhibiting force in Greece which it was in earlier societies. The word *religio* in Latin means a sense of awe or respect for what is sacred. The Greeks had a full measure of this feeling toward their gods, but they never transferred any of it to an established priesthood. Like other peoples in the ancient world, they felt themselves dependent on the gods and were careful about their relations with them. Their anxiety lest they give the gods any offense is seen in their frequent use of native and foreign purifiers, men who knew the proper rites for exorcising the pollution of some great crime or sacrilege. Periodic sacrifices to the gods were also conducted throughout Greece, just as in older societies, and priests were employed to see that the rites were properly performed. Yet these priests always remained employees of the state for specific functions and were never considered as having special powers of their own or as shepherds of their flocks. Since political authority in Greece was of men rather than of gods, the priests did not assume a power even remotely equal to that of the dominant priesthoods of earlier sacred societies. Thus religion, while important to the Greeks, never permeated all aspects of their society or became the end of all, as it did among the Egyptians and the Hebrews. Its place was more akin to the one it holds in the present Western world—a part of life, but not so large a part as to inhibit individuals who prefer to think about something else.

It is true that officials, whether in a monarchy, aristocracy, tyranny or democracy, were bound to secure the favor of the gods by attending to the proper sacrifices. But the contractual character of Greek religion which, in essence, said "we do this for you and you do that for us," left a wide area of human activity outside any religious consideration. While the works of the epic poets and the playwrights implied moral teachings, there was never anything doctrinal or binding in these implications.

In the Greek experience it was the absence of an all-inclusive commitment, whether political or religious, which made a variety of thought and action possible.

### The Brash and Candid Archilochus

Whether composed as entertainment or as partisan comment, the poetry of the Colonization Age had a personal tone. Homer only once mentioned himself in his works and that was to thank the muses for inspiration. Hesiod's comments on his own life were brief and restrained. There could be no more startling contrast than that between these men and the brash and candid Archilochus, a native of the island of Paros, who lived during the first half of the seventh century. This was the time when the tyrants began to appear in Greece and, so far as we know, Archilochus was the first poet to mention them. A character in one of his poems says that he cares nothing for their wealth or power. The remark is typical of the outspoken, often defiant, attitude of the new poetry which is perhaps best observed in the verse of this disgruntled soldier of fortune—or maybe he was just a pirate. In any event, when he says he depends on his spear in order to drink, he sounds like the familiar gunslinger of the Old West. Yet he was also a man with a thirst for strong words and, while only fragments of what he wrote remain, almost any line of his is sufficient to mark a definite break with the past. Homer's warrior and Hesiod's farmer may not have had much in common but both were serious about whatever it was that seemed important to them, be it revenge for a fallen comrade or getting a barn repaired on time. They were predictable, but Archilochus was not. He was, in fact, the first Greek to announce in writing that he made up his mind on the spot. He says that in battle one day he had a choice between recovering his shield, the ancient badge of honor, or getting out with his life. He guessed that he could buy another shield and so he ran for it. On second thought, is it so extraordinary that a man who was hired to fight might sometimes ask himself what a battle was worth? The attitude was new, of course, but then so was the money.

Archilochus was born the bastard son of a nobleman who had sired him, unnobly, by a slave woman. His father was apparently willing to care for him, but the code of the aristocracy allowed only legitimate sons to inherit status. Under the circumstances, Archilochus became a wanderer and lived in outrageous defiance of polite society, turning its honored values upside down.

Unlike the earlier poets who described the misfortunes and sufferings of men long since dead, Archilochus talked deliberately and incessantly about himself and his bad luck. Instead of addressing the muses, he spoke to his friends, calling them by name.

While poets continued to use the measures of the traditional epic, they were at the same time introducing new metres more in keeping with the excitement of their own feelings. Archilochus, for instance, is credited with the invention of the iambic metre, which replaces the stateliness of the old dactylic hexameter with the beat of the poet's emotions. It is explosive and unpredictable. Some poets even mixed metres when they felt like it. Moreover, as might be expected, they used everyday speech in their verse and so gave the new poetry a less formal, more familiar tone.

## Theognis Could Be Sentimental

Archilochus' verse displayed the rudeness of a young age toward the passing glories of an old one. Some other poets were bound to be exactly the opposite in sentiment. They were men driven from their native cities by popular tyrants or leaders of the new democracies, and they lamented the fate of the well-born, the better people. No one among them lamented more keenly than Theognis. How many of the bitter poems attributed to him were actually his has long been disputed, but some surely were, and all of them revealed an unhappy frame of mind over the way things were going. He observed that men who used to dress in goatskins were coming into the city dressed like everybody else and seeking to get ahead. They had neither high birth nor good breeding, but had managed somehow to acquire money and with it power. Worse, their wealth enabled them to marry their sons and daughters into the best families and so, according to Theognis, mix bad blood with good. Theognis never doubted the natural superiority of the well-born and well-bred and he saw money as an awful agency by which this good stock was being contaminated.

Theognis was not only a spokesman for the discontented of his native Megara; he served also as an example, for his property was confiscated and he was forced to leave the city. It is not likely that men who were promoting a democracy would sit still while he compared the new mixture of blood to an indiscriminate mating of barnyard animals.

Theognis could be sentimental too. In one of his quieter moments he echoes Hesiod, when he writes that he can hear the call of the crane but his fields are no longer his to plow. And when he was not being bitter about his loss, he could allow that the selfishness and greed of his own class were part of the trouble. He remained true to his colors, however, and his pleasantries about proper conduct were addressed only to men of good blood and breeding. The substance of his advice was that they should seek poise and self-control and avoid the company of common men, those who drink and talk too much. In his youth Theognis wrote of loves, won and lost, regular and irregular; in his old age he despaired of life or of having lived at all. This is a familiar pattern with poets and says little about Theognis personally. In the end what remains valuable is his singularly sharp reaction to his times, for he confirms our notion of what was happening when he says, "it happened to me."

## *The Honesty of Sappho's Emotions*

It could also have happened to the renowned Sappho, but we would never know this from what she wrote. Her words are of love and almost never of politics. Nor does she say much about herself. She was born on the island of Lesbos and spent nearly all of her life there. It is possible that as a young girl she went into exile with her parents and other members of the aristocracy, but this is not certain. Although she was married and had a daughter, her husband is only a name and very possibly died as a young man. All that is added to these few details is the statement that she was a small and slight woman with dark features. The only Sappho we really know was a woman of intense personal feelings. This much she herself revealed. In her poetry she described how she felt about those she loved and how she suffered when they were gone. Occasionally she mentioned other topics, but they were minor. Love was the central theme.

Few women have ranked so well in the arts as Sappho yet it must be admitted that she had to withdraw from a man's world to achieve her fame. Other poets not happy with their native city went wandering in search of an audience. Sappho created her own where she was. She gathered young girls about her and gave them training in singing and dancing. Whether this association was a formal school or not has been the subject of scholarly debate for the very good reason that there is not enough evidence to be sure. However, that girls were being given any instruction outside the home is an interesting piece of news and suggests a modernity of living on this eastern Aegean island in the late seventh century.

Sappho describes her girls in her works. There is a certain gentleness of the eyes, a daintiness in the way they gather flowers. All is innocence and freshness—a moment of life in which Sappho delighted. Others too found these young girls beautiful and lovable and were jealous of those who stole them away, but it was Sappho who voiced her feelings aloud. The Greeks, who greatly admired her choice of words, considered her the greatest of all their women poets. Her likeness appeared on coins in Lesbos and a statue was erected in her honor in Sicily. Yet in later times, both in crude pagan comedy and in early Christian writings, Sappho was cast as a lesbian. Modern scholars have busily defended her name against the grosser implications of this charge and they may be right, but nobody knows. Since Sappho's poems include frequent references to Aphrodite, it has been suggested that her girls were members of a cult which celebrated the festivities of this goddess. Emphasis on the religious vocation of the community in the service of a deity who expressed the most refined qualities of love, especially beauty, has of course been used to discount the notion that feelings in the grove were sometimes uncontrolled.

Actually all that remains to us is the honesty of Sappho's emotions and the intimacy of her verse, neither of which is shocking. Those who write about her poetry usually speak in terms of love rather than passion. Sappho's own good taste suggests the choice.

Archilochus, Theognis and Sappho are representative of the writers of the seventh and sixth centuries. Each of them was outspoken, maybe eccentric, certainly sensitive. And there were many, many Greeks who for one reason or another took exception to what they had to say. Thus these poets remained outsiders among those very Greeks who are so often heralded as the discoverers of man and his mind. During these early years, it was in an "exile" of one kind or another that these three talented poets were free to write as they pleased. They were not the spokesmen of a new kind of man. They were only what some human beings in any age may be, given the chance and having the courage to take it.

### In Honor of the Gods

Those who traveled in Greece during the seventh and sixth centuries saw more than political and social changes. Everywhere there were evidences of a great building program.

The tyrants have been described as the patrons who gave encouragement (and money is encouraging) to the arts. They also channeled artistic effort toward a new purpose. What they ordered was for public enjoyment and use, not private. In the earlier Mycenaean period, the tombs and palaces of the nobility and the rich jewelry found in them indicate that the artist was serving the interests of a particular class. The skill and imagination lavished on a single golden cup were the same as an artist might devote to any object, but the end of the cup was a private collection and finally a tomb. It never belonged to the community. Artistic talent was used for private purposes. This would always be so to some extent, but the tyrants and other wealthy men in the Colonization Era opened up a new direction. The tyrant sought unity within the city-state and one way of securing it was to build temples, theaters, and aqueducts which would serve a community purpose.

The temple of the patron deity was especially designed to serve as a focal point for the community-wide celebrations in honor of the god responsible for the well-being of the city. At Athens, the annual celebrations in honor of Athena involved a procession of the citizenry to the Parthenon—a temple which takes its name from Athena Parthenos, Athena the Maiden. Gifts were offered, of course, and in the Great Panathenaea, every fourth year, a robe (*peplos*), newly woven for the goddess by the women of the city, was presented. The statue of Athena in full armor standing in the temple was not an idol for worship, but rather a physical representation which was appropriately located in the place where intangible devotion might express itself by the offering of a material gift.

As in the cities which sent out colonists, so in the new settlements, the temples were a sign of prosperity and stability as well as an expression of devotion. For this reason, some of the best-preserved temples of this early period are found outside of Greece itself. Of special interest are those in southern Italy. About sixty miles south of Naples, in a ruined city known by its Roman name of Paestum, there remain today three remarkably preserved Greek temples which make the place a modern tourist attraction.

A temple without its statuary is still an impressive sight to the modern visitor in the Mediterranean world, but the ancients would have been troubled by what was missing. The structure and the sculpture were parts of a whole in their view.

Apparently about the middle of the seventh century, Greek artists learned from the Egyptians how to carve large figures in stone. By this time various contacts existed with Egypt and certainly the earliest statues in Greece bear an unmistakable likeness to the older Egyptian figures. About a hundred or so pieces which are collectively termed *kouroi* (youths, or less exactly "Apollos") have been recovered from various sites in Greece (Pl. 32). They are male nudes and they all stand solidly with both feet flat on the ground, the left foot slightly forward. The arms are held at the sides with the fists clenched and the eyes, which are large and stylized, stare straight ahead. It would be difficult to look at these figures and not be reminded of the *Ka* statues in Egypt. The *kouroi* even wear typical Egyptian-styled wigs. Seemingly the only item lost in the transfer was the loin cloth, for the Greeks never shared the Egyptian aversion to nudity. It might be said that the only item added was a smile. Yet this is not really true because earlier artists did occasionally allow for some facial expressions. However, it is still safe to say that nowhere else was a smile the idiom which it became in Greece.

The Greeks probably used these *kouroi* as funerary monuments or as votive statues of some deity, perhaps Apollo, and so they were serving the same purpose as their counterparts in Egypt. But whereas in Egypt, century after century, this type of statue continued to satisfy the same need, in Greece other interests soon led to innovations. The desire for decoration within the pediments of the Greek temples, for example, offered a new use for free-standing sculpture and encouraged experimentation with different poses.

Pediment is an architectural term for the triangular gabled area at either end of the Greek temple. It was recessed and in fact offered a kind of stage on which sculptured figures could be placed in a tableau to tell a story. The pedimental figures portrayed well-known scenes from the Greek past much as earlier Egyptian myths were retold in hollow relief on the walls of Old Kingdom tombs, or as Biblical stories would be carved in stone in the tympanums of medieval churches.

An obvious arrangement to fit the space within the pediment called for a central standing figure and then at either side, as the roof slanted, figures which crouched or kneeled, followed by others

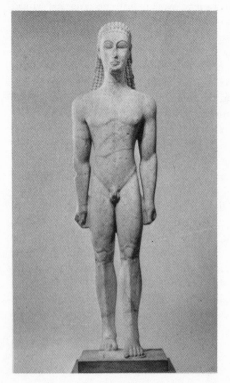

*Pl. 32 Attic* kouros,
circa *600 B.C.*

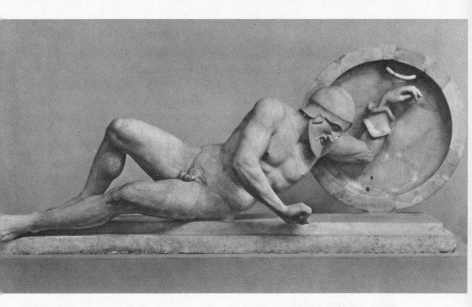

*Pl. 33 Fallen Warrior, from eastern pediment of temple of Aphaia, Aegina,* circa *480 B.C.*

which reclined (Pl. 33). At times, various animals were used in the corners and serpents seem to have been especially popular.

Some of the best-preserved pieces of pedimental statuary are in the Museum at Olympia. They were recovered in a series of excavations begun in 1875 by the German School of Archaeology. The great temple of Zeus, various other shrines, treasuries, *stoas,* residence halls, the *gymnasion,* the *palaestra* and the *stadion* were gradually reduced to ruins by a series of catastrophes beginning in the fifth century A.D. The process began with the wanton raids of Gothic tribes and was continued with the premeditated destruction wrought by the Emperor Theodosius II (401–450 A.D.) who decreed that all pagan temples be destroyed. The earthquakes of the sixth century finished the job. In the ensuing centuries earth washed down from nearby Cronion (the Hill of Cronos) and sand from the flooded Alpheus buried the fallen columns and statuary.

When the Germans began to dig, they knew what they were looking for. Pausanias' guidebook to Greece includes a description of Olympia in the second century A.D. He says that the East Pediment of the temple of Zeus, built during the first half of the fifth century B.C., told the story of the famous chariot race between

Oenomaus and Pelops. Excavators recovered the statues of both these figures and also Zeus who stood in the center, the overseer of the race. A broken kneeling figure has been identified as Myrtilus, the unfaithful charioteer. Fragments of the horses and a variety of crouching and reclining statues suggest how the pediment was completed.

The scene in the West Pediment is more famous because of the well-preserved statue of a majestic Apollo. He stood at the center with one arm outstretched, his serene countenance in sharp contrast with the violent struggles of the Lapiths and Centaurs on either side of him.

Excellent examples of Greek pedimental statuary are to be found outside of Greece; many of these sculptures were carried away from their original sites by French, German and British excavators. Among the best are those preserved in the Glyptothek in Munich. They represent warriors and they were originally part of the pediments of the temple to Aphaia in Aegina. Those from the western end of the temple were perhaps in a scene intended to depict the Trojan War, while Heracles, seen among the figures from the eastern end, suggests a mythical theme. Whatever the story, the active poses of these figures, shown kneeling and charging, are in sharp contrast to the earlier, always erect, *kouroi*. The bodies have a greater volume and are

*Pl. 34 Heracles, from eastern pediment of temple of Aphaia, Aegina,* circa *480 B.C.*

more natural appearing in keeping with the new liveliness of their postures (Pl. 34).

These statues are not smooth and refined products, nor are they altogether finished on the unseen side. Since they were intended to be placed up high, far removed from close examination, a certain roughness would not have made any difference. Viewed from the ground they gave the desired impression of a majestic moment or dramatic action from the past.

The Greeks used statuary for the same decorative, commemorative and inspirational purposes as it is used today, only more so. The most striking difference in subject would be the prominence given to the athlete. Such statues have been found not only in or near *gymnasia;* they were prominent everywhere and especially at the famous religious sanctuaries where the major games were held. The honored gods were represented at Olympia and Delphi and also the winners themselves. Among the dedicatory works at Delphi was a charioteer group, including man, horse and chariot, given early in the fifth century by Polyzalus, the tyrant of Gela in Sicily, who had himself been a recent winner. Of the whole arrangement only the now famous *Charioteer of Delphi* has been recovered. It was found by the French during excavations in 1895 (Pl. 35).

The Charioteer stands in the Museum of Delphi today as if frozen alive while posing for a portrait. He is alone in the center of a special room. The smallish head and arms suggest a youth of about seventeen. The figure is very slender and has an air of delicacy about it which photographs seem unable to capture. The upper part of the youth's garment is bloused over an encircling band high above the waist. The carefulness with which the many folds of this garment are arranged matches the serenity of the motionless body. Yet the treatment of the drapery is fine and numerous small variations give enough irregularity to avoid the impression that the whole is a routine pattern with each fold exactly alike. The details were conceived by the sculptor as he worked on his original model before the casting of the final bronze product and the success of the work reveals what had been learned from the experience and the mistakes of earlier artists.

The achievement of greater naturalism of body and posture for the nude male, and a more realistic treatment of drapery for both male and female figures, show the early concern of artists for a better representation of the physical. The desire to have their figures express a mental attitude was to mark the next development. Already the *Charioteer of Delphi* stood at the threshold. His dignity is that of a refined youth, with a sense of presence, a confident control over himself and his mood. He has the look of effortless poise which became a mannerism of the Golden Age.

## Even Very Poor Pieces Have Value

The changes in style and technique in Greek painting can only be observed in their pottery. All other examples of painting from this early period, including large wall scenes, have been lost, yet the abundance of well-preserved pottery amply testifies to the skill of the painters. Museums everywhere, from New York to Moscow, boast of major collections and almost any art museum will have a case or two of examples. Pottery was one of the major products of the ancient world, and for cities like Corinth and Athens it was a mainstay of

*Pl. 35 Bronze* Charioteer of Delphi, circa *470 B.C.*

*Pl. 36* Loutrophorus *(marriage vase), third quarter of fifth century B.C.*

*Pl. 37 Attic* hydria, circa *530–520 B.C., showing Ajax and Achilles*

the economy. Indeed, Athenian ware replaced the Corinthian product in the Mediterranean market at about the same time that Athens surpassed Corinth as the dominant commercial city in the Greek world.

Most of this pottery was as common as "pots and pans," but there was also a large market for decorative and ceremonial pieces.

*Pl. 38 Attic Comast cup,* circa *580–570 B.C.*

These were carefully preserved as objects of value, in fact hidden, and so are still to be seen in large numbers. Now as then, these objects are valuable because of their intrinsic worth as vases of superb craftsmanship and imaginative design. Among the finer pieces, the *loutrophorus,* or marriage vase, is an excellent example of the kind of vessel used in Greek ceremonial (Pl. 36). It also shows how wealth could make itself conspicuous in the ancient world.

In the post-Dorian revival as in the earlier Bronze Age, artists first used geometric designs for decoration; they then turned gradually to the more interesting, and at the same time more challenging, representations of mythical stories and human events. Down to the latter part of the sixth century, it was customary to paint the figures in black against the natural red of the clay and then add details by means of incisions on the silhouetted figures (Pl. 37, 38). This "black-figured" pottery was gradually succeeded by "red-figured" work on which the figures were etched against the red clay and the background around them painted black. The greater versatility and naturalness allowed by the painting of details on the lighter surface caused the red-figured vases to predominate by the time of the fifth century. The further choice of a white slip background had also become popular and the tall *lekythoi* used for funerary rituals were usually given a white ground (Pl. 39, 40).

The painted scenes on Greek vases have more than an aesthetic interest. Where armor, weapons, or musical instruments are shown in detail, the vases act as a kind of illustrated catalogue of objects and serve to clarify certain points which are not mentioned in the litera-

ture. In addition, while the majority of the scenes are taken from
the myths or depict historical happenings, some of them illustrate
everyday occupations and amusements (Pl. 41, 42, 43).

The athlete and the warrior again join the gods as the most
popular subjects for representation. As is true in statuary, a distinct
preoccupation with masculine interests is shown. While the goddesses
are given their proper place, the secondary position of women in
Greek society, especially at Athens, is reflected in their correspondingly

*Pl. 39 Attic white
lekythos, circa
440–430 B.C.
showing youth and
woman at stele.
Museum of Fine
Arts, Boston,
Pierce Fund*

*Pl. 40 Attic white
lekythos, circa 440–
430 B.C., showing
man and woman at
stele. Museum of
Fine Arts, Boston,
Perkins Collection*

Pl. 41 Attic amphora, late black-figure style, showing shoemaker's shop. Museum of Fine Arts, Boston, Pierce Fund

Pl. 42 Column-crater by Myson, circa 490 B.C. Warriors are struggling over a fallen comrade

Pl. 43 Athenian cup by Makron, circa 490–480 B.C., showing late-night party (game of kottabos)

small role in these painted scenes. Typically they appear as flute girls or dancing girls serving as entertainers, a wife saying goodbye to her warrior husband, or a mother holding a spear for her son while he puts on his armor. Women are thus usually represented as accessories to the enjoyment and the occupations of men (Pl. 44).

Frequently, the names of gods or men shown in a scene are placed next to the figures so that there can be no mistake about who they are. The artists and their patrons who paid for the work were also concerned about identifying themselves; and this is to be expected, for the Greeks as a people were not given to anonymity. From the earliest times, vases can be attributed to artists by name and even when the name is missing the known idiosyncrasies of certain painters allow for identification. These active men, no less than the poets, architects, and sculptors, belonged to a talented minority. It is assumed that the type of patronage they enjoyed enabled them to do what they pleased and that in any event they were leading rather than following popular tastes. With the philosophers it will be another story, for most men will welcome or suffer changes in literary or artistic styles far more readily than they will alter their cherished beliefs.

*Pl. 44* Pelike *by the Altamura Painter,* circa *460 B.C. A woman pours libation for departing warrior*

## An Intellectual Tradition And Not A Popular One

A frequently repeated exaggeration about the ancient Greeks is the statement that they made a religion out of reason. If so, the Greeks as a people altered their mental processes in a way no people had before their time or have since. The statement is dangerously misleading because it fails to emphasize two points which may be of interest in the continuing debate over the role of the intellectual in a popular democracy. To begin with, only a small minority of Greeks ever abandoned the magical, mythological and supernatural common beliefs in favor of a speculative approach toward the universe around them or their own behavior in it. Speculation about the origin of all that exists, the conflict between being and becoming and the essence of virtue, is not a popular pastime. The vast majority of human beings in all places at all times have spent most of their existence in the honorable but routine process of making a living. The majority of the Greeks were no exception and they never gave up their belief in a god of the winds or a god of the sea. They lived, as do most Greeks in the modern world, by instinct, habit and faith. The assistance of the saints today replaces the assistance of the gods of yesterday. It is no misfortune that such help and comfort are always available.

Secondly, the minority, insofar as it gave expression to views contrary to accepted beliefs, was no more popular in Greece than such a minority has ever been anywhere. At the height of the Periclean democracy in the fifth century, the philosopher Anaxagoras was driven from the city on the charge of atheism. There may have been some politics involved, but even if the charge of atheism was a smoke-screen for the real reason, it was apparently calculated to win popular support.

Much more agreeable to the popular viewpoint were the comedies of Aristophanes, which pictured the sophistic intellectuals of the fifth century as undermining the moral structure of society by their persistent doubts and endless quibbling. Aristophanes in his play the *Clouds* presented Socrates as just such a man and his caricature of Socrates is thought to have contributed to the downfall of history's best known freethinker.

The impression of Athens in the fifth century as a haven of freedom where strangers were welcome and no man spied on his neighbor was enshrined by Pericles in his famed *Funeral Oration*. It is true that an extraordinary amount of free and open discussion took place on matters of politics as it does in Greece today. This achievement of a public forum on any subject was truly a remarkable advance over all previous societies—so remarkable indeed that there is no need to exaggerate the point in order to credit the Greeks with progress.

However, the average Greek considered politics a subject more open to discussion than he did religion. When has this ever been different? Respect for the gods was a very serious matter. It was believed that they could help or hinder a city and so any man who offended them was not only putting himself in jeopardy; he was risking the welfare of everybody else as well. The worship of Athena at Athens was not a matter of religious choice. It was an act of patriotism. The great democrat Pericles, who entertained non-conformists like Anaxagoras in his home, may have had his own doubts about the gods but he never expressed them in public. He was the most successful politician in the history of the Athenian democracy and he did not win his place by making mistakes.

So the Greeks as a people never did make a religion out of reason. For a brief time in certain cities, Athens especially, an atmosphere was provided wherein a tolerated minority of men were free to pursue their doubts and speculations and to keep alert the minds of other men. That they were generally tolerated does not mean that they were liked. Nor were they disliked only for their ideas. Their own persistent quarrelsomeness and frequent obnoxiousness had something to do with it.

This emphasis on the correlation between individual expression and the variety of thought is not intended to suggest that Greek creative works were only produced by those who broke with established convictions. The great dramatic poets, Aeschylus and Sophocles, treated the traditional themes in a respectful and meaningful manner. The building of temples, theaters, and much Greek statuary was a reflection of the desire to honor and offer worship to the gods. Their beauty was inspired by a faith common to a whole people. Yet the traditional and accepted does not of itself admit the diversity which is best gained through tolerance of the experimental, the unusual and the unorthodox. The history of rationalism in Greece is an intellectual tradition and not a popular one. Some men did find an opportunity to doubt and speculate and write what they would. The result was the best argument for why they should.

## He Had a Question

No one knows who first began to speculate about the nature of the universe in scientific terms. We simply know that in Greece the man of record was Thales and that he was a native of Miletus. The place as well as the man was important to the beginnings of philosophy.

Miletus, the largest and most prosperous city in Ionia, a busy port with ships going to and from her numerous colonies, became a gathering place for colonists and a market place for traders. In this city of contrasts and diversities, a crossroads for east and west, the strange was a commonplace and the new only incidental. If there were to be a startling breakthrough in man's thinking, a shift toward rationalism, Miletus was the place for it. It is therefore a convenience to the historian that this is where it happened.

The stories about Thales picture him as a man of varied talents and interests; he is seen both as a dreamer lost in his thoughts and as a shrewd business man. One tale describes his practice of studying the stars while out walking, and reveals that on at least one occasion he fell into a well. Another relates how his meteorological studies enabled him to predict that there would be a large olive crop, whereupon he obtained a monopoly of the local olive presses and made a sizeable profit. Both stories may be legendary yet they serve to illustrate the kind of reputation he had with ancient writers. We know no more of him than they did.

There seems to be little doubt that Thales was interested in the practical application of his varied knowledge. In this connection he is credited with having discovered the constellation of the Little Bear and first pointing out its usefulness as a guide to sailors. For such a man the chance to study reliable records of the movements of the stars dating back over a century or more was undoubtedly a bonanza. The Babylonians had been keeping such records and it seems certain that Thales had access to them. It is possible that he traveled all the way to Babylonia, or he could perhaps have acquired this data by visiting Sardis, the capital of nearby Lydia.

The Babylonians, like the Egyptians, while able to calculate well enough to fascinate future ages with their engineering accomplishments, never theorized beyond practical considerations. Their accumulated data about the stars was used mostly in the pseudo-science of astrology, and so their thinking was fixed at about the level of those millions of our contemporaries who make astrology the profitable business it is today. Events which to us appear natural remained for them in the realm of the supernatural. Isolated instances of rational thinking did occur, however. In both Egypt and Mesopotamia at a very early date, treatises were prepared by physicians who took a wholly objective view of the body and whose writings were altogether free of the magical formulae so characteristic of the treatment of diseases by their contemporaries. Yet these exceptional men did not inaugurate a tradition in rationalism and their failure to do so pointed to the forces at work in these earlier societies which prevented it.

On the other hand the milieu in which Thales lived had not committed him to any kind of traditional thinking. He looked at the Babylonian records from the outside, the way a modern Western visitor might view the sacred Ganges. When he correctly predicted an eclipse early in the sixth century, it was for him a starting point toward new knowledge, not merely confirmation of an old belief in omens. To him the eclipse was a natural event about which a curious man might wonder and perhaps learn more. To the Babylonian priests it was a message from the gods. These divinities were all knowing, and man could only learn by observing their signs.

The submission of Near Eastern man to the overpowering knowledge of the gods was more than one of his thoughts; it was actually the context in which he did his thinking. He accepted the idea that man cannot learn anything on his own as readily as we insist that he can. This earlier man did not reject rationalism; he rarely thought about it.

Here is the essential difference between the priests and Thales. They had an answer and he had a question. His question was the starting point of Greek philosophy and science, which at the time were one and the same. What, he asked, is the primal stuff of which everything else is made? There have been many answers to the question since, but Thales' answer was water. Seen in the light of his own day, it was not as unreasonable as it sounds. In the Babylonian mythological accounts of the origin of all things, there was in the beginning only water. The various stories differed in colorful and imaginative detail, but in all of them the great god Marduk did establish the earth and so divide the waters below from those above. So, too, in Egyptian myth the earth was bounded by water. The many boats found in the tombs of Egypt were intended for transit of the heavens, not the Nile. It does not seem unlikely then that Thales was seeking to find natural reasons to account for the significance of water in the accepted stories of creation. It is also entirely possible that in a physical sense he envisioned the earth as floating on water. Aristotle suggests that his reasons for deciding on water may have resulted from his observations on the significance of moistness in seeds and semen and the growth of living things. It has also been conjectured that he attached significance to the fact that water appeared as vapor, liquid, and solid. As with the eclipse, so with the concept of water. Thales was looking at old knowledge in a new way. His steps may have been stumbling but the direction was momentous.

Thales' students followed the master's shift from supernatural to natural causation and then went off on their own. Anaximander, perhaps a relative of Thales as well as his pupil, was not content with simply finding some rational explanation for old stories. He boldly abandoned the naive insistence on a single known substance as the primal stuff of all things and postulated instead an indefinite "something" which was unknown to man's experience. This "something" has usually been described as the "infinite" or the "boundless" and its character has been endlessly debated by ancient and modern writers. Still, the proposal was unquestionably more provocative than that of either his teacher or of his younger contemporary Anaximenes, who suggested air rather than water as the primal source of all matter. Today, on the basis of man's latest experiences, we would be tempted to call Anaximander's "something" energy. While he could not himself have imagined such a hypothesis, he did in answer to another question make an astoundingly good guess. He suggested that life had first originated in the sea and therefore man was himself in some manner related to fish. The reports that he spoke of men as originally having been born and sustained within fishes and then brought to dry land reveals merely the limitations of even a brilliant mind in these early years. Yet his proposal was closer to currently accepted scientific theories about man's physical origin than are the numerous accounts of a special creation which flourished then as now.

As a group, Thales, Anaximander and Anaximenes make up the Milesian School. They are also sometimes called the Monists, for each of them did search for that "one" something or other from which came "the many." Anaximander and Anaximenes were also pioneers in the use of prose. Their cold and impersonal speculations about the nature of the universe were in sharp contrast to the earlier imaginative stories of creation, and out with the fable went the language of romance.

The Monists introduced rationalism to the educated circles of

Miletus where its influence was soon to reach beyond the investigation of only natural phenomena. Toward the end of the sixth century, Hecataeus began his *Genealogies* with the complaint that many of the myths told by his contemporaries were foolishness and that he would set the record straight. For the most part, he was only inspired by the new spirit of inquiry to abandon wrong myths in favor of the right ones by freeing the traditional stories from divers accounts which had crept in here and there; but on occasion he rejected the colorful stories altogether in favor of the plain truth. Hecataeus' more objective approach to history was startlingly new, but the title "Father of History" went to his popular successor Herodotus whose writings were more interesting. Herodotus also observed from time to time that a story might not be true, but if it was good, he told it anyway.

### Other Questions

Hecataeus, like Thales, helped to establish Miletus as a center of Greek intellectual life and so it remained until destroyed by the Persians in 494. The name of the city is closely associated therefore with the Pre-Socratic period in Greek philosophy. However, the best known of the Pre-Socratics did not live there. The mathematician Pythagoras left his native Samos about 530 to escape the rule of the tyrant Polycrates and established his school at Croton in southern Italy. Aside from this, we do not know much about Pythagoras personally and it is equally difficult to define his doctrine. Like certain other famous teachers, he did not write anything himself and so his words were passed on orally from generation to generation, perhaps with alterations in the process. Presumably they were not written down until a century or so after his own time. Another difficulty is that both his thinking and that of his students were permeated by a strong strain of religiosity which is difficult to unravel from their philosophical views. Finally, it is impossible to be sure who is responsible for what tenets in Pythagoreanism, because it was the custom of later writers to attribute everything to the founder and nothing at all to his successors.

From the beginning, the Pythagorean circle was different from the other Greek schools such as the Monist group at Miletus. It was a religious community in which the members followed rituals and taboos which were foreign to the spirit of rationalism. The secrecy which served to create a bond among the initiates was indicative of the esoteric nature of the movement.

The central doctrine of Pythagoreanism on its religious side was the reincarnation of souls, a belief which had been held by earlier peoples in Thrace and which would later reappear in Socrates' teachings. There was a tale often told that Pythagoras once chided a man for beating a dog because he said he heard the soul of a friend in the bark. This idea that souls might be reborn into lower animals naturally implied the kinship of all life and led to a prohibition against eating flesh. The soul was conceived of as moving in and out of matter, and from this developed a dualistic view of man in which soul and body were actually antagonistic. To best serve the soul, therefore, the body must be subjected to discipline and the result was a life of asceticism. The Greeks as a whole never accepted this dualistic view of man nor did they see any benefits in the denial of the flesh. Yet here, among some of them at least, was an example of precisely the kind of solution so prevalent in the religions of the East and one which would be offered again explicitly in Plato's *Phaedo.*

It should be added that the convenience of using familiar terms often endangers accuracy because it suggests that the philosophers were progressing more rapidly in their thinking than they actually did. The soul need not at this early date have been thought of as incorporeal. Today a distinction is made between the corporeal electricity which passes in and through the body and the incorporeal soul. Before the time of Plato in the fourth century, the Greek thinkers assumed that what existed had both quantity as well as quality, albeit perhaps, as in the case of the soul, it happened not to be in a visible state.

The same point of view was emphasized in the Pythagorean mathematical studies where again, as with the idea of the soul, number was an entity itself and in fact all physical objects had their own particular number. The unity of nature seen in the kinship of all life was coincident with a unity based on number. The argument was from the notion of proportion. According to tradition, Pythagoras was the first to observe that proportion was the difference between music and mere noise. The length of a string determined the pitch. From this simple observation he went on to argue that there was a proper proportion in all things and this gave order to the whole universe.

Thus both on its religious side and on its philosophical side the Pythagorean tradition stood for order and harmony. It seems, too, that the Pythagorean brotherhood won control over Croton and tried to impose an orderliness which was too much for the uninitiated to share. Tradition says that Pythagoras was driven out of the city and that he died only a short time later. Exactly when this took place is not known, but it was presumably in the late sixth century.

After the time of Pythagoras, his disciples carried on elsewhere and spokesmen for the tradition flourished into the fourth century. But they were never without their critics who looked at the same world and came to other conclusions. Chief among them was one Heraclitus, who was in his prime about the year 500 B.C. in his native Ephesus, a city on the Ionian coast north of Miletus. In direct contradiction to Pythagoreanism, Heraclitus wrote that all that exists is in a state of flux. He based his argument in part on what he saw in the physical world around him and was known for his remark that a man could not step into the same river twice. The same river, forever changing, would be a fair analogy to his view of all that existed. His thoughts were obscure and have been much debated, but he seems to have been suggesting that everything was involved in a never ending process, like an eternal fire which as it burns both destroys and creates. His other main idea was that the balance of nature is maintained through strife rather than harmony. If this hard truth sounds like Darwinism, it should be remembered that the Greek thinker was not concerned with an evolutionary concept but with nature in equilibrium. The controlling principle, or *logos,* provides for a condition whereby all things are constantly shifting from one state into another. Nothing is lost and nothing is gained. The world is always the same physical reality, but, like one of its rivers, is not really the same from one moment to the next.

The Pythagoreans had insisted on permanence and harmony, yet Heraclitus saw only change and strife. A third position held that in a sense they both were right. If the world was as Heraclitus described it, and for many it seemed to be, then the order and permanence which the Pythagoreans envisioned must be somewhere else. This was the conclusion of an ex-Pythagorean named Parmenides. He abandoned the senses as grounds for evidence and relied exclusively on reason as the better guide. Thus he argued that it was logically impossible for that "which is" to become that "which it is not" and so insisted that only the changeless is real. Parmenides implied that the senses deceive man about the true nature of reality and this conclusion was later enshrined in Plato's famous Allegory of the Cave. If it was Socrates or Plato who found the way to the modern concept of the soul, it was assuredly Parmenides who had suggested where to look. While it is difficult to be sure what Parmenides had in mind, it is not far from what he said to the position that matter is an illusion altogether and that reality and permanence are to be found only in the non-material world of thought.

When Socrates (*circa* 470–399) was about twenty years old, he had a chance to listen to the seasoned Parmenides who was probably in his sixties when he visited Athens in the middle of the fifth century. As part of his own legacy, Socrates left the assertion that justice, love and beauty were themselves realities and existed apart from men who expressed them. Back of this profundity or nonsense, depending on what you think of it, was Parmenides' provocative suggestion. And still in the future was St. Paul's observation that faith is the substance of things hoped for, the evidence of things not seen.

The Greeks were not the first people to use their minds or to express themselves as individuals, but qualities which were elsewhere only transient and exceptional became characteristic of Greece, especially Athens. Athens was no utopia, to be sure. Philosophers with new ideas came and some were asked to leave. Not everybody was happy about everything. They never are. Yet, if men are capable of creating a free society, this was one, for a generation or two. Then it was over and Socrates was executed, not for what he was saying, but because he insisted that it was his duty to say what he pleased. Within a century the Athenians were to find freedom and then abandon it. For those who had nothing to say or contribute, it could hardly have made any difference. For Socrates, what happened at Athens was the difference between life and death. Moreover, he said that men would remember these events and some have. The story has often been retold but there is hardly another story which can better stand retelling.

# The Formative Years at Athens

**VI**

Accounts of Athens and her accomplishments loom so large in history that for convenience sake the terms "Athenian" and "Greek" are often used interchangeably. Such a mistake belies the significance of the variety of Greek life, but it flatters the Athenians and they deserve it.

By the fifth century, Athens was the largest and most prosperous city in Greece. News of her wealth and free institutions spread wide, and to her came the writers, sculptors and philosophers whose works, along with those of native citizens, have given Athens a unique place in all of human history. By comparison with the condition of other cities of the ancient world, Athenian cosmopolitanism and democracy were spectacular and startlingly modern.

In classical times, the city-state of Athens included all of Attica, a triangular shaped peninsula which juts out into the Aegean Sea from the Greek mainland. The rich clay beds of this region offered raw material for a flourishing ceramics industry; the silver in Mount Laurium provided the wherewithal for ships to export this pottery; and the marble of Mount Pentelicus went into temples which thanked the gods for all these gifts.

Nearly everywhere in Attica the sea was in sight, but land was scanty. The growth of a large influential *polis* was made possible only by exporting local products and importing food. The decision to do this was part of the wisdom of Solon who lived about 600. Before that, not much is known for certain.

The collective memory of a whole people is like that of a single individual. The stories a man may tell of his boyhood on a farm may be longer or shorter by the time he is writing his memoirs, but the farm is still there. So it was with Athens. By the time her history was written down, many discrepancies existed in the various accounts, but there was enough agreement to allow at least an outline of the past.

In Mycenaean times, Attica was divided apparently into a number of small groups of villages, each ruled by a local monarch. According to tradition, the king, whose palace was on the Acropolis at Athens, managed by conquest or persuasion or both, to unite all Attica under his rule and so gave to the whole area a common citizenship. The exciting Theseus, who may have reigned as early as 1250 or as late as 900, has always been a popular choice for this role. According to the accounts which feature him as a heroic figure, the unity he achieved gave the Atticans the strength to end the impressment of their young men into the Cretan navy. This is the history behind the familiar tale which tells how Theseus slew the Minotaur, the monster belonging to the Cretan king Minos.

The story which portrays Theseus as a great king of remarkable deeds appears long after his day however, and may actually be a dramatic substitution for a process which was in fact gradual and possibly not completed until sometime in the eighth century. If the various communities were assimilated only piecemeal under a common rule, there would have been a number of kings jointly responsible for this accomplishment. So it is that modern speculation has found an uninteresting alternative for a spectacular myth. Either way, unification and common citizenship were in fact achieved and this was important to the future of Attica.

How long the monarchy lasted is unknown. Even the name of the last full-fledged king remains undecided, although among ancient writers the popular choice was Codrus. All accounts agree, however, that because of some changes which took place before the seventh century, the kingship was no longer what it once was. While the title *basileus*, king, remained attached to an office on which were entailed the old sacred duties, the real power passed to the nobility who substituted their own privileged rule for that of the monarch. These were of course the same men who had long surrounded the king with advice and, very likely, intrigue.

It is not certain whether the usurpation was carried out by the whole aristocracy acting in concert or by a single powerful clan. By whatever means, the reduction of the kingship took place gradually. Tradition states that the later kings had become weak and effeminate, which, if true, would explain why the first encroachment on the monarchy was a demand by the nobility that a commander-in-chief (*polemarchos*) be elected from among their own ranks. Later the king's civil duties devolved to another elective magistrate, the *archon eponymos*. The title meant that each year would henceforth be recorded in the name of the man who held the office. By subtraction the king was left with only the administration of religious matters, although the office of king was still for life and was retained in the same family.

In time, the magistracy was further expanded by the introduction of new officers who took over some of the routine work, such as recording laws, which formerly belonged to the archon. These lesser officials were also accorded the name archon, and in addition the title was attached to the established offices of polemarch and king. As a consequence, the aristocratic constitution finally included nine archons who made up a kind of executive board headed by the *archon eponymos* who was also the chief judicial officer in the state.

In the familiar tripartite division of government amongst Indo-European societies, there was a king, a council of elders and an assembly of the people. The later Athenian story that their council, the Areopagus, was founded by Athena simply meant that it was very old and nobody knew how it got started. In any event, this body was left uninjured by the shift in power from king to archons. It had been an aristocratic stronghold even under the monarchy when it was very likely made up of the heads of the noble families. Under the aristocracy all ex-archons were added as members for life. Age, prestige, and experience were built into the council and during its long career at Athens it appears to have performed a task similar to that of the later Senate at Rome. It was the anchor of the state, with a general supervision over all areas of the government; above all it acted as a preserver of custom and public decency. Magistrates were subject to its questioning both during and after their term in office, and it may even have had the right to deny office to anyone elected whom it considered unfit. Furthermore, its traditional role as a court of last appeal gave it an authority in Athenian political life which lasted until the very eve of the popular democracy.

The Assembly of the Athenian people was more of a theory than a practice in earliest times. Consistent with the pattern common to other Indo-European societies, the people were asked to voice their formal support in times of danger, but under the monarchy this earliest Assembly was more akin to a rally of aroused tribesmen than to a meeting of informed citizens prepared to vote.

When the aristocracy assumed control, this folk gathering was replaced by a regularly constituted body which may even have been given some voice in the election of magistrates. It is unlikely that it elected them directly, but it may have nominated men from whom the Areopagus made the final choice or it may simply have met to approve the selection of the Areopagus acting independently. Participation in this Assembly was limited to men with some amount of property, yet the requirement of noble birth continued to exclude the majority of those in the Assembly from holding any office. So the "elections," if there were any, were held by voters who themselves ranked above the poor and who selected the magistrates from among the nobility. Furthermore, only those matters of state which the Areopagus chose to bring before the Assembly would receive its attention. Operating under such restrictions, this body could not have acted as an agency for broadening the base of power below the level of the well-born. The political imbalance in turn reflected the social and economic favoritism within the society.

Hesiod had never lived in Attica, but he would have recognized the government we have described as similar to the one he knew in Boeotia in the eighth century. It was a situation in which the few who owned most of the land had also a monopoly of political power. As observed earlier, the collapse of such a system was usually coincident with a major shift in the economy including the introduction of trade, manufacturing, and a new moneyed group.

The Athenian commercial development was late compared to that of other parts of Greece. The settling of Athenian colonies, the large-scale export of pottery, and the introduction of coinage came roughly a century later than at Miletus and Corinth. The first attempt to establish a tyranny at Athens was correspondingly late and even then it was premature. In 632, Cylon, a young Athenian nobleman who had married a daughter of the tyrant of Megara, borrowed armed support from his father-in-law and attempted to seize Athens. Not only was his timing off, but he had the wrong kind of backing. His fighting men from Megara caused resentment and offended the citizenry whose support was necessary for his success. The attempt was doomed beforehand, although this was apparently not obvious to Megacles, the chief archon that year. Even after the citizenry had rallied to block the attempt, Megacles and members of his family, the Alcmeonidae, killed those involved in the plot although they had sought sanctuary near the image of Athena. This bloodshed brought pollution on the whole city and no amount of gratitude to those who had acted to save the state could overcome the fears of the populace. Subsequently the Alcmeonidae were found guilty of sacrilege and sent into exile. They eventually returned, but all or some of the members of this active and powerful family were to be driven out many times in the future and the memory of Megacles' mistake was forever kept alive by their political enemies. Nevertheless the men of this house, including the renowned Pericles, played more prominent roles in Athenian history than did the men of any other family.

That a tyranny was even attempted was an indication of growing problems. The times demanded a concession. This came with the appointment of Draco as a magistrate for the purpose of preparing for the first time the existing laws in written form. His name has been ill used in the familiar term "draconian" which suggests cruel or unjust legislation. Property was ranked well above human life and the death sentence was inflicted for simple theft, but this was customary in early codes. Similarly, the custom of debt slavery was of long standing and in no way the fault of Draco. On the positive side, Draco is credited with the introduction of a court of appeal which consisted of fifty-one judges (members of the aristocracy, to be sure), who might listen to appeals in matters of homicide where the case was not otherwise reserved for the Areopagus. This was especially pertinent since Draco's code specifically distinguished between premeditated killings and other acts such as self-defense.

Aside from these inferences about his work, Draco left only his name, and it is impossible to know whether he was a reformer at heart or merely hoped to forestall a political crisis. Whatever his intentions, economic changes were taking place which inevitably meant further trouble.

## Giving Everybody Something, Nobody Everything

As had happened at Miletus, Corinth and elsewhere, the planting of colonies overseas with the accompanying increase in trade led to an impasse at Athens between the entrenched aristocracy, still in control of the government, and the ambitions of other men, especially the new rich. The chance that all parties in any city might agree to arbitration and dictation by a single legally elected official seemed very remote. But early in the sixth century at Athens an extraordinary man made this chance possible. For one reason or another, Solon (*circa* 638–*circa* 559) was acceptable to all sides. A number of stories about him help to explain why this was so.

According to one old tale, Cyrus, a triumphant king of Persia, was about to burn alive a conquered king of Lydia. While there was still time, the king at the stake called out the name of Solon three times. The king who remembered him was Croesus; in happier days he had received Solon at his court. According to tradition, Solon was at the time in retirement and much celebrated for his judicious settlement of affairs at Athens. Croesus arranged a lavish display of his wealth and then presumptuously asked Solon whom he considered the happiest of all men. Solon named three. None of those he named had been wealthy in the king's sense of the word, and all of them were dead. Solon described how each had lived with honor and courage. He then stressed the point that they had died without having suffered from any reversal of fortune such as so often befalls a man unexpectedly. Solon advised Croesus to consider himself happy only when he too had managed to reach his last day without misfortune. Croesus had been made unhappy by this reply, but as he faced the flames he realized that he had lost everything except the memory of this advice. Yet it saved him after all. Cyrus, the Persian king, was eager to hear more about Solon and the last day for Croesus was postponed.

It is annoying perhaps, but true, that Solon could have been dead before Croesus even began his reign. The ancients themselves were doubtful whether the chronology of the sixth century would allow for any conversation between them. Nevertheless, the import of the story remains. Moreover it is a theme which repeats itself again and again in Greek literature. They die happy who choose to live rightly and who escape the miseries which may happen in any event.

There is no harm in giving Solon credit for this advice. Nothing we know about him would make us believe that he could be deceived by either wealth or power. He was a cautious man in all respects. His fame is firmly established as a great lawgiver, but in one of his poems, when speaking of his laws, he says that they were not really the best, but only the best possible.

Solon's life story has benefited from the imagination of ancient writers and the speculations of modern ones. He wrote poetry (this was the accepted means of self-expression then) and his verse leaves no doubt of his moderation and common sense, but his poems were not autobiographical in the usual sense. His life, therefore, remains little more than an outline. Election to the archonship was in itself evidence of his noble birth. However, for some reason never explained, he found it necessary when young to travel as a trader and earn money. So that he entered public service as a man well-born who had also a background sympathetic to the budding commercial community. He was elected archon for the year 594/93 and then in 592/91 was given a temporary commission to reorganize the government.

It is clear that Solon considered the rapaciousness of wealthy landowners to be the greatest evil of the day. He was therefore determined to get the poor out from under their crushing debts. On the other hand, he had distinct reservations about these same much-abused people. He had refused to be moved by their clamor for a redistribution of the land, and he further let it be known that he had no confidence in the judgment of common men who enjoy too much prosperity. When he came to reorganize the government, he says that he gave to the common people only a limited responsibility, as much as he thought they could handle.

Solon was aware that poor men see the rich as hoarding what they do not need, and that rich men see the poor as coveting what they do not deserve. As far as he was concerned, any man—rich or poor—was easily deceived by selfish material interests and was likely to lose sight of more enduring values. This observation and others like it were no more unique then than they are now, yet they helped win Solon a place among the seven wisest men in antiquity. The evidence that he actually practiced what he taught convinces us that he deserved his honors.

Upon taking public office, his first orders were aimed at easing tensions. He writes that he freed the land of those who had fallen into debt slavery both at home and abroad. His statements about these matters are simple and offer no details, for everyone at the time would have known what he meant. He does not explain, for instance, how he managed to buy back men sold abroad for debt. It is possible that the wealthy classes, in addition to their losses from the debt cancellation, were held liable for this cost. The situation may have been critical enough for these men to consider themselves lucky in having avoided the redistribution of land which Solon had blocked. Admittedly, nobody was altogether happy with Solon's arrangements. This, however, would have reassured him; for he insisted that good laws followed a middle course—giving everybody something, but nobody everything. For the time being at least, he established an accommodation between those with too much and those with too little. In Greece this was not easy to do then, nor has it been since.

In order to open up a wider range for Athenian trade, Solon abandoned the coinage of the Aeginetan standard and shifted to the lighter coins used by Corinth. Athenian products could now more easily enter the markets of the western Mediterranean. The olive oil *amphora* seen on the new coins was itself a clear indication of what Solon had in mind. Although he banned the export of other food-stuffs from Attica during a time of necessity, he never stopped the shipment of olive oil. Pottery was another major product of Attica and Solon saw the need for skilled craftsmen to increase the Athenian output and to provide a better quality of goods. He recruited artisans from Corinth and elsewhere by offering citizenship to all who would come with their families and settle in Attica.

Solon's support and encouragement of the business life of the city had little meaning so long as the government remained largely in the hands of aristocrats whose wealth was in land. It is a testament to his abilities that although he refused to become a tyrant and steadfastly avoided partisanship, he was able to effect changes which tyrants had managed to achieve only with extra-legal force. Solon opened public offices to men of proven ability on the premise that they could not have earned their wealth without some brains. The monopoly of the well-born was abruptly ended. As in the past, however, citizens were assigned to classes based on income and the assessment was still stated in archaic terms of bushels of produce. The wealthiest citizens were called "five-hundred bushel men" while those of the lowest class produced less than two hundred.

All men were admitted to some degree of participation in the government, although responsibilities were still heavily weighted from the top brackets down. How this principle worked itself out in every detail is not known but the overall intention seems clear. It is apparent that offices were on a graded scale with the nine archons, for instance, being chosen only from the first class. Lesser magistrates were elected from the second and third classes, but the poorest citizens were excluded from the magistracy altogether. Solon's decision to bar the most numerous class from public office was balanced, however, by his admission of all citizens to serve as jurymen. In effect, decisions by magistrates belonging to the upper classes could now be challenged by an appeal to popular judgment.

A new Council of 400, open to members of the top three classes, was created for the purpose of directing the day-to-day business of the state. It discussed and weighed all policy questions and proposed laws, and decided which matters were to be brought to the Assembly of all citizens for a vote. As such it took over the prerogative which the Areopagus had had during the time of aristocratic domination. Since the Council was in the hands of the upper three classes, the fourth class of poorest citizens still had no chance for radicalism. In other respects too, so far as both the Assembly and the courts were concerned, what the poorer citizens had been given in theory was very likely different from what they had in practice. For one thing, they would be the least likely to spare the time from making a living to come into the city and participate in government business. Their lack of experience in public affairs, their depressed circumstances, and their inability to afford any education must also have discouraged large numbers of them from taking steps to claim their rights. Indeed, under the Solonian constitution it was apparently not expected that they would. While Solon has always been credited with giving the common people a place, it has been plain that he intended them to have only a limited role in the government and did not by any means intend that they should have the last word. More than a century would pass before a more experienced and better-informed majority would take the ultimate power for themselves. It was as though Solon had invited the hired hands into the house—and at first few of them knew how to behave but after several generations they owned it! Democracy was not a sudden invention.

Because historians will continue to re-evaluate bits and pieces of information from sometimes obscure and even contradictory sources, there can never be any final decisions on questions which Solon himself left unanswered. It is unlikely, however, that the overall significance of this man will ever be altered. His laws and administrative changes, although not made for the purpose of establishing a democracy, did remove certain roadblocks from its path. His greater significance is as an example of the man who, because of who and what he is himself, exercises an influence far greater than that of men of lesser character, whether they hold office legally or simply rule by force. Solon won the willing confidence of all parties because they saw in him the strength to solve their problems. Surrounded by men who sought his help to gain their own ends, Solon only wanted to be what he already was. Rather than possess the power of a tyrant, he preferred to have the will to refuse it. Plutarch reports that Solon once told a friend that tyranny was a high place from which there was no easy way down. No one should use this statement to rob him of his good motives by suggesting that he declined tyranny for fear of its consequences. But at the same time he was human, and there is no reason to insist that he never thought about it.

After his retirement, Solon traveled for about ten years. Before leaving, he advised the Athenians to put their trust in laws rather than in men. His advice went unheeded. The large landowners sat on their estates north of the city, still bemoaning the insolence of all change. The hard-pressed farmers who tried for a living in the marginal soils of the foothills had been helped temporarily, but not permanently. Between these two classes was another group made up of producers, exporters and shipbuilders who had plans of their own. These were the three major factions jockeying for position during the three decades after Solon's retirement. On at least two occasions, orderly government broke down altogether and it was not even possible to elect archons. In a literal sense that is what anarchy means, no archons.

It is said that Solon was bitterly disappointed by what happened. Perhaps in spite of his acute observations on human nature, he still expected too much from men as yet inexperienced in self-government and others too long sated with privilege. It may only have been the viciousness of the struggle which disturbed him, for it is hard to believe that he would have expected the years following his archonship to be without trouble. More likely, he was determined to give the citizens a chance to govern themselves, even at the risk of an uneasy adjustment. But he was wrong either way. He had staked everything on his refusal to be a tyrant. In his old age, he saw another man take his place.

### The Model Tyrant

Peisistratus, like Solon, was an aristocrat with a popular appeal. In the years following Solon's retirement, he had succeeded in establishing himself as the spokesman of all who would be benefited by more drastic reforms. His main support came from the poor farmers, but he took a footing wherever he found it. Among his backers were those citizens newly enfranchised by Solon, as well as other persons of mixed descent whose hope for citizenship might well depend on trading their present support for future favors. Peisistratus was an opportunist in the beginning and he remained one until his power was firmly established. In later years, however, with unchallenged authority, his program revealed a fairness worthy of Solon himself. His career offers a good example of that not unfamiliar type of political figure whose actions while in power contrast favorably with his methods in getting there.

Peisistratus had charm and good looks, but he never made anybody's list of wise men. Still, he was astute enough to know that Solon's hope for a government under law was premature. If there was to be a tyrant, then Peisistratus may have been the best choice. In any event, he was his own choice. According to the traditional story, he wounded himself and then claimed his wounds as proof of an imminent danger to the cause of reform. The Assembly voted a bodyguard for his protection and with these very same protectors he captured the Acropolis and seized control of the government. The story has been doubted. Yet it remains true that some of the St. Georges in history have indeed made their own dragons, and there are some modern examples.

The enemies of Peisistratus were not easily silenced and twice mustered enough force to drive him into exile. By 546, however, he had sufficient backing to establish himself in power for the last nineteen years of his life. His most determined enemies amongst the nobility were driven out of the city and others, it is said, were forced to hand over their children as hostages. The rest of the aristocracy were apparently won over by fair dealings and their own good sense of self-interest.

As the holder of unchallenged power, Peisistratus became the model tyrant. He sought to hold power, not by force alone, but by allaying the fears of all classes through judicious acts and hard work. He seems to have exercised restraint and to have used his power only where he felt it absolutely necessary to sustain his program. He never put himself above the state in any personal sense, nor did he live in any extravagant or unseemly manner. He kept the system intact as Solon had arranged it, and managed to direct the affairs of state without ever himself holding a legal office. By one means or another, no one knows how, he must have rigged the electoral process to insure himself the help of archons who were friends, if not relatives.

Peisistratus became the promoter of policies designed to bring further prosperity to the city, of building projects to beautify it, and of festivities to glorify its patron goddess Athena. These were causes which all citizens could join and for which they might freely thank Peisistratus. His reputation as a man of selfless dedication to the welfare of the city was well established in Athenian tradition. This does not mean that he was merely cunning, a man who plotted his place in history. It is rather to say that by the time he had established himself at Athens he was a man of considerable political experience and that he behaved accordingly.

The tradition says that Peisistratus favored the farmers, especially when they were at home and busily at work. His plan of having judges travel through the countryside to try cases, and his own frequent tours of inspection, were designed to keep these rural citizens away from the city and thereby minimize at least one source of trouble. His interest in the farmers, however, did not prevent him from collecting taxes on all their produce. A standard anecdote is often told about Peisistratus which mentions both the tax and his own good humor. It is about a farmer with a wretched plot of land who, during one of Peisistratus' tours, failed to recognize the tyrant. One of Peisistratus' attendants asked the man how much he got out of his farm. The farmer answered that his return was in aches and pains and he wished that of these Peisistratus might have his ten per cent. Peisistratus must have laughed for he forgave him all his taxes. It was a story worth votes, if tyrants had risked elections.

But there is also a more serious story. A citizen had accused Peisistratus of homicide but was afraid to appear against him in court. We are left with the impression that he was not afraid because Peisistratus was cruel and he need fear retaliation, but rather because Peisistratus was so popular. Thus the man did not fear the tyrant, but rather those who supported him. Having involved his own welfare so successfully with that of the majority of citizens, Peisistratus had convinced them that a threat to him was also a threat to those he loved and served. The people became a shield and a weapon. One despotism may be no better than another, but despotisms of men sincerely dedicated to the welfare of the majority are inevitably more subtle and secure.

Peisistratus brought a season of quiet years to Athens. His foreign alliances, especially with cities toward the Black Sea, helped Athenian trade and facilitated the import of grain. As the population of Attica was constantly growing, and the city proper continuing to swell with the influx of families from the countryside, more food was badly needed. So was water, and Peisistratus, like most tyrants of the time, was well remembered for his provision of a new aqueduct.

The unemployment problem was not so easily solved. Here again

Peisistratus followed the pattern of tyranny by beginning an ambitious building program which created new jobs. Significant among the projects was an addition to the so-called Old Temple of Athena, later burned by the Persians. But even a busy building campaign could not solve Peisistratus' problem, and the promotion of overseas colonies remained the best solution for taking care of men unable to find permanent employment.

Those who did manage to settle in the city brought about certain innovations, for they retained the cycle of seasonal celebrations which had always been part of rural life. These festivities included singing and dancing contests which of course are not unfamiliar country pastimes; in Greece, however, these gatherings involved more than the social activities of a country fair. They had a religious side. Dionysus, a god of fruitfulness, was being honored. Because worshippers more readily changed occupations than gods, Dionysus came along to the city.

In the course of the sixth century these informal and unorganized activities were gradually transformed into regular events on the civic calendar. It is recorded that a poet by the name of Thespis won first prize in 534 for his composition in a city-wide celebration. So it seems that by this date at least, the old country festivities had been assimilated and were contributing to the tyrant's plan for the community.

Thespis was more than just a prize winner. He was also presumably the first man to step forward to recite alone, or perhaps to carry on a dialogue with the chorus. Formerly the contests were only between groups of singers. He had become a "thespian." So it was that at some time after the middle of the sixth century those forms began to emerge which later, around the beginning of the fifth century, Aeschylus and his contemporaries would blend into tragedy as we know it. Peisistratus' policy of promoting civic unity through regularly scheduled community festivals had helped to lay the foundations of Athenian drama. It was also Peisistratus who ordered a theater constructed on the south slope of the Acropolis, and there has been one there ever since. The original structure, however, was remodeled several times and what remains today cannot be dated any earlier than the reign of the Roman Emperor Nero in the first century A.D.

Peisistratus came to power by means of military force and always depended on it to a certain extent, but he could never have remained at the top as long as he did without popular support. His willingness to work within a system in which all citizens were members of the Assembly and eligible to sit on juries was sound politics, for those who stood to gain the most by his rule were also the most numerous. And ironically enough, it was during the time that a majority of the citizens willingly accepted a government manipulated by one man that democracy became a real possibility.

When at the beginning of the century Solon gave the ordinary citizens a new status, they lacked both the practical experience and the confidence to do much with it. The older generation had been raised under aristocratic domination. Their lack of familiarity with public duties or obligations resulted in feelings of awkwardness and inadequacy. But in the course of the sixth century the city had grown in size and wealth and, what mattered most, the common people had become more sure of themselves. They had a higher standard of living, more leisure time, and were better informed than their ancestors had been. Since the tyrant sought to give his power a broad popular base and welcomed the support of the commoners, it was during his reign that the average citizen was provided with the political experience his ancestors had lacked. Furthermore, since men continued to qualify for office on the basis of wealth and since the level of incomes rose steadily during the sixth century, there was a higher and higher percentage of citizens being included in the operation of the government. So as time went on, the tyranny outlived its usefulness.

While Peisistratus lived, however, there was no real danger of a movement in favor of a change. Aristotle says that after the tyrant had once established himself he became popular with both nobles and commoners. He knew how to talk to his own kind, and how to act toward the others. To the one he gave respect and to the other benefits. Neither got all they wanted, but it was enough. Peisistratus died in power and in bed.

### The End of the Tyranny

The two sons of his first marriage, Hippias and Hipparchus, succeeded to Peisistratus' position as he had always intended they should. It was the earliest brother-team this side of mythology, but Hippias, the elder, was the actual tyrant. By all accounts he was also the more responsible of the two, and the more attentive to the duties of the state. Hipparchus was something of a dandy, a poet of sorts, and only interested in the finer things of life. Any time he spent in the public interest was devoted to promoting Athens as a center of the arts.

With Hippias minding the civil and military affairs and Hipparchus attending to the muses, the brothers managed in fair fashion to continue the work of their father for thirteen more years. In 514, the first crack in the wall appeared to give warning of their downfall and the end of the tyranny at Athens. The immediate cause of trouble was a private affair, which is beclouded by conflicting accounts and did not originally have any political significance. According to one version, Hipparchus was angered because a personable young nobleman named Harmodius refused his proffered friendship. He sought revenge against him by the petty means of having his sister disqualified from participating in a festive procession. It was an instance of enormous power being used for a very small purpose—exactly the kind of mistake which Peisistratus had been careful to avoid. Indeed, so had Hippias. Harmodius, who already had a friend named Aristogeiton, plotted an assault against the tyranny. Their chief target was the powerful Hippias, but they only succeeded in murdering Hipparchus. In the ensuing melee Harmodius was also killed. His companion Aristogeiton managed to escape from the scene but was later captured and executed.

The conspiracy was bound to have raised suspicions in Hippias' mind, and either because of this, or for revenge, he began to act hastily, executing some men and driving others into exile. This new policy of suspicion and repression now turned the good will of the citizenry into contempt. Hippias' actions after the assassination plot transformed his would-be assassins, Harmodius and Aristogeiton, into popular heroes. At the time of the conspiracy they were hardly doing more than settling a private grudge, but later their names became associated with the cause of freedom.

After the death of Hipparchus, everything seemed to go wrong. Hippias alienated his popular support, and he also made the mistake of refusing to allow the Alcmeonidae family (again recently outlawed) to return to the city. So he brought their wealth and influence into play against him. This family had busied itself recently in the rebuilding of the temple of Apollo at Delphi which had burned. At the same time, the oracle was repeatedly advising the Spartans to overthrow the tyranny at Athens. This is not thought to have been merely coincidental.

As usual, it took time before the Spartans could be persuaded to take overt action, but goaded on by an unusually dynamic king, Cleomenes I, they finally intervened. With their help Hippias was driven out. It was not the last, however, that Athens would hear of him.

The Spartans were fearful of ambitious and energetic tyrannies and it was their policy, wherever possible, to restore more passive aristocracies to power. At Athens they gave their support to a certain Isagoras who favored a program of reaction which, if successful, might have revived the conditions of pre-Solon days. Even with Spartan help it was too late for that. The citizens of the city, now aroused to their own potential, besieged Cleomenes and his men on the Acropolis. After a two-day impasse the king thought better of his ambitious project and he and his Spartan contingent were permitted to leave peaceably.

### The Founder of the Athenian Democracy

The Athenians, now free from a long tyranny and the threat of oligarchy, gave their support to Cleisthenes, a member of the Alcmeonidae family which had returned to favor. Almost nothing is known personally about this man and yet he, if anybody, was the founder of the Athenian democracy. Solon and Peisistratus may have indirectly prepared the Athenian people for democracy, but it was the reforms of Cleisthenes which actually put the power in the hands of the *demos*.

Up to this time the political structure of Athens had rested on the four Ionian tribes. This age-old tribal arrangement, based on birth and an assumed common ancestry, had never permitted the average citizen to act as a free agent in any decision making. The tyrants had superseded tribal influence and actually sought to curtail its power, but the Council of 400 which survived as a basic institution was still organized on the old tribal basis.

Cleisthenes introduced a radical change. He "secularized" a man's place in the state by replacing the four old tribes by ten new ones based on residence rather than birth. The effect of this change was to remove a major barrier to popular democracy. It is a commonplace to say that block voting of large ethnic or religious groups is a deterrent to the ideal of democracy, which calls for each citizen to make a private decision on the basis of his own knowledge and experience. So long as the old tribal system persisted at Athens, the city was dominated by a minority of families whose influence through custom and wealth was sufficient to secure for them a disproportionate power—one inconsistent with any truly democratic government.

The basic unit in the new arrangement was the deme, a term which in the countryside could mean a village and in the city would be equivalent to a neighborhood. The new tribal groups were composed of demes taken at random by lot from each of the major economic regions; a few each from the city proper, the rural area and the district along the shore. In this way each tribe, while not containing the same number of demes (for they varied in size and population) did contain a representative cross section of the various factions amongst the citizenry.

The political identity of a citizen was henceforth based on where he happened to live. Indicative of this change was the decision to register all citizens in the records by their first name and the name of their deme, rather than by their father's name as in the past. Common usage probably made use of both, but the official designation now dropped the connection with ancestry. No one could tell from the records whether a citizen belonged to one of the oldest families or had only recently been enfranchised. In Athens, ancestry would always count for something, even if only socially, but it no longer meant anything in a legal sense. The change is of course analogous to the present-day efforts to lessen racial and religious prejudice by dropping all mention of them in official forms and job applications.

Cleisthenes now introduced a new Council of 500 which replaced Solon's old Council of 400. In the new organization each tribe nominated candidates, and from among these names fifty were chosen by lot from each of the ten tribes. The pre-selection of candidates by the tribes at the deme level eliminated persons who for some reason were considered unfit for public service. After this the lottery device confirmed the belief that one citizen's judgment was as good as another.

Although Cleisthenes' reforms had broadened the base of power, tyranny was not easily forgotten. It seems reasonable then that the practice of ostracism, as a hedge against some would-be tyrant, was introduced immediately, and Cleisthenes has usually received credit for the idea. By this plan a vote would be taken every year to determine if at least 6,000 citizens felt that there was anyone in the community whose presence was a threat to their freedom. The citizens cast their votes by scratching names on a broken piece of pottery—*ostracon*, from which comes the term "ostracism." When any man was so "elected" he was asked to leave the city for ten years after which he could return with full rights, obviously older and presumably wiser. It sounded like a good idea. In practice it was something less. In the following century a popular politician who could convince the citizenry that his enemy was also their enemy could conveniently rid himself of a rival, real or imagined. Among the *ostraca* found in excavations and now on display in the Agora Museum at Athens there are some which bear the same name written in the same hand. These "votes" prepared in advance show how an ostracism could be rigged. The antidote to one kind of power became the instrument of another.

After the establishment of these domestic reforms Cleisthenes' name disappears from the historical sources without our knowing what happened to him. He may have suffered an eclipse because of his foreign policy. Herodotus reports that about the time Cleisthenes was in power, agents were sent to the Persian king's viceroy in Asia Minor and they accepted an alliance which recognized the Great King's pretentious claims in the Aegean area. These aides were punished for their submission when they got home and Cleisthenes may have been too if he is the one who sent them. When Herodotus was writing in the mid-fifth century, members of Cleisthenes' family, the Alcmeonidae, were his patrons and friends. His silence on the question of Cleisthenes' involvement suggests that it was still a touchy subject.

### Mixed Feelings Toward the Persians

The question of whether Cleisthenes was or was not "soft on Persia" had a greater significance than its influence on the career of one man. Throughout Greece, there was an ever increasing concern about the ultimate intentions of this Goliath on the doorstep; yet in 505, when Athens was again endangered by a coalition of her neighbors, she sought Persian friendship. At this time the Persians made the restoration of the ex-tyrant Hippias, presumably under their guardianship, a condition for any cooperation. The offer was abruptly refused by the Athenians. They had sought the friendship of equals, but the Great King, who ruled the mightiest empire the Near East had ever known, continued to speak as a superior. The Athenians considered their refusal to restore Hippias a matter of free choice. To the Persians it was unexpected insolence.

Over and over again the same story is told. The weak and their principles face the strong and their pride. In the course of two generations, Athens herself would play both parts. Later, at the height of her own imperial power, she too would deny to weaker powers the choice which Persia denied her now. When she did, she would argue that there were extenuating circumstances and that the strong could not afford to let the weak defy them. Darius could make the same claims when after fifteen years of brooding and suspicion, threats and defiances, he finally sent an army into Greece.

Perhaps the Persians had a right to be surprised by the stubbornness of this handful of Greeks. The history of their empire for the previous half-century had been one of constant success and growth. Under Cyrus I, the founder of their empire, they conquered all the lands between what are now the states of Iran and Turkey. Since the Greek cities along the coast of western Asia Minor had long been under Lydian rule they now by circumstance fell to the Great King. Cambyses, Cyrus' son, added Egypt to the Empire, and in 513 Darius, his successor, invaded Scythia, a land north of the Danube.

From Egypt to India, Persian rule brought the familiar mixed blessings of imperialism. Their system, shaped by experience, was not intolerable in a world already conditioned to despotism. In fact, here and there the efficiency and mildness of their rule may have been a distinct improvement. The center of power was distant and the quality of local rule from satrapy to satrapy could vary enough to make a judgment of the whole difficult. The Persians, however, were foreigners, a fact on the side of trouble—and like all imperialists, even those who do good, they had a tendency to stay forever.

Nevertheless, for nearly fifty years those Greeks who lived under Persian rule seem to have remained quiet. These Ionian cities were at the western extremities of the important trade routes to the East, all of which were under Persian control. They were governed either by a tyrant who in these circumstances favored the commercial class above all others, or by an oligarchy of well-to-do traders who managed for themselves. Certainly such men had no reason to consider their Persian masters any more abusive than the Lydians. Sardis, the former capital of Lydia, became the seat of the local Persian satrapy. Taxes were taxes, and they were going to the same place.

The widespread anti-Persian feeling ran most strongly among the less well-to-do citizenry who did not share with the commercial class any good reason for accommodation. This group was also inclined toward democratic reform, which was a further incentive to upset the ruling puppet governments. Therefore, the uprising against Persia, when it came, was a matter of local politics, class conflict, and, for those who would benefit by it, freedom.

The situation awaited an incident and this was provided by the ambitious Aristagoras, the tyrant of Miletus, who started out by seeking to help the Persians and ended up by leading the rebellion against them. The chain of events began with a revolt of the democrats at Naxos, an island in the central Aegean, which caused the established interests there to appeal to Aristagoras for help. He in turn, seizing this opportunity to ingratiate himself with Artaphernes, the Persian satrap at Sardis, convinced him that Persia should intervene and win a valuable island base for her trouble. The Persians sent a force and besieged the island but after four months the expedition proved an utter failure. Two points were now obvious. First, somebody would have to be punished for the mistake. Second, the Persian effort, like the Scythian campaign, had been such a dismal performance that it gave encouragement to any future attempt at revolt. Aristagoras saw both points quickly. He gave up the support of the wealthy, sought the backing of the populace at large, and then led an uprising against Persia.

A general revolt developed in 499 with the other Ionian towns soon joining the cause. In the long run, the Persians were able to bring their superiority by land and sea to bear and ultimately to crush the insurgents. The renowned Miletus was destroyed in the process. By 492, the Persians had recovered full control. In the same year, a campaign in Thrace recovered territory first won during the Scythian campaign but lost during the Ionian trouble.

Only Athens and Eretria, a city on the island of Euboea, had sent aid to their Greek kinsmen in Ionia. This, on the surface at least, offered the best explanation why Darius prepared and sent an expedition against Greece. No one then could be sure if he was bent on conquest pure and simple, or only intended to punish the offending cities for their interference. We still do not know, and the fact that he sent ahead messengers asking for "earth and water," symbols of submission, does not decide the issue. Such emissaries were usually sent in advance of Persian movements and they could have presaged either wholesale conquest or a campaign of revenge.

It was easy enough for some Greeks to argue that lip service would secure a cheap peace. For others it was offensive to have this foreign despot making any demands at all. Everywhere two parties arose, with one or the other gaining the upper hand. Those who favored getting along with the Persians were willing to assume that the foreigners were only intent on punishing Athens and Eretria. Such men were called "medizers." To them the substance of independence was all important and the shadow not worth fighting for. Thus if they were in fact left alone, it did not bother certain Greek states what power might want to claim suzerainty. Others, like Aegina, acted as much out of hatred of Athens as for any fear of Persia. Under the circumstances the policy of the "medizers" could be called one of shrewd calculation; it might also be called base appeasement. Either way, they were often reminded that it was not what saved Greece.

Athens too had its Persian party, but the general feeling in the city was one of pride and independence. Nor was there any reason for the Persians to have doubted that Sparta would be as intransigent as Athens toward an invasion of Greece. Both cities could be troubled by the attitude of the oracle of Delphi. The priestess predicted that if the Greeks chose to fight, Athens would be burned and Sparta would either be ruined or lose a king. These were not implausible predictions, but the oracle's advice that it would be better not to resist at all sounded more like politics than prophecy.

The actual course taken by the Persian fleet seemed to confirm the guess of the "medizers" that Darius was only intent on punishing those who had first interfered with him. After taking Naxos, which had embarrassed them so much earlier, the Persians proceeded to the island of Euboea and placed Eretria under siege. Here the mixed feelings toward the Persians proved disastrous. After seven days the city was betrayed and subsequently burned to the ground. From there the Persians sailed to Attica and at a point about twenty-six miles northeast of Athens, they came ashore at a plain near the village of Marathon.

# PART TWO

*The Fifth Century B.C.*

## The Persian Wars and After

## VII

The Athenians never forgot their victory at Marathon and they never let anyone else forget it. It was one of the great debuts in history.

The Spartans were the best fighters in Greece and the Athenians had not expected to face the Persians without them, but as the enemy approached, Sparta was in the midst of a religious festival and sent word that her men could not march until the next full moon. Half of the ten Athenian commanders favored stalling off the Persians until the Spartans could arrive; Miltiades led the other five in insisting that the right moment for action was more important. Moreover, the polemarch Callimachus promised he would break the tie if the right opportunity presented itself. It did, and 10,000 Athenian *hoplites* with only the help of 1,000 Plataeans, attacked the more numerous Persians. No one knows exactly how many of the enemy actually came ashore at Marathon, although ancient estimates had them outnumbering the Athenians two to one. Whatever the count, they wore trousers and this, said Herodotus, was itself an unnerving sight to the skirted Greeks. But if the defenders felt some trepidation about attacking these strange appearing invaders, it must be admitted that, given the order, they made the most of it.

The time was early in September in the year 490. The Persians were deployed in the plain of Marathon along a line facing to the northwest with the bay at their backs. More than a mile away, the Athenians were encamped on rougher terrain in the approaches to Mount Kotroni where the uneven ground ensured their safety from attack. The Persians, with their cavalry to guard the plain, were equally secure. For a time there was only waiting. Then came a break. A few Ionians who had been pressed into service by the Persians brought word to the Athenian camp one night that the cavalry was gone. (The horses were perhaps being watered in the marshes to the north.) This was the moment which Miltiades had dared to hope for, and by chance (according to a rotation system) he was the commander for the day which was at hand. To overcome the disadvantage of his inferior numbers, he strengthened his line at either end and left the middle weak, hoping that the Persians would rush into the trap.

The attack came at dawn and speed was an essential part of it. The Athenians moved across the plain very swiftly, and while they may not have been running for the mile which separated them from the enemy, it may be assumed that they increased their speed the closer they came. Their spirited onrush in defense of native soil was possibly a surprise to the invaders. Surely the "morale" of the Athenians was an advantage. And upon making contact, their armor and equipment also proved to be better. The Persians, as expected, routed the Greek center, but the strong wings of the Athenian line then converged on their rear and cut into them with a fury which never relented even after the Persians fled toward the shore. In fact, the Athenians followed them there and captured seven of their ships in the ensuing struggle at the water's edge.

The plain of Marathon is today a quiet, fertile stretch of land with olive groves and plots of garden vegetables between the hills and the sea. In the midst stands a man-made mound of earth, thirty-six feet high, overgrown with grass and wild flowers. It marks the spot where the Athenians buried their dead. Stone stairs lead to the summit of this hillock which offers a view of the historic battlefield. At the foot of the stairs there is a simple commemorative *stele,* a copy of the original memorial now in the National Museum of Archaeology in Athens.

Herodotus reports that the Persians left about 6,400 men dead at Marathon as against an Athenian loss of only 192 which included the polemarch Callimachus. Although Herodotus' figures appear more flattering than factual there is no question that the Athenians had proved to be the better soldiers.

The Persians may have expected the same kind of help at Athens as they had received at Eretria. At the moment they managed to get back on their ships, a signal from inland was flashed to them by means of a shield raised to the sun—or so it was reported. Whether or not this sign was intended to mean that Athens was to be betrayed from within was never cleared up.

Herodotus, writing about forty years later, mentioned that the Alcmeonidae had been accused of giving this signal and, as a friend of the family, did his best to discount the rumour. A more likely source of treason would have been the allies of the Peisistratidae, for Hippias, the exiled tyrant, was with the Persians and would likely have been restored to power as their puppet had the invasion been successful.

In any event, whether a signal had been given or not, Miltiades rushed the army back to Athens in time to forestall any further action. The Persian fleet made an appearance at Phalerum but it did not remain long, and Athens was free to celebrate its great victory and to receive the praise of the Spartans who arrived the following day.

A story about a young man who ran from Marathon to Athens and shouted *"Nike"* (victory) before falling dead first appeared in the literature about six hundred years after the battle. This is of course the basis of the Marathon run in the Olympic Games. The story does not appear in the writings of Herodotus, however, and this argues against its truth for Herodotus liked a good story and it is unlikely that he would have missed this one.

## The Man of the Hour

Success made Miltiades the man of the hour in Athens. He had proposed sending the army to Marathon in the first place; he was responsible for the right strategy there; and he had brought his men home in time to prevent any further effort by the Persians. His career soon took a sharp turn, however, for in the following year he involved the Athenians in a disastrous affair. It began with his proposal that Athens follow up her victory by punishing the islands in the Aegean which had defected and made the Persian advance so easy. According to tradition, Miltiades did not spell out his plan, but said simply that if the Assembly would vote to give him seventy ships, he would show them a profit. Miltiades selected the wealthy island of Paros to be his target and sent word to the Parians that they must pay a fine of one hundred talents. When they refused he attacked the island, but the venture was a failure; after a long and costly siege, he returned home empty-handed. This blunder added a sour note to the happy harmony of recent events, and those who had been quick to praise Miltiades were now just as quick to blame him. Although he had been wounded and had developed gangrene in one leg, he was carried into court and tried for having deceived the Athenian people. He was found guilty and condemned to death but this sentence was quickly reduced to a fine of fifty talents, or half the sum which the Athenians might have received from Paros. Miltiades died soon after the trial.

## The First Commoner

Miltiades dominated the story of Marathon and the name of Themistocles, who succeeded him in popular favor, was rarely mentioned in connection with that event. Yet he was there and, along with his comrades, could claim a share of the glory which belonged to them all. As a man of common birth with high political ambitions, he needed all the credit he could get. Leadership in Athens still belonged to the well-born class for men of high breeding and good family pursued a public career by custom. Those invisible lines of influence which modern men associate with an "Establishment" prevailed then too, and the sources for this period show clearly that Themistocles was an outsider. Yet the times were dangerous and Themistocles, who had the right ideas and the courage to make himself heard, carried more weight than his social standing would ordinarily have allowed. Thucydides praises him as a man of "natural" ability and specifically mentions his good judgment in areas in which he had had no formal training.

By making preparedness his cause, Themistocles won wide popular support from the average Athenian citizens who, like the majority of the Ionians, were violently anti-Persian.

Themistocles has been best remembered as the builder of the Athenian navy, for it was sea-power which made Athens a city of destiny. The navy was to be important not only in the forthcoming Greek victory at the Bay of Salamis but was to effect momentous consequences for the future of Athens and the whole Greek world. At home, the large number of rowers needed to man the new ships constituted a block of votes which any politician in the future had to reckon with. The increasing dependency of Athens on its fleet was to be a decisive factor in the evolution of its popular democracy. Also of importance to the rest of Greece was the fact that Athens had built a navy with which to resist the Persian Empire and that, in the course of a few decades, this force would become the arm of an empire of her own.

According to Aristotle, it was during the ascendancy of Themistocles that a change was made in the method of selecting archons which tended to diminish the importance of the office. Instead of being elected directly, as had been true apparently since the overthrow of the tyranny, the archons were again chosen by a system of lotteries as they had been under the Solonian constitution. The process began at the deme level, and ended with nine names being drawn out of one hundred at the tribal level. Because of the various stages of the process, the chance of a "people's choice" finally arriving at an archonship was made more remote. The popular leader was more likely to be one of the ten generals (*strategoi*) who, from about the turn of the century, had been elected directly by the people, one from each tribe. Since the archonship had been most closely associated with the aristocracy, it has always been assumed that this constitutional change favored the rise to power of Themistocles, the first commoner in Athenian history to direct the affairs of state. A man could not hold the archonship for two successive years whereas a general could be re-elected year after year, so long as he held popular favor. The way to continuity in office, with all the power that this implied, was open only through a generalship. A dynamic, clever or intelligent, well-spoken leader might well dominate the board of generals, and especially so if he was supported by the citizenry at large. In theory, the system outlawed one-man rule, for ten generals were elected. In practice, however, Themistocles, then Cimon, and finally Pericles were able to exercise an extraordinary amount of influence within a democratic state.

Themistocles enjoyed his greatest fame in the decade between the first Persian invasion in 490 and the second more massive onslaught in 480. How the practice of ostracism could favor the ascendancy of a popular favorite was amply demonstrated during this period. Coincident with Themistocles' rise to power was the downfall and ostracism of those who disagreed with him.

When Plutarch wrote the life of Aristides he used the occasion of this noble man's ostracism to point out the irrational behavior of the Athenian commoners. He told the story of an illiterate citizen who did not recognize Aristides, and so approached him and asked if he would write the name "Aristides" on his potsherd (ballot). When he was asked why he had chosen this man to be ostracized, he replied that while he knew nothing against Aristides he was simply tired of hearing him always called "the just." Plutarch leaves the implication here, as on other occasions, that such behavior was to be expected where men varying in their capacities were given a vote apiece. However, there is no reason to assume that a majority of the votes cast against Aristides were of this kind. Rather, it seems that the citizenry decided in 482 to remove all opposition in order to give Themistocles a clear mandate for his policies, which were widely favored at the moment. Aristides may well have preferred the traditional dependency on the army, rather than Themistocles' new emphasis on the building of a fleet, as the surest defense for Athens and the lifeline of her commerce.

Themistocles' influence with the members of the Assembly was clearly seen in a decision which they made in 483. In that year a new lode of silver had been discovered at Mount Laurium. At first, the citizens were tempted to divide this bonanza amongst themselves but Themistocles talked them into spending it on two hundred warships instead. There could not have been any better testimony to his abilities. He was helped in part, to be sure, by the fact that recent encounters with the navy of the nearby island of Aegina had shown the Athenians that they were unprepared for even a small challenge. What would they do if the Persians sailed against them?

The Greeks had no illusions about the future. An uprising in Egypt in 487 and the death of Darius in 486 may have caused the Persians to alter their timetable, but it became increasingly clear toward the end of the 480's that the new king Xerxes was making elaborate plans for another invasion of Greece. In fact, he was so confident of his overwhelming superiority that captured spies whom the Greeks had sent into Asia Minor were allowed to return home by the Great King with the awe-inspiring news of his mighty preparations.

No one believes that the Persian forces came anywhere near the five million persons claimed by Herodotus. Still, the army was too large to be transported by sea. It took the land route through Thrace and Macedonia and the fleet followed along the coast. This entailed a slow and laborious progress toward Greece, but if numbers were to determine the outcome, the Persians had no intention of losing. Unlike Darius, who had remained at home during the previous invasion, Xerxes came along to direct the conquest of all of Greece. As was the custom, he sent agents ahead to receive "earth and water" from those Greeks who were in no mood, or no position, to fight. Envoys were not ordered to Athens or Sparta. According to Herodotus, the ambassadors sent to those cities by Darius had been murdered.

Sparta was the rallying place for the Greek resistance. Her army was the finest in Greece and her long-standing system of alliances gave her further advantage over Athens, who had been at constant odds with neighboring states in the past two decades. The Athenians also had an alliance with the Spartans and they sent representatives to a general conference which was summoned. The crucial decision facing the Greeks was where to make their final stand. This decision was especially important to those who would be left on the wrong side of the defense line. It was finally decided that a delaying action should be fought in the north at Thermopylae. At the same time, an attempt would be made to do as much damage as possible to the Persian fleet which would be standing nearby. The final line of defense, however, would be the Isthmus, and the Persians would be kept out of the Peloponnesus at all costs. This meant that Athens had to be sacrificed.

An inscription found in 1959 at Troezen, in the northeast corner of the Peloponnesus, purports to contain a copy of the plans which Themistocles made for evacuating Athens. The text, first published by Professor Michael H. Jameson of the University of Pennsylvania, offers evidence which questions Herodotus' hallowed account of this period. There has been some discussion about its authenticity, for historians, like archaeologists, must ever be on the alert for forgeries which have been ingeniously planted in appropriate places either by the ancients who wished to alter or fabricate an account to suit their own interests, or by modern rascals who delight in fooling the experts. The appearance of the *stele* and stylistic clues in the presentation of the text suggest that this particular inscription was not prepared until sometime in the third century B.C. But the date of the physical inscription and the origin of its text are separate matters. Inaccuracies and anachronisms in the text may be explained by the probability that it is a copy of a copy of a copy and has suffered from faulty editorship. It seems doubtful that its message represents an outright effort to falsify the facts.

The inscription sets forth the provisions made for removal of women and children from Attica to Troezen, where the monument which bears the inscription was erected long afterwards to commemorate the event. Detailed plans for the outfitting of the ships are also described. Half of these ships were to meet the enemy in the north; the other half were to guard the waters around Salamis in order to support the final Greek defense line at the Isthmus. In addition, mention is made of the recall of the exiles. Among these was Aristides who, unmindful of old feelings, gave his support to Themistocles in subsequent debates over strategy.

This new evidence would seem to indicate that the decision to abandon Athens to the Persians was not a last minute affair, as Herodotus had it, but rather a part of a total plan. Obviously the Spartans who commanded, at least technically, all the land and sea forces of the allies were unwilling to risk the defense of any territory other than the Peloponnesus in the face of the overwhelming numbers of the Persian army. As it turned out, the crucial battle was fought in the Bay of Salamis and Themistocles and his new Athenian navy made the difference there.

Before the battle of Salamis the Persians were halted at the pass at Thermopylae, which will always be remembered as the place where three hundred Spartans, including their king Leonidas, made a valiant stand and died to a man. There is a monument there which says so. Today, however, we can no longer believe that they remained to face certain death simply because no Spartan ever gave ground. The Spartans knew that a strategic retreat in search of better ground was not cowardice, and the Troezen inscription shows that they were never intended to fight to a decision at the pass. With hindsight, we might wonder why it was ever believed that the Greeks would have expected three hundred Spartans and a few thousand of their less skilled allies to hold the whole of the north against the several hundred thousand men under Xerxes' command. Even so, according to a story retold by Herodotus, Demaratus, a disgraced former king of Sparta who was in the Persian camp, advised Xerxes that any Spartan was worth ten Persians. The king was amazed and maybe, after the second day of direct assault on the Spartan position, even convinced. In the end it did not matter. A Greek traitor showed the Persians a hidden pass by which the Greeks could be surrounded. Informed of the danger, the Spartans and the Thespians held their ground while the other allies made good their escape. Only the Thebans surrendered but, as Herodotus observes, they had been forced to stay against their wishes in the first place.

The revised version of the story of Thermopylae, which makes the engagement only a delaying action, does not detract from the reputation for skill and bravery of either the Spartans or their less heralded allies who stood and fell with them. The monument which says that the Spartans remained obedient to their laws is right. They stood against hopeless odds and resisted to the dusty and bloody end. Those who had lost their swords fought on with their hands and teeth.

As the battle of Thermopylae was being fought, both sides sought to dominate the narrow stretch of sea between Euboea and the mainland. The tradition says that Delphi counseled the Greeks to "pray to the winds." Considering the small size of the Greek fleet sheltered at Chalcis, it was by all odds the thing to do. The Persians with their numerical superiority might have won had it not been for two violent storms which cost them a total of six hundred ships.

There were three engagements fought near Artemisium, the promontory at the northeast tip of Euboea, and the Greeks were proud to have at least held their own. It was the bad news from Thermopylae which prompted their eventual retreat.

After the breakthrough in the north, the Persians marched to Athens and burned the now evacuated city. According to plan, the Greeks on land and sea were supposed to defend the Isthmus leading to the Peloponnesus.

Many of the allied commanders were apprehensive of an entrapment in the Bay of Salamis and wanted to leave. Themistocles, fearing he could not hold them to their duty for long, sent a slave to the Persian fleet with instructions to tell the commander that there was dissension among the Greeks—a story which was never hard to believe. He was also to say that some of the allies were planning to escape from their position. The Persians immediately attacked in order to prevent these allies from getting away. Themistocles had his way. The whole of the Greek forces were committed to a battle then and there.

Themistocles advised the Greeks to maneuver in such a way as to draw the Persians into the narrow waters around the island of Salamis. This would minimize the enemy's superior numbers. Only a few of the allies followed his advice but it did not matter. The Persians actually defeated themselves. As the first ships which had engaged the Greeks sought to draw back, they created disorder amongst others which were hastening forward. Part of the difficulty was owing to the eagerness of the Persian commanders to impress Xerxes, who was seated on his throne and viewing the scene from nearby Salamis. With few exceptions, they could not have impressed him less. His scorn was summed up in his remark that his men had behaved like women.

Again, as at Marathon, Herodotus assigns a disproportionate share of the losses to the Persians. As he explains it, the Greeks when necessary were able to swim to shore, but because the barbarians did not know how to swim, more of them were lost in the water than were killed in the battle itself.

Xerxes, who was worried about his greatly extended supply lines, so vulnerable at places like the Hellespont, made immediate plans to retreat. His son-in-law Mardonius, who felt that some way might yet be found to salvage the Persian cause and his own reputation, persuaded Xerxes to let him remain with 300,000 men and fight a decisive battle. Xerxes was pleased with Mardonius' spirit, a quality heretofore best exhibited by Greek commanders. Nor did the King feel that he was leaving Greece in complete frustration. No matter what the outcome of Mardonius' plans, the Great King had come to burn Athens and this at least he had accomplished. There was, of course, nothing in his past experience which would allow him to anticipate what manner of city would arise out of the ruins.

In the following year, the final battle of the second invasion was fought near Plataea in Boeotia. As in the past, there were Greeks who continued to expect a Persian victory and so served on the "wrong" side. Herodotus says that most of them fought half-heartedly, but he singles out the Thebans as having viciously opposed the Athenians, suffering greatly in the process.

Herodotus gives the main credit for the Greek victory to the Spartans under Pausanias, cousin and regent for the infant son of Leonidas. Although the Greeks all along the line were victorious against the Persian auxiliaries, it was the Spartans who withstood the best the enemy had to offer. He also credits the finest of the Persian forces with having fought valiantly until Mardonius himself was killed. On the death of their leader, the Persians fled from the scene and the battle ended in a rout.

On the same day as the crucial contest at Plataea, another battle was fought near Mycale on the coast of Asia Minor. Since the Persian king still claimed Aeolis and Ionia, this engagement was a counterattack by the Greeks. Encouraged by reports that the Persian ships were not battle-ready, and aware of the dubious loyalty of the Ionians to their Persian masters, the allied fleet sailed under Leoty-chides, king of Sparta. The Persians beached their ships at Mycale and took up positions on the land. The defection of the Ionians, as expected, made certain a decisive victory for the Greeks who burned the Persian ships as if lighting a signal for a general uprising all along the coast.

Leotychides sailed on to the Hellespont to destroy the bridges which he thought were still there, but upon arrival found that they had already been torn apart by the rush of the water. He and his Peloponnesian supporters sailed back then to Greece. The Athenians, under Xanthippus, father to the better known Pericles, stayed and laid siege to Sestos, the most powerful of the Persian bases in the area. Artayctes, the Persian satrap in command of the fortress, was unprepared for the siege and surprised as well by the Athenian daring. With winter coming on, it was customary for the Greeks to return home as the Spartans had done.

Sestos was one of those occasions which the Athenians were fond of recalling in later years. They prided themselves on their flair for the unexpected and on their superiority over men who tied their plans to the seasons. Herodotus, however, reports that not all of the Athenians present at Sestos dreamed of being so well remembered and that some of them petitioned their general to take them home. Xanthippus, well aware of the significance of this siege, for the Athenians were no longer operating under orders from the allied command but were on their own against the Persians, refused to depart unless ordered to do so by the Assembly at Athens.

Before long, the fortress was starved out and Artayctes, whom Herodotus describes as an evil-doer and much hated by the natives, was executed along with his son. Then, with an eye for the dramatic (something the Spartans seemed to lack), the Athenians gathered up the cables which had connected the broken bridges to Hellespontine shores and carried them home as an offering to the gods.

The Athenians had been the first at Marathon and the last to leave the Hellespont. It was therefore natural that Herodotus should end his account of the Persian Wars with the episode at Sestos. For those who would one day trace the causes of the Peloponnesian War, fought a half a century later among the Greeks themselves, Sestos was also part of a beginning. There, as elsewhere, the Athenians gave evidence of a willingness to take positive and unexpected action where Spartan thinking had been retiring or merely routine. Even so, although Athens in her ambitious climb to power gave other Greek states good cause to hate her, Sparta was not one of them. The Spartans did not see the Athenians as oppressive or cruel, but rather as a people filled with energy, ingenuity, and the will to win. They did not hate the Athenians but they gradually became jealous and then fearful of them. In the end, it came to the same thing.

In the years immediately following the Persian Wars, the Spartans were especially embarrassed by the disgrace which befell a favorite son. Despite the brief spectacular success of the Athenians at Sestos, the Spartans had not yet abandoned the leadership of the allied cause and Pausanias was chosen in 478 to lead an expedition designed to sweep the Persians out of the Aegean.

At first, Pausanias proved worthy of this assignment. He drove the enemy from the Greek cities on Cyprus and recovered the strategic colony of Byzantium, thus re-opening the Black Sea route. The campaign therefore was a success; unfortunately, the man turned out to be a failure. Pausanias ignored the petitions of the smaller states to be consulted on political matters, and in fact began to treat all the allied officers in a high-handed way. Some of them were provoked enough to carry their complaints to the Athenians and they could not have found more willing ears.

The ephors in Sparta were naturally displeased with Pausanias, whose behavior so seriously undermined Sparta's relations with her allies. More than that, they had also heard rumors about behind-the-scenes deals with the Persians and in 476 Pausanias was relieved of his command.

Five years later, the ephors obtained proof that Pausanias was again plotting secretly with the Persians, presumably in an effort to arrange a deal whereby he would rule all of Hellas in the name of the Great King. A helot uprising was a part of the plan. Before he could be arrested, Pausanias perceived his danger and ran to a temple for sanctuary. When the ephors located him, he had taken refuge in a small room. The Spartans were careful not to violate the sanctity of their temples and so the ephors made no attempt to lay their hands on him. They sealed up the door and he starved to death.

On the basis of the record, it might be assumed that Themistocles would be the man to take Pausanias' place and become the leading personality among the Greeks in the post-invasion years. Yet Themistocles, in spite of all he had accomplished, somehow lost his footing in Athens, and as the years passed he drifted farther and farther away from his fame.

Nobody can say for certain exactly why it was that Themistocles failed. Plutarch offers a simple and provocative explanation when he writes that the citizenry grew tired of listening to him. In a democratic society, such a suggestion is not to be ignored. However, there must have been other reasons. One of them was surely his opposition to Aristides and Cimon, who continued the policy of cooperation amongst the Greek states and faithfully pursued the popular purpose of ridding the Aegean of the Persians. On the other hand, immediately after Salamis where the Persians had been repulsed a second time, the acute Themistocles was among the first to foresee the implications of the increased Athenian naval power. It would allow the city to grow and prosper through commercial expansion. It would also draw Athens into direct competition with other Greek states. So, although Athens now supervised the Greek effort against Persia, Themistocles was not unmindful that she might soon have to defend herself at home. Consequently a difference in emphasis developed between him and the aristocratic leaders like Aristides and Cimon, who were always more pan-Hellenic and less competitive in their thinking than were the commercial interests. They would favor friendship with a state like Argos for the same reason they favored it with all Greek states, whereas Themistocles would advocate friendship with Argos because this city was the arch-enemy of Sparta and the alliance might be useful in the years ahead. It may have been, therefore, that his concern about domestic problems in Greece put him at odds with the citizenry, for whom Persia remained the crucial issue. In the long run, Themistocles was right; but he was right too soon. He was ostracized in 471.

The ironies in Greek history cannot be surpassed. Both Pausanias and Themistocles, each of whom had been the most prominent leader of his city in the war against Persia, strangely enough became involved with the enemy.

During the inquiry about Pausanias in 471, the Spartans had turned up information which implicated Themistocles in the planned helot uprising. Since Sparta and Athens were still technically allies, the Spartans lodged a strong protest with the Athenians over the interference of one of her citizens in the internal affairs of Lacedaemon. Themistocles was already under the ban of ostracism and the Athenians consented to the Spartans seizing him wherever they could find him. He was never taken and eventually, about 465, he fled to Persia and sought refuge at the court of Artaxerxes I, the son of his old enemy. The king may have thought he could use him as his father might have used Pausanias. In any event he was well received and eventually given a governorship in one of the Persian satrapies. The hero of Salamis, the champion of the Greek fight against the barbarian, lived out his life in the pay of the Persians.

Remembering what had happened to Miltiades, Pausanias, and Themistocles, was it any wonder that the Greek poets and playwrights seemed at times obsessed with the theme of inexorable fate? Each of these men had reached the summit of popular acclaim and each of them died in despair. Modern men speak of how they chart their course and earn their destiny. The ancients with simple resignation re-echoed again and again the line which Homer gave to the valiant Hector: "At last, my fate has found me."

## An Outdoor Aristocrat . . . A Man Among Men

Cimon and Aristides stepped in where Pausanias had failed and supplied the leadership for the campaign which freed Ionia, and in fact the whole of the Aegean world, from the still feared Persians. Aristides, who had been allowed to return from exile during the Salamis crisis, became increasingly more sympathetic to popular interests as time went on and remained a power in Athenian politics until his death in 468. Cimon it was, however, who won the heart and favor of the citizenry. He was elected *strategos* every year from 476 to 462 and during this period dominated the Athenian political scene.

Cimon was the son of Miltiades who had died in prison. Under the circumstances, if this young man was to have a successful career of his own it would be due to his own gifts. And so it was. According to writers of the day, Cimon grew up a tall and strong youth, good-looking, with an abundant crop of curly hair. His education in music and the arts was considered somewhat deficient, but this was due perhaps to his temperament since he showed a preference for action rather than for patient study or casual conversation. In his younger days he had a reputation as a heavy drinker but, like his other faults, this weakness was in the open for all to see. No one ever accused him of being secretive, petty or deceitful. He was a warrior, an outdoor aristocrat. His good-hearted frankness and robust habits made him a man among men.

Cimon was old enough to fight at Salamis in 480 and his performance there apparently won for him an excellent reputation. So much so that when Themistocles began to slip in popular favor Cimon was the natural choice to take his place. Ancient writers stressed Themistocles' craftiness and Machiavellian maneuvers. If this was true, then Cimon's candor and unassuming service may well have been a refreshing change.

At Athens, the poets and playwrights made Cimon's generosity a legend. He dispensed food, clothing and money personally to those who needed it and his open house was famous at home and abroad. Such kindnesses could in no way harm his popularity, but we know too much of his personal traits and interests to attribute this behavior to mere calculation. Apparently he had a very high regard for Spartan "virtue." As a frequent visitor to Sparta he had been impressed with the relative simplicity of life there and he admired the way the Spartans actually, in practice, put other values ahead of mere riches. His naming of one of his twin sons Lacedaemonius was an obvious gesture and ready proof of his feelings. It hardly needs to be added that Cimon was, in turn, the Spartan's favorite Athenian. In the years immediately following the Persian Wars, when Athens was busy building her future, Cimon's leadership did not conflict with his partisanship for Sparta. Later, as the rivalry between these two cities began to mount, it meant trouble. Then the Athenians began to resent his chiding them for their faults and pointing to Sparta as the good example.

In the meantime, ironically enough, Cimon was responsible as much as any man for the growth of Athenian power which would increase the anxiety of Sparta. He was one of the architects of the Delian League.

## An Ancient N.A.T.O.

In the years following the second invasion, the Greeks were determined to drive the Persians out of the Aegean world. They were well aware that adequate defense against any future trouble required the organization of a league of those states most likely to be menaced by Persian aggression. Over 150 *poleis* joined forces, including cities in Thrace, the islands of the Aegean, and the maritime centers along the coast of Asia Minor which had recently been liberated from Persian control. Athens quickly assumed the leadership of this movement. In the best sense she was the guiding spirit for the other members, but her wealth, experience and powerful navy made it a dangerous partnership.

The states which joined the league did so voluntarily. They contributed money, ships and manpower with which to pursue the common goals, which included keeping the Aegean free of pirates as well as Persians. Customarily, the larger states sent ships and men, while the smaller states contributed only money. Policy for the league was to be decided by a synod of representatives meeting regularly at the island of Delos where a sanctuary to Apollo was especially sacred to the Ionians. Therefore the organization (an ancient N.A.T.O.) was called the Delian League.

From the beginning, the Athenians monopolized the offices of the League and presumably its operation as well, yet during the early years their leadership did not arouse any suspicions about possible abuse of a favored position. Aristides managed the assessments against the various member states for their share of the League's needs, and his well-established reputation for fair-mindedness and honesty was enhanced by the way he handled the assignment. Furthermore, Cimon, who was the leading Athenian commander, was not likely to arouse any apprehensions among the allies. Both men were members of that faction of the Athenian aristocracy which traditionally favored cooperation of all Greeks against the barbarians. In other words, they were pro-Greek and anti-Persian, not just pro-Athens. To be sure, they were "patriotic" Athenians and certainly desired Athens to be the leader of the Greek world. At the same time they opposed the policies of men like Themistocles and the later imperialists who sought greater power and prosperity for Athens at the risk of endangering the unity of Greece.

The first fifteen years of the Delian League were those in which Cimon was the most influential figure in Athens. Therefore, the moves made by Athens during this period, acting on her own or in concert with her allies, have inevitably been linked to his leadership. The actions which he supported seemed at the time to be justified by his pan-Hellenic outlook. There was an irony to Cimon's career, however, for while he promoted the Delian League as an instrument of Greek solidarity, what he built was to become something quite different in the hands of his successors—men who before any other consideration were pro-Athenian. No man knows the future, and the decisions taken in good faith by one generation may have unforeseen consequences for the next.

Among the first actions of the League was a campaign which

resulted in the subjugation of the island of Scyros in the central Aegean and the establishment of an Athenian military outpost there. In modern times this small island has been better known as the last resting place of the poet Rupert Brooke, whose burial plot is the "corner of a foreign field that is forever England."

Scyros had long been a center of piracy, and, since the League sought to make the seas safe for all, there was ample reason for the attack and subjugation of the island. This action was important to Athens in particular for two reasons. First, Scyros lay athwart the main shipping lane from the Black Sea region to Athens and its control would be insurance for the safe import of grain. Athens as the central power and mainstay of the League felt it deserved such protection. The second reason was sentimental. Taking the island made it possible for Cimon to bring back for ceremonial re-burial in Attica the remains of the great king Theseus which had long been entombed at Scyros.

The next action by the League, an attack on the city of Carystus which was located at the southwest corner of Euboea, involved a different issue altogether from that of Scyros. Like many other cities, Carystus had decided against joining the League but its location close to Athens did not allow for a free choice. To a military man like Cimon it was unreasonable to build an elaborate system of defense and then allow so vulnerable a spot to remain outside the plan. Thus, the city was coerced into joining the League for strategic reasons. The charter members had acted voluntarily. Carystus was forced to join against her will. This was a dangerous precedent.

The most serious action taken by Athens during Cimon's tenure was the refusal to allow Naxos to withdraw from membership at her own discretion. The question of whether a city-state which had voluntarily joined the League could "voluntarily" secede had apparently never been resolved. In any event, the Athenians argued that local interests must be subordinated to the greater goals attainable through union. No single party to the original agreement had the right to destroy the compact; it could only be dissolved by all participants acting in unison. This decision meant that Athens assigned to herself a veto power. Consequently, about 468, the stubborn Naxians were besieged by the stubborn Athenians and forced to remain in the League, albeit on less favorable terms.

According to the Athenian point of view, military actions such as those against Scyros, Carystus and Naxos, were for the purpose of insuring a proper defense of the Aegean Sea and allowing a more efficient operation against the ever pressing problems of piracy. Yet by each of these moves it was Athens who benefited the most, for she had the most at stake.

In addition to these operations at home, the League also took the offensive against the Persians. Cimon won his greatest military honors in three battles, one after the other, in the year 466. By this time the Persians had withdrawn from the Aegean and their fleet stood near the entrance to the Eurymedon River in southeastern Asia Minor. As Cimon moved eastward along the coast, the Persians were awaiting the arrival of eighty ships manned by the Phoenicians, their chief naval mercenaries. To gain time, they retreated within the mouth of the river but Cimon followed them and captured two hundred ships in the ensuing engagement. He then landed his battle-weary men who fought successfully against fresh forces on the shore and captured an enormous store of booty. Finally—as Plutarch has it, "like an athlete going from contest to contest," Cimon rushed out to intercept and defeat the approaching Phoenician ships and so made a clean sweep of the enemy's strength. No Athenian general had ever fought so far away from home, or so gloriously.

Under inspired Athenian leadership, the Delian League had been successful in greatly diminishing the chances of another barbarian invasion. As the anxieties of the member-states declined, so did their enthusiasm for the League. When threatened from outside, they judged Athenian actions one way; but after the danger was past, the same events were recalled in a different light. The attempt by Naxos to withdraw from the League may have seemed premature in 468, but after the decisive victory at the Eurymedon, two years later, other states might think more about the harsh Athenian punishment of Naxos than of Naxos' hasty action. So long as Cimon remained at the head of the League, however, the allies felt reassured with respect to the policy of the organization, for he was always considered a good friend.

Cimon's generosity to the contributing states was part of their undoing. When the immediate danger in the Aegean was over, most states were anxious to return to their normal pursuits and those which had been sending ships and men to Athens sought to send only money. Except for Cimon, the Athenian generals seem to have felt that the allies should be held strictly to account for the actual military service which they now sought to escape. Cimon, partly for pragmatic reasons and partly because of a misguided sense of friendship, allowed the allies to stay at home and took more and more Athenians into the navy in their stead. In terms of uniform training and discipline this system had its advantages, but the Athenians gained the experience in warfare and the allies, growing ever weaker, were paying for it. As Thucydides observes, those cities which took the easy way out and refused direct service had only themselves to blame when they found in the long run that they were defenseless against Athenian power.

Cimon thought that all Greeks would benefit by the growth of Athenian power, but even during his own time the gulf between practice and the ideal was growing wider. Leaders arose who were increasingly more outspoken in favor of Athenian self-interest. As the Persian danger subsided, the old views of Themistocles became timely. Athenian plans were to be promoted at the expense of the other Greek states, even if the Delian League had to be used to do it. Cimon was a representative of the first generation of the fifth century —the generation of Marathon—men who built a great naval force and organized an effective alliance. The men of the second generation used these instruments to make Athens the most glorious and the most feared city in Greece.

The shift in the purpose of Athenian foreign policy was made plain by the course of events which began to unfold after the battle at the Eurymedon River. The next year, 465, the Athenians turned their attention to the coastal area of the northern Aegean Sea. The routes through Thrace were important connecting links between Greece and the Black Sea settlements. With the sea lanes secured, Athens now became interested in the connections by land. A strategic crossing place on the Strymon River was chosen as a site for a new colony. To the west of the river was Macedonia and to the east was Thrace. The Athenian intention of planting a colony at a place known as the Nine Ways was an obvious bid to take up a position commanding in both directions. More was involved than a military objective. The region was rich in silver, timber and grain.

The Athenian intrusion aroused the apprehensions not only of the Macedonians and the Thracians but of the citizens of nearby Thasos as well, for these islanders had their major investments on the mainland. Thasos, one of the largest and most prosperous of the Aegean islands, was a member of the Delian League. Her citizens were especially resentful of the Athenian action because their future would be directly affected by any further competition in this area.

Since the victory at the Eurymedon River, Athens was actually a greater threat than Persia. Therefore, Thasos withdrew from the League in the same year, 465.

The Thasians had a larger navy and greater wealth than Naxos, the first of the Delian members to challenge Athens, and so their withdrawal was more serious. The siege of the island began under Cimon, but he did not enhance his reputation by a contest which dragged on for over two years. On the contrary, he returned to Athens before it was over to face sharp criticism from ambitious new leaders who had reason to believe that he was not wholeheartedly committed to the campaign. The actual charge placed against him, however, concerned another matter. It was said that he had been bribed by the king of Macedon to remain out of his territory.

Among Cimon's accusers was the young Pericles. By coincidence, it was Xanthippus, the father of Pericles, who had led the prosecution against Miltiades, Cimon's father. The charge against Cimon underscored the growing conflict between the leaders of the tradesmen, rowers, and laborers—men who were bound to gain by an expansion of Athenian commerce—and, on the other hand, the spokesmen for conservative and pan-Hellenic ideals. Cimon had been interested in establishing an outpost on the Strymon River primarily as a military project. He was naturally wary of any exploitation of this region which might cause trouble with the allies.

The effort at the Strymon proved a dismal failure. An inspired Thracian uprising decisively forestalled the Athenian attempt to establish a base of operations at the Nine Ways, and the idea of a colony had to be abandoned, at least for the time being.

The surrender of Thasos in 463 was the sole accomplishment of the northern campaign. The island was reduced to a humiliating position as a subject state, but this was hardly worth the time and money which Athens had spent and the northern campaign, on the whole, was a severe set-back for Athenian ambitions. Presumably, Cimon's political enemies had hoped that the citizenry would turn against him because of this dismal showing but they had miscalculated the strength of his personal popularity. His fund of good will saw him through the crisis and he was acquitted on the charge of having accepted a bribe. Plutarch reports that Pericles was only a perfunctory prosecutor, which suggests that the future statesman had an ear already well tuned to public sentiment.

If Cimon was to be brought down in order to make way for the more progressive, if chauvinistic, leaders, it had to be on another issue and he supplied it himself. He remained friendly with Sparta, as he had always been, and it was this well-meaning loyalty which proved his undoing. He had maintained consistently that a partnership between Sparta and Athens would be the best insurance of peace and unity within Greece, and therefore the strongest defense against the barbarians. For their part, the Spartans had always been interested in friendship with Athens but they were even more interested in the *status quo*. Recent Athenian policies, especially toward the Delian League allies, clearly forecasted a shift in power which could be viewed as dangerous. In fact, the Thasians had appealed to Sparta for help in their struggle with the Athenians and they might have received it, except that Lacedaemonia suffered a severe earthquake in 464. Sparta needed help herself, for in addition to the loss of life and the destruction of property she faced an uprising of enslaved helots who sought to take advantage of this unexpected gesture of support from the gods.

The fact that Sparta turned to her allies, even to Athens, for aid was a clue to her desperation. At Athens, the Assembly heard Ephialtes, the leader of the popular interests, argue against assisting a city which had showed so much suspicion of recent Athenian growth. Nevertheless, Cimon was able to carry the citizenry with him when he argued that Spartan power was still a mainstay of the Greek defense. With Athenian help, the Spartans survived their troubles and in 463 they again took the offensive against the Messenians. Once the crisis was passed, the Spartans saw no further need for Athenian forces on their soil and (with what was probably no more than their customary boorishness) summarily asked the Athenians to leave. The Spartans may not have intended any insult or ingratitude by this request, but the Athenians chose to see it as both. The incident was extremely embarrassing to Cimon, and it was the opportunity his political enemies had been waiting for. He was ostracized in 461.

The downfall of Cimon left the way clear for further democratization of the Athenian constitution. The Areopagus, the remaining stronghold of the aristocracy, was the chief target of the reformers. Ephialtes proposed and carried measures by which this ancient body was stripped of all its powers, except the right to hear cases of homicide. It was natural that the traditionalists within the aristocracy bitterly resented both Ephialtes' policies and his success. Therefore, when he was assassinated a short time later, his death was attributed to the machinations of a stubborn nobility. Nothing was ever proved.

With Cimon in exile and Ephialtes dead, power came to the man who would give his name to the era that followed. Pericles was the dominant political figure during those middle years of the fifth century when Athens reached the height of her success and was praised and feared because of it.

Earlier, when Pericles was still a boy, the city had not yet begun to rival Sparta in power, nor was it a dazzling cultural center. These were years of struggle for the fledgling Athens. Yet in spite of her future power and prominence, they may have been the best years after all.

# The First Generation:
# The Whole Man

**VIII** The remark that a gentleman was a man who could play the flute, but not too well, expressed the Athenian ideal of a balanced education. Young men should learn to sing some poetry, but they should not neglect the wrestling school on that account. The development of the "whole man" required training both of body and mind.

Pericles, whose speeches were the best publicity Athens ever had, boasted that the Athenians followed this middle way. His fellow citizens, he said, unlike the Spartans, had not sought manliness by conditioning themselves to brutality. At Athens, youths spent only part of their time exercising their bodies—but enough to keep any concentration on music or philosophy from turning them into soft or effeminate men. The Athenians avoided the excesses of either the physical or the intellectual side of life; at least Pericles liked to think they did. But his famous declaration of principles, delivered in 430, came long after there had developed, especially among the aristocracy, an unsettling preference for purely intellectual pursuits. In fact, if there was ever a time in Athens when a balanced education was the rule it appears to have been during the heyday of the Marathon generation.

The Athenians who defeated the forces of the Persian Empire were men who had been born before the year 500. They were the first generation of the fifth century. During the next thirty years, as a result of other victories, they built an empire of their own. Yet, as it often happens to men and nations, what Athens won in the way of power and wealth altered her habits and even her values. So that these men, the builders, behaved and thought somewhat differently than their sons, the second generation, who managed the inheritance during the middle years of the century.

The collective experience of the men of the earlier generation had been one to inspire confidence in themselves and their heritage. They had participated in events, both sad and glorious, from which Athens emerged as the first city in Greece. In 480, ten years after their momentous victory at Marathon, the same men who had saved the city abandoned it to be burned rather than compromise their freedom. After the Greek victories at Salamis and Plataea, the Athenians led the campaign which carried the fight to the Persians and eventually swept them out of the Aegean world. Finally, because of Athenian initiative, the Delian League was founded and in its early years became an effective arm of defense for all Greece. No matter what happened later, Marathon was always the great moment for the men who fought there. They had been put to the test physically and mentally and had proved themselves worthy. They had fought in the way their fathers had taught them to fight and they believed in what their fathers told them they were fighting for. In the years after Marathon, they did not spend their time speculating about what might be done, or if it should be done, or what others might think of how they did it. They went ahead and acted, neither timidly nor in a foolhardy way, but with a confidence born of experience and success. And it was their boldness which decided the future of Athens and won for her a reputation for future thinkers to think about.

It is always difficult to assay the mood of a generation. In our own day, we speak perhaps glibly of a time before World War I, indeed before the works of Freud and Einstein, when there seemed to be an attitude of certainty about values and behavior which is generally called Victorian. Invariably, this term evokes thoughts of the British Empire and of the brave soldier who may not have reasoned why. This soldier took orders from an officer who may not have reasoned either, for England during the Crimean War was a society of rank by classes in which army commissions were obtained by virtue of birth or wealth and not necessarily because of brains. The question arises then: to what extent has the usual impression of the Victorian era, as derived from art and literature, reflected the standards and tastes of only a particular class with a particular education? Were the hired hands and factory workers also "Victorians," or were they merely living in the Victorian Age? The same question is pertinent for Athenian society, because any consideration of mood or values in the early years of the fifth century must be based almost exclusively on the writings of aristocrats. From two of them in particular, we learn about the Athenian ideal of the "whole man."

The glorification of the physical side of life was best expressed for all the Greeks by the poet Pindar (522–443), a Theban aristocrat who admired and often visited Athens. In his victory odes, he lavished praise on the winners in the great athletic festivals; more than any other man he established the Greek reputation for adulation of athletes. His exaltation of the beauty and skill of the victors raised them to a level only a little lower than the gods—and contemporary sculptors, as if to illustrate his verse, gave admiring attention to physical excellence in their statues of the winners. The emphasis on athletics had a practical side of course, since daily exercise and preparation for the games kept the Athenians ready for any emergency. Marathon had proved that.

It was Aeschylus (525–456) who exemplified the intellectual life of this same period. He was a native Athenian, the first of the three major writers of tragedy of the fifth century, and, like Pindar, an aristocrat. His talents won him recognition as the foremost poet of his generation, and his words, true to the times, placed an emphasis on courage and idealism.

Aeschylus had fought at Marathon and well might he remember it, for his brother was killed there and was buried along with the rest of the fallen beneath the mound which marks the spot. Aeschylus was destined to be buried long afterwards in distant Sicily but his epitaph recalled that day of battle so memorable in the minds of the first generation. The inscription did not mention his poetry; it asked only that he be remembered as a brave man. Courage was a quality admired by his contemporaries who in 480 had refused to come to terms with Xerxes.

As a playwright, Aeschylus was a spokesman for a generation of men who had kept the faith of their fathers. But when he left Athens, toward the end of his life in 458, it was already being asked in certain intellectual circles if the old ways were good enough. This skepticism characterized, in part, the thinking of the second generation. Earlier, when Pindar and Aeschylus were in their prime, the good life followed the traditional pattern and Odysseus was still the model.

Homer's words, the first any Athenian boy would learn, implanted in young minds the ideal of the "whole man." Odysseus, the archetype, strove to excel in both physical and mental deeds of agility. Although physically tough, he was not brutish; although intelligent and a good talker, he was not an intellectual. He was a leader of men.

### The Body

During the first generation of the fifth century the good life was an active one, especially for those who had the leisure time to pursue it. The cheapness of slave labor meant that even men of modest means could spend part of their days exercising in the *palaestrae*. It is not possible to reckon what percentage of the Athenian citizenry was in fact able to follow this routine. At that time, a man and his family could live on what we would call pennies a day, but there were many citizens who were fully occupied in obtaining even this. These men earned their living as rowers in the fleet or as laborers in the shops and kilns, and they often worked alongside slaves who were publicly or privately owned. Nevertheless, the prominence given to athletics in both the art and literature of the times suggests that for an important segment of the citizenry there was a daily concern with the conditioning and enjoyment of the body.

For the aristocracy this had always been true. Although men were born into the nobility and never had to prove their right to belong to it, there was still a code of behavior which served as a badge of membership. Aristocrats considered themselves better than other men and this sense of superiority accompanied the good name and wealth which passed from father to son. Many attitudes were also transmitted, and among them was the idea that the worth of a man was not alone what he inherited but also what he could prove himself to be by his deeds. For instance, a skilled charioteer exhibited a certain poise based upon training and practice. His confident handling of the horses was the mark of a nobleman. Common men who lived meager and routine lives did not own chariots.

Before the Dorian invasions in the Achaean period which Homer described, fighting had been the major occupation of the aristocracy, and exercise and competition were the means by which a nobleman stayed fit, and so alive. The Achaean nobility were not athletes but warriors who lived an athletic life. They knew nothing of gymnasiums or stadiums or training schools. Later, after the Dark Ages, when their descendants no longer roamed the seas and the old citadels had given way to cities, a place was marked out for exercise. But in the earlier times contests were held wherever noblemen happened to be. When Achilles wanted to have a chariot race, he chose a tree stump to be the turning point of his improvised course. The Achaeans, as Homer described them, were no closer to the later Olympian tradition (which called for games at arranged times and places) than were the American Indians to the World Series.

The earliest literary description of Greek athletics is in Book XXIII of the *Iliad* where an account is given of the contests which Achilles provided for the funeral of his friend Patroclus. The chariot race was the most honored among them, and for the competitors in this "sport of kings" Achilles offered prizes which would interest roving raiders. First, there was a woman, probably captured along the way, who was described as skilled in handiwork. Along with her went a valuable tripod, a three-legged vessel of some sort. There followed four other awards including a six-year-old mare, a caldron, two talents of gold, and a two-handled urn.

The boxing and wrestling contests which followed were rough and even brutal, for this was natural in a combat between strong opponents. Yet those who witnessed these contests, brutal or not, were would-be contestants themselves and the motive in the matches was to win a contest of skill—not to provide amusement for gaping spectators.

Numerous passages in the *Iliad* are all blood and bowels spewed forth in hard battle, but in contrast to these scenes, the contests which Achilles staged were true sport, fair and clean. At times the behavior of the Greeks demands unequivocal praise and this is one of them. There were winners and losers, but those who lost remained alive and were in fact honored for their effort. In Homer's account of the wrestling match between Odysseus and Ajax, the prize for the winner was to be a tripod worth ten oxen. But since the contestants fought to a draw, Achilles urged them to take equal prizes and not to suffer any further strain.

Cruel practices, masked as sport, did eventually appear in Greece but at a time of decline when there was a general deterioration of standards. Centuries after the refined *Charioteer of Delphi,* a statue of a seated boxer was sculptured whose weary body and battered face show him to be a fighter and nothing else. In keeping with the later Roman tradition and unlike Homer's warriors, he is not the finest boxer among men who can all box a little, but a killer watched by men who cannot box at all. So it happened that what was best, and uniquely so, in the Greek tradition came to an end. The sight was all the sorrier for what had gone before.

The ideal of physical excellence remained a part of the aristocratic code after the Achaean period. It was the mark of the man who did not earn his living by work in the fields or by service to others. During the Colonization Era (750–550), a new class of wealthy men gradually emerged who borrowed the manners and the ideals of the aristocracy and so adopted the code of athleticism. During this period the establishment of regularly held contests at various sites, such as Olympia, reflected the "settling down" which followed the disorders of the Dark Ages. Furthermore, the growth in popularity of these festivals coincided with the shift of political power away from the privileges of birth to those of wealth. At first, perhaps only the aristocrats had the opportunity to stay in training for such events, but gradually the new rich found the time. So the great games were opened to Greeks of all classes and commoners were encouraged to acquire the athletic skills which had formerly been the mark of an aristocratic warrior. The festivals introduced to many men the activities and values once possessed by only a few.

No one knows when the Olympian Games began. The official list of winners dated from 776, and that year has passed into tradition as the date of their founding. Between then and the fifth century, in addition to many local contests, there developed three other major pan-Hellenic festivals. The games held at Nemea, a valley in northern Argolis, were sacred to Zeus like those at Olympia. At Delphi, the games were dedicated to Apollo, and at the Isthmus of Corinth to Poseidon. By age and custom, the festival held every fourth year at Olympia, in the northwest corner of the Peloponnesus, enjoyed the greatest prestige amongst the Greeks. For this reason we know more about it than we know of the others.

The Olympian festival may have evolved slowly from a repetition of contests held to honor some dead chieftain, perhaps Pelops, after whom the Peloponnesus was named. Pelops does appear in a legend which explains the origin of the games, and Pindar is among those who repeated it. According to the traditional story, of which there are variant versions, Pelops was the last in a long line of suitors who sought the hand of Hippodameia, the daughter of a local ruler named Oenomaus. The father had challenged all hopefuls to a chariot race and had successfully defeated, and then killed, thirteen of them down to Pelops. But this young man, perhaps wary of the odds, arranged for some tampering with Oenomaus' chariot, and with the further help of horses sent from Poseidon, won both the race and the girl. The deed seems hardly befitting a man for whom these famous games may have been founded, yet according to Pindar's account it was at the tomb of Pelops that Heracles inaugurated the festival. Greek myths are fanciful tales, but they do occasionally contain some uncomfortable truths.

It is a fact that nothing is known for certain about Pelops or the origin of the games. It is also a fact that in classical times the erection of a great temple to Zeus with an imposing cult statue of gold and ivory made Olympia, like Delphi, one of the major shrines of all the Greeks. Only Greeks were allowed to compete. In wartime, hostilities ceased during the celebration of the games (usually held in August and September) and no arms were ever allowed in the area. Persons traveling to or from Olympia were supposedly safe from harm, although this presumption did not always mean that they were.

The traditional contests, already described in the *Iliad,* continued as the major events in the more regular athletic festivals. The chariot races even carried over the aristocratic flavor, for few men outside of the old families could afford horses. Now, however, there was more to win than Achilles had offered. Victory meant widespread fame and prestige. Like the kings before them, the tyrants made the chariot race their favorite.

A race in full armor reflected recent changes in the economy. The new *hoplite* class, which had played a prominent role in the rise of the tyrants, was made up of men who could afford heavy armor and with a new contest designed for them the games kept pace with the times.

True to the old tradition, however, emphasis was placed on all-around training by the introduction of the pentathlon which combined five events in a single contest: running, jumping, throwing the discus, throwing the javelin and wrestling. Because exact information is missing, it is not known if these events were performed in exactly that order, nor is it certain that a man had to excel in all five to win or if he could take the prize on some kind of point system. In any event, the pentathlon called for an amateur in five sports rather than a professional in one.

In Homeric times, although athletics were natural to the life of the participants, prizes of real worth were awarded them. This practice was presumably continued in the later festivals but abandoned in the seventh century when, upon advice attributed to the oracle of Delphi, a crown of wild olive leaves became the sole reward for victory. This wreath was thereafter a symbol of amateurism. Such was the spirit which the games promoted among men who were no longer exclusively warriors but who exercised regularly to keep fit and to add balance to their education and life. At the very time when wealth and the things it could buy began to abound in Greece the festivals offered a brake to the subtle influences of materialism.

At Athens, it was not until the latter part of the fifth century that the increasing democratization of all aspects of life had its impact on athletics, and the support of wealthy patrons enabled even the poorest of men to engage in athletic competition. Some men then began to train for a particular skill and the resulting specialization broke down the old ideal of the all-around athlete. Not all who exercised and competed did so as a way of life; for some men it was a way of making a living.

These changes came after Pindar's day, when a statue and a poem or two were the honorable means of rewarding an athletic hero for whom victory itself was the prize. His joy may have been alloyed with egotism, but not presumably with acquisitiveness. The victor knew that he was the best man in a given contest, and he knew it better than anybody else. His moment of triumph was akin to that of an artist who finishes a work knowing that it is exactly right. Here was the spirit which Pindar glorified, and mixed the glory with sadness. The work of art could not be saved. Although the likeness of the athlete in his prime might be captured in a poem or a bronze statue, the reality lasted but a day.

According to custom, a young man who came home victorious from the games was given a celebration by his family and friends. The occasion included the singing of a special choral ode prepared especially in his honor. These were the lyrics which Pindar wrote for love, and because he was no amateur, for money—in fact, they probably financed his travels from one end of the Greek world to the other. Although he treated other subjects as well, it is forty-four of his victory odes which have survived.

His poems are not always paeans to a single winner. Those who ordered and paid for them often had other ideas about their content. For instance, it is not unusual in a poem about a certain youth's triumph, to find that his father's great moment of glory is also recalled. And if any other member of the family had won at the games, he might be mentioned too. Customarily, the shining performances of the living are linked to great feats of the past, for as a rule the main body of the poem revives memories out of history or myth.

Pindar's ties were with the past. He was a traditionalist and his odes reflected the aristocratic view of life which Homer first described centuries before. The winner was glorified. The best man stood alone. Above all, Pindar was a spokesman for an "outdoor" civilization, one in which honesty, loyalty and piety were the accepted rules of a gentleman. Yet this same moralizing, amidst sonorous references to ancient heroes, gave his poems the air of period pieces. By the middle of the fifth century they would have sounded dated to sophisticates who had turned a critical ear, and perhaps a jaded eye, toward all traditional values.

## The Mind

On regularly scheduled occasions the Athenians sat down together to listen to a series of tragedies presented by competing playwrights. The theater was an integral part of the community. Never again has the Western world witnessed a comparable situation in which citizens of an autonomous state have been so much involved with one another in common political, religious and social activities. Perhaps the closest parallel would be the Italian communes of the later Middle Ages, yet they were more comparable to those ancient Greek cities which were under the control of oligarchs.

Nowadays, where democracies exist, the citizenry is so numerous that it is necessary to elect a few representatives to meet and decide important questions for all—and to take the blame when things go wrong. Rarely, except in small towns, do people debate and pass their own ordinances. Even when they do join together to deliberate and make laws, the citizens do not all worship at the same shrines. At Athens, the life shared with one's fellow citizens was the good life and the theater was part of it. Today in the Mediterranean world, at least on certain occasions, there still exists in small communities a "sense of belonging," reminiscent of a quality so characteristic of the ancient *polis*.

A tourist may witness this phenomenon if he happens to be visiting in a small town in Italy or Greece on a feast day in honor of the local patron saint. The bunting and flags seem worn and tattered from too much use and the lights strung across the facade of the church look gaudy rather than colorful. In comparison with the sparkling outdoor displays in large cities, especially at Christmastime, the trappings of a little town often appear poor and amateurish. Still, like the old-fashioned trimmings for a Christmas tree which we bring out year after year, the decorations of such a town have a special value, for they belong to a family which on this occasion is the community—the whole town gathered together for a parade, a pageant and a good time. On the same date every year these people honor the saint who cares for their town and for them, and, on that day at least, those who have joined the celebration belong to one another. Amid such scenes the visitor is a stranger, trained to be one by the busy city which along with its glamour and glitter offers anonymity for all.

The ancient Greek *polis,* in at least one respect, was like such a modern small town. On certain traditional dates, festivals were held in honor of various gods; and naturally the patron deity was especially honored. These festivals were organized and administered by priests who were city officials, and the religious and patriotic character of these occasions guaranteed their popularity. Among a people who accepted and worshipped many gods, rather than just one, there was no difficulty in introducing still one more. Thus, in the sixth century, no barriers prevented the whole citizenry from joining in the worship of the newly popularized Dionysus, and as the festivities in his honor slowly developed into full-scale dramatic presentations, they became at the same time community-wide programs.

The high level attained by the Athenian drama does not mean that all the Athenians were "intellectual" any more than does the popularity of opera in Milan make the Milanese "intellectual." It was a matter of circumstance. The Athenians were accustomed to the competitive nature of the drama. The festivals were occasions for performances of high quality and the citizens expected this, as men today expect better English in a lecture hall than on a street corner. Besides, the theater was not a commercial venture. There was of course a nominal admission price, but even this was subsidized by the state during the heyday of the popular democracy. Many costs, for instance the expenses of a chorus, were paid by wealthy men who were expected to donate to public causes. A rising young aristocrat, hopeful of a public career, might purchase favorable publicity by such beneficence. Thus the theater was supported in part by private funds; but this did not mean that the playwright was in any way bound by the wishes of those who contributed the money. Actually he was doing them a favor, not the other way around.

The playwright's success depended on the decision of a few judges and not upon the approval of the spectators. There was therefore an emphasis upon quality. If there was any accommodation, it was the audience which rose to the poet's level; he did not debase his talent to theirs.

In 472, the young Pericles paid for the chorus of a play by Aeschylus. It must have been a great honor for the budding careerist because Aeschylus was the leading poet of the day—in fact, he has often been called the founder of Athenian tragedy. Aristotle says that he was the first poet to make use of two actors instead of one. It will be recalled that in Peisistratus' time, during the sixth century, Thespis had stood apart from the chorus and declaimed a speech of his own. Now Aeschylus moved further away from the old choral form by adding a second actor and so creating dialogue in the sense that we know it.

In the early years of the Greek theater, the playwright was more than a poet. He gave instructions to the chorus in singing and dancing and sometimes even took a part in the play. In our terms, he was writer, actor, director and producer. It was in these multiple roles that Aeschylus introduced certain devices which thereafter became conventions in the theater. For instance, he provided his actors with highly stylized masks and elaborate costumes. These additions, along with buskins (high platform shoes), lifted his performers out of the realm of the ordinary and gave them a solemn grandeur well suited to his verse.

It is impossible to say what impact Aeschylus' words may have had on the average citizen in his audience, but the impression he made on the judges is clear. At the height of his career, in the sixteen years between 484 and 468, he was awarded first prize thirteen times. It is estimated that he wrote about ninety plays of which over eighty titles remain. Of these, seven have survived: *The Suppliants, The Persians, Seven Against Thebes, Prometheus Bound,* and his only extant trilogy, *The Oresteia,* which includes three plays, *Agamemnon, Choephoroe,* and *Eumenides.*

In each of these plays, human existence is inextricably involved with suffering. Yet Aeschylus insists that man must persevere because in spite of terrifying sequences of crime there is a moral order, and all things do work together eventually for good. The intelligent use of power is better than brute force, and resistance for the sake of principle is more to be valued than a compromise to win some immediate goal. Again and again, Aeschylus presents protagonists who have to decide whether to safeguard their own interests by abandoning their principles or to remain in tune with the universe by following the will of the gods, no matter what the consequences. Each of his heroes makes the right and unselfish choice.

## The Uses of Power

About the year 460, Aeschylus offered his Promethean trilogy, consisting of three plays: *Prometheus the Fire-Bearer, Prometheus Bound* and *Prometheus Unbound.* In the surviving *Prometheus Bound* he presents a theme familiar in the works of Greek poets, the conflict between "right motive" and "brute force."

Prometheus was a Titan, one of the early deities who had ruled the universe prior to the usurpation of power by the Olympians. According to legendary stories which mirrored man's own dynastic struggles, Uranus was overthrown by his son Cronus and Cronus was in turn unseated by his son Zeus. In this struggle, Prometheus was already an exceptional figure. Unlike the other Titans he supported Zeus and helped him to win his throne. This heightened the irony of his future suffering at the hands of the new ruler.

Prometheus' determination to be a friend to man had momentous consequences for himself and for the human race. He chose to be helpful by various means, of which the best known was the gift of fire. In addition, he eased man's mental pain by taking away his capacity to foresee his own doom and planted in him instead a merciful "blind hope." Zeus on the other hand had no such plans for man. On the contrary, for some unknown reason he intended to replace him with another creature. In any event he was angered by Prometheus' independent action, and especially because it was an act of defiance early in his reign. Since new rulers among gods or men must quickly show their firmness, he ordered Prometheus chained to a rock in desolate Scythia, there to suffer from the sun by day and the winds by night. After a time, a thunderbolt drove Prometheus, rock and all, into Tartarus, and much later he was bound on Mount Caucasus where he was tortured daily by an eagle sent from the vengeful Olympian. Through all of this, Prometheus persevered in order to prevail. He finally did.

Myths took different turns in the writings of various poets. While the Promethean story was always recognizable, the details often depended on who was telling it. An author might choose to add a little or leave out a little, and his choice shaped the message he intended to convey. For instance, in Hesiod's *Theogony,* the legend begins as usual with Prometheus stealing fire from Olympus and giving it to man in direct defiance of Zeus' orders. Then we are told how man's fortunes became mixed as a result of the favor. Prometheus, the open friend, has aroused to action a powerful and devious enemy. Zeus decides to send man some offerings of his own and the conveyor of these gifts is to be the first woman. Pandora, wicked in mind and seductive in body, is sent to Epimetheus who, although warned by his brother Prometheus not to accept any presents from Zeus, finds her tempting and marries her. When she opens the chest which holds her dowry, out come all the ills which have troubled mankind ever since. An alternate version, kinder to Pandora, claims that in opening the chest she was not being wicked, just curious. Women are nowhere credited with composing their own accounts of the origin of evil and they do not fare any better here than they did in the Garden of Eden.

In Aeschylus' *Prometheus Bound,* attention is centered exclusively on the conflict between Prometheus and Zeus. Aeschylus uses these two figures to personify a familiar conflict between intelligence and blind power. All other episodes, including the Pandora story, are eliminated.

The *Prometheus Bound* begins with the beloved patron of mankind being chained to the rock in Scythia. Thereafter, the play consists quite simply of his dialogues with the Chorus and with his visitors, including the goddesses Oceanus and Io, who join in his recitation of the cruelties of Zeus. His last visitor Hermes is less sympathetic. He has been sent from Zeus to demand that Prometheus reveal a secret which he holds over the mighty Father's head.

Instead of Clymene, Aeschylus substituted Themis as the mother of Prometheus. She is a goddess who, like Apollo, knows the future and Prometheus has learned from her that if Zeus has a son by a certain goddess, Thetis, the same offspring will dethrone him. He stubbornly refuses to reveal his secret unless Zeus releases him and

repays him for what he has endured. Far from making any concession, however, Hermes now adds the threats of Tartarus and the
liver-devouring eagle. So the play ends in an impasse. Prometheus
in his last speech again cries out against the injustice which he suf-
fers. The words are spoken by a god, but any man who has endured
cruelty at the hands of a despot might have said them.

It has been assumed that in the final play of the trilogy, which
has been lost, Zeus allows Heracles, another friend of man, to effect
Prometheus' release. So it would appear that the Father of the gods
finally recognizes that the use of power unguided by moral precepts
brings a hollow victory. The body of Prometheus is enchained and
tortured but his spirit cannot be captured. This is the lesson which
Aeschylus might have wished to impart to his audience. Power of
itself is neutral. If used selfishly or ignorantly, it breeds trouble. If
used with wisdom and temperance, it brings harmony to the universe.

Aeschylus produced his Promethean trilogy at a time when
Athens was approaching the zenith of her power, but not necessarily
her greatness. As the same clay may be given different shapes, so
the Delian League, organized for the benefit of all its members, was
slowly being molded into an empire for the profit of Athens. Increasingly, as we have observed, Athenian leaders were following a career
of expediency and calculation, even toward their friends. The design
was for winning, no matter what ideals might be lost in the process.
However, Pericles, one of the leaders of the popular party, insisted
that the allies benefited by Athenian paternalism. Some did. But
not all of them wanted to be so well taken care of. They preferred
to be free to decide their own course, no matter what the cost. So
the question of self-determination arose and many members of the
old Athenian aristocracy took sharp issue with Pericles about it. It
seems likely that Aeschylus would have too. Certainly Pindar, although rarely interested in politics, found his long-term friendship
with Athens sorely tested.

Aeschylus said that his plays were only restatements of the Homeric view of man. In the *Iliad,* Achilles knew he must die if he
stayed to avenge Patroclus. Yet he stayed because it was right that
he should. He would rather die than betray his honor. It was in such
a man, doomed to suffer while making the right choice, that Aeschylus had found his tragic hero. Under the circumstances, he could
scarcely have seen any nobility in policies which built the fortunes
of Athens on the betrayal of the trust of her allies.

## Private Vengeance Gives Way to Public Justice

The *Oresteia* was produced in 458. The three plays tell how violence bred violence, one generation after another, until the gods established a court of justice wherein passion gave way to reason. The trilogy retells only the final sequence of events in the turbulent history of the accursed House of Atreus. The legend went back to Pelops, the same who married Hippodameia and became the king of Pisa in Elis and in whose memory Pindar said the Olympian games were founded. It will be recalled that the victory of Pelops over Hippodameia's father had been due, in part, to the treachery of Oenomaus' chariot driver. When this man (Myrtilus) demanded too much for his services he was murdered by Pelops who thereby brought a curse of blood upon himself and his family. It took bitter effect in the next generation. There ensued strife between Pelops' two sons, Atreus, the king of Mycenae, and Thyestes who stole his brother's wife and conspired with her to win the kingdom. At first, Thyestes was forced to flee for his life, but actually Atreus had something else in mind. Feigning forgiveness, he welcomed him home with a feast at which the unwitting father was served the flesh of two of his own sons. Thyestes then renewed the curse on the murderer and his progeny. So it came to pass that Atreus' son Agamemnon offered his own daughter Iphigenia as a human sacrifice to Artemis in order to win calm seas for the venture against Troy.

The *Agamemnon*, the first play in the trilogy, begins with the return of the victorious king after the defeat of the Trojans. While he was away, his wife Clytemnestra had been living in adultery with his cousin Aegisthus, another son of Thyestes, and they plot the murder of Agamemnon. Each sought revenge for a former crime against a loved one; Clytemnestra for her daughter, and Aegisthus for his father. Together, in this play, they commit a crime of their own.

The second segment of the trilogy, *Choephoroe* or the *Mourners*, is named for the chorus of captured Trojan women. It tells how Orestes, the son of Agamemnon, who had been sent away before the murder of his father, comes home to avenge the death by killing those who killed him. He and his sister Electra, who has only lived for his return, plot the murder of their mother and her lover. The play ends as Orestes, standing over the bodies of Clytemnestra and Aegisthus, sees the Furies, avengers of kindred blood, swarming around him and continuing the curse to the third generation.

In the final play, the *Eumenides,* Orestes is pursued by the twelve Furies who relentlessly seek his destruction by haunting him everywhere he tries to run. Although it was the will of Apollo that he avenge his father, he had shed his mother's blood and the Furies would not release him from this stain. At this point, the goddess Athena establishes in Athens an institution which will put an end to the savage process by which one crime breeds another. The Areopagus is the tribunal which tries and then releases Orestes, with the goddess casting the tie-breaking vote. Furthermore, Athena transforms the avenging Furies into helpful protectors of justice and they become the Eumenides, or good spirits.

There is no word from Aeschylus as to why he introduced into this legend an account of the origin of the Areopagus, but many writers since have made suggestions. Almost nobody thinks that it was to supply a happy ending. Some have seen the interpolation as a "patriotic" gesture, for it might be assumed that the founding of the Areopagus was symbolic of the birth of the *polis,* an event which marked the transformation of disorderly folk into a community of citizens. Private vengeance gave way to public justice. According to this view, the *polis* among the Greeks fulfilled a purpose akin to that of the Law among the Hebrews. As with Yahweh, so with the Olympians. There was imposed on the lives of men a pattern of behavior without which they were unruly and vengeful, obeying only their own selfish inclinations.

The emergence of a tribunal of the state as a means of ending the chaotic succession of one crime avenging another was unmistakably Greek. Aeschylus, who has been described as a deeply religious poet, is not here upholding the "trial by ordeal" of sacred societies wherein God protects the innocent and gives a sign of the guilty. The playwright has Athena place in man's hands an institution wherein men might seek out motive and fix degrees of guilt. Under trial by ordeal many an innocent man might die, yet reliance on a jury was not a perfect means of justice either and the system was often abused. The first method, however, was based on submission to an outside power; the second required the best that men could do of themselves. Athena remained the guardian of the laws and the Athenians were grateful to her for that; at the same time they listened to the evidence and determined a man's fate by their own decision. All of this has a modern ring.

An outright attack on the Areopagus and the reduction of its powers came in 462, only a few years before the *Oresteia* was presented. It is a matter of opinion whether Aeschylus' glorification of this body in the *Eumenides* was intended as a comment on the recent democratic reforms, one way or the other. It might be assumed that he was warning the popular leaders against tampering with this sacred institution. He makes Athena counsel against anarchy. On the other hand, he may actually have been supporting the reforms by showing that the Areopagus had originally only considered cases of homicide as it would continue to do. This difference of opinion leaves the question open as to whether his departure for Sicily a short time later was in protest against the political climate in Athens or only in response to a request to produce one of his plays there. In any event, he never returned, for he died and was buried in Sicily in 456.

## The Peace of Reconciliation

Aeschylus focused his attention on man in agony. This is what he knew of life. The sombreness of the tragedies was born of experience and he had no revelation to guide him further. Nor was there any well-charted heaven or hell by which the injustices of the here-and-now might be balanced in the hereafter. In this life, the only life he knew, the righteous often went unrewarded and the wicked did often flourish. No man, surely not Aeschylus, knew why they should. But he did know that men must live with this knowledge about human existence and that it was acquired through suffering. Each tragedy unfolded before his audience an old story, true to life, and men were confronted, like Job, with what they could not understand. Yet in their recognition and acceptance of the insoluble conditions of life, it is presumed that at least some men found the peace of reconciliation which has been called "tragic pleasure."

Unlike Job, this calm of theirs did not mean submission to a single all-knowing, all-powerful deity. It resulted from an acceptance of the limitations of man, due in part to his own weaknesses, in part to the power of the gods, and above all to the mysterious workings of fate. A man could learn only that he must accept suffering. There was no escape from it.

As in the works of Homer and Pindar, there was in Aeschylus' verse a frank acknowledgement of the strange, intertwined strands of harmony and discord, hope and despair, which although only dramatized in the lives of certain men, were really the condition of all humanity. This view of life was a balanced outlook, sometimes called maturity, which accepted life for what it seemed to be and recognized at the same time the necessity to carry on bravely, even creatively, to the inevitable end. The tragedies were not alone sorrowful tales, overwhelming and numbing, but portrayals by which a man might see his own life as a part of all existence and so turn hopefully from a consuming self-pity to sympathy for humanity.

Aeschylus stressed obedience to moral law. Yet, he was not teaching an abandonment of self as a means to union with a greater power, as is central to all the higher religions. Nor was he describing saints who draw ever closer to a perfect God. It was rather that, in the midst of a universe in which all actions were contingent on the will of the gods, his tragic hero was a man, expressing the best that a man could be. The honesty in Aeschylus' plays has lasted the ages. Shocking horrors and treacheries were to be found in his plays, but there was nothing akin to the exhibitionism of the modern theater which so often depicts man as a dreg. Aeschylus did not stress only the weaker side of man's character as though this was all there was. In fact, later in the fifth century, Aristophanes in his play the *Frogs* has Aeschylus rebuke Euripides for encouraging immorality by picturing man in a hopelessly debased condition. True to his own times, Aeschylus included in his works examples of the heroic spirit, which he had himself seen in action, but suffering and violent death befell the innocent and the guilty in his plays, the good as well as the bad. This was a hard truth for men without a heaven of rewards, and it still is.

In sum, Aeschylus offered an answer somewhere between the depressing hopelessness of earlier oriental societies and the later hope-filled promises of the higher religions. There was not, as in Judaism, the promise of the Covenant; nor, as in Christianity, the assurance of the Resurrection; nor, as in Islam, the rewards for those who obey the Koran. Essentially, Aeschylus saw the fulfillment of human life in the living of it. He offered man the nobility, often magnificent, of a lost cause.

## Variety in the Theater

In spite of the high moral tone and purpose of Aeschylus' tragedies it would be wrong to consider him a single-minded man. It was customary for the same playwright who presented a serious trilogy in the morning to offer a diversion in the afternoon by writing and producing a satyr play involving buffoonery and humor of the broadest sort. Although all of the satyr plays which Aeschylus wrote have been lost, his reputation for success with them has survived to suggest the range of his capacities.

From various fragments and the one satyr play which is extant (the *Cyclops* by Euripides), it seems apparent that these productions were often prepared in haste and, as might be expected, lacked the polish of the tragedies. The pictorial evidence, supplied by bits and pieces of relief sculpture and especially vase paintings, leaves no doubt about their ribald character. The members of the chorus were often represented in grossly padded costumes appropriate to their role as satyrs, those busy demigods of Greek myth who pursued sensual pleasures with great abandon. Included in the standard by-play of these frolicsome dancers was an obvious preoccupation with phallic props which were sometimes attached to their tights.

The babblings of the satyr plays were far removed from the sublime intonations of the tragedies, yet the Athenians who witnessed the one also witnessed the other. The companionship of the *polis* has been mentioned before, and here was another example. There was not on the one hand a theater which catered to the elevated tastes of those who enjoyed the finer things (or thought they should), and then another theater which appealed only to those who were at ease listening to parodies on serious themes, or watching licentious pantomime. Athenian audiences were presented with the entire range in the same theater on the same day. This experience was among the binding forces which helped to create the unusual fraternal life so characteristic of the *polis*.

## The Old Mood Lingered On

During the first three or four decades of the fifth century, the spirit of Marathon set the tone. There was an emphasis on strength of mind and body, including all the great Homeric virtues. The poets Aeschylus and Pindar remained attached to the romantic notions of heroism. This idealism was to be expressed not only in poetry, but in sculpture. The qualities of Aeschylus' hero and Pindar's winner were blended in the minds of the sculptors who created the statues of athletes which became characteristic of this era.

No original works by Myron or Polycleitus have ever been found, yet they are among the best known of the Greek sculptors because their fame was extended by the Romans who ordered marble copies of their bronze masterpieces. The most famous examples are the *Discus Thrower* by Myron and the *Spearbearer* by Polycleitus, both of which are dated in the first half of the fifth century. These represent athletic types, gracefully posed, with the anatomy treated carefully and naturally. On the other hand, neither figure is individualized in the sense that a particular person is represented; they are idealized conceptions. In fact, among ancient sculptors, the *Spearbearer* was con-

LEFT: *Pl. 45 Discus Thrower* (Discobolus). *Roman marble copy of Myron's bronze original.* RIGHT: *Pl. 46 Spearbearer* (Doryphorus). *Roman marble copy of Polycleitus' bronze original.*

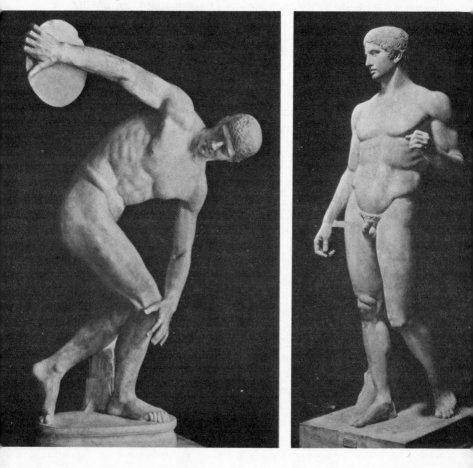

sidered to be a canon, representing the ideal proportions of the male body. Again, as with the *Charioteer of Delphi,* the facial expressions reveal an inner sense of calm and even detached reserve, a certain air of superiority. As in the poetry of Pindar and Aeschylus, the emphasis is on the exceptional, not the average (Pl. 45, 46).

In our own century, the change in mood between the so-called "Good Years," of about 1900 to 1910, and our own less homey times has often been described in terms of the theater, the novel, paintings, or the movies. These barometers have been used to study material changes, as for example an accelerated urbanization, and also the shifting of intellectual interests. It is by similar means, with fewer resources, that the "sense of things" in Athens has been reconstructed.

Herodotus, writing during the middle years of the fifth century, talked to the aging veterans of the Persian Wars and his glowing account of the great Athenian victory at Marathon recaptured the idealism of the past. And so the old mood lingered on. The heritage handed down by these brave men was recalled also in the speeches of the democratic leaders who appealed to the popular majority of tradesmen, laborers and rowers, not to be less mindful of the glorious past than they were of a prosperous future.

Such men, however, did not aspire to heroism; they were hard workers with a dream of their own. The life of Odysseus could not be scaled down to fit the experience of a rower in the fleet or a worker in a kiln. Gradually, the heroic code was overshadowed by new standards and aims, more popular and open to all. Average citizens were not inclined to attack the satisfying romanticization of great deeds, nor to speculate about the hallowed values of the past. They accepted the gods and the established standards of morality. So that it was not a change in their beliefs but an upgrading of their status in the popular democracy and the commercial empire which caused a drastic change in circumstances. The interests of common men, who made up a majority in the Assembly, now became paramount.

These citizens had no time for theorists but they were led in time to listen to men of action, bellwethers who promised them anything, including a larger empire and a greater prosperity. And who could blame them, except that their plans failed in the end and the last years of the fifth century were as dismal for Athens as the early years had been glorious.

Before that happened, however, there were the middle years, the time of the second generation when Athens was in her prime.

# The Second Generation:
# A Popular Democracy Ruling
# an Unpopular Empire

**IX** Sons too young to fight with their fathers at the battle of Marathon and, of course, all those born after 490, grew up as the second generation of the fifth century. Among them, as we have seen, was the famous Pericles who was already well launched on a brilliant career when the aging Aeschylus left Athens. Most of Pericles' contemporaries liked him, a few did not, but every man in the second generation felt his influence. The period between the late 460's when Pericles rose to power and his death in 429 may conveniently be called "their" time. These middle years of the century are usually considered the best that Athens ever enjoyed and in some respects they were. Never before or again would a single city in Greece know comparable power or prosperity. The Parthenon, a magnificent temple and the most famous architectural masterpiece of all time, was dedicated in 438 as an expression of devotion and gratitude to Athena. It was also a symbol of an imperial city with a healthy treasury.

The era of the second generation was the heyday of the Athenian democracy. All power was vested in the citizenry and every citizen, rich or poor, had a single vote. At the same time, the majority relied so often on Pericles for his advice and leadership that the observation could be made (and it was made by Thucydides) that the government was really by one man. Any power Pericles possessed, however, was given to him by his fellow-citizens and on occasion they took it back.

The citizens were not content merely to watch their government from the outside; they were in it themselves. Before mentioning how they managed this, it should be noted why the term "the people" is being avoided here. The Athenians had a democracy with many admirable qualities; however, even though the term *demos* meant "the people," "the people" did not mean everybody. In Athens, only men over eighteen could be full citizens with all political rights. In 451, a special law, which Pericles passed through the Assembly, limited citizenship even further by insisting that all citizens must furnish proof that both their parents were Athenians. A large number of foreigners had settled in Athens and there had been a correspondingly large proportion of mixed marriages. To the average native, it was one thing to welcome a stranger who brought news or talent to the city—"sharing the wealth" with him or his offspring was something else. Because of Pericles' measure, close to 5,000 men were removed from the rolls.

By the middle of the fifth century many benefits had accrued to citizenship, including the guarantee that the widow and children of a fallen citizen-soldier would be cared for at the state's expense. There were other benefits as well, and on one occasion when the government distributed free grain, those "in" could be grateful for a man like Pericles who had kept others "out." At the height of the democracy, discrimination based on an inherited name or money had been abolished and inherited citizenship had become the prize.

If there were in Attica during this period some 40,000 men who were citizens, plus 40,000 women, 50,000 foreign born, and another 100,000 slaves, it will be seen that those who had voting rights made up less than twenty per cent of the total population. Under the circumstances this group was hardly entitled to be called "the people" in our sense of the term. Given this qualification, however, those who were eligible for citizenship did in a real sense govern the *polis* through the election of officials and by sharing in the work of the Council of 500, the Assembly, and the courts.

Most of the public administrators were selected by lot, which meant that out of a large number of names pre-selected at the local (deme) level, those who finally reached office did so by chance. There were, however, certain officers—the treasurers and water commissioner, and especially the *strategoi* or generals—who required a more careful selection and continued to be elected by a direct vote of the Assembly. The great majority of jobs, however, were filled by sortition and one of the most creditable aspects of the Athenian system was this obvious effort to encourage the widest possible participation in public affairs.

The delegation of authority to elected officials for the performance of specific duties was the same as in our representative system, but the Athenians did not elect professional politicians to manage the rest of the government. They actually operated it themselves. The Council of 500 had been designed by Cleisthenes for this purpose. Citizens over the age of thirty were eligible, and each of the ten tribes chose fifty of its members by lot every year to carry on the work. This Council then, which looked after the finances of the state and managed all its properties including harbors and military installations, was made up of five hundred citizens chosen at random who served for a year at a time. In practice, each tribal committee of fifty (*prytany*) conducted the business for one-tenth of the year. The order in which they served was again decided by lot.

During the thirty-five or thirty-six day term of each committee, a chairman (*epistates*) was selected by lot for each twenty-four hour period. This man was the presiding officer of the whole Council when it was called into session. He was also, technically speaking, the titular head of the state during the day of his chairmanship. While a citizen could sit on the Council for two terms, although not consecutively, he could serve only once as the chairman for the day. This unusual turnover in personnel kept more of the citizens better informed about the working of their government; it kept particular factions from entrenching themselves in power; and it brought the most unlikely politician imaginable—the outspoken and irreconcilable Socrates—to the head of the government for a day.

For nearly two decades after the Persian Wars, the hallowed Areopagus acted as an upper-class counterbalance to the more popular Council. The prestige which the older body enjoyed stemmed in part from the leadership and services which the aristocracy and the wealthy had provided during the invasions. There was also its tradition and ancient sanctity which Aeschylus chose to emphasize in his *Eumenides*. In time, however, the members of this elite group came increasingly under fire from the democratic leaders on charges of corruption and favoritism and finally, in 462, as a result of the reforms of Ephialtes, the powers of the Areopagus were sharply curtailed. It was then, Aristotle says, that the "guardianship of the laws" became the responsibility of all the citizens. Consequently, it is assumed that the Council of 500 in particular exercised a critical eye thereafter over the fitness and conduct of all public servants. The archons were no longer comfortably accountable to the Areopagus, whose members by custom came only from the upper two classes and in which they would themselves sit for life. Now, like all other officials, their actions were subject to review by the Council which could bring them before the Assembly for an accounting. As in all democracies, the prestige and pomp of office became something less and service to the community something more.

In a technical sense, the eclipse of the Areopagus was the end of aristocratic power in Athens and the beginning of a truly popular democracy. But in actual practice this was not so. Throughout the middle years of the fifth century, until after the death of Pericles, the Athenians depended exclusively on aristocrats for leadership. There was never in this period another commoner like Themistocles who had managed to come to power during the Persian crisis in the 480's without the backing of one of the old families. Aristocrats like Aristides, Cimon and Pericles were committed to the democracy and accepted its ideals. These men of the highest social standing offered their leadership to those who had not had their advantages of wealth and education. In order to lead, however, they had to be popular and Cimon's generosity in allowing anyone to stop by his estate and pick what fruit they would was an example, not only of good-heartedness but of excellent public relations. It gave rise, in addition, to a topical joke about how Cimon paid the citizens out of his own pocket, while Pericles, with his occasional boondoggling, paid them out of theirs.

Neither man, however, abandoned all principle or prudence in an effort to win power. Like Solon, they had disavowed the narrow perspective of their class, but, also like Solon, they were unwilling simply to cater to the desires of the populous poor. Each of these aristocrats conceived of his role in a democratic society as that of a responsible leader who advised the Assembly to follow what he thought was the best course. Cimon, in particular, supported policies which were more in agreement with the thinking of the aristocracy than with the citizenry at large, yet he was successful on a number of occasions in convincing the Assembly that he had the right idea. It was in this conclave of all citizens that the final decisions were made.

In modern democracies, the collective judgment of the people is registered only from time to time, usually every two or four years. In Athens, in theory, all of the citizens came together in an Assembly which met about once every eight or nine days. They could, if they cared to do so, maintain an almost day-to-day control over current developments. In practice, however, it would appear that only the excitement of an emergency or the appeal of an anticipated clash between popular orators would attract a large attendance. When only routine business was being considered, it was probably too much to assume that farmers and dock workers would put down what they were doing in order to attend. Even men with leisure time were often reluctant to break off an interesting conversation to hear a debate on a bill which did not interest them. Furthermore, it might be supposed that during the period of Pericles' greatest influence, the continued acquiescence of the Assembly in his policies was a further reason for not bothering to attend.

It is not known how many citizens actually assembled on an average day. Using our previous estimate of 40,000 citizens (which is low as such guesses go), the requirement of a 6,000 vote to ostracize someone gives an idea of what was considered a reasonable showing.

A meeting of the Assembly was an extraordinary phenomenon since major questions of domestic and foreign policy were placed directly before the citizens for a decision. Moreover, although proposals were usually introduced by the leaders of the various factions, it was possible for any citizen to take an idea to the Council of 500 and ask that it be presented to the Assembly. This right was matched by a strong deterrent against irresponsible legislation because any law could be challenged on the grounds that it was unconstitutional. In such an instance, the man who had proposed it in the first place was tried before the Assembly according to a device known as the *graphe paranomon*. If found guilty he could be fined or even executed, depending on the seriousness of his intention to deceive and the temper of the citizenry at the moment. On the other hand, hasty charges of unconstitutionality were discouraged because at least one-fifth of the votes had to be cast in favor of the "prosecutor" or he would be liable to a fine himself. As with the practice of ostracism, the *graphe paranomon* served a useful purpose, but it was also open to abuse and in time, like ostracism, became a political tool. This was especially so in later times when demagogues commanded a majority of the votes in the Assembly and used their power ruthlessly.

In the best days of the democracy, "government by the people" was realized as closely as it could be, given the limitation of who "the people" were. Pericles in his *Funeral Oration* stressed the importance which the Athenians attached to freedom of speech and the right to dissent. The requirement that every man be given a chance to speak in order that all opinions might be heard is the strongest link between the Athenian system and every democracy that has ever existed. Yet, despite Pericles' optimistic statement, the open forum has always been fraught with aggravation. To the well-informed, the empty mouthings of ignorant if well-winded men are at best exasperating; to the underprivileged, the arguments of their more affluent and articulate opponents are mere words to disguise some selfish motive. And there are always those who test the patience of free men by pleading for tolerance in order to subvert freedom and institute some more perfect plan of their own. Midst the delays and confusion of the democratic process, such men constantly point to the inadequacies of the process for getting anything done. Yet the weaknesses of a democracy are always the best guarantee that it is intact, for no other system allows such inefficiency. Democracy recognizes that whenever men of differing temperaments, experiences and education are actually free to follow their own ideas and interests there will be a scramble.

During the early years of the full democracy in Athens, the Assembly called upon a number of generals to carry out its orders, including Myronides, Charitimides, Leocrates and Tolmides. In time, however, Pericles emerged as the most consistently popular among them and after the death of Ephialtes he became the chief spokesman for democratic interests. His reputation as the best orator of his time did not mean that his voice always carried the vote, but Thucydides says that as long as the citizenry listened to him everything went along fairly well. This praise carried with it an implication that Pericles may actually have been responsible for a weakness in the Athenian system. It suggests that the citizens had not been educated to make good judgments for themselves, but rather to rely on a man of destiny, who would, as if by magic, continue to supply an endless series of victories and a greater prosperity. Such a state of mind left them prey to demagogues, who, unlike Pericles, would promise them anything as a means to power.

A more serious accusation, often voiced by his contemporaries, was the charge that Pericles had set in motion certain tendencies which eventually undermined the democracy altogether. The innovation which caused the most controversy was a proposal which he passed through the Assembly in 451, providing for the payment of jurors. There was a good argument for an allotment, no matter how small it might be. If democracy meant that all citizens should participate equally in the government, and if it was admitted that men with money and time to spare would have more opportunity to do so than others, then some kind of subsidy, at least for the sake of the destitute, seemed advisable. As far as Pericles was concerned, the payments were considered a kind of poor relief, especially for the elderly. There appeared to be good reasons at the time for what he did, yet good reasons today may permit bad precedents to be set for tomorrow. Although Pericles was praised by many, he was sharply criticized by a few. The critics argued that if men were paid for public services they would no longer consider them duties which patriotic citizens should perform for the good of all, but rather as a means of gaining something for themselves. Eventually they would want to be paid for everything they did, including attendance at the Assembly. This was what in fact happened. Not in Pericles' time, for then it would have been unthinkable. Within a century, however, citizens were indeed paid to attend the Assembly.

The issue of pay for jurors was important because there were so many of them. Every year, six thousand citizens over the age of thirty were chosen by lot, six hundred from each tribe, to compose the Heliaea from which juries, large and small, were selected to hear individual cases. Customarily, 501 citizens would make up a jury; larger juries up to 1501 were not unknown. A simple majority decided a case, and the safety in numbers reflected the usual Athenian confidence in public opinion. It also made bribery or any kind of illegal pressure difficult. As an additional safeguard, each jury was composed of men chosen daily by lot. No one knew who was to serve on what jury until the hour was at hand. Yet, no matter what the number of jurors, or how they were selected, there was no insurance against the Athenians being moved rather frequently by emotional appeals, or basing their judgment of a man, not on the facts of the case, but on how his actions had affected the best interests of the state.

Recourse to Athenian courts could be risky, therefore, not because of outside influences but because of the character of the jury itself. The jury was all important. The archon who conducted the proceedings maintained order and saw that certain procedures were followed, but he did not perform the judicial functions we associate with judges today. Charges and the evidence supporting them were presented in writing and then the jury listened to oral testimony supporting or denying the validity of the written statement.

Both the defendant, who spoke in his own defense, and the "prosecutor" were private persons. Their speeches, however, were often written for them by experienced professionals. These men were not lawyers in the sense that they would find and cite precedents, because Athenian juries decided each case on its own merits without recourse to any previous interpretations of the law. They were specialists in preparing effective speeches which pled their clients' cases according to the law and were also calculated to appeal to the sympathies or the prejudices of an average jury. Their preoccupation with the latter point earned some of them an unsavory reputation.

Given the proclivity of the Athenians for argumentation and invective, we may suppose that most of them joyfully attended and served in their courts without the added attraction of Pericles' small payment. Moreover, they would not be listening to the trials and tribulations of strangers. One speech which has been preserved was prepared for a trial which had all the spice of a tabloid feature story. It was charged that the children of a certain Neaera, posing as the wife of a prominent citizen, were illegitimate because they were born while she was still a prostitute. The defense insisted that the woman was only the mistress of this man and that the children were his by a former marriage. Athens was a small town and the dirty linen which was washed in court were the secrets of friends and neighbors. This has never been a losing attraction.

## The Pastime of Politics

The Athenian democracy was a government by amateurs—an informal operation, like that of a small town in which everyone knows the councilmen and the mayor keeps the budget in his hat. The city was not beset with bureaucratic experts such as seem so necessary to the conduct of a modern democracy and are so chilling to its spirit. In Athens, there were inefficiencies, delays and petty arguments, but men dealt with one another and not with mimeographed forms.

The poets joined freely in the pastime of politics by launching scathing attacks on certain prominent figures. The plays of Aristophanes show us how a talented playwright, chosen to compete in the annual festival, used his opportunity to present the city-wide audience with an uninhibited attack on the public leaders he roundly disliked. The Athenians treated one another with a brutal frankness. At times they must have been telling the truth, but the atmosphere was conducive to muckraking. Since there was no elaborate book-keeping of state funds, or any formal budget presented, it was always possible to claim that an official had misappropriated money. Pericles himself was faced once with this charge, althought he came as near to being a sacred cow as the Athenian temperament would permit. Even so, the poets delighted in making references to his head which apparently was ill-shaped and reminded some of them of a turnip. What it really looked like is hard to say for the surviving portrait busts show him with his helmet on, and appropriately so, for he always wore it.

Even in his heyday, Pericles was unable to keep his friends from being prosecuted on all manner of charges and, as Plutarch has it, they were in fact harassed because of him. His good friend Phidias, the sculptor, was accused of pilfering some gold assigned for a statue of Athena. In addition, certain sensitive persons took exception to the fact that he placed his own likeness and that of Pericles among the warriors fighting the Amazons on the goddess' shield. To our way of thinking, he was no more presumptuous than Rembrandt who placed himself at the foot of the Cross. Yet Phidias was sent to jail, for "sacrilege" presumably, and Pericles had to exert himself to get him out and away from the city. Even Aspasia, Pericles' second wife, was charged with impiety, and there is a tradition that Pericles shed tears when pleading for her before the jury. Probably not, but she was acquitted and an impassioned plea on his part may very likely have accounted for it.

## Conflicts at Home and Abroad

Many men viewed the Athenian democracy with alarm from a distance, and it was not popular with everybody at home either. In Athens, there were always critics who bitterly opposed the transfer of power to the plebeians. Such men were mostly unreconciled aristocrats who banded together in small cliques which have often been called Clubs, although they were not really formal organizations. Before the demise of the Areopagus, these informal groups had considerable political power—and even afterwards they supplied the spokesmen for the old-line aristocracy. Naturally, this faction opposed the policies of the democratic leaders who promoted Athenian naval and commercial supremacy, for these were the means by which men like Pericles won the support of the rowers and the working classes. Nor was it only the political implications which bothered them; they were anxious lest Athenian ambitions crowd other cities to the point where there would be a general war. These aristocrats whose estates were outside the city walls had nothing to win and everything to lose if Attica was invaded. Their personal concern was justified. What they feared was to come upon them during the Peloponnesian War.

Other aristocrats in Athens, while not opposed to the democracy itself, were genuinely concerned about the welfare of all of Greece. They agreed with Cimon, who advised that the Athenians should remain on good terms with Sparta because these old allies could withstand any future invader and could also maintain the peace amongst the Greeks themselves. But the Athenians had other plans. Even in the best times, the growing population of the city and chronic unemployment made the founding of new colonies and the expansion of overseas trade desirable. Conflicting purposes knotted the problem. Cimon, in effect, asked the Athenians to scale down their own ambitions in order to give Sparta reassurance that Athens was not really aiming at hegemony over the whole of Greece. Yet his keynote was one of caution, and in the long run this idea made little appeal to men who believed that their success so far had been due to daring.

The hope of any permanent alliance with Sparta was doomed perhaps from the start. It was too much to expect that the other cities would let the Spartans forget the dangers inherent in the continued growth of Athenian power. Corinth in particular had much to lose if the Athenians sought to dominate the sea routes to Sicily and southern Italy in the same way that they controlled the Aegean. Corinth had of course been replaced long ago by Athens as the major exporter of pottery to the west, but her commercial interests were still in a westerly direction and she had valuable connections with Syracuse, her prize colony, which had grown rich and powerful on its own.

Besides Corinth, there was Thebes. The determination of this city to dominate Boeotia caused smaller towns, particularly those on the border of Attica, to turn to Athens for help and the Athenians had often lent them aid.

Under the circumstances, any ambassador who carried a complaint of some state against Athens would find a sympathetic ear in Sparta, Corinth, or Thebes. It is not surprising then that, about 460, the Athenians were quick to seize a chance to check all three.

It was about this time that Megara, the dominant city of the Isthmus, was threatened by Corinth and asked the Athenian Assembly for help. Megara received it in the form of an alliance which was in effect a declaration of war against the Corinthians. The opportunities were too good for Athens to refuse. She could not only rebuff Corinth, but by controlling the Isthmus she could also close the land bridge between Sparta and Thebes. Furthermore, Megara owned two strategic ports, one on the Saronic Gulf (Nisaea) and one on the Corinthian Gulf (Pegae).

The Megarian position had always been precarious. The city was located about a mile from the Saronic coast and needed a means of protecting her lifeline to the sea in order to avoid being starved out. The Athenians, with their usual initiative, immediately corrected this fatal weakness by building a walled corridor to the port of Nisaea. Indeed, the advantages of this solution were so obvious that within a short period of time they would begin to erect their own "long walls" at home.

Corinth's suspicions of Athens had probably been as deep-rooted and as long-standing as any other city's, although there had been friendly relations between them from time to time. Now, in two bitter engagements the Athenians twice routed them from the Megarid, and their suspicions gave way to a feeling which Thucydides bluntly called hatred.

It was only a matter of time before the Megarians would share their attitude. They had been saved from Corinth and their new ties with Athens were profitable commercially, but their walls continued to be garrisoned by Athenians. Moreover, their protectors made it clear that they intended to stay. The harbor at Pegae provided Athens at last with a "window" to the west, and subsequent moves at the other end of the Corinthian Gulf confirmed the intention of Athens to stand guard over that waterway. In the long run Megara received more help than she had bargained for. She learned in the process, as others had before her, that a friendly embrace from Athens could also be a squeeze.

In the years ahead, the Spartans, while anxious about the growth of Athenian power, never seemed as aroused as the Corinthians or the Megarians because there was never actually any direct interference with their primary interests. Because of Spartan indecisiveness, the Athenians had no trouble in completing their long walls to the harbor at Piraeus by 456. From then on, so long as the Athenian navy remained intact, the city could not be starved out. If Athens were to be defeated, it would have to be at sea. That was where she was strongest, and it would take some time. It took fifty years.

During the 450's, the Athenians felt secure enough at home to engage in an overseas campaign on behalf of the Egyptians who were in revolt against their Persian masters. The chance to embarrass the Persians was appealing, but the real reason for Athenian intervention was probably to win access to the plentiful wheat available in Egypt. Thucydides says that they gained nothing and lost a great many ships. Rarely, in the course of her best years, had the calculations of Athens gone so far awry.

An obvious consequence of this disaster was renewed anxiety about Persian aggression in the Aegean.

When Cimon returned from his ten years' exile in 451, only three years after the Egyptian debacle, there could not have been a better atmosphere for renewal of his peace-in-Greece policy. It was therefore through his good offices that a five-year truce with Sparta was arranged. Whenever Athens and Sparta came to terms, so did everybody else. Even Argos felt compelled to enter into a thirty-year alliance with her old enemy Sparta.

In 449, Cimon was again the commander of a fleet sailing against the Persians, but his comeback was shortlived. He died during the siege of Citium and his previous triumph at the Eurymedon in 466 was to stand in the record as his last and greatest victory. The Greeks went on to whip the Persian forces decisively at Salamis, the chief city of ancient Cyprus, but not without suffering sizeable losses of their own. This battle was followed by a standoff during which the Persians and the Athenians worked out an agreement on spheres of influence. This "understanding" has been called the Peace of Callias, because an Athenian soldier-diplomat by that name visited Artaxerxes in 449. However, historians were still in disagreement a hundred years later as to whether there had been anything more to his visit than conversation. Whatever happened, the standoff became a period of peace which lasted for forty years.

The peace of course was with Persia and not among the Greeks themselves. The old ill-feelings continued and some of them were well justified.

## An Emerging Empire

Fear of a sudden attack by the Persians had supplied the pretext for the transfer of the treasury of the Delian League from Delos to

Athens in 454. Obviously, while weakened at sea, the fortunes of the League would be safer there. Under the circumstances, it would have been difficult for any of the contributing states to object and, as a matter of fact, Samos first proposed the move. Athens had again an excellent excuse for a change which in the future could be counted among the other small injuries by which the Delian League was killed—or rather metamorphosed into an Athenian Empire. The freedom of cities or men is most easily encroached on with patience, step by step, a little at a time.

There were economic as well as military ties between Athens and the allies. The relationship with Phaselis has become better known than the others through the chance survival of an inscription which reveals the contents of a commercial treaty. This agreement is known to us because it was customary for the Athenians to inscribe such a treaty on a slab of marble (*stele*) and set it up on the Acropolis, with the cost being paid by the other friendly party. Some of these inscriptions, or copies of them, have survived.

If some members of the League were contemplating a return to the old easy independence, a crucial clause in the text of this treaty shows how differently Athens was thinking. The evidence is clear that she intended to use her powerful advantages to win concessions from those who wanted to do business with her. It was stated that in the event of litigation over a contract made at Athens between an Athenian and a Phaselitan, the suit was to be tried in Athens before the archon polemarch who was in charge of matters concerning foreigners. Because of the preponderance of contracts which would be closed at Athens rather than in the smaller city, this was a commitment of far-reaching significance. There were side issues. The expense of traveling to Athens was a burden placed on the outsider. The chances of a foreigner in an Athenian court could by no means be considered fifty-fifty. However, such matters of principle were not likely to have bothered the shopkeepers in Athens, or those with room and board to offer. These people were among the staunchest supporters of such one-sided arrangements, as if those coming to Athens were happy conventioners instead of disgruntled litigants.

The insistence of the Athenians that their courts alone have jurisdiction over certain cases involving the allies was to become a sharp issue in the years ahead. But it was only one issue among many, including the crucial matter of Athenian intervention in the domestic affairs of the allied states. The aristocrats everywhere remained obdurately hostile to Athens. She was the champion of the popular will. Beginning with Naxos in the early 460's, Athens took it upon herself to establish democratic governments among her allies, and also to keep a close eye on their operations. The degree of control which she retained varied from place to place. In some cities, troops were garrisoned to ensure that order was maintained, even though the presence of a powerful military commander was hardly conducive to self-government.

An extant inscription shows the kind of terms Athens imposed on her allied states. In this agreement with Chalcis, an oath appears which was taken by the Council of 500 at Athens, promising to protect certain minimal rights of the Chalcidians in return for good behavior. The officials of Chalcis were obligated to betray any fellow citizens suspected of subversion, lest they be implicated themselves. Those holding office were required to swear that they would inform the Athenians about any person who was working to upset the *status quo*.

Certain actions by the Athenians affected the prerogatives even of those states which retained their autonomy. For instance, the close commercial dealings between Athens and her allies made it desirable that coinage and weights and measures be standardized. Athenian silver coins were declared henceforth to be the common currency and, except for a few cities which handled gold, all local currencies were abolished. This was a practical move but it was also a serious blow to allied morale, for any interference with old customs cut deep.

Even more tangible evidence of Athenian intentions was the increased use of a special kind of military colony called a cleruchy, a listening and watching post placed here and there through the Aegean area. The cleruchy, which takes its name from *kleros* meaning land allotment, differed from the ordinary type of colony in that its members retained full Athenian citizenship. It was not an independent settlement, but as much a part of Athens as if it were in Attica. Under Pericles, as trouble with the allies increased, so did the number of cleruchies. It need hardly be added that the appropriation of good land for these bases, whether on Euboea, Andros, or the Chersonese, became another issue in the long list of allied complaints.

By the middle of the fifth century these complaints had become permanent. In the subsequent resolvement of the "Persian question," the allies not only failed to regain their freedom but it became apparent that they never would—short of help from Sparta.

The cost of subsidizing full employment, the payments to the jurors and the numerous state officials, plus the expense of the army

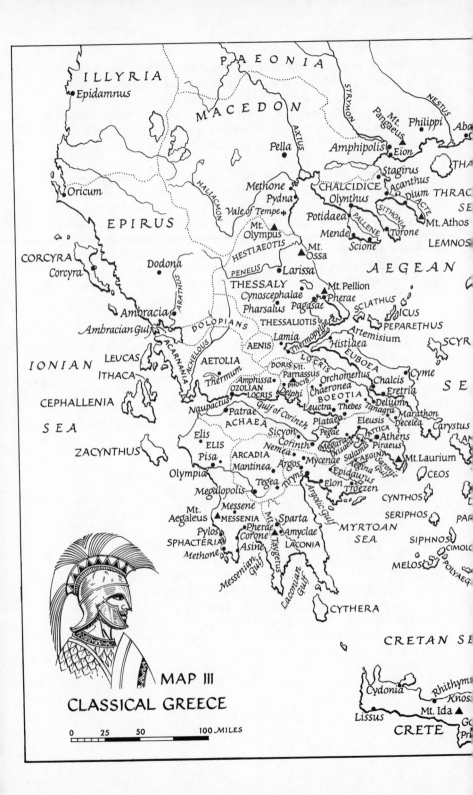

MAP III

CLASSICAL GREECE

0    25    50         100 MILES

PONTUS EUXINUS
(BLACK SEA)

THRACE

AGRIANES

BOSPORUS

Heraclea Pontica

HEBRUS

nea
esembria

Selymbria
Perinthus

Byzantium
Chalcedon

Astacus

Aenus

PROPONTIS

BITHYNIA

THRACE Cardia

Cius

Chersonese

HELLESPONT

Parium

Cyzicus

Dascylium

SANGARIUS

Aegospotami
Sestos
Abydos
Cape Cynossema
Sigeum
Troy (Ilium)
NEDOS

Lampsacus

GRANICUS

RHYNDACUS

PHRYGIA

SCAMANDER

PHRYGIA

TROAS

Adramyttium

MYSIA

Assus

MECESTUS

Mytilene

Pergamum

CAICUS

SBOS

AEOLIS

LYDIA

PHRYGIA

ARGINUSAE IS.

Cyme

HERMUS

Phocaea

Mt.
Sipylus

Magnesia

Ipsus

Erythrae

OS

Smyrna

Sardis

Chios

Clazomenae

IONIA

CAYSTER

Teos

Colophon

Notium

Celaenae

Ephesus

Magnesia

Tralles

SAMOS

Samos

MAEANDER

CARIA

Priene

Mt. Mycale

Alabanda

ONOS

LADE I.

Miletus

CARIA

PISIDIA

Mylasa

LEROS

Halicarnassus

AXOS

COS

Cos

Caunus

AMORGOS

Cnidus

TYPALAEA

Telmessus

LYCIA

Phaselis

ANAPHE

RA

Camirus

Rhodes
Ialysus

Xanthus

RHODES

Lindus

CARPATHOS

Dicte
icte
ierapytna

Praesus

SAM! H. BRYANT

and navy, all added up to more than Athens could afford. The obvious answer was to use the money in the Delian treasury for domestic expenses. As a result of the "peace" with Persia, however, the regular contributions from various member states had stopped coming. So, by 448, when the Athenians used force to make the collections, the allies had in fact become satellites. The Delian League was dead.

With such a solution, Pericles was able to finance a government in which nearly a third of the citizens, including military personnel, were on the payroll, and also to launch a great building program and start a "war chest." The two faces of the city were now plain. Athens was a popular democracy ruling an unpopular empire.

Pericles insisted that the strength and prosperity of Athens was in fact good for all of Greece, even though not all of the Greek states had the good sense to see it. The other states must recognize that if they were divided and quarreling they were lost. If Athens had to cut a corner here or there for the sake of unity, it was for the benefit of all. When a local boundary dispute between Samos and Miletus erupted into a small war in 441–440, Pericles demanded that Athenian arbitration be accepted. Samos was severely punished for refusing to accede. Bringing her to terms meant a heavy loss of young men. (Pericles said that the spring had been taken out of the year.) Regardless of the cost, the Athenians continued to insist that there must be a centralizing, peace-keeping force in Greece, and they chose themselves for the job. To support their claim they could point to the evidence of Spartan inadequacy, which had been especially obvious after the Persian invasions earlier in the century.

There was some practical truth in the Athenian position, a truth which died hard. A century later, when the Greeks were faced with invasion from Macedonia, the famed orator Demosthenes was still using this argument for Athenian leadership. However, the rest of the Greek states, with a few notable exceptions, were never willing to accept Athenian hegemony. Nor was it because they did not really understand the Athenians. Earlier, many of them had yielded to Persia and others would later give in to Macedon rather than be ruled from Athens. They had to know the Athenians well in order to feel that way.

## The Thirty Years' Peace

The Athenian navy gave Athens control of the Aegean but her fortunes on the mainland were always shaky. In the autumn of 447, serious trouble arose when the oligarchical interests in various Boeotian cities overthrew the democratic governments which were friendly to Athens and repudiated the Athenian alliance. The Assembly at Athens underestimated the danger. Tolmides received the Assembly's approval for a campaign in Boeotia which Pericles strongly opposed as being too risky. He was right; it was, and the Athenians met with a severe setback. Tolmides was killed at the battle of Coronea and most of his men were captured. In order to secure the return of the prisoners, the Assembly was forced to disavow any further Athenian interference in Boeotia.

Any Athenian reverse was encouraging to the long-suffering, tribute-bearing states. In the summer of 446, there was a serious defection in Euboea and Pericles led the expedition to put down the rebellion. While he was there, the Megarians took the opportunity to rid themselves of their Athenian "protectors." With the help of the Corinthians, they overwhelmed the garrison within the city and wiped it out, although the ports of Nisaea and Pegae remained in Athenian hands. But now, the five-year truce with Sparta which Cimon had arranged in 451 was at an end, and the Spartans were again on the march. The uprisings in Euboea and Megara and the Spartan move toward Attica gave Pericles a severe test. It was like him to have solved it by diplomacy rather than to have risked the military odds.

Exactly how Pericles maneuvered the Spartans out of Attica was never made public. It was only known that they turned around shortly after he hurried back from Euboea and went home without a fight. It seems reasonable to assume that Pericles was able to convince the Spartan King Pleistoanax that Athens would soon agree to a long-term pact giving ample protection to both sides. This in fact happened during the following winter. There was also an item of ten talents which was recorded on Pericles' expense account and never explained. The matter was allowed to rest at Athens, but not at Sparta where the about-face at Eleusis was very embarrassing. The exile of the young king and his military aide left no doubt that the ephors thought that a bribe had been taken.

Athenian subject states, which had looked to Sparta for help, had once again been left to Athenian mercy. In the case of Histiaea, none was forthcoming. Pericles returned to Euboea, scored a smashing victory, and then forced the Histiaeans to evacuate their land and seek homes elsewhere. In their place he established an Athenian cleruchy.

The Athenians continued in the mastery of their empire; at the same time, Pericles' willingness to compromise in matters of direct concern to Sparta made the signing of the Thirty Years' Peace possible. Athens, while holding on to Aegina and Naupactus, agreed to abandon her interests on the Isthmus and so gave up the Megarian ports of Nisaea and Pegae. She also terminated her alliances with Troezen and Achaea. In essence, this meant that she recognized the Spartan domination of the Peloponnesus. In return, Sparta agreed not to interfere with the Athenian maritime empire. Each side also promised to negotiate any problems which might arise on the borders of their separate worlds. It was co-existence. However, only the Spartans seemed really satisfied with the arrangement. The Corinthians could not be happy so long as Athens remained entrenched at Naupactus which guarded the exit from the Corinthian Gulf. Nor were the Athenian citizens pleased to see the fruits of many endeavors vanish overnight. It was this timely and realistic, but unpopular, treaty which caused the temporary eclipse of Pericles' power in 444.

Pericles knew that Athens must expect setbacks in the long run, but, as Thucydides observes, the continued prosperity and success of the Athenian citizens left them unprepared for any reverses. Cautious forethought is not easy to teach to men who are for the first time enjoying a better life.

When Pericles was re-elected in 443, his chief opponent was an aristocrat named Thucydides, customarily called the "son of Melesias" to distinguish him from the historian of the same name. As the successor of Cimon, Thucydides was the spokesman in Athens for those who deplored the "imperialistic" policies which invariably involved Athens in conflicts with her neighbors. Now that Pericles had achieved a working agreement with Sparta, there was less for them to complain about—but that did not mean they were quiet. During the same years, Athens had embarked on a building program by which the Acropolis was to be beautified by the addition of new temples and an impressive entrance gate. As Thucydides and his friends often observed, the construction was to be financed with other peoples' money. The use for this purpose of the tribute collected forcibly from the "allies" was admittedly a touchy question, but Pericles did not back down. He boldly told the citizenry that the allied states were paying for protection, and, since they were receiving it, Athens could do as she pleased with the money. The citizenry must have believed him. Thucydides was ostracized in 443 and Pericles, the champion of the democracy, viewed this action as a strong vote of confidence.

During his remaining fourteen years in office, Pericles continued to strengthen the navy and to build up a substantial surplus in the state treasury. He was known to have remarked that peace could mean valuable time to Athens, and it is possible that he always knew there would be a final reckoning. However, it is not necessary to think that he wanted war simply because he was determined to be prepared for it. When the war finally came in 431, he was again the center of controversy. His enemies claimed that his policies during the peace had provoked the new hostilities. His friends insisted that he had only been taking precautions. The Corcyrean affair was a case in point. In 433, Corinth and her rich colony Corcyra were again embroiled with each other and Pericles intervened on behalf of the Corcyreans. This island was a strategic base commanding the sea lanes to the west and it had a fleet second only to that of Athens, so that there were good reasons for Pericles to risk trouble by blocking a Corinthian victory. It has often been suggested that if Pericles felt there was going to be a war anyway, this was the right move to make; for it would keep the Corcyrean navy out of Corinthian hands. Whatever his reasons, the Corcyrean imbroglio was one of the incidents which led to the outbreak of the Peloponnesian War in 431. Two years after the war began, Pericles died. He was about sixty-five years old. The young Athenians who carried on the war and lost it were the men of the third generation.

## Pericles: In Public and In Private

Pericles was the most talked-about man of his times, yet little remains to be read about him today. The only extant biography was written by Plutarch, who lived five hundred years later. Even so, at that time there were more sources available on Pericles than there are now. Most of this source material had been written by aristocrats who were strongly opposed to Periclean policies. Two of the three prose writers used by Plutarch were foreigners. Ion of Chios, a wealthy traveler, gave a more favorable picture of Cimon than he did of Pericles, whom he seems to have considered pretentious, perhaps even overbearing. Stesimbrotus, coming to Athens from much abused Thasos, could hardly have been expected to be any friendlier, and in fact he was the chief source of the scurrilous stories about Pericles which Plutarch found so "out of character." In any event, since we are almost totally dependent on Plutarch's quotations for our knowledge of these accounts, there is not much known about Pericles' personal life beyond what that well-read gentleman chose to preserve.

Pericles was about as well-born as a man could be. His father, Xanthippus, was a noted general, active in the Persian Wars, and remembered for his prosecution of Miltiades. His mother, Agariste, was the niece of Cleisthenes, who has been called the founder of the Athenian democracy.

As a youth in the inner circle of Athenian society, Pericles became acquainted with certain leading intellectuals of the day. They were his teachers and in time his closest friends. Plutarch reports that their influence on Pericles was always viewed with suspicion, especially in conservative quarters. Among Pericles' associates was the Ionian philosopher Anaxagoras, who spoke of *Nous*, or mind, as being the source of all order. If he did not actually deny the existence of the popular gods, he certainly ignored them.

Although Pericles rarely expressed any radical opinions in public, Anaxagoras' naturalistic views did apparently make a strong impression on him. On one occasion, which Plutarch mentions, Pericles went aboard a ship ready to sail at a time when the sun was eclipsed. Those with him were greatly afraid, but he held up his cloak in front of a man's eyes and explained that what had caused the darkness was only some larger object in front of the sun. In seeking to allay the superstitions of those around him he was attacking ignorance, not religion, a point which can be missed by those who confuse the two.

The question whether Pericles' role as the champion of the common man was adopted by conviction or for convenience is similar to the disputes over the motives of better known figures of recent fame, and is no more resoluble. Unless, of course, common sense suggests that it was something of both.

Through all that was reported about Pericles there ran two refrains: one which praised his reserved bearing, intelligence and good judgment; and the other which pointed to his compromising, even perhaps unprincipled, efforts to win popular support. These variant characteristics, however, seem to have been well blended by a consummate politician who kept his own counsel and knew exactly what he was doing at all times.

There were other reasons for Pericles' success besides his skill as a politician. His style of speaking won for him the nickname "Olympian." On or off the platform his demeanor was appealing. Aristotle once observed that if a man kept his actions slow, his voice low and his words controlled, he would command respect. This was Pericles. He made an uncommonly good impression upon the Athenian citizens. He did not appear too frequently in public and almost never accepted invitations to private parties. Moreover, when he did make an appearance there was a presence about him which discouraged familiarity. Plutarch says he planned it that way. Obviously, Pericles knew that dignity and high-mindedness are best guarded by a distance which lends enchantment.

However, there are at least two standards of greatness for a man. If measured by his accomplishments in the glorification of Athens and the management of her affairs, then Pericles was great. If on the other hand the appellation demands quieter qualities, including a sense of graciousness and helpfulness toward those of less ability who could not serve his purposes or his pride, then maybe Pericles missed the mark. He was greatly admired by the Athenian people whom he served so well and whose support raised him to pre-eminent heights in the Greek world. Yet his own family was estranged and his eldest son apparently hated him. Undeniably a success where all the world could see, Pericles appears to have been a failure in private. This was not because of his divorce which merely ended a loveless marriage. Given the social customs of the times, his casual relationship with his wife was not unusual.

Pericles might well have settled for the marriage he had, except that he fell in love with the beautiful Aspasia from Miletus who, during his middle life, served not only his emotions but also his desire for intellectual companionship. In her native Ionia, women had a better chance for some education outside the home than they did in Athens, and Aspasia took full advantage of this greater freedom. She became a knowledgeable cosmopolite who could live anywhere. In a man's world, this meant that she was a courtesan. In fact, it was said that in Athens before she married Pericles she had used her house as a school in which young women were trained to emulate her dubious role in a male society. Afterwards, when living with Pericles, she was accused of exercising undue influence over his thinking, especially where the interests of her native Miletus were concerned. She was always a topic of gossip. Plutarch, in his biography of Pericles, repeats some of it but he also stresses her wide knowledge of public affairs and her brilliance as a conversationalist. His claims seem justified because Socrates enjoyed talking to Aspasia and he was known to be careful in such matters.

Pericles did not marry Aspasia until he was fifty or so and their son, his namesake, was only a boy when his father died. It was Pericles' relations with the sons of his first marriage, Xanthippus and

Paralus, which suggest that his well-known aloof demeanor may have helped to disguise a lack of generosity. When they were young, Pericles left these boys to tutors and servants as was, and is, the custom sometimes of busy men of affairs. But when they were grown he paid very little attention to them, and this was not customary.

Pericles' unbending attitude toward his sons was as though their inadequacies were a personal offense to him. Because Xanthippus was the elder, first in line for his father's mantle, he especially felt the sting. This young man was probably less resentful of criticisms than he was of the fact that his father ignored him altogether, a subtle means of telling him that his company and conversation were of no value. Plutarch reports that Xanthippus with bitterness revealed unknown incidents in the past life of his father and comments which Pericles had made in private conversations with his intimates. It was obvious that his father's neglect had wounded him very deeply.

Plutarch accepts the tradition that Xanthippus was a profligate and so perhaps unworthy of sympathy, but he tells another story which again raises a question about Pericles' true character. This one concerns the statesman's old friend and teacher Anaxagoras. It seems that Pericles had become too engrossed in his own affairs to be aware that the elderly philosopher had become destitute. When he heard about it, he of course rushed to his side voicing his solicitations. Yet Plutarch adds the casual observation that his concern was not so much for Anaxagoras' plight as for fear that he would be denied the advice of a sage. It may be that humility was another quality of greatness which Pericles lacked.

Plutarch's life of Pericles has value because it allows for some reading between the lines. There are weaknesses balanced against strengths. However, Plutarch's obvious admiration of the man shines through in the scene where Pericles lay dying. Tactfully wearing the amulet which the women had placed around his neck, he listened to those assembled recount his virtues. Finally, he spoke up in his own behalf and said that he wished only to be remembered as a man who had never used his enormous power for any selfish purpose, such as revenge against a private enemy. Like Solon, he had resisted the corrupting temptations of office and of this he was proud, for it was not an easy thing to do. To Plutarch, a cultured gentleman living during the affluent days of the Roman Empire, it was a noble valedictory.

Thucydides' *History of the Peloponnesian War* is the only surviving prose work of the fifth century which mentions Pericles. Although

Thucydides knew Pericles and wrote about him not long after he died, he did not speak of him in a personal sense, nor did he mention the contemporary works of Ion or Stesimbrotus even to refute them. He treated Pericles entirely in the light of his political and military capacities. It is unlikely that the great statesman will ever escape Thucydides' blunt evaluation of his role in the Athenian democracy. He states that Pericles managed the citizens for their own good. When they became over-confident, he tried to dispel their arrogance. When they were discouraged, he sought to inspire them and his famed *Funeral Oration* was delivered on such an occasion. This masterful panegyric for the first fallen in the Peloponnesian War displayed the aging statesman's unswerving devotion to Athens and her free institutions.

In the years gone by, Pericles had held himself aloof and majestic. Now he could comfort the Athenians, for men are consoled by those they respect. His fellow citizens were reassured as he reviewed the great deeds of their ancestors and the wondrous advantages of their democracy. His dignity, intelligence and courage embodied all that was Athenian. As long as he was with them, nothing had changed. Yet it really had, and when he was gone they knew it.

## Public Places:
## Some Private Questions

**X**  In the fifth century the Athenian Acropolis was an impressive sanctuary sacred to the gods, especially glorious Athena. It has since become a shrine of Western civilization, a symbol of the greatness of the Greeks. Without Pericles, it might never have been so glorious. He envisioned his native city as a model community of freedom and beauty and he coaxed his fellow citizens into acceptance of their destiny. At the same time, they were no more enthusiastic about spending their own money than any other people. It was their willingness to authorize the use of the tribute from subject states for local purposes which made them partners with Pericles in the Golden Age.

From the earliest times until the sixth century the Acropolis was a citadel for the open countryside. Its usefulness as a place of refuge is readily apparent. Not only would it have been very difficult to scale its sides, but an enemy could not have approached from any direction without being seen. Peisistratus ordered walls to be built around Athens and thereafter the Acropolis was the chief religious center of the enclosed city. There is still a sense of peace and serenity for those who stand today on the heights of this celebrated rock and look down upon the mundane world below. The lasting impression is of a shrine, a sublime expression of religious dedication.

In 480, the buildings and statuary of the Acropolis were destroyed by the Persians. Significantly, Athena's own temple which Peisistratus had improved was lost. Pericles promoted restoration on a grand scale.

War and weather in league with time have left the Periclean buildings broken and hollow. It is tempting to imagine how they might have looked originally, all parts put back together, the whole neatly balanced—but the Athenians never saw all of them finished either. Most of the south wing of the massive Propylaea or gateway to the Acropolis is missing today. It always was. Like other buildings in the master plan this structure was never completed. When the Peloponnesian War broke out in 431 it was one of the projects affected by a sharp cut-back in expenditures (Pl. 47).

*Pl. 47 The Propylaea, from the west. The temple of* Athena Nike *is at the upper right.*

In essence, the Propylaea was the superstructure of a gatewall which ran from north to south on the western side. Those coming up the slope passed through a Doric portico into a broad, covered passageway which served as a foyer to the wall with its five openings. Within the Propylaea, the central roadway for carriages and chariots was bordered by Ionic columns; it passed through the major entrance, thirteen feet wide. Pedestrians walked up steps to the four smaller doorways, two on either side of the main road. Beyond the wall, the inward side had simply a Doric portico through which those riding or walking reached the plateau. The original plan for the Propylaea included galleries which were to be built at both the north and south ends of the central structure and used as halls for the display of paintings and sculpture. The one on the northern side was finished.

The entire summit of the Acropolis, 350 feet above the surrounding plain, was sacred ground but there was not much of it. The area measured only 1,000 feet from west to east and 500 feet from north to south. The modern visitor can only imagine how the proliferation of inscriptions, memorials and statues in addition to the temples must have crowded this small space.

Not all of the ground was sacred to Athena. The priests who served other deities claimed plots here and there and this may have been one of the reasons why certain buildings were left in an incomplete state. Apparently there existed a certain amount of rivalry among the various priestly groups over encroachment of other buildings on their allotted land. Obstinate refusal to allow a few feet for the wing of some new structure may even have prevented the completion of a symmetrical plan.

This point has been made by some who have attempted to explain the curiously irregular plan of a temple begun during the war and finally completed in 404. Although named for Erechtheus, the Erechtheum was also sacred to Athena and Poseidon (Pl. 48). Indeed, it was said to have been built on the very spot where they conducted their contest for Athens. That the various priests involved each had a different plan and all had their own way, is another suggestion which has been advanced to account for the unorthodox design. Certainly the temple looks like the work of a committee. Even so, the unevenness of the ground in this area has provided yet another explanation for its peculiarities. The traditional character of Greek temple architecture has hindered the claim that the design was a feat of originality.

Instead of the usual arrangement of columns on all sides or on

*Pl. 48 The Erechtheum, from the southeast*

opposite ends, the Erechtheum has an Ionic portico on the east and
north sides, with the north porch lower than the rest of the temple
and reached by a flight of steps. It is the south side of the temple
which is most often photographed because of the famous Porch of
Maidens, or Caryatids, from the story of the young girls abducted
from the town of Caryae in Laconia. Today, on the western side
of the temple there is an olive tree which commemorates the place
where the ancient sacred tree of Athena stood.

The Erechtheum was the most elaborate building on the Acropolis, but nearly all of its decorative effects have been lost. The statues
from the three pediments (including the one belonging to the north
porch) are missing. Only fragments remain of the marble figures
once attached by pegs to a band of grey stone which encircled the
temple. In contrast, the Caryatids gracing the south porch are intact except for one which is gone, but not missing. A Portland cement

copy substitutes for the original statue now housed in the British Museum.

Despite the representation of other deities—Poseidon for instance —the patron goddess of the city, Athena, was the dominant figure on the Acropolis. Phidias' fame as a sculptor rested in part on three monumental statues, his great Zeus at Olympia and his two colossal statues of Athena, both on the Acropolis at Athens. Unfortunately all three of these works have been lost, the metals in them having been put to other uses in later, less happy times. However, there is no doubt about their general appearance or where they were located. The information comes from references by ancient authors, engravings on extant coins, and best of all from small replicas which have survived.

One of the statues of Athena stood on the left side of the Sacred Way as it began its course from the Propylaea to the east door of the Parthenon. The statue was erected during Cimon's day in gratitude to the goddess for the victory at Marathon. It was paid for out of the spoils collected in that battle. A prototype of the Statue of Liberty, this imposing Athena served as a landmark from about the year 470 onwards. Its height has been variously estimated from thirty feet to sixty feet, but it was tall enough to be seen by the sailors of approaching ships.

Surviving coins of the Roman period show that the goddess wore a helmet and was dressed in a robe which reached to her feet. She held a spear in one hand and stood like a sentinel guarding the city. One coin even shows the statue in its place atop the Acropolis near the Propylaea. It was known to the ancients as the "bronze Athena" but nowadays is usually referred to as the *Athena Promachos,* or literally, "Athena, the first in battle." This term suggests the goddess' role as the guardian of the city, but the ·actual demeanor of the figure was apparently one of majesty rather than sheer might. In any event, it was not as grandiose as the *Athena Parthenos* which stood inside the Parthenon and was the major cult statue of the goddess and the one to which the presentation of gifts was made on ceremonial occasions. It was perhaps forty feet high and was placed at the rear of the great east hall where double rows of Ionic columns across the back and along both sides supported a flat timbered ceiling (Pl. 49, 50).

The *Athena Parthenos* wore robes and armor of gold. Ivory was used to simulate the flesh of the face and hands. It must have been an awe-inspiring sight to ancient viewers. To a few it was also a

LEFT: *Pl. 49 Roman coin of Athens showing the* Athena Promachos
RIGHT: *Pl. 50 Roman coin of Athens showing the* Athena Promachos *on the Acropolis*

tempting one. There were a number of thefts reported and Phidias himself was accused of pilfering some of the gold before his work was finished. Various sources reveal that the statue was laden with detail. For instance, the goddess' helmet was adorned with a sphinx in the center and a griffin on either side. In one hand, she held a small statue of Victory; with the other she grasped a spear. Taken as a whole the work was stylistically related to Phidias' gigantic statue of Zeus at Olympia. Zeus, while seated, also bore a Victory in one hand and a sceptre in the other. Even as Michelangelo would one day offer his impressions of Moses and Jeremiah, so Phidias furnished his contemporaries with likenesses of their gods and goddesses.

A relief on the base of the *Athena Parthenos* recorded the birth of Pandora. Resting on this base near the feet of Athena was a large serpent, reminiscent of the earlier snake cult associated with the Mother Goddess of Crete. Alongside Athena stood a bronze shield decorated with elaborate relief carvings. On the convex side, the battle with the Amazons was depicted and on the concave side the battle of the gods and the giants. It was in the execution of this shield that Phidias had involved himself in difficulty by including among the mythical heroes, not only Pericles but his own bald-headed likeness (Pl. 51).

It has been mentioned that Phidias' troubles were partly political owing to his close association with Pericles. However, professional jealousy may have been involved. He was the foremost sculptor of his time, but other artists may not have been so dazzled by his masterpieces as to forget that he received all the treasured assignments. Another of Phidias' commissions was for a smaller statue of Athena which also stood on the Acropolis although we do not know exactly where. It was a dedication from the settlers who went to Lemnos between 451 and 448 and has appropriately been called the *Lemnian Athena.* The original work which has been lost was probably in bronze, but there is no direct evidence for this. A Roman piece which some critics believe to be a copy of the *Lemnian* has survived in marble, but it is not intact; the torso is in Dresden and

*Pl. 51 Roman*
*"Varvakeion statuette"*
*after Phidias'*
Athena Parthenos

*Pl. 52 Head of
the* Lemnian Athena

the head is in Bologna. This is not unusual, considering the ancient
practice of using a finer grained marble for the head and then at-
taching it to the body by means of pegs (Pl. 52).

Ancient critics were lavish in their praise of this beautiful Athena
whose delicate and serene countenance stressed the qualities of beauty
and intelligence. Some writers consider the work to be Phidias' finest
representation of the goddess. There were of course many ways in
which she could be presented. The meditative features of this helmet-
less Athena were in sharp contrast to those of the more determined
warrior-queen images, such as the *Promachos* and the *Parthenos*. These
three statues showed how the ancient artists depicted their deities
in various moods, even as medieval painters and sculptors offered
Christ on one occasion as a stern judge seated in judgment and on
another as a suffering lamb of God.

*Pl. 53 Traditional view of the Parthenon, from the northwest*

Athena's image was everywhere to be seen. Her temple, the Parthenon, dominated the Acropolis. It was the most famous building in antiquity, a symbol of classicism, the gold in the Golden Age. It is now a magnificent wreck, as it has been since it was hit by a Venetian bomb in A.D. 1687. Before that date it had had a variety of tenants. After having served as Athena's chief shrine in ancient times, it became a Church of the Virgin Mary during the Middle Ages. Under the Turks in the fifteenth century it became a mosque. The Venetians' suspicion that it was also a storehouse for arms brought its actual usefulness to an abrupt end (Pl. 53).

In recent times the Parthenon has been partially restored, but not as much as it could be. Early in the nineteenth century during the Turkish rule in Greece, Lord Elgin, the British ambassador to Turkey, with the permission of the Sultan, removed certain priceless sculptural pieces for their own good—and for his own too presumably. In any event the building was left permanently estranged from some of its most beautiful adornments.

What distinguished the Parthenon among the marvelous structures of the ancient world was the attention lavished on details. The temple was intended to be beautiful and even as a ruin it still is. Enough remains to impress the viewer with that sense of balance and directness which are the essentials of classicism. Only in this respect was it extraordinary; not if one prefers size, or the solution of problems of spatial engineering. The Parthenon measured 230 feet by 100 feet. It did not cover thirteen acres like the Egyptian pyramid of Kurfu. It did not involve the architectural intricacies of a variety of rooms and arcades as did the later baths built by the Roman Emperor Caracalla. The Parthenon consisted of two halls back to back with an entrance to each, one on the east and the other on the west.

The construction of the Parthenon began in 447 and it was dedicated in 438 as the gift of Athens to Athena. (This temple was built on the site of an earlier structure which is called the Older Parthenon even though its construction was scarcely begun before the Persians burned the Acropolis in 480.) Excepting the doors, the interior ceilings and the roof, the entire building was constructed of marble from Mount Pentelicus. Although built with blocks and drums of stone, the fineness of the marble permitted such careful tooling that the exterior achieved an amazingly smooth appearance. The iron in the stone caused the temple to take on eventually its present brownish, some say golden, hue.

The Parthenon was a product of the best creative talent which the city possessed. Pericles, a careful observer and visitor to artists' workshops, knew where the talent was. He commissioned Ictinus and Callicrates as architects and he could not have chosen more painstaking craftsmen. Aware of the previous experiments of other architects, they were prepared to expend time and money to make the Parthenon the final expression of all that had been learned about the construction of a Doric temple. For instance, they knew that mathematically precise lines in a structure of the post-and-lintel type gave it a frozen, "drawn by a ruler" appearance. Therefore subtle variations were introduced and the resulting elasticity and fluidity gave the Parthenon a unity which a pattern of perfectly straight beams and columns would not have achieved.

It had long been the practice to give fluted columns an entasis, a slight swelling in the middle, which saved them from an overly rigid appearance beneath the weight of the roof. Also it was not novel to alter the horizontal of the stylobate. Others had given this base on which the columns rested a very slight bulge in the center. The architects of the Parthenon did not stop with these alterations. They also corrected the entablature so that it too curved slightly upward in the middle. The columns standing between the stylobate and the entablature were made to lean a minute degree inward, with the corner columns angled twice as much as the others. In addition the corner columns were slightly larger than the rest. When the temple was completed these small variations were not obvious to the viewer; he was only aware that the building looked very right. That was because it was all slightly wrong.

Ancient writers marvelled at the pains taken by the Athenian architects to make these slight adjustments in order to compensate for optical illusion, particularly in the glare of the sun. Frontinus, an engineer in charge of Roman aqueducts in the first century A.D., was especially amazed at the time and effort which the Greeks expended for only an esthetic purpose. Only, indeed! It was the aim of Ictinus and Callicrates to achieve quality. Unlike quantity and practicality, such a goal required more than time and money. It demanded patience and painstaking effort from all concerned—the architects down to the kneeling, sweating masons. It also called for a special attitude toward the uses of intellectual talent. There were in Athens artists for whom a beautiful idea perfectly consummated was worth a lifetime, let alone ten years of hard work. The money, the time and practical considerations were beside the point. There was also Pericles who was both willing and able to give such men free rein to bring to reality their marvelous conceptions. The city could be grateful for the coincidence.

The Parthenon exhibited how plentifully sculpture was employed in Greek buildings. Aside from the cult statue, the *Athena Parthenos,* figures in the round were also sculpted for the scenes in the pediments (gables) at either end. In addition, two different types of *bas relief* encircled the temple (Pl. 54). Pericles placed his friend Phidias in charge of this sculptural work, as we have seen. In brief, Ictinus and Callicrates supplied the building and Phidias decorated it.

Much of the original sculptural work (including the *Athena Parthenos*) has been lost, but there are still pieces which may be seen and studied. Drawings made of the Parthenon by a visitor to the Acropolis in 1674 provide a record of how the pediments looked in that year. Most of this statuary was destroyed a few years later in the explosion; a few pieces, however, have survived.

Both pediments of the Parthenon depicted episodes from the

Pl. 54 Detail of the northwest corner of the Parthenon showing the west pediment and the Doric and Ionic friezes

legends about Athena. In the East Pediment, a tableau symbolized the birth of the goddess. It is not possible to know what this scene actually looked like, for even by 1674 the middle section was missing. It is generally hypothesized, however, that a great seated figure of Zeus occupied the center. There is no unanimity of opinion about the extant works which we do have. Some critics have thought that the so-called "Theseus" in the British Museum was actually intended to represent Dionysus; others have argued that the figure was a symbol of Mount Olympus where Athena's birth took place (Pl. 55). There is more agreement about the vividly rendered horses' heads which appeared in the corners of the pediment. Obviously they were a novel and interesting device for filling these awkward spaces. They also created the illusion of a chariot rising at the left and another chariot descending at the right. Helios the sun god was arriving and Selene the moon goddess was departing. True to the myth, the time

*Pl. 55 The so-called "Theseus" (perhaps Dionysus or a personification of Mount Olympus), from east pediment of the Parthenon*

for Athena's birth was set at dawn. As would be expected on such an occasion the Three Fates were present. However, the famous triad in the British Museum, composed of one seated goddess with two reclining goddesses beside her, long identified as the Three Fates, is no longer thought to have represented this group. A later Roman reproduction of the scene in the East Pediment suggests that the Fates stood on the left near the center and so are among the missing pieces. There are now various proposals about the figures in the British Museum which are shown on the right of the center in the 1674 drawing. For instance, the seated figure may be Hestia, with Thalassa, the Sea, resting in the lap of Gaea, the Earth (Pl. 56).

The conflict between Athena and Poseidon for the possession of Attica was represented in the West Pediment. These two figures dominated the center. Athena stood at the left striking the ground with her spear, and Poseidon was at the right holding his trident. Athena's gift, the sacred olive tree, stood between them. Next to

Athena was her chariot driven by Victory; beside Poseidon was his chariot with an Amphitrite holding the reins. To the left and right of these chariots were figures in various poses, but they are not now identifiable. In the corners were reclining figures, a usual device for filling those spaces.

The Parthenon has been considered the definitive expression of the Doric temple. Its pediments, in comparison with earlier examples, would appear to have benefited by the experience of previous efforts. The figures were more relaxed and the scenes more fluid by contrast with the somewhat artificial appearance of the pedimental groups in the earlier temple of Zeus at Olympia. The architects of the Parthenon wanted to avoid a static appearance. So too, Phidias, presumably the designer of the pediments, sought to make his scenes more life-like. He abandoned the tradition of making one side of the pediment a mirror image of the other. Monotony was avoided by balancing a female on the left with a male on the right, and a nude figure on one side with a draped figure on the other.

*Pl. 56 The so-called "Three Fates" (perhaps Hestia, Gaea and Thalassa) from the east pediment of the Parthenon*

*Pl. 57 Aphrodite, Eros and magistrates (or Attic heroes) awaiting Panathenaic Procession. Section of east frieze of Parthenon*

Certain parts of both the Doric and Ionic friezes of the Parthenon remain in their original places. Generally speaking, the terms Doric and Ionic refer to different styles of architecture differentiated by the kind of columns used for the exterior of a building. Doric columns carried simple block capitals, a type primarily associated with the Peloponnesus. Ionic columns were capped with more elaborate volutes and were used by the eastern Greeks, especially in Ionia. Similarly the terms Doric and Ionic designated the types of friezes commonly employed on the exteriors of such temples. In Athens, where all influences found their way, both styles were used in the same buildings. The Parthenon, a Doric temple, had a Doric frieze on the entablature and an Ionic frieze on the cella.

A Doric frieze consisted of alternate sections called triglyphs and metopes. The triglyphs were projecting blocks decorated with three vertical channels, reminders of the old wooden crossbeams used in earlier temples. Alternating with the triglyphs were metopes, sculptured scenes in high relief. On the Parthenon, there were ninety-two metopes each about four feet square. Forty-three of them are *in situ,* although some of these are now very indistinct. Fifteen are in the British Museum. Fragments of others are to be found in the Louvre, in Copenhagen and in the Acropolis Museum. Like the shield of the *Athena Parthenos,* the metopes depict the mythical battles between gods and giants and between Athenians and Amazons. They also show centaurs and lapiths in conflict as well as scenes from the Trojan War. Since the victory over the Persians was the unforgettable event of the recent past, this emphasis on contests of strength

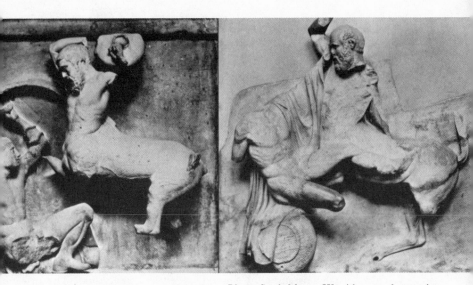

*Pl. 58 South Metope IV with casts of heads (presently in Copenhagen)*

*Pl. 59 South Metope IX with casts of centaur's head and right arm and lapith's right knee (presently in Athens)*

*Pl. 60 South Metope VII with casts of lapith's head (in Louvre) and centaur's head (in Athens)*

*Pl. 61 South Metope XXVII with cast of lapith's head (in Athens)*

was to be expected. Artists could not help recalling the invasions in pictorial combats between the forces of light and darkness (Pl. 58–61).

Unlike a Doric frieze with its alternating triglyphs and metopes, an Ionic frieze was a continuous band of sculpture. A viewer moving inside the columns of the Parthenon and looking upward on the wall of the cella may still see, on the west and south sides, parts of the frieze which once encircled the enclosed portion of the temple. Well over half of the extant pieces of the original frieze are in the British Museum where the various pieces are beautifully displayed in the spacious galleries presented by Lord Duveen of Millbank (far from the corrosive chemicals which now infect the air around Athens.) An especially beautiful section depicting a group of maidens is in the Louvre. There are other parts and fragments in the Acropolis Museum. The surviving pieces readily show that the workmanship of the continuous frieze was superior to that of the metopes, but in either instance Phidias must have assigned various sections to other sculptors who presumably worked under his supervision. The unevenness of the work simply reflects an unevenness of talent. Phidias has usually been credited with the execution of the best parts, and as the directing genius behind it all (Pl. 57, 62, 63, 64).

*Pl. 62  Horsemen in Panathenaic Procession. Section of west frieze of Parthenon* (in situ)

The Ionic frieze recreated in stone the Panathenaic procession, which wound its way through the city and up the Sacred Way to the Parthenon bearing tribute to Athena. This band of sculpture was about three feet four inches in height and originally ran a course of about 525 feet (of which 420 feet have survived). The formation of the procession was realistically portrayed. Young horsemen, perhaps participants in the Panathenaic Games, prepared to mount their horses. The procession moved along both the north and south sides of the temple. Priests, public officials, musicians and armed youths were shown making their way toward the east end. There the twelve gods, six on each side of the center, awaited the arrival of the worshippers who brought with them the sacrificial cattle. Between the gods, directly over the east door, a priest was shown receiving a large folded cloth from an attendant. This was undoubtedly the *peplos* or cloak, newly woven for Athena and intended to be draped around the shoulder of the *Athena Parthenos*. Even as images of the religions today, both East and West, are bedecked with jewels by devout believers who are moved to express their feelings in this fashion, so too the Athenians decorated the representation of their patron goddess.

As with other sculptures of the Parthenon, brilliant paints were used to enliven this scene of pageantry, but very little evidence of painting remains. There were, however, other features of Phidias' design which may still be appreciated. As in the temple itself, calculated distortions were introduced. To achieve a harmonious effect the artist "adjusted" the size of his figures as had been done in the pediments. The youths riding the horses were carved to smaller dimensions than those standing. The horses were also made smaller than they should have been by comparison with the human figures. These alterations were too subtle to be obvious, but other devices used by the sculptor were more readily apparent. For instance, there was an obvious preference for showing the heads of persons walking in the procession at the same level as exemplified by the maidens in the Louvre scene (Pl. 64). But there was no rule about this, and in the slab in Athens which shows boys carrying *hydriae* one boy is stooping to lift his jug (Pl. 63). Although parts of the relief which show figures in a row suggest the Greek predisposition for simplicity and harmony, Phidias did not present his processioners as static soldiers in a line. His figures twist and turn and strike various poses. Again, it may be observed how classical sculptors, famous for their symmetry, avoided monotony by subtly underlaying an appearance of

*Pl. 63 Boys carrying* hydriae *in Panathenaic Procession. Section of north frieze of Parthenon*

orderliness with a variety of detail. A swirling cloak caught by the wind was a way of adding dash and filling space. This device incidentally captivated early Renaissance painters and sculptors.

Despite the fact that sections of the Panathenaic frieze show horses one behind the other, with a clutter of horses' legs in a jumbled appearance, the frieze as a whole has an arranged rather than a candid appearance. Specifically, in contrast to later Roman examples, a desire is shown to avoid the crowdedness and clumsiness of an actual procession. Phidias sought a compromise with the commonplace. The natural activity of the actual occasion was altered by his desire to present not a procession only, but a beautiful one. His success could never be equalled. Not because there would never be another sculptor equal to Phidias, but because for this particular building, given his subject and the material at hand, Phidias created a unique work of art.

It is a commentary on the times that this brilliant artist who had given Athens such a magnificent work had later to flee the city.

There are two other structures on the Acropolis today besides the Propylaea, the Erechtheum, and the Parthenon. Situated on a bastion at the southwestern corner is a reconstructed gem of Ionic architecture—the temple to Athena *Nike* (Athena as the personification of Victory). Built during the years 427–424, it was torn down during Turkish rule in the seventeenth century and rebuilt rather clumsily by the Greeks in 1835 using much of the original material. It was much more accurately restored in the late 1930's. The temple is a one-room structure with four Ionic columns on both the western and eastern sides. The Ionic frieze seen on the building today was made from casts taken of the original pieces now in the British Museum. Despite these reservations, this temple is an excellent example of the elegance and charm of the smaller types of shrines once common in all parts of Greece (Pl. 65).

A modern museum is located at the opposite end of the Acropolis at a lower level than the Parthenon. On display here are several archaic statues which show the orientalizing influences in Attic art

*Pl. 64 Maidens in Panathenaic Procession. Section of east frieze of Parthenon.*

*Pl. 65 Temple of* Athena Nike *on the Acropolis in Athens, from the north*

prior to the fifth century. In the same room where sections of the Panathenaic frieze are exhibited, there is one of the most appealing of all Greek reliefs: *Nike Tying Her Sandal* (Pl. 67). This sculptured section, once part of the parapet beneath the small *Nike* temple, is worn, but the technique in the treatment of drapery in stone remains a marvel to behold and typical of the excellence synonymous with the Acropolis.

Not all of the beautiful relief sculptures in Athens were paid for by public funds and used in public shrines. There was a profitable private market, especially in funerary monuments. A large collection of these memorials, set up mostly by the well-to-do, may be seen today in the National Museum of Archaeology in Athens. Unlike the grim and stolid figures which decorated *stelae* in Egypt and the Near East, these Greek *bas relief* scenes were taken from everyday life and were presumably reminders of the deceased as they were most pleasantly remembered. For instance, a touching scene of farewell is suggested as a figure clasps the hand of a loved one. An especially well preserved *stele* shows a woman selecting a piece of jewelry. Another memorial pictures a man with a dog. The sentiment is universal. The simplicity and the subtle restraint with which this sentiment is exhibited are unmistakably Greek (Pl. 66).

Pl. 66 *Attic* stele *of Hegeso*

Pl. 67 Nike *(tying her sandal), from the parapet of temple of* Athena Nike

## The Agora

For the modern visitor to Athens, the Acropolis is the center of attention. Aside from other considerations, it happens to be that part of the ancient city which is still there. To the average Athenian in the fifth century, the Acropolis was a special place to be sure, but he spent most of his time elsewhere. The busiest place in the city was the *agora*, the "gathering place," located northwest of the Acropolis.

The *agora* was "downtown." Any traveler entering Athens by one of its gates had only to follow the street he was on to reach this central piazza or public square. Criss-crossed shaded walks cut through the open space in the center. All around were markets, shrines and government buildings—with barber shops and wine shops, those age-old institutions of conviviality, crowded in here and there.

In a city of politicians, the *agora* was the hub of politics. For the men of Athens, it was not a question of going there occasionally, hoping to see someone they knew; they went there all the time, expecting to see everybody. A stranger stood out. All other faces were familiar. News and gossip were exchanged side by side with goods and currencies. Here was the public forum of a free society where men could gather to discuss the issues of the day. It was also a place for political shenanigans, including an occasional deal.

The Athenians practiced their democracy out-of-doors. The Assembly met in a place called the *Pnyx*, located to the southwest of the *agora*. The arrangement was presumably like that of a theater, with seats cut into the side of a gradual slope and the overflow sitting on the ground in front of the rostrum. At Athens, the informality of such a setting was in agreement with the tone of the proceedings. Other gatherings of the citizenry, for the purpose of an ostracism for instance, were held in the *agora*. Political, religious, social and commercial activities were mixed together in this heart of the *polis*.

As in Mediterranean countries today, good weather encouraged open-air market stalls. In Athens they lined the east side of the *agora*. Haggling over prices was expected and a careful look at the fish was wise. There were other items on sale and more expensive ones. The *kapeloi* (retailers) offered imports such as jewelry and cloth from eastern ports. These goods were obtained from *emporoi* (travelers) who rented space in a ship and carried products from place to place. Then as now the *naukleroi*, who owned the ships, were among the richest men in town. By modern standards, the volume of import business was small and the list of products limited but those with inherited or borrowed money could invest it with hope. In any event there was enough low-key capitalism to insure a "whig" interest in keeping the sea lanes safe and profitable.

A banker went into business by setting up a table. He sat with his assistants and received deposits which were guaranteed by his life rather than the government. He also listened to loan applicants and offered advice which might prove profitable or ruinous. It was, as always, a touchy business and in lieu of air-conditioning best conducted in the shade. So, the bankers were usually found in the *stoas* or roofed promenades. The most famous *stoa* in Athens, the *Stoa Poikile* or painted porch, was built about 460 along the north side of the *agora* and was so named because of its colorful paintings by Polygnotos.

It is difficult to be sure of much about the appearance or even location of the buildings which stood in the Athenian *agora* during its earliest years. The area was destroyed along with the rest of the city during the Persian occupation in 480. After the defeat of the Persians, the practical needs of the government and business required that restoration of the *agora* should take precedence over the more expensive work on the Acropolis. It was largely rebuilt under the direction of Cimon.

The famous religious shrines of the Acropolis, once in place, had the permanence of monuments, but the changing needs of government and commerce meant that the *agora* would undergo various "renewals" during later Hellenistic and Roman times. Eventually the later buildings also passed from the scene, but their traces have naturally been easier to find than those of the earlier ones they replaced.

In recent years, the major restoration work in the *agora* has resulted in the reproduction of a building erected by a Hellenistic king, Attalus II (220–138) who ruled over the kingdom of Pergamum in northwest Asia Minor for twenty-two years during the second century. In these later times, Athens was no longer the power she had been three hundred years before. She had become an *alma mater,* renowned for her culture, and was still the epitome of the best that was Greek. Attalus II had the money to match his affection for Athens. He presented the city with a magnificent *stoa,* and it is the modern copy of this building which now brightens the eastern side of the *agora* where the original once stood. Though an impressive

*Pl. 68 The* Stoa *of Attalus. The Athenian* agora *is in the foreground.*

structure, it does not belong to the great days of Athens when *stoas* were built on a less grandiose scale. It does, however, serve as an excellent museum and houses finds from the Neolithic period onward which have been recovered in and near the *agora*. Included are fragments of inscriptions ranging in importance from official tribute lists of the Athenian Empire to the common *ostraca* used in voting (Pl. 68).

A variety of buildings stood in or near the *agora* where magistrates conducted their business. The state archives were kept in the Metroön. Not far away were the Bouleuterion where the Council of 500 met, the Tholos which housed the Council's executive committee and the Prytaneion with the city's sacred fire dedicated to Hestia, goddess of the hearth. In addition there were temples, large and small, and of these the Hephaesteum is still there. This Doric temple, built on a hill which dominated the western side of the *agora,* has been better preserved than the Parthenon or any other temple in Greece. It was for a long time called the Theseum on the assumption that the bones of Theseus were buried beneath it. They were not. In fact it is still not known where Cimon erected a shrine to house the great king's remains, although an area near the *agora* which Pausanias called "a sanctuary of Theseus" is now favored. In any event the Theseum has become the Hephaesteum. The ample evidence of metal-working around this hill has led to the current assumption that it was a temple built by metal-workers in honor of their patron deity Hephaestus. Standing apart from the *agora* proper, it escaped the later renewals. Today for those who visit the restored *stoa* of Attalus, the Hephaesteum is only a short walk away. It is also three centuries earlier, and original. Sculptured figures which are thought to have stood in the east pediment of this temple are exhibited in the Agora Museum (Pl. 69).

Roads are at times easier to trace than buildings. The Sacred Way cut diagonally across the *agora* from the northwest corner to the

*Pl. 69 Temple of Hephaestus (formerly called the Theseum) in Athens*

southeast corner. Its course is seen today as a neglected path of small stones and red dirt. In the fifth century, like the great avenues of modern cities famous for stately processions, the Sacred Way had a special significance. Over this route passed the annual Panathenaic procession in honor of Athena. The road began at Eleusis in northwest Attica where the great temple of Demeter was located. It entered the city proper through the Dipylon Gate in the west wall. Then it passed through the *agora,* up the slope of the Acropolis, through the Propylaea and ended at the east door of the Parthenon.

There were two other prominent roadways which passed through the *agora,* one along the north side and the other along the west side. These arteries intersected with the Sacred Way at the northwest corner of the *agora,* which on a map looks like the busiest spot in the city. Not far away was the altar of the twelve gods, the point from which all distances were measured.

## Beyond the City Walls

A network of roads brought the Attican villagers to the city. On the way in, they would pass other men leaving, perhaps going to one of the *gymnasia* beyond the walls. These were not buildings, but pleasant groves situated here and there in the countryside. Nor should they be thought of in the American sense as exclusively places for exercise. A *gymnasion* was rather (as the Europeans use the term) a place for education both physical and mental. Ancient writers, familiar with the usually cramped and dirty quarters of the city, spoke fondly of the greenery, the cool shade and bucolic peace of these surroundings. Statuary added to the beauty of the walks which wound through the area. There were of course altars to the various gods, with Heracles, Apollo and Athena being especially honored. Along with the statues of the gods were those of famous athletes, and in time there may have been a cluttered profusion of monuments.

The term *gymnasion* comes from the word *gymnos,* meaning naked. The Greek acceptance of nudity was a part of their characteristic behavior, which set them apart from the other peoples of the ancient world. Only the Greeks seem to have put the exhibition of trim bodies in action above other considerations. Although the notion that the body was a corrupt prison of the soul had long since been introduced by the Pythagoreans, it was a doctrine as yet only pondered by intellectuals. For the average man on the road to the *gymnasia,* the ideal was still the whole man—a sound mind in a firm body. He did not as yet consider himself a battleground between a soul and the senses. He had no self-conscious concern about the corruption of the flesh; on the contrary the flesh was pleasing. Corruption occurred to be sure, but then in some degree it always had and it was not generally believed that the body was more to be blamed than the mind. Nor was it thought that to be "absent from the body" would necessarily solve the problem.

The nudity of the *gymnasia* and the preoccupation with the nude in Greek art exhibited a comfortableness with the body which other peoples in the ancient world—and peoples ever since—have failed to share. Some might find nudity suggestive of license. Others might say it showed a healthy absence of false modesty. Boys who grew up in Athens during the fifth century undoubtedly took it for granted.

At the *gymnasia*, males of all ages stripped for action and engaged in running, jumping, boxing and wrestling contests. A central area was suited for a variety of exercises, but two specialties, wrestling and running, required their own special facilities. A *palaestra* was ground used exclusively for training and wrestling. A city depending on its size might have several of these sites. They were not always located in a gymnasium, but every gymnasium would have one. Nearby would be a *stadion*, a stretch of two hundred yards of flat land suitable for races. Where natural mounds were not available, banks of earth were thrown up along both sides of the track to allow more spectators to see the contests.

Surrounding the central exercise area of the *gymnasia* were buildings providing dressing rooms and baths. There were also *stoas* where those who wanted to watch could stand in the shade. Here, too, informal talks and discussions were held on learned topics ranging from astronomy to metaphysics. Altogether, the *gymnasion* was a complex of various facilities, exercise areas, pleasant spots for resting or listening to speakers, and buildings to serve the practical needs of those using the area.

Athens had three *gymnasia*, financed and operated by the city. To the northwest, less than a mile from the walls, was the famous Academy where the original structures may have been part of the extensive building program under the tyrant Peisistratus and his sons. The Lyceum, east of the city, took its name from a nearby shrine to *Apollo Lyceus*, or "Apollo the Wolf-Slayer." To the south, across the river Ilissus, was the Cynosarges which never acquired quite the reputation of the other two and seems to have had a less distinguished clientele.

Modern archaeological studies and references by ancient authors have made possible a general picture of what a *gymnasion* looked like. As might be expected, the earlier *gymnasia* of the sixth century were less complex than those of the fourth century at which time schools founded by Plato, Aristotle and Antisthenes grew up on adjacent ground.

## The House and the Home

From dawn to dusk, the Athenians were to be found gathered together amid familiar surroundings—the Acropolis, the *agora*, the *Pnyx*, the courts, the *gymnasia*, or on the roads and pathways in between. Home was where they did not go. Their dwellings appear to have been mostly places of accommodation. In any event the limited space within the city walls did not allow for the building of elaborate houses.

The available evidence of house architecture in Greece is scanty and the appearance of the residential area of Athens is a matter more of imagination than fact. What is written on the subject must be derived from bits and pieces of archaeological and literary evidence, including hints obtained from comparable cities elsewhere in Greece.

Originally, Athens had grown by spreading out from around the base of the fortified Acropolis. No formal planning was involved and dwellings were erected helter skelter with the streets eventually following an irregular pattern. The customary disorder of Greek cities was a familiar cause for complaint by ancient writers who at the same time recognized that for the purpose of defense the maze of passages could be a blessing.

Systematic grid arrangements of streets apparently began before the time of the Milesian architect Hippodamus. However, this man, who gave Piraeus a plan in the fifth century (but came too late to save Athens), is the first town planner of whom we know. He probably gained valuable experience in city planning when his native Miletus was rebuilt after the Persians had destroyed it in 494. Aside from this report, and the tradition that he applied his talents in such widely separated places as Thurii and Rhodes, there is little known about him, except that Aristotle says he had long hair.

So much publicity has been given to the houses of well-to-do Romans in Pompeii in the first century A.D. that there may be a temptation to think of houses in general in the ancient world as being on that order. For fifth century Athens, the image of Pompeii would be especially misleading. In Pericles' time, narrow streets bounded small sections within which several houses stood attached to one another in a solid block. The poorest of these might have only one or two rooms, but the average would have four or five. They were built of wood and unbaked brick with tiled roofs. There may well have been small paved courtyards within these houses, but they would have contained cisterns to catch water rather than elaborate pools, columns and statuary. There was no central open space, or peristyle, around which the various rooms were spaced as was true of the Pompeian homes. The Athenian courtyard could be square or rectangular, and it might be at one end of the house rather than in the center. Many houses had two stories and it is believed that the second floor was customarily reserved for the women. The ladies of the house and their female slaves were partly occupied there in making clothing which in ancient times was a household occupation.

The limitations of available space allowed little variation in design between the wealthier houses and the poorer ones. Great wealth would have been displayed by the presence of better pottery and by extra decorative effects, including more elaborate sculpture and wall paintings. The very finest houses had mosaic floors. As is true in many parts of the Mediterranean region today, the exteriors of both rich and poor residences were likely to be unimposing, simply presenting a wall to the street.

Only the country houses belonging to aristocrats who lived in the plains northeast of Athens might have rivaled the Pompeian homes. Space on which to build and money to spend would have made this possible, but we do not know what these villas actually looked like.

The social life of the Greeks is not well documented and what notes we have concern the better appointed households of the wealthy. Athenian hosts did entertain at elaborate dinner parties with hired singers and dancers on hand. More often perhaps, the company simply enjoyed long hours of drinking and lively conversation. From references in plays and scenes on Greek vases, we learn about the after-dinner game of *kottabos* in which the guests by a dexterous throw of their wine-lees sought to hit (or upset) a target placed in the center of the room (Pl. 43).

Plato offers a few glimpses of the life of the aristocracy. His *Symposium* is set in a Greek house which obviously provided a comfortable haven for the master and his companions. Missing from the literature are any Dickensian accounts of jolly family gatherings in which the home is pictured as a refuge for a father and his own.

It has generally been assumed that the absence of "togetherness" in the Athenian home reflected, in part, the sexual mores of the Greeks. The late beloved Miss Edith Hamilton avoided this subject in her popular work *The Greek Way*. The more specialized *A History of Education in Antiquity* by H. I. Marrou perhaps gives it disproportionate attention. Case histories, whether from modern studies or from ancient chapter and verse, as in the Bible or Homer's epics, suggest that: "That which hath been is now; and that which is to be hath already been; . . . ." (*Eccl.* 3, xv.) It is the attitudes of societies which vary, and with them the degree of tolerance given any form of behavior. In the ancient world it was commonly believed that women were inferior to men, mentally as well as physically. Nor was there much opportunity for most women to prove the contrary. At Athens, marriages were arranged for convenience sake. A girl had no expectation of any education outside of her father's house, much less any public duties, and so marriage came early, usually at the age of about thirteen or fourteen. On the other hand, a young man, with military service and education to occupy him, plus the time spent in becoming initiated into the life of the community, customarily did not marry until close to thirty. Marriage was a matter of good family, good dowry, and good health. Given the differences in ages, education and experience, there were no real grounds for companionship. Bearing children and managing a household were all that would ordinarily have been asked of a wife. She had a place, a function, a service, but she was not an equal. Her husband spent most of his time with his friends and perhaps some of his time with the *hetaerae*.

The *hetaerae* were courtesans, state-owned slaves or other foreign women, who were engaged primarily in serving the comforts of single men. They were not common prostitutes; rather they played a familiar role as female companions in a society wherein "respectable" women did not mix in the social life of men. The *hetaerae* were often well educated. In cosmopolitan Corinth and Athens where they flourished, their profession was not considered immoral. Nevertheless, it was not until after the breakdown of the "old morality" of the Marathon generation that married men could escape censure for openly keeping company with them. Pericles' marriage to Aspasia, the most famous *hetaera* in Greece, contributed no doubt to the increasing laxity in these matters. Aspasia's rare gifts for conversation and rhetoric, however, were undoubtedly exceptional among the *hetaerae* whose talents were generally more basic.

The segregation of the sexes in Greece is presumed to have given rise also to widespread homosexuality. (Some prefer to say bisexuality because marriage and a family were only rarely excluded.) Beginning in Homer's *Iliad* with Achilles' shameless grief for Patroclus, there are to be found a number of relationships between friends in Greek literature which seemed acceptable at the time, but less so now. In Sparta, the circumstance that men lived away from home altogether has been useful in explaining the pederasty which ancient observers so often associate with that city.

In general, however, with respect to homosexuality, the available information is supplied primarily by the intelligentsia. This does not mean that the prevalence in the literature of love poetry between persons of the same sex and the well known historical incidents of homosexuality have been misleading. Public toleration, if not approval, of this behavior, did allow for a free expression of feelings. At the same time, it should be stressed that there has always been a gap between the preoccupations of the *literati* and those of the man in the street. Today, the overly publicized views of "sensitive" playwrights and "honest" novelists are scarcely representative of the outlook and habits of Americans who punch time clocks in the morning and watch television variety at night. Nor need they be. It is the difference that is worth remembering.

Marriage may have been a stronger institution in ancient Greece than some think. Certainly, affectionate family scenes depicted in vase paintings suggest as much. More stress should perhaps be given the probability that husbands and wives, despite the differences of age and education, might have experienced a love "forsaking all others" in cohabitation. Plutarch mentions Cimon's "unusually passionate affection for his lawful wife Isodice," and says that this was indicated by the sentiments expressed by Cimon's friends when she died. Discounting the comedies of Aristophanes which offer the sporting side of marriage (a kind of "battle of the sexes"), we find only a few serious references to married life. Xenophon writes in his *Hellenica* about a certain Theban leader, Leontiades, who dined alone according to custom but reclined after dinner beside his wife who was working her wool. The scene has all the passion of an evening in Plymouth Colony, but it is not unpleasant.

# Knowledge and Entertainment

**XI**

The commingling of the Athenians in the *agora* was one of the pleasant graces of life they took for granted. To all the other attractions of this place there was added education and amusement. A typical Greek *agora* had provisions for an audience to gather and listen to a speaker or watch a show. Where a small hill was available, rows of steps could be cut to provide seats; on the western side of the *agora* at Athens there was precisely such an arrangement. Here local politicians or famous teachers from abroad had no difficulty attracting a crowd. There were also occasions when writers, both native and foreign, read from their works. The *agora* offered the public a free "chautauqua" the whole year round.

According to tradition, Herodotus (*circa* 484–*circa* 430), a refugee from Halicarnassus, won the hearts of the Athenians on the *agora* "platform." He liked them and they liked him. Indeed, it is reported that the citizenry showed their appreciation by awarding him the rights of citizenship and money besides. No doubt he was a man of ability and charm. He also had a sharp eye for timely subjects.

By the mid-fifth century, the Athenians had become internationalists. They were interested in learning more about the history, geography and customs of other lands. At the same time, an account of their own glorious past could not have been more welcome. Herodotus combined all of this in a book which men have been reading ever since. The finished work covers events from the founding of the Persian Empire in the mid-sixth century through the story of the Persian invasions of Greece—in all, a period roughly from 546 to 478. Interspersed here and there are lengthy digressions about various peoples living in the Near East and around the rim of the Mediterranean Sea. It would appear that Herodotus' book grew with his travels (Pl. 70).

*The Persian Wars* remains a standard and indispensable source of knowledge about the ancient world. Because of it, Herodotus has been given the title "Father of History," yet he borrowed generously from the earlier, less popular, Hecataeus who probably deserves to be called the first historian. Thucydides, who wrote at a later date, was the only one of the three who consistently followed scientific methods.

Herodotus fares best when he is read and judged less as a historian than as a raconteur. Much of his history reads like a travelogue and the reader moves along at a leisurely pace to a momentous climax. Essentially, Herodotus writes about two different worlds and then describes the clash between them. First, he tells about the rise of the Persians, a story of conquest by which an empire is built stretching from India to the coast of the Aegean. In the process, many despots are supplanted by only one—the Persian king, the Great King, whose word is law.

Everywhere in this Eastern world there is an acceptance of an absolute ruler, an hereditary nobility, and a priesthood who possess powerful secrets. To the multitudes who till the soil, these dominant few are as established in their power as the stars are fixed in the sky. They rule as much by hoary custom as by force. The king of Persia becomes the Pharaoh of Egypt, but the Egyptians never change. Nor does it ever occur to them that they should.

By way of contrast, Herodotus stresses the variety of the Greek political systems which allow for varying degrees of citizen participation. His highest praise is saved for Athens where leaders are elected and thus dependent on their followers for support. In the East where the slightest hint of insubordination might mean a cruel death, the Athenian democracy is incomprehensible. (Parts of the world which the Great King once ruled have never had such an experience to the present day.)

*Pl. 70 Head of Herodotus*

To say that Herodotus offers a choice between two systems, one slave and the other free, may sound superficial, yet it is not entirely unfair. He does in fact take sides and the freedom-loving Athenians are without question the heroes of his history but to leave the matter there would be misleading. Herodotus was too well informed and too fair to present the Persians as totally barbaric while he put forward the Greeks as the enlightened possessors of all truth. He found much to praise in Egyptian, Babylonian and Persian customs. He also found much to blame among the various Greeks. Since he and his family had been driven out of their native Halicarnassus by the tyrant Lygdamis, his special distaste for tyranny is not unexpected.

Herodotus was impressed by the Persian willingness to learn from others, even if they were not an inventive people themselves. He also praises their abhorrence of lying or indebtedness. A boy was taught to ride, to shoot straight and to tell the truth. No Athenian would object to that. He reports also the reasonable Persian habit of considering a man's previous good record against a single misdeed before passing sentence. The Persian priests, called Magi, are another matter; they seem to enjoy killing animals indiscriminately whether making a sacrifice or not. Herodotus, in a rare moment of tartness, says it is their habit and they can have it.

The basic fault which Herodotus discovers in the Near East is a smallness of spirit. The good life is only for the few and a man must be born to it. Law and order are maintained by a rigid control of masses of illiterate peasants and soldiers. The Athenians had advanced far beyond this level of thinking. The *agora* with its social and political give-and-take among citizens of all classes is altogether foreign to the Persian mind. Herodotus reports a remark by the Persian conqueror Cyrus that he could not have any fear of men who gathered in market places to deal with one another. How could discipline be established among men, each of whom is entitled to have his own say? The vast spaces of the East and the hordes of different peoples who had to be ruled did not prepare the Persians to understand what strength could be mustered by a few free men living together around a single hill.

Herodotus tells later how the soldiers of the Great King are driven into battle with whips. There are no issues at stake for such men, only the will of their masters. Nor are these soldiers any match for Greeks who fight because they have voted to fight and know what they are fighting for. Freedom, Herodotus insists, makes all the difference even among the Greeks themselves. When the Athenians were under a tyrant they were no better than other men, for all were equally subservient to masters. In a condition of freedom, when each Athenian is his own master, he is the superior of those still enslaved.

*The Persian Wars* has a plan and it has a message, yet only the endearing qualities of Herodotus himself could have made it one of the great books of all time. He was easy company—a man who was interesting because he was interested in subjects outside himself. His curiosity about the world and the people in it provided his history with an abundance of incidental information. There were for instance the customs he found in Babylonia. The one which Herodotus admired the most was a plan by which the villagers disposed of their marriageable girls. It was a simple arrangement with the least amount of disorder and nobody left over. In each village, the girls old enough to be married were brought together with the men who were seeking wives. Each girl was offered in the order of her physical attributes, from the most attractive down to the ugliest. The would-be husbands made their bids. The most money took the most beautiful girl and so forth, until in the course of nature a point was reached where the bidding stopped. Then the money which had been paid in began to be paid out. A prospective husband might be willing to take the next girl in line if money were offered in the bargain. By the end of the session, the money paid for the beauties had been paid out to assist the plain, the books were balanced, and every girl had been taken by somebody. Herodotus admits that not everybody was satisfied with this arrangement but he personally thought it was a good idea. Because of his silence about a wife and family of his own, it has been assumed that he was a life-long bachelor, which of course could be an excuse for his judgment.

Herodotus did not by any means approve of everything—for instance, a requirement that every woman devotee of the local love goddess must at one time enter into the deity's sanctuary and there offer herself to the first stranger who tossed a coin in her lap. Rich or poor, high of station or low, women of all sorts came to the temple and submitted to this "holy" prostitution. Afterwards they refused to endure such an indignity for any price. Herodotus thought the practice distasteful and says so, but he does not dwell on the matter although with his customary thoroughness he mentions that some women had to wait for as long as four years.

Herodotus states his own opinions here and there in his book, but he is never contentious. In his travels he saw many sights and heard many tales, some of them strange. All of this he passed along to his readers the way it came to him. Occasionally, he heard a claim which offended his sensibilities. There was a diver from Scione, for example, who wanted to quit the Persians and go over to the Greeks. Herodotus reports that it was popularly believed that the man made his escape by swimming under water from Aphetae to Artemisium, a distance of ten miles. He adds that he personally thinks the diver went in a boat. Concerning a story of a floating island, he says that he has never seen it float. Concerning two statues which were said to have fallen to their knees, he states flatly that he does not believe it. He does not, however, interrupt his narrative to berate those who do.

Herodotus would have been the last to offend the feelings of the devout. The Delphians told him that they were saved from the Persians by Apollo who had caused a mighty storm which sent rocks rolling down upon the enemy. He reports the event without any mention of possible coincidences. Herodotus was willing to accept the idea of divine intervention, but there were some stories which he feared had become garbled over the years and he made an effort to straighten them out. The manner in which the oracle of Dodona originated was a case in point. Herodotus sought to make an old story more plausible in a new day.

He apparently was first intrigued with this question as a result of a story told to him by priests at Thebes in Egypt. They claimed that the Phoenicians had once captured two women who had served in the temple and had eventually sold one in Greece and the other in Libya. As a consequence these women carried the oracular arts of Egypt into other lands. So, they said, the shrine of Zeus at Dodona had begun.

The women who currently conducted the oracle at Dodona told Herodotus a somewhat different story. They said that a black dove once came to Dodona from Thebes and perched on an oak tree sacred to Zeus. Speaking with a human voice, the dove gave instructions for the founding of an oracle. The women said that a similar black dove had gone to Libya. Of these two versions, Herodotus preferred the reasonableness of the first. It seemed plausible to him that a woman, carried far from her homeland, might build a shrine under an oak tree and establish an oracle similar in operation to the one she had known in her native land. She would also pine for her sister who had been carried to Libya. By making assumptions, Herodotus was able to explain the second story in terms of the first. He felt that the woman had perhaps been called a dove because her peculiar language sounded like a bird's. She was a black dove because of her dark Egyptian skin. The miracle of the human voice occurred when she had learned enough Greek for others to understand her.

Herodotus sought to refine the Dodona story but he did not question the validity of oracles. Nor did he ever raise any suspicions about the existence or the power of the gods. He supported the same orthodoxy that Aeschylus had presented in his *Persians*. In this drama, the only extant fifth century play about a contemporary event, Xerxes is meted out a full measure of retribution for his *hybris*—that is, his delusion that worldly power and wealth made him unaccountable to the gods. Both Herodotus and Aeschylus in their time were much like cultured gentlemen of the nineteenth century who were willing to take a long look at the story of Jonah in the whale, but were born too soon to be bothered by Darwin or Freud. In the mid-fifth century, Herodotus tried to amend old religious tales with common sense. Later on, Thucydides, under the full impact of sophism and scientific objectivity, dismissed them altogether.

In spite of his caution in matters of religion, Herodotus' cosmopolitan acceptance of the ways of other people may have helped to encourage the relativism which the Sophists of the time were promoting. Although Herodotus did not philosophize about his material, what he offered spoke for itself. It was apparent that habits which men found offensive in one part of the world were perfectly acceptable in others. Thus, the Greeks were monogamous, but the Persians took many wives and concubines as well. The Persians, like the Greeks, considered themselves superior to all other people. Those who lived nearest to them they thought the next best, and so on down to the most distant who were, in their view, the most inferior. Therefore, since many peoples with different ways each thought their own to be best, could not the moral code in any locality be simply a matter of custom?

Not everyone who listened to Herodotus or read his book was provoked to speculate about this new information any more than modern tourists necessarily return from their travels with more than pictures and souvenirs. But for some (always a few) fresh knowledge sparks an entirely different outlook on the world around them. Undoubtedly, Herodotus would have disapproved of some of the conclusions reached by his contemporaries, but this loquacious traveler brought the news of the world to the main corners in Athens and men already enlightened became enlightened even more.

Herodotus was well known because the *agora* was a place where "everybody" went. For that very reason the area was viewed with distaste by a few. It was probably noisy and crowded most of the time. Regular officials were assigned to keep the area clean and to maintain order, but the Athenians were rightly proud of their freedom to speak and behave as they pleased. Given the range of human proclivities, this could mean sublime philosophical debate on the one hand and loud-mouthed vulgarity on the other. Yet more importantly, the *agora* represented a sharing by the citizens of a common experience which gave the *polis* its special meaning. It should be kept in mind that this experience was an education. And since the capacities and desires of men were as different then as they are now, all those in attendance did not benefit equally. Would it have been wonderful to have been alive in Athens during her Golden Age? It depends on who you are. For the majority of the Athenians the conflux of new ideas did not result in any radical alteration of old habits.

## New Ideas

Among those who arrived in Athens about the middle of the fifth century was Anaxagoras from Clazomenae, the teacher and intimate of

Pericles, whose speculations about the planets became too imaginative even for the Athenians. His contemporary Oenopides of Chios tried to convince the Athenians to accept a solar year in place of their clumsy lunar reckoning. Among his students in mathematics was Meton who calculated the year to be 365 days, 6 hours and 19 minutes which was only 30 minutes too long as we reckon time. His Metonic Cycle whereby solar and lunar calendars could be brought into agreement over a period of 19 years was undoubtedly useful to the Athenians. Be that as it may, they belied their reputation for innovation by refusing to abandon their lunar calendar.

The majority of the Athenians were also reluctant to accept any other means of curing disease than that offered by the temples where they slept overnight in the hope that they would be cured. Offerings and prayers were made and magical amulets were worn to ward off further dangers. There can be little doubt that some persons did walk away cured after a night spent in a temple. If this had not happened at least occasionally, the practice would not have been continued for so long. During the later years of the fifth century, the sick went especially to the sanctuaries of Asclepius, the god of healing whose cult was introduced into Athens by bringing one of the sacred snakes from Epidaurus in the northeast Peloponnesus, site of the most famous of this god's shrines.

At Epidaurus, the best preserved theater in Greece still offers evidence of the popularity and importance of this once flourishing religious center. Little remains today of the temple and sanctuaries where the cures took place, but the local museum displays a large number of the votive offerings brought by pilgrims from all parts of Greece.

The priests who acted as caretakers of these places and who performed the required rites also gave advice to the sick who came for help. Since these priests saw many kinds of illnesses they were bound to make observations and to accumulate gradually a certain amount of medical lore which they could pass along to others. The dependency on divine help did not preclude the use of common sense based on rudimentary observations. However, a purely objective approach to medicine was best exemplified by the work of Hippocrates (*circa* 460–*circa* 400) who lived on the island of Cos. He wrote concerning the disease called "sacred" (epilepsy): "It is not, in my opinion, any more divine or more sacred than other diseases, but has a natural cause, and its supposed divine origin is due to men's inexperience, and to their wonder at its peculiar character."

There is almost nothing known about this man aside from his writings; and indeed some of the so-called Hippocratic *corpus* was written by others. It is even possible that the oath for which Hippocrates is so famous was written long after he was dead. As with Pythagoras, the writings of students and the later members of the school were all attributed to the master, thereby confusing the record.

It seems certain, however, that whereas the temple priests only casually observed the symptoms of familiar diseases, Hippocrates urged the gathering of data so that observation might become systematic. The purpose of his *corpus* was to supply case histories which would allow future practitioners to know what to expect, given certain conditions. As for remedies, Hippocrates stressed rest and diet. In his writings, herbs having medical uses are prescribed but he distinctly favors allowing nature to take its course wherever possible. "Time is the great physician." In Hippocrates' day, this familiar saying had more opposition from the superstitious than from pill manufacturers, advertisers and sellers of popular medicines.

The Hippocratic School viewed the body as functioning like nature as a whole. It was a balanced system and any disorder tended to be redressed within the system itself. Abuse of the body by improper eating and drinking or loss of sleep was a major cause of imbalance, i.e., sickness. Such a point of view was in keeping with the Ionian philosophical tradition, wherein one thinker after another sought to explain the universe in terms of some unifying substance, operation, or principle. The philosophical emphasis on man's capacity to study, reflect and then hypothesize about his environment and experiences created the intellectual climate for the Hippocratic view of medicine.

This same climate continued to give rise to various speculative theories about the nature of the universe. During the middle years of the fifth century, a doctrine of absolute materialism was taught by a certain Leucippus of Miletus, a figure so obscure that his very existence has been doubted. His atomistic theory became known through the writings of his disciple Democritus who apparently expanded it in the process. Democritus traveled widely. He came to Athens from his native Abdera in Thrace sometime in the latter half of the fifth century. Although an excellent writer whose books covered a variety of subjects, he was best known for his exposition of atomism. *A-toma* in Greek literally means "uncuttable." Democritus describes all material objects as composed of such atoms. These bodies are indivisible and vary in shape and size (and so weight). Nothing exists except atoms moving in all directions through infinite space and combining to form the objects we know through our senses.

If an item is soft, its atoms are not closely combined and so can be pressed together. The closer together the atoms, the harder the object. Because of the diverse ways in which atoms are combined, light is reflected as different colors. Light itself is composed of very small round atoms. Democritus did not conduct experiments. He perceived a conclusion and then arranged his data to fit it. All phenomena were explained in terms of a single idea. Yet his idea had significant ramifications.

While Democritus did not stress the fact that his hypothesis ruled out all claims for a non-material soul or any purely "spiritual" existence, it was such a notion which later became central to the teachings of Epicurus. This fourth century philosopher sought to rid men of their anxieties about death by arguing that because the soul itself was material, immortality was impossible. Man, being pure matter, was dissolved in death. Epicurus found comfort in the thought that he would one day be altogether dead. His followers have always been in a minority.

The ancient "atomists" had neither the knowledge nor instruments for discovering the atom as it is known today. All things considered, pure speculation had led to an amazing hypothesis. Nevertheless this materialistic view of the universe was in direct contradiction with the philosophical conclusions of Pythagoras and Parmenides. What indeed could a man be sure about amid this spectrum of opinion in Athens? Among the intellectuals, there was a definite shift toward skepticism and secularism. And it was precisely this air of speculation and controversy which spawned the rampant sophism of the later years of the fifth century.

Certain teachers, called Sophists, advanced the notion that there was no way at all to know an absolute truth in the sense that it was true for everybody. Protagoras, a friend of Pericles and a noted grammarian, has been better known for the dictum: "Man is the measure of all things," i.e., what each man believes to be true is true for him. Out of this relativism came the familiar byway to nihilism. The celebrated Gorgias, who visited Athens in 427 as an emissary from Leontini, was a well-paid teacher of rhetoric and famous for his saying that a man could not know anything. And if he could, he could not describe it and if he could describe it, nobody could understand him.

The Sophists examined the "whole man" and found that his ideals were rooted in literature and custom. So, they raised doubts about stuffy standards of behavior which circumscribed what a man should be. A man should decide for himself. And if he chose to quit the *gymnasia* and lead a life of contemplation or conversation, that was his own affair. To young men who caught the new spirit, Aeschylus and Pindar sounded old-fashioned. Moral standards, formerly accepted as a matter of course, were now subject to debate.

There were two sides to the sophistic movement. At their best, the Sophists introduced a refreshing re-examination of accepted values, many of which may only have been receiving lip-service. Some of the Sophists were high-minded men whose musings were purely speculative. They sought the freedom to sweep away old conventions as a means by which to find a better understanding of the universe, the gods and themselves. Many of their students, however, carried the new relativism into practice. In their dealings with other people, in politics and in the courts, what mattered was to win by any means possible. Their attitude appeared totally destructive and left man unprotected from his baser inclinations, or, worse, gave him a pseudo-scientific basis for giving in to them. It was the behavior of these Sophists which created the stereotype of them all. The comic poets pictured them as men of dubious morals and sharp practices and this is how the suspicious public saw them.

The reality of the human propensities and the necessity to control them by some means or another are the basic premises of civilization. There were young men in the *agora* who grasped for the freedom and forgot the responsibilities. They were educated enough to be dangerous, but not intelligent enough to see beyond self-interest. They represented a new kind of individualism which plotted a solitary and irresponsible course. It was not the individualism of the hardy Marathon fighters who had faith in the *polis,* the gods, and each other.

## Sophocles

Herodotus, Anaxagoras and Democritus were typical of the talented men who came from abroad to join the galaxy of thinkers and writers in Periclean Athens. Yet no man added more to the glory of the city than one of her own native dramatists, Sophocles (496–406), the premier playwright of the second generation. Actually he was more than that. Because his life almost spanned the fifth century, he was the major tragic poet in Athens for over sixty years. Sophocles won first prize in 468 with his initial entry at the age of twenty-seven. Moreover, as a young man he had shown confidence in his own abilities by offering significant innovations in the theater. He was apparently the first playwright to expand the possibilities of a dramatic scene by the use of a third actor. Aeschylus, whose ingenuity made him the founder of Greek tragedy, flattered his young competitor by adopting the change.

Although Ion of Chios observed that Sophocles showed no real enthusiam for official duties, his long record of public service as ambassador, treasurer and priest shows that he was well liked and considered to be a person of responsible leadership. Plutarch has passed along Pericles' gratuitous remark that as a soldier Sophocles made a fine poet. This was of course the evaluation of a good friend rather than a critic, for Pericles and Sophocles had grown up together. In fact, according to Plutarch, they were close enough friends for Pericles to criticize Sophocles for his irregular emotional interests and to remind him bluntly that a man's eyes should be as clean as his soul. Sophocles was known for his pleasant personality but he also had his failures and his weaknesses. Without them he could scarcely have written about human life with such insight and sympathy.

During his long career Sophocles appears to have written a minimum of one hundred and eleven plays. At least, there are that many titles attributed to him. Out of this number, part of a satyr play and seven tragedies have survived.

The *Philoctetes* and the *Ajax* are plays about men and war. The *Women of Trachis* is a tale of a wife's good intentions gone astray. In each of these dramas, amid scenes which depict the woeful ways of human passions and weakness, there are also men and women of innate decency. Sophocles' talent for characterization and his discerning view of human nature are always evident, yet these plays were not the mainstays of his reputation. On the other hand, the *Oedipus Tyrannus* alone could have justified his fame as a dramatist.

## Man and His Fate

Today, everybody knows what an Oedipus complex is. Yet Oedipus never had one. In fact his mother was dead before he knew who she was. In brief, the story of the *Oedipus Tyrannus* is this. While Oedipus was still a baby, it was learned from an oracle that it would be his fate to murder his father Laius, king of Thebes, and to marry his mother Jocasta, the queen. To forestall such an unhappy course his parents had his feet bound (whence the name Oedipus, meaning the swollen-footed) and gave him to a trusted servant with instructions to leave him in a desolate place to die of exposure. Instead, the herdsman, having no heart for the deed, hands the baby over to an itinerant shepherd. Oedipus is then carried to Corinth and there adopted into a childless royal family. He never learns his true identity but when he is grown to young manhood he does learn about his fate. Fearful that he would inflict these wrongs on the king and queen of Corinth, who he thinks are his real parents, he flees from their court.

In the course of his subsequent travels Oedipus encounters, quarrels with, and kills a stranger at a place in Phocis "where three ways meet." The victim is Laius, his real father. Proceeding on to Thebes he solves the riddle of the Sphinx and slays the monster which has devoured so many earlier victims. For this masterful deed he is hailed as the king of Thebes. He then marries Queen Jocasta, his real mother, and together they have children of their own. It comes to pass, however, that a plague falls upon the land and the oracle of Delphi reports Apollo's oath that the pestilence will last until the murderer of Laius is discovered and punished.

Oedipus is a responsible king. The city has been delivered from the dreaded Sphinx and it will be saved from this more recent plight. He announces to the harassed Thebans that he will discover who is guilty no matter what the cost. The grave irony of this pronouncement sets the mood of the play. In a rare poetic tapestry of foreshadowing and suspense, Sophocles permits the truth to be made apparent, first to one person and then to another, and finally to Oedipus himself. The audience knows it all the time. Yet the play is a spellbinder and to read it over and over is like watching a skilled artist paint the same picture again and again.

Shortly after his declaration that he will find the truth, Oedipus is warned by an aged seer, the blind Tiresias, not to pursue his investigation too seriously. If he does learn the truth it will be to his own sorrow, for he is himself the guilty party. To Oedipus, the statement is too fantastic to be believed. At first, he accuses Tiresias of serving some rival for the throne and Creon, Jocasta's brother, is the prime suspect. Oedipus ridicules the soothsayer's alleged powers and then sends him away.

In the scene which follows, Oedipus behaves rashly, even unfairly, toward his brother-in-law. Creon keeps his wits about him. When Oedipus demands to know why it is that Tiresias had not at the time of Laius' death revealed the name of the murderer, Creon replies simply that he did not know. He adds that he keeps quiet about matters of which he knows nothing. With such a line, Sophocles may well have provoked some glances among his impetuous and talkative fellow citizens. In any event, he obviously has given Creon the better part of this exchange and in so doing makes Oedipus a truly believable human being. The bluster about a plot by Creon does not successfully cover up the fact that, like any man, Oedipus is badly troubled by Tiresias' blunt accusation.

Jocasta tells Oedipus why he should ignore the seer's unsettling words. As an example of the falsity of oracles she relates the story about her own unhappily fated baby which was supposed to have one day slain its father. But, she explains, this never happened because the baby was shackled and exposed to die and Laius was eventually slain by robbers. In the telling, however, she mentions casually that the murder was committed at a place "where three ways meet." This chance reference, a seemingly unimportant remark, is a thunderbolt. Her intention had been to comfort Oedipus, but now he is more disturbed than ever. He too has killed a man at such a locality. The sudden shift in the wind is a Sophoclean trademark.

The *Oedipus Tyrannus* is a showpiece of the master's stagecraft. In the crucial scene in which the soothsayer's words prove to be true, sad news sounds like good news. In the end it could not have been worse. A messenger from Corinth announces that Polybus the king has died of natural causes. Thus, the foretold fate of Oedipus could no longer come true. Jocasta again scoffs at the oracles, unaware that she will be the first to suffer when the real meaning of the news is known. Oedipus, reacting impulsively, joins her in denouncing the claims of Delphi and boldly states that oracles are worthless.

There was a bitter cup awaiting both Jocasta and Oedipus for their outbursts of sacrilege. The stress which Sophocles placed on this point has been interpreted as an obvious display of his religious orthodoxy. It might also be taken as a sign that he felt such orthodoxy was in trouble. When he was writing, the sophistic movement was at its height in Athens. It is conceivable that the *Oedipus Tyrannus* reflects an apprehension about the growing tendency of certain intellectuals to question any and all beliefs. Whether Sophocles did in fact intend his words as a warning to those who lacked faith in the oracles cannot be known. There is no doubt that he told the story of sacrilege and its consequences with dramatic power. Jocasta, excited and relieved at the news which she hopes will rid her husband of his fears, tells him that life is only a matter of chance and that men should live free of care, unbound by the old religious beliefs. Yet she is herself only moments from disaster, for the messenger has not finished telling all he knows. Surely, to the faithful in the audience it was no coincidence that her defiant speech occurred at such a juncture.

Oedipus does not give himself over to complete abandon. There remains the danger about his mother. The messenger, eager to please and happy to be able to allay all of Oedipus' anxieties, hastens to inform him that he has no reason for any fear. He was not the real son of Polybus and Queen Merope in the first place. The messenger identifies himself as the very shepherd who had carried Oedipus to Corinth from the region of Mount Cithaeron. Where did he obtain the baby? From the hand of a fellow shepherd whom he had known for three seasons in this region. When the man is described, it is apparent that he is the same servant who carried back the news of Laius' death and then, seeing Oedipus at the palace, asked permission to pasture his flocks in fields some distance from Thebes.

Oedipus demands that he be brought in immediately so that the final piece of the puzzle might be put in place. Jocasta does not await his coming. She already knows who Oedipus is, for the shepherd from Corinth has told how the baby he received had had its feet pinned together. Unable to stop Oedipus in his relentless pursuit of the truth she withdraws to the palace.

Now the herdsman arrives. The final moment is at hand, but not quite. There is a suspenseful hesitation as the herdsman balks at being called a common slave. His insistence that he had been bred in Laius' house as a servant, and not bought in the open market, was precisely the kind of point about status which an average man might make on suddenly finding himself in the spotlight. This excellent characterization is also an historical note. The herdsman's objection confirms the impression that in fifth century Athens the customary treatment of household servants was appreciably superior to that of slaves bought for work in the quarries or the mines.

After some impatient prodding, Oedipus finally learns that the baby was from Laius' house. Suddenly all is simple and direct. Concerning the baby, Oedipus asks: "Jocasta gave it to you?" "She gave it to me." All was done.

Oedipus knew that it was right to search out the truth and he stubbornly performed his duty. This admirable quality ruined him completely.

Athenian audiences often heard the sound of outcry and anguish in the drama, but rarely saw any scenes of violence. They heard what happened subsequently to Oedipus from a messenger who tells the chorus that the king found and took down the body of his mother-wife who had hanged herself. Overcome with remorse, he then took the brooches from Jocasta's dress and gouged out his own eyes. It was an act of supreme repentance. He would never see his mother again even in the after-life, for Sophocles, like Homer, saw no physical change between this world and the underworld. Blindness here would be blindness there. Even death would not allow Oedipus to escape his self-inflicted punishment.

It was folly for even a king to try to escape his fate. The most respected and able man of Thebes was now an outcast. As Oedipus departs into exile, the chorus intones a familiar warning. No man should call himself happy until his life be over.

Critics who have detected a strain of fatalism in Sophocles' plays have had no difficulty in accounting for it. During the last twenty-five years of his life, the Greek states clawed at each other in a demoralizing and destructive war. The total collapse of Athens came only two years after he died. In his lifetime he had witnessed the rise and fall of the mightiest city in Greece. Moreover, the astounding reversal of fortune which caused Athens to plunge from the heights to the depths in so short a time had been paralleled in the lives of some of her most prominent citizens. Here today and gone tomorrow offered little comfort.

Even so, these recent events had not evoked a mood which was entirely new. A sense of pessimism about man and his fate was a major thread in Greek thought and literature from Homer onward. The truly tragic warfare was not the pathetic wars which men fought amongst themselves, but the conflicts between foolish or arrogant men and the gods. Pitiful man forever pitted against hopeless odds! Sophocles' *Oedipus Tyrannus* is a variation on a very old theme.

## Between Heaven and Earth

It is not known when Sophocles produced his *Antigone*. Perhaps it was written before the *Oedipus Tyrannus*. On the basis of the story, we would call it a sequel. Oedipus' daughters, Antigone and Ismene, had accompanied their father into exile. After Oedipus died they returned to their native Thebes. In the meantime their brothers,

Eteocles and Polyneices, had struggled over the throne, a story which supplied the background for Aeschylus' *Seven Against Thebes*. As it had been prophesied, the brothers were killed, each by the other's sword, whereupon Creon, their uncle, became king. Sophocles' *Antigone* tells of the events on the first day of Creon's reign. He has ordered full religious rites for Eteocles who had been the legal ruler. The body of Polyneices, Creon declares, is to be counted among the enemy dead which, according to Theban custom, were never buried. The corpse, left rotting and unattended, will be a warning to other would-be usurpers.

In ancient belief, the performance of a proper ceremonial was all-important, almost magical. Without the burial rites, Polyneices could not join his parents in the underworld. To Antigone, the denial of the rites is an intolerable offence against her brother and therefore against herself. Worse, it is an impious act, an outrageous insolence against the gods. In her subsequent quarrel with Creon, she makes it plain that she is defending the laws of heaven and not some mortal opinion of her own. It is Creon who dares to countermand a divine ordinance by substituting an expedient order for ancient custom.

Antigone takes matters into her own hands and seeks the help of her sister Ismene in covering their brother's body. But her sister holds back. She feels that they should acknowledge their place as women and as subjects, and therefore submit to Creon's order, distasteful as it may be. To Antigone such an argument evades the issue. There is only one answer: her brother must join his parents in the underworld no matter what the cost. She goes alone, not once but twice, to place earth over the corpse. The second time she is caught and brought to her uncle.

The guard who arrests Antigone has been worried lest the body be covered and he be blamed for the deed. He is unconcerned about the principle at stake. Still, Sophocles does not treat him as a perfunctory go-between. As with the herdsman in the *Oedipus Tyrannus,* he gives this man a characterization of his own. By custom, tragedy dealt with clashes of strong-willed personalities, men and women of divine or royal, at least noble, blood. It was unusual for much attention to be given those in subservient roles. Yet Sophocles' talent was not easily contained. The guard is uncomfortably real, a whining, self-centered person, concerned for his own skin. Unlike Creon and Antigone who seek to justify their opposed positions, he represents those who want only to escape the responsibility of having one.

Face to face with Creon, Antigone continues to defy him. She insists that his order of the moment has broken a law which even kings must obey. Characteristically, Antigone, the idealist, is upholding an eternal principle, and Creon, the realist, is arguing the merits of a particular case. It is not a successful dialogue. Antigone's insolence alone is enough to doom her. She is sentenced to die, entombed alive in a rocky sepulchre.

After Antigone is led away, her betrothed, Haemon, Creon's son, engages his father in a raging argument. It begins in an ordinary way, with the father urging his son to renounce his cousin who has set an example of defiance for others to follow. Haemon, who knows the feelings of the Thebans, cautions Creon not to be deceived by the silent acquiescence of his subjects, for this is a sign of fear and not agreement. The king, angered at being lectured by his young son, impetuously makes a bolder claim. He declares that the city belongs to him and he will not obey any laws save his own. Whereupon Haemon, in frustration and despair, withdraws to join Antigone. He is too late. Believing that she had been abandoned, even by him, she had hanged herself.

Meantime, the aged seer Tiresias tells Creon that his refusal to allow the burial of Polyneices has aroused the gods. The usual sacrificial offerings will not burn on the altar. At last, remorseful and seeking to undo what he has done, Creon goes to the cave. There Haemon spits upon him, and then before his father's eyes stabs himself to death.

The audience learns of this horror-filled scene from a messenger who describes it at the palace. Creon's wife Eurydice listens and turns away silently. She goes to an altar and in supplication praises her dead son and curses the living Creon. And there she dies. Whether from shock or from her own hand is not said.

Creon has had his way and he is ruined by his triumph. Grief-stricken, he realizes that he has learned the truth too late. The chorus observes in closing that this is not unusual.

Creon was a man who in self-justification could say he had tried to do the best job he knew how. Yet he failed because he lived by the book and never calculated the depth of the feelings and faith of others. Still, the tragedy was neither in him nor in Antigone, but between them. It was an inevitable conflict between a person who must take strong, practical action to accomplish the needs of the moment, and a person who cares nothing for the passing scene and will not bend to circumstances. Melodrama presents a sad situation, yet one in which the victim may yet be saved. Tragedy is uncompromising. It does not allow a way out. Both Antigone and Creon inevitably had to suffer. The dilemma, stated in Sophoclean terms, was a conflict between the order which men seek to work out by their own wills and the eternal order of the gods.

Such conflicts between heaven and earth have always existed. In 1940, in Nazi-occupied Paris, the French playwright Jean Anouilh produced a modern *Antigone* closely patterned after that of Sophocles' play. The implications in his drama were obvious since the lines between resistance and collaboration were sharply drawn. The expedient Creons, the shy Ismenes, the defiant Antigones, the subservient guards were all there, offering the same old arguments, pleading the same old excuses.

Perhaps it was Sophocles' close friendship with Pericles which kept him active in government affairs. Even so, he was an aristocrat on the conservative side and need not have felt required to be enthusiastic about the program of the popular democracy. There were no passages in his plays which touched directly on a controversial issue in the way Aeschylus mentioned the Areopagus in his *Eumenides;* nevertheless, as in Aeschylus' *Prometheus Bound,* it might be possible to read into Sophocles' works an oblique commentary on the baser aspects of Athenian imperialism. The *Antigone* was concerned with the familiar problems including the right of the weak to disagree with the strong. Did Sophocles intend to allegorize the conflict between Athens and her allies? There is no positive evidence that he did. Nor is there anything wrong with suggesting it. In other ages, men like Anouilh have seen analogies. Some plays have a timeless value. Should it be any wonder if they had political overtones in their own day?

## Vengeance

Athenian playwrights used the same stories in different ways. Aeschylus related the bitter tragedy of the House of Atreus in three parts. First there was the murder of Agamemnon. Then the vengeance of Orestes and Electra against their mother and her lover. The final play in the trilogy told of the intervention of Athena who founded a court of justice and ended the chain of killings which had linked one generation to the next. Sophocles had a sharper focus. He concentrated on the story of the vengeance alone and he told it in a single play. In the *Electra,* Orestes appears at the beginning and at the end, but the rest is a tale of the irrepressible hatred of a daughter for her mother. Electra's thoughts, vividly drawn, give the play an air of midnight and even outweigh the horror of Orestes' final act.

The play begins with Orestes standing before Mycenae, plotting how he might enter the palace without arousing the suspicions of his intended victims. Beside him is an aged friend—the servant to whom Orestes had been trusted as a baby with orders to carry him away secretly and care for him until he has grown to manhood. This guardian, now changed with the years, will go to the palace and announce that Orestes has been killed in an accident at the Pythian Games. Then in due time Orestes and his friend Pylades will arrive, posing as messengers and bringing a bronze receptacle presumed to contain the ashes of the fallen prince. In the interval Orestes will place a lock of hair on his father's tomb.

In the scene which follows, Electra appears, accompanied by a chorus of Mycenaean women. When she speaks, it is apparent that her mind is overstrained by grief and hatred. Thoughts dart in all directions and moods overlap. A moment of despair is quickly followed by a cry of defiance. Tearfully, she speaks of the years she has had to endure the agonizing sight of her mother and the cowardly Aegisthus enjoying the throne and the bed of the man they murdered. As yet she has no inkling that this day will bring deliverance.

Her sister Chrystothemis joins her and they renew an old quarrel which makes plain a difference in attitude toward the problem which they both face. Chrystothemis insists that she feels as badly as Electra does about what happened to their father, but argues that they are helpless and so they must be sensible and make the best of things. At all costs they should not make matters worse by disobedience. Electra will not bargain even for her life. She mocks Chrystothemis for claiming love for Agamemnon while living in peace with those who butchered him. When Chrystothemis warns Electra of other punishments to befall her, her sister simply asks what could be worse than her present condition? Chrystothemis leaves before her mother arrives.

In the scene which follows, the exchange of speeches between Electra and her mother poses a familiar conflict. On the one hand is the excuse of circumstances; on the other, a devotion to moral law. Clytemnestra seeks a general pardon for murder, adultery and a stolen throne, by arguing that she killed her husband because he had slain their daughter. Iphigenia, she claims, was sacrificed to make possible the recovery of Helen from Troy. Did not Helen's husband, Menelaus, have two children of his own to offer? It is a clever question, but Electra cannot be fooled. She corrects the story by stating that Iphigenia was sacrificed because of an offense of Agamemnon against Artemis and not because of Helen. Then, more tellingly, she asks, if Clytemnestra lives by the law of a "life for a life," why should not her own life also be forfeited? Yet Electra denounces such a law for it leads only to an endless cycle of killings.

When the aged guardian arrives with the false report that Orestes is dead, Clytemnestra is ecstatic. The news gives her a new life and she is free from the fears which have torn her night and day. To Electra it means the end. Left alone, she asks for death. When Orestes appears, he is a stranger to her yet she pours out her heart to him for she believes the small urn he carries contains the ashes of her brother. In his sympathy to see her so, Orestes reveals his true identity and explains to her his plan for revenge. As in the *Oedipus Tyrannus,* a strikingly dramatic effect is achieved through the realization that a piece of news has exactly the opposite meaning than that which first appears. Electra's mood changes to hysterical joy and Orestes has to calm her lest her excitement betray his mission.

After Orestes enters the palace the audience hears only his mother's screams for mercy. What they see is Electra, standing before the closed doors, exulting in the act of vengeance. When Orestes strikes Clytemnestra with his sword it is Electra who shrieks, "Again!" True, Apollo had sanctioned the death of Clytemnestra, but earlier in the day when Electra attacked the rule of a "life for a life" she did not mention this. Rather she entered a plea for higher unwritten laws. These same laws are now forgotten in the murder of her mother. Sophocles has it exactly right. The emotions often do betray the mind.

After Aegisthus is slain the chorus concludes that the House of Atreus is free. With that pronouncement Sophocles ends the story.

Aeschylus had gone on further. He felt that the guilt of these final killings had also to be resolved. Both playwrights were part of the same tradition. Man was to be reconciled to the human condition through suffering. Yet Sophocles' tragedies were preoccupied with how men behaved in the midst of suffering whereas Aeschylus was more interested in the end of things. Technique aside, their works had a difference in tone and emphasis, something like the difference between the books of *Esther* and *Job* in the Old Testament.

Sophocles' plays have life because he wrote about believable people. His characterizations of women were especially noticeable in contrast with Aeschylus' plays and in view of woman's usually secluded role in society. Women actually come alive in Sophocles' plays though only on paper to be sure, for men played the parts.

The more cautious sisters, Ismene in *Antigone* and Chrystothemis in *Electra,* are feminine and dependent. Neither has any compelling interest in principles or revenge. It is a world they never made, and for the most part they seek to escape its problems by living unseen, hidden in sweetness and submission. The other sisters, Antigone and Electra are "Friday's children, full of woe." They would find a problem in heaven. Intelligent and restless, each insists on the righteousness of a cause to the point of death. They have an admirable stubbornness and make more trouble than their less courageous sisters. They also get more done. Those who edge the plow forward do often suffer for it; those who follow cautiously behind benefit from the courage of others. Sophocles does not pass judgment on this juxtaposition of human attitudes and temperaments. He simply describes them exactly as they still are.

Sophocles' *Oedipus at Colonus* was his last play, written a short time before he died in 406. It is a strange play, indeed hardly a play at all. It records a series of incidents at the end of the exiled Oedipus' life. He has been granted refuge in Athens and in gratitude the deposed Theban king sings the praises of his new city, her laws and her citizens. The singular outbursts of patriotic fervor in this drama are not difficult to understand. By this time the wealth and confidence of Sophocles' beloved Athens have been drained by a ruinous war.

## The War Against
## "What Might Happen"

**XII**

Through the years the Greek cities had fought intermittently and had accumulated unsettled accounts of enmity. Finally, in a long and bitter civil war, Greek brothers, like the sons of Oedipus who destroyed each other, were to do more harm to their homeland than the Great King Xerxes might ever have dreamed of. The Peloponnesian War (431–404) is the classic example of the trouble men make for themselves.

There were two periods of actual conflict from 431 to 421 and from 414 to 404. The seven years between were an uneasy interlude which has been called the Peace of Nicias. Today such a peace would be called a "cold war" and that is exactly what it was.

A history of the Peloponnesian War was written by Thucydides, an Athenian general. There can be no synopsis of this conflict which does not quote or paraphrase his work. There are other references to these times in Greek literature, but Thucydides' account is the standard, the only history of the war. It may seem regrettable that no other major source exists for this important period yet there could scarcely be a better one. Thucydides was an eye-witness. He reported events conscientiously with a minimum of personal bias and took pains to be sure that his facts were straight. In short, unlike Herodotus, he has not included strange tales for the sake of adding interest. It was his intention to write an honest account, even if it might also be somewhat dull. He succeeded on both counts. His work has always been a model of objectivity and there are several long and dry passages to prove it.

Sparta had the strength to challenge Athens; other cities supplied the reasons. According to Thucydides, Corinth was the most vocal plaintiff. Her relations with Athens had been marred by commercial rivalry for over a century. Feelings steadily worsened after 459, the year that Athens checked Corinthian ambitions in the Megarid. Two years later, Athens established a base at Naupactus near the mouth of the Corinthian Gulf, a direct threat to Corinthian trade with the west. By 433, the breaking point was reached. Corinth was again having trouble with her colony at Corcyra and this time, as we have previously noted, Pericles sided with the Corcyreans to keep their sizeable fleet from falling into enemy hands. His interference raised the issue whether Athens had violated the Thirty Years Treaty with Sparta. The pact stipulated that neither party should become involved in the affairs of the other's allies. Corinth, a staunch friend of Sparta, charged that Athens broke faith when she made an alliance with Corcyra. Technically speaking, however, Corcyra, although a colony of Corinth, considered herself a neutral and was free therefore under the terms of the treaty to join either camp. Athens, in feigned innocence, insisted that she had been within her rights. In a sense they were both wrong, and that made the argument hotter.

In the late summer of 433, the Corcyreans and the Corinthians fought out their differences at sea. Athens with the least effort was the actual winner. The presence of her ships near to Corcyra discouraged the successful Corinthians from pressing their fight. To Pericles that was all that mattered.

The Corcyrean affair was quickly followed by another flare-up between the same powers. Again, the action was far from the home scene; again, it concerned a Corinthian colony. Potidaea was located on the three-pronged Chalcidic peninsula which juts into the northern Aegean Sea. Her ties with Corinth were strong; in fact, she still received magistrates from the mother city. Nevertheless, like other commercial towns in the area, Potidaea had joined the Delian League and had become eventually a tribute-bearing state of the Athenian Empire. The dual ties to Corinth and Athens invited trouble. When the Potidaeans decided to withdraw from the Empire, the Corinthians sent reinforcements to assist them and the Athenians in turn besieged the city. The war in the north was on. Not at home, however. There the Thirty Years Treaty was still observed and the Spartans and the Athenians remained at peace.

Corinth called for a meeting of the venerable Peloponnesian League, now almost seventy-five years old. The representatives met at Sparta amid a rising tide of resentment against Athens. Each state was able to present its case directly to the Spartan Assembly. Aegina, who had been forced to join the Athenian Empire, sent envoys in secret to bewail her loss of independence. That was an old story. The complaint of the Megarians was new. The Athenians had retaliated for the massacre of their garrison in 446 by excluding all Megarian goods from the ports they controlled. This economic boycott was hard on the Megarian clothmakers. It was also a handle which the Athenians intended to use in order to return to the Megarid. More significantly, the Megarian Decree, as it was called, was a warning to all that Athens would use any means possible to punish those who defied her will.

After the complaints of smaller cities had been heard, the Corinthians came forward and stated boldly that the root of the problem was in Sparta, not Athens. Who was more to be blamed—a strong power which energetically exploited weaker neighbors, or an equally strong power which stood by and let it happen? The Athenian intervention at Corcyra and the siege of Potidaea were ruthless acts of aggression. If Athens dared that much without knowing the Spartan reaction, what would follow should it become apparent that Sparta would not intervene? These questions were put politely but the Corinthians had no intention of being diplomatic. They bluntly recounted the Spartan failures. Spartan indecisiveness and ineptitude had allowed the Athenians to erect long walls to the sea, and so make their city an impregnable island. Furthermore, the Spartans had failed to come to the aid of those who stood up to Athens. Even worse, by promising help and not sending it they had caused other states to miscalculate their needs. Only an occasional Athenian blunder had thwarted her growth. Sparta in some respects had been a silent partner in the process.

The Corinthian argument need not have been novel at the time and certainly is not now. Peace, they said, was only possible when a strong power maintained its strength and made it absolutely clear to others that this potential would be used to thwart any and all aggression. It was a good point, but the decisive one was saved for the last. The Spartans were bluntly warned that if they did not lead the Peloponnesian League in a war against the Athenians they would lose their position of leadership. The allies would be forced to turn elsewhere.

A few Athenians happened to be in Sparta on other matters, and even though they were not official representatives they asked to be heard. It was typical of them to insist that they would not make excuses for the past actions of their native city. Instead, they warned against challenging Athenian power. They also asked why Athens should be blamed for acting in self-interest? Which of the Greek states did not? Actually, they insisted, Athens had behaved with greater moderation and justice than was necessary under the circumstances. Where were the thanks for that? Their proud and high-handed attitude gave substance to the Corinthian claim that the time was getting late for any action at all.

For the Spartans, there was now a clear choice. The Corinthians had urged them to abandon their usual cautious habits and act with haste. The Athenians advised them to reconsider the many risks involved. The Thirty Years Treaty, they said, provided a sure means of solving all problems by arbitration.

Archidamus, one of the Spartan kings, favored the slower route. He for one had not been impressed by the fast-talking Corinthians. He argued that instead of a rash declaration, the Spartans should parley with the Athenians and at the same time prepare for any eventuality. Both sides should be given time to assess the seriousness of the situation. His advice was in keeping with the traditional character of the Spartans and he was not ashamed of it. What the Corinthians had described as a lack of daring, he called self-restraint. The Spartans might admit that they were not well-read or sophisticated. Yet neither had they produced Sophists who questioned ancient law and made clever remarks about the gods. They were soldiers, methodical and deliberate. Because of these fixed habits they had succeeded in the past. There was no reason to change.

The tempered words of Archidamus were followed by a brief emotion-laden speech in which one of the ephors, Sthenelaidas, took the opposite position. He observed that the Athenians had done little more than pat themselves on the back. It was obvious they had no intention of admitting that they were in the wrong. The Peloponnesian allies expected the Spartans to act immediately to relieve their injuries, and act they must or lose this valuable support. The point was not pertinent as to whether the Athenians had or had not broken the Thirty Years Treaty, yet the two ideas were now wedded in the Spartan mind. The Assembly voted that the treaty had indeed been broken. As it was well said, the Spartans finally followed in order to lead.

The war, Thucydides observes, resulted not so much because of what had happened, as for what the Spartans feared might happen. This is what he means when he says that his history will be an object lesson for all time.

The decision by the Spartan Assembly was crucial, but the Peloponnesian League (known more precisely as "Sparta and her Allies") was an organization of autonomous cities and a majority vote was needed for a declaration of war. Before this momentous decision the Spartans sent envoys to ask the advice of Apollo. The priestess at Delphi relayed encouraging news. If they pursued the war energetically they would win. Apollo was with them.

When the Peloponnesian League met to make the final decision, the Corinthians spoke only of victory and the representatives voted for that. War was declared and preparations for the invasion of Attica began immediately.

In spite of this threatening action there continued to be strong sentiment for peace, especially at Sparta. King Archidamus had not abandoned his hope that the Athenians could be brought to their senses and he sent word to them that war could still be avoided if they would foreswear interfering with the independence of their fellow Greeks.

The Athenians as usual listened to a variety of suggestions about how to respond to this overture. As usual too, they followed Pericles' advice. He took a hard position. Any compromise would be judged as weakness and other demands would follow. Furthermore, he argued, there was no need to accept the Spartan offer since the Peloponnesian alliance was neither sound enough nor wealthy enough to await a drawn-out decision. And drawn-out it would be. Pericles planned it that way. The enemy would invade Attica and lay waste the land but the Athenians would remain safe behind their walls. They must not risk heavy casualties in a fight against superior land forces. Pericles had no illusions about the loyalty of the Athenian allies. He bluntly acknowledged that they would not remain loyal for long after hearing of Athenian losses.

Athenian aggression would be at sea, where her superiority would permit hit-and-run raids along the coast of the Peloponnesus. Pericles advised his fellow citizens that brief forays inland burning crops and barns would do more harm to the Peloponnesian cause than a set battle outside the walls of Athens. His plans were cautious. Time would win the war for Athens. Specifically, he warned against any drastic or costly ventures.

Finally, Pericles scored the Spartans for claiming to champion freedom and pointed to their own self-interest in dealings with their neighbors, not to mention the enslavement of Messenia. Could these men dictate terms to a city which had resisted the Persian Empire? The Athenians would not hear of it. They must live up to the memory of their ancestors. The Spartans and their allies would also be worthy of theirs. The trumpets took over. Communications were broken off.

## The First Year of the War

The insurance which had been written for thirty years had lasted fourteen. Time enough for five-year-olds to become eager youths of nineteen. The moment for reliving the heroic tales of the past had come round again. These young men were the third generation of the fifth century.

The Spartan king Archidamus, although criticized at home because of his anxious desire for peace, continued to delay the assault on Attica in the hope that the Athenians would have a change of heart. At Sparta, militarism may have blunted the imagination of most citizens, but old men are the same everywhere. In his long life, Archidamus had observed that wars caused much suffering and solved few problems.

By midsummer it was apparent that the Athenians would remain adamant. Those who lived outside the walls had hurried into the city bringing everything they could carry. Some families were forced to move in with relatives who were perhaps no happier to see them than they were to come. Others had to be content with uncomfortable makeshift shelters. Their livestock was taken to the island of Euboea where the navy could offer protection. Everything else was abandoned to the enemy.

Archidamus knew what he had to do. The Peloponnesian cities had gathered the largest force they had ever assembled. This mighty army moved into Attica and put a torch to the land. The grain, ready for harvesting, was burned. From the walls of the city, the Athenians could see the smoke rising from their fields, orchards and barns. Those awesome dark clouds were a horrifying sight to men who were used to punishing others. Pericles would not fight. He kept to his waiting game. The citizenry, now that their land was actually invaded, found his calculations less appealing than they had seemed at first. They openly criticized him for his reluctance to do more than employ the cavalry to keep raiders from the suburbs. Ignoring their grumbling, he stuck to his original plan. This included sending one hundred ships to raid the coast of the Peloponnesus with orders to do as much damage as they could with as few casualties. At the same time the Aeginetans were finally expelled from their island. They fled as refugees to the Peloponnesus and the Athenians occupied Aegina.

When the Peloponnesian allies had exhausted their supplies and any expectations that the Athenians would come out and fight, they returned home. Later that summer, Pericles sought to placate his critics by leading the Athenian army in a counterattack against the Megarians. The Athenians burned crops and pillaged the villages of the Megarid, just as had been done in Attica.

### The Funeral Oration

No major battles were fought in the first year of the war. It was a contest of endurance. That was Pericles' strategy and he was himself the mainstay of the Athenian spirit. During the winter he delivered his famous *Funeral Oration* in honor of those who had fallen during the preceding months. He was well aware of the anxieties of his listeners and his words were intended to bolster their morale for the trials ahead.

These men have died, Pericles said, to protect the heritage which we have received from our ancestors. He spoke of the Athenian democracy in glowing terms. It was a government by majority rule, and one in which every citizen's chance for promotion was based on ability rather than class. There was also equal justice for all citizens under the law. Furthermore, he stated, we Athenians are free to speak and act exactly as we please. The lack of specific written laws detailing how men should act does not make us wanton or disrespectful of public order and decency. There are higher unwritten laws. We might be free of the control of each other, but not of the gods or our own consciences. Slaves and barbarians might display animality, but we know how to behave. It was a flattering account. Each of those present, however, could perhaps have named a few exceptions.

The *Funeral Oration* cannot be understood in its proper perspective unless it is realized that Pericles was talking about ideals. Athenian aims were high, and for that they deserved praise. Unfortunately, however, romanticists have on occasion allowed the speech to be taken literally. This might lead to the impression that all Athenians behaved according to exalted principles. It is a disservice. They were more human than that.

The passage in the *Funeral Oration* on Athenian foreign policy has a familiar sound. Pericles described the relationship between Athens and her allies as similar to that of a creditor who cares for indigent debtors. Those who receive the help feel that they owe something, and dislike the creditor for it. The Athenians, Pericles said, are not self interested, they only want to help others. Debtors seem unwilling to accept such reasoning, then or now.

Pericles' boastful, one-sided praise of Athens offered reassurance to his audience. In his most eloquent passages toward the end of the speech he spoke again of the dead. Their lives had been richer in every way than those of other men. They had given up life itself that their fellow citizens might continue to enjoy the benefits they had known. Since there were many ways a man might die, what better way than in the service of his homeland? To these fine words Pericles added a note which jars the modern ear. He urged those parents who had lost loved ones to comfort themselves by having more sons. They would ease the pain of the present loss and in their turn provide a future defense for the city. This hard advice has not found a place in the picture of Pericles as the romanticists would have him. It does sound very like the practical war leader whom Thucydides knew.

In closing, Pericles remarked that the government would care for the widows and their children. In return he suggests that the women behave honorably and not provoke any kind of talk whether good or bad. It is fatherly advice. In keeping with this paternal mood he tells his audience that the funeral is over and that they may go home.

Thucydides' report of this famous speech has a special value. Not only the content of the oration is important, but also the style. If this was the way Pericles addressed the Athenian people it speaks well for them. The speech has dignity. It praises all things Athenian, yet it is not a sentimental harangue. Pericles did not talk down to his audience. Only at the end is there a touch of that familiar aloof air which infuriated his enemies.

### The Plague

In the second year of the war, 430, the Spartans again invaded Attica and again the walls of Athens were a sure defense against them. Yet not against a far more deadly enemy which crept into the city unseen. From the East by ship came the germs of a hideous plague. Before it had run its course nearly a third of the population died. Victims suffered from a fever which ran through their bodies and were consumed with a thirst no amount of water could quench. Thucydides recounts the various stages of the disease with a clinical eye. Death, he says, came usually on the seventh or ninth day. There were survivors lucky enough to have lost only toes or fingers. Others were left blind or insane. For some unknown reason a few came through the ordeal without ill effects. Thucydides was one of them.

Neither previous good health nor the best living conditions provided immunity. The hardest hit were the refugees from the countryside. They had no permanent residence in the city and were crowded into makeshift shacks where sanitary conditions were especially bad. The near dead were unable to attend the dead and the more fortunate were wary of both. Bodies lay in the streets; other bodies were thrown helter skelter on funeral pyres already burning. Dying men fled to the temples to join the dead already there.

Life and property were cheap. No man could be sure he would survive. With the city in a state of shock, the scaffolding of morality collapsed. Those who had restrained themselves from wanton pleasure to protect their future reputation found themselves without a tomorrow. The pious who revered the gods were struck down as frequently as those who did not. What difference did it make? When the fragile threads of moral restraint gave way, cautious men spent money wildly, honest men became thieves, and decent men repulsive. Thucydides describes this shocking behavior as clinically as he had reported the course of the disease. Given the circumstances created by the one, the other was not surprising.

Amid the desolation, men nodded their heads and reminded one another of an old saying that a Dorian war would bring much suffering to the Athenians. Thucydides airily observes that the prediction was quoted variously and could be interpreted now to mean the plague, but would have been equally useful no matter what befell the city. He was aware that in times of widespread suffering few men find comfort in the suggestion that their misery has happened by chance. There must be a reason. In addition to this prophecy, the report was ready at hand that Apollo had given his support to Sparta through the oracle at Delphi. Naturally mortals could not presume to understand the decisions of the gods. Nor was it the first time that Apollo had aligned himself against Athena. Would the goddess let them lose? They could not pass judgment on her. But they could on Pericles.

## Pericles' Last Years

Since the beginning of the war, the Athenians had been living cooped up in their crowded city with food in short supply. Under these circumstances the best news could only have been consolation. In fact, the news had been very bad. In two years the devastation of the Attican countryside plus the effects of the plague had eroded Athenian morale to the point where many citizens were willing to test the Spartan sentiment for peace. Pericles vigorously opposed this move. Spartan coolness toward the peace feelers may have been more important in ending the overtures.

Nevertheless the citizens were in a mood to take some kind of action. They fined Pericles for having misused state funds. No amount of protest or proof of his honesty would have served to check their resentment; even so, they never doubted that he was the man who could win for them. A short time later they re-elected him as a general. Yet it was not to be his war after all; in the following year, 429, Pericles was himself a victim of the plague. After his death the war continued for another quarter of a century before ending in 404 with the ignominious defeat of his once glorious Athens. Pericles was no part of this. His name remained associated with the golden days of the Empire and the democracy at its best.

Two busts of Pericles have survived. They are marble copies of works attributed to the fifth century sculptor Cresilas. One is in the British Museum (Pl. 71); and the other in the Vatican. They show the statesman to have been a handsome man, intelligent looking with strong features. Both exhibit his head with a characteristic tilt, the way he might have appeared when speaking to the Assembly.

*Pl. 71 Head of Pericles. Roman copy of a fifth century B.C. original, probably by Cresilas*

Although these portraits may be somewhat idealized, here, we feel, is the Pericles of history—calm, confident, admired, victorious.

### Stalemate

The predicament of the Athenians in 430 had not encouraged the Spartans to consider an amicable settlement. Ironically, a few years later the Spartans asked for peace, at which time the Athenians had their chance to refuse. Hostilities lasted a decade until the despair was finally equal on both sides. This early period of the Peloponnesian War (431–421) has been sub-titled the "Archidamian War" after the Spartan king. Although Archidamus did not live to see it, he would not have been surprised that these years of conflict ended in stalemate. It had always been apparent to him that neither side had a clear advantage. A victory here was balanced by a loss there. In 430, the Athenians scored by finally taking Potidaea, the Corinthian colony where the fighting had begun in the north. The following year the Spartans began their successful siege of Plataea. In each instance the city was starved out.

When Potidaea capitulated, the entire population of men, women and children were driven out. Then Athens sent settlers and established a colony of her own. At Plataea, those who remained loyal to Athens paid for it with their lives. The Thebans insisted that every male defender be executed. The women were sold as slaves. Afterwards, the Thebans levelled the city to the ground.

Thucydides had no use for the legends of poets. To him, sober history was sufficient to show that man's own perversity and wicked-mindedness were the causes of human misery.

The revolutions within various Greek cities during the course of the war provided other examples in proof of this thesis. The ferocity of partisanship was everywhere the same. In was not necessary for Thucydides to offer details of the convulsions in each city. He chose the revolution in Corcyra in 427 as typical of all the rest and his description of this event is one of his best known passages.

Most Greek cities harbored the same competing factions as appeared at Corcyra. There were the oligarchs, who favored a narrow franchise or maybe none at all, and the commoners who wanted a democracy with the leadership responsive to public opinion. Between these two groups were the moderates who worried about the short-comings of both positions and sought some kind of compromise.

During the Peloponnesian War, local revolutions were by-products of the general trouble. Food shortages made old antagonisms more acute. Besides, each faction could depend on outside help. The Athenians could always be expected to aid the democrats while the Spartans and their allies, especially Corinth and Thebes, supported oligarchs. As always, the lack of support for moderation was a chronic cause of instability. Wherever these revolutions occurred, the goals of either side were lost in the fanaticism of a vendetta. Loyalty meant blind obedience to a leader no matter what mistakes he might make. The slightest hint of a willingness to compromise with the enemy was considered treasonous. In such an atmosphere, men were more willing to burn their city to the ground than to hand it over to a rival party. Neither oligarchs nor democrats considered a loyal opposition possible. Each party hid its true intentions behind an appeal to principle.

At Corcyra, the poor complained about poverty. Thucydides observes that they wanted power in order to make the rich as poor as they had been. The oligarchs were no better. They maintained order by enforcing only those laws which perpetuated their own advantages. Thucydides found selfishness to be a prime factor in human action. Although, to be sure, men were ashamed enough to try and hide it from each other, Thucydides was not deceived. His observations agree with those of Solon. Angry and spiteful men who differ in temperament and motive feel compelled by circumstance to kill each other.

## The Democracy After Pericles

Democracy asks for a special talent. The ideal leader of a democracy accepts his responsibility to the electorate and also realizes that he may have to sacrifice his own popularity and position in order to guide the state on the correct course as he sees it. Athens never found a better man for the job than Pericles. Twice during his career the citizenry removed him from the leadership and both times they took him back on his own terms. Pericles commanded respect. It may have been grudging from those who opposed his policies, yet on major issues it was apparent that he had made up his own mind and was not swayed by the impulsive wishes of the majority. At the same time, although Pericles knew that the majority could be wrong, he did not denounce their right to choose their own leaders. Most of the time they chose him. It was the secret of their success.

After Pericles was gone, the scramble for power was among men who would not dare defy the majority as he had done. Cleon, who succeeded him in public favor, had no desire to try. He ran roughshod over all opposition to the war and openly served the interests of those who had the most to gain by it. Furthermore, he abandoned the Periclean pose of self-defense and adopted an aggressive policy which openly committed Athens to all the grandiose ambitions which Corinth had accused her of. Pericles had sought to restrain the appetite of the citizenry. Cleon whetted it.

The authors of this period marked Cleon down as an uncouth, power-hungry demagogue. We have no word from his friends. Even Thucydides for all his objectivity could not hide his aristocratic bias. He was plainly disgusted by the manner in which this low-born man cultivated the baser instincts of his followers. They wanted an aggressive policy and that is what he gave them. Yet his ruthlessness toward rebellious Lesbos in 427 was even more than they could stomach.

The Lesbians had long shared the fears of the Corinthians that the Athenians aimed at nothing less than the total subjugation of Greece. They decided to break their alliance with her and actively join her enemies. Their plans became known too soon, however, and swift action by the Athenians caught the rebellious ally ill-prepared. The Lesbians asked the Spartans for immediate help. Victory for Lesbos would encourage other cities to revolt.

The Peloponnesians took the Lesbians into their alliance. What happened next did not encourage other would-be defectors. The Athenians besieged Mitylene, the chief city and center of defense for Lesbos. The Peloponnesian fleet arrived too late to help their new friends. Cleon carried a resolution in the Assembly that every man in Mytilene be executed and that every woman and child be sold into slavery. The order was duly dispatched by ship.

The next day, the Athenians reflected on how ordinary men like themselves had been condemned for the treachery of their leaders and they decided to reconsider the matter. Cleon chided them for this show of weakness. An empire was best maintained by muscle, not loving-kindness. Others argued that common sense would be a better guide. It was the aristocratic clique in the allied cities which threatened revolt—not the common folk such as those who had insisted on surrendering Mytilene. To kill the members of both parties would only unify dissident groups elsewhere. What hope had the men of any faction if the Athenians were to treat them all alike? The previous order was reversed and a second ship was sent to rescind it. Although the conscience of the Athenians arrived in time to save the populace, one thousand or more Lesbian leaders were executed and the Athenians took possession of the island.

Thucydides' version of this incident portrays Cleon as a vicious man, but his history of the war was not published until later. It was the playwright Aristophanes who attacked the demagogue to his face. His comedies, ingenious mixtures of earthy humor and political satire, showed Cleon to be as ruthless toward his enemies at home as he was toward those abroad.

## Comedy: A Mirror of the Times

Comedy, like tragedy, evolved from rustic beginnings. Yet it never evolved as far. There always remained in comedy an earth-bound robustness vividly reminiscent of earlier rites of spring.

Winter is boredom. Everywhere, in all times, spring brings newness and with it a desire to escape from routine. Carnivals in Rio de Janeiro and New Orleans offer present-day examples of this spirit. Although in modern cities the fun is better organized than in the ancient countryside, the mood has always been the same. It reflects the urge to dress in fantastic costumes, to make sport of the old and tried-and-true, and especially to deflate the pompousness of mortal "chieftains" who take themselves too seriously. In short, by occasionally succumbing to his wilder side, man admits that he is not all his customary dressed-up manners proclaim him to be.

A revel is an inning of brutal honesty about life and its sometimes pitiful pretences. The archaic *komos,* or revel, dedicated to Dionysus, the god of wine and fertility, was the prototype of all springtime frolics and also marked the beginning of Greek comedy. Country folk dressed up as animals or grotesque creatures and in these "unhuman" disguises danced and sang with all the abandonment that new wine could provide. Life was basic and so were the symbols carried, worn and made the center of attention. The buffoonery and ecstasy created an atmosphere in which the usually subservient folk of the community felt free to voice their complaints about their problems and their leaders. The baiting of hooks for the "big fish" was licensed by custom and excused by laughter. From the beginning the *komos* bore the seed of satire.

The steps by which amateurish fun-making reached an established form of comedy in the early fifth century may only be surmised. In the sixth century, perhaps one man voiced the sentiments of all, as was true of Thespis in the beginning of tragedy. Later, it would appear that small groups held mock debates on topical subjects. When the comic playwrights finally introduced invented, plotted narratives, they found various ways of including harangues and debates in their scripts. By 487 comedies had become part of the annual festivals and prizes were awarded for the best productions.

The only extant comedies of the fifth century are those by Aristophanes. These eleven plays are enough to show that comedy was only an updated and intellectualized version of the ancient *komos.* The scurrilous character of the earlier revels was still there. Here again, as with the satyr plays, Greek audiences were greatly amused by ribald mockery of the body and its functions. Only a few years ago parts of Aristophanes' plays were considered obscene in the United States at a time when obscenity was less difficult to define.

Aristophanes (446–388) was fifteen years old when the Peloponnesian War began. He was the son of a wealthy aristocrat, and his family was inconvenienced (to say the least) by being forced to move from their roomy country estate into the crowded and unhealthy city. The war had cost them dearly and not even victory would repay them for their loss. They did not share the prospects of the workers and rowers whose interests were closely tied to an aggressive imperialism. Later—and in the light of his background it is not surprising—Aristophanes figured as a spokesman for those who condemned the mistreatment of the allies and also the catering to the interests of the many instead of the best. While Pericles, a well-born and dignified man was at the helm, the policies of the state seemed bad enough, but the sight and sound of Cleon, a tanner by trade, were near intolerable. Aristophanes represented those who opposed this mean man's regime whether for logical reasons or out of mere prejudice.

Cleon's foreign policy was believed by Aristophanes and his friends to be the greatest danger to the state. They also viewed his domestic policies with disgust. This was evident in the *Wasps* which won first prize in 422.

Certain persons mentioned in the *Wasps* are still not identified, and much that was amusing then naturally has no fun in it now. Yet the play contains lines which are as hilarious today as when they were first written. The profundities of many ancient authors have survived the ages, but the humor of Aristophanes stands alone. No other poet has evoked so much laughing aloud. At the same time, on the serious side, his plays presented a view of the popular democracy through the eyes of an acute, if not altogether friendly observer.

The *Wasps* was a satire on Cleon's crafty use of elder citizens for his own purposes. The principal characters were Philocleon (Love-Cleon), an aging juror, and Bdelycleon (Hate-Cleon), his son. The opening scenes of the play are concerned with the efforts of the younger man to keep his father from joining the other elderly pensioners who tramp into the city daily to serve on the jury courts. The house is covered with nets; slaves guard the doors; and the son beats his father with a stick to keep him from coming out of the chimney. It is apparent that the old man has been mesmerized into a totally unrealistic sense of self-importance. He keeps insisting that he must go to the city in order that no wrong-doer escape his punishment. Soon the house is besieged by the other jurors. They too have been flattered endlessly by Cleon and now believe themselves the purgers of all villainy in the state. The foes of Cleon had little chance to escape the righteous indignation of these loyal jurors. Otherwise old and forgotten, they feel themselves young again and useful as they march forward to cast their votes into the urn of guilt, or more rarely into the urn of innocence. There is also the money. They each receive three obols a day and it is their livelihood. They live off litigation and worry about how they will eat on the days when the courts are not in session. For certain crimes, a defendant might be stripped of his property if found guilty. What chance did a rich man have when the prosecutor reminded the jurymen that their pay depended on such revenue? He could, of course, bribe an official to prevent the trial in the first place. If, as it often happened, he faced a trumped-up charge, he might as well pay at the start.

The jurors could not see beyond their own meager handouts and, according to Aristophanes, were completely deceived by cunning grafters who played the poor against the rich for an easy profit. Cleon, when prosecuting his critics, had only to mention that they opposed his influence with the courts. The jurors were quick to unleash their stings against anyone who endangered their precarious security. Aristophanes dressed them as wasps.

Looking alike, thinking alike, these garrulous and rambunctious chorus members typified the mass of citizens, the *demos*. They have become the slaves of a clever man who hypocritically calls himself "the servant of the people." A typical demagogue, he claims to be a foe of tyranny; he teaches his followers to use the word, but not to understand its meaning. "Tyrant" becomes the stock epithet for any uncooperative person who refuses to accede to popular wishes. And by extension to anyone at all. In the market, if a shopper purchases a fish from one stall and nothing from the next, the second merchant gives him a long look. He knows a man who favors tyranny when he sees one. Hate-Cleon attempts to show his father and the other jurors how they have been duped by a real tyrant. After that he too is suspect.

### Cleon Victorious

By the time Aristophanes produced the *Wasps* in 422, Cleon had been riding the crest of popularity for some time. He need not have been as base and ruthless a man as Aristophanes made him out to be. Satire is a cartoon. It exaggerates. Even so, Cleon was unquestionably a politician who boasted loudly and promised much. Such a man had to deliver in order to keep his place. To the amazement and discomfort of his enemies Cleon did just that. Like his fellow citizens he was experienced in politics, but his background was in the hides business—not in soldiering. And yet he managed to bring off the most amazing military coup of the war. He captured a group of Spartans who surrendered with weapons in their hands.

The incident occurred at Pylos on the southwestern shore of the

Peloponnesus in 425. Cleon reaped the harvest, but the real credit belonged to a general named Demosthenes. A man whose fame has been overshadowed by a like-named orator of the following century, Demosthenes was carrying out the usual Athenian attacks on the Peloponnesian coast and had established a beachhead on a narrow strip of land which curved outward from the mainland. We might call it "Cape" Pylos. Very near the tip of this peninsula a long island, Sphacteria, extended southward and together with the "Cape" formed a bay.

The Athenian fleet managed to surround the island of Sphacteria and trap those Spartans and their allies who had taken up positions there. Although the Peloponnesian forces held strong positions on the mainland, the Athenian advantage in the bay made the situation of the men on the island hopeless. The Spartans, not wishing to abandon them and alert to find some honorable means of getting them out alive, sent envoys to Athens in a bid for peace. They argued that a treaty arranged between their two cities would restore quiet to all of Greece. No lesser power could challenge such a settlement.

Cleon vehemently opposed any talk of a conditional peace. His rallying cry had been a war for profit; he might not fare so well in peacetime. Of course peace was always possible at a price, if Sparta would accede to certain exorbitant demands. The trapped men must be surrendered and then held at Athens to insure that all other promises would be kept. These included the return to Athens of Nisaea, Pegae, Troezen and Achaea, places which she had been forced to give up in the Thirty Years Peace. At that point the negotiations broke down and the test of endurance was resumed at Pylos.

Cleon who had blocked the chance for a favorable peace declared that the island should be taken by assault. Speaking before the Assembly, he chided the Athenian generals for not having the courage for the job. Whereupon Nicias, at whom Cleon pointed a finger, rose and announced that he wished to relinquish his command in favor of Cleon who could then carry out his own plans. The surprised Cleon tried to escape the trap by admitting to his lack of experience. The citizens, however, were in a petulant mood and enjoyed his embarrassment. They insisted that he accept the honor. In fact, Thucydides remarks, there were those who were delighted with such a turn of events. They would be pleased if Cleon took the Spartans, or if the Spartans took him.

At Pylos, Demosthenes had been considering the possibilities of an assault and a chance fire which destroyed much of the wood cover on Sphacteria enabled him to see the size and layout of the Spartan encampment. When Cleon arrived with reinforcements, the Athenians had the advantage of superior numbers. Nevertheless, it was a long and furious fight before they gained the high ground surrounding the final position to which the Spartans could retire. At that point Cleon and Demosthenes halted the attack and offered the encircled men their lives if they would surrender where they stood. After some consultation they did. Of the 292 prisoners taken to Athens, 120 were full-fledged Spartan peers. For Cleon there could not have been a better prize.

To the rest of Greece the news was electrifying. Spartans had surrendered with swords in their hands! Was Thermopylae a myth? Thucydides reports that one of the Spartan prisoners was later asked if it was not true that all the men of honor had died on the battleground. The Spartan, with a sharpness he was not supposed to have, replied that it is a valuable arrow which can pick out a brave man to kill. Are events determined by chance? Although Thucydides insists that he will stay out of his history, his opinions do seem to be hidden here and there in anecdotes.

The Spartan prisoners were used as pawns by Athens. Sparta could only expect to get them back at a high price. Certainly if Attica was again invaded they would be killed.

## The Knights and the Acharnians

Nearly everybody in Athens was enthusiastic over Cleon's success. There is no reason to include Aristophanes among the enthusiasts. In the following January he unleashed another attack on this popular politician in a comedy entitled the *Knights.*

In a modern musical show, the book may be thin yet a sufficient framework on which to hang one song or dance after another. In ancient comedy the story line allowed for episodes of fast repartee and powerful speeches. Aristophanes used both devices in the *Knights* and kept punching away at Cleon from beginning to end. His chorus of knights—the well-to-do gentry who were strongly anti-Cleon—added to the vocal clamor.

The play is an allegory in which Athens is a household owned by *Demos,* a personification of the citizenry. The slaves of *Demos* are represented as generals, in this instance Demosthenes and Nicias. These two "slaves" complain about the ill-treatment they receive from the master's chief steward, who of course is Cleon. One of them has discovered an oracle, however, which predicts that this leather-seller will eventually be displaced in the master's favor by a seller of tripe. When the tripe-seller appears he proves to be more disreputable than Cleon and there is an uproarious exchange of indignities during a scene in which Aristophanes dredges up every possible damning fact or fiction and hurls them at Cleon. He is a liar, a blackmailer, a grafter who has deceived his master *Demos* and abused his slaves. Much of the banter is amusing as any exchange of insults can be when written by a master wit. But if Aristophanes had seriously hoped to undermine Cleon's standing with the audience he was doomed to disappointment. Cleon was too popular to be ruined by satire. He remained the dominant political figure in Athens from the death of Pericles in 429 until his own death in 422.

Cleon was the principal target in the *Knights,* but Aristophanes also managed some side-swipes at other despoilers of the community. He turned a sharp eye on the growing number of luxurious young fops for whom the recent prosperity of the city had provided an incubator. Aristophanes was an aristocrat who harked back to the sturdy values of Pindar and Aeschylus. He was disgusted with effemi-nate young men who lounged about the city filling the air with per-fume and endless sophistical chatter. At the end of the play, the tripe-seller who has succeeded in displacing Cleon turns out to be a reformer after all; he had only adopted Cleon's tricks to win power. Now he wields a fresh broom and among those to be swept up are the unathletic dandies.

The boldness with which Aristophanes stated his opinions, espe-cially about the leading politician of his day, has always served as a proof of the free Athenian climate. Yet Aristophanes did not escape trouble altogether. After the *Knights* was produced in 424, Cleon counter-attacked by declaring that Aristophanes had a forged an-cestry and therefore was not truly a citizen. This charge was em-barrassing and difficult to prove false. In fact, Aristophanes had to pay court to Cleon to get him to drop the case. Because of Cleon's lack of humor, the playwright took a different target in the following year when he satirized Socrates in the *Clouds.*

Aristophanes' attitude toward the war is clearly shown in the *Acharnians.* This comedy, named after its chorus of hardy Attican villagers, was staged in 425, the sixth year of the war. The Athe-nians had suffered much and gained little. Aristophanes offers an argument for peace. Dikaiopolis, an old Athenian farmer, is the chief character and spokesman for the poet's views. This man has the

independence of mind, stubbornness and common sense which New
England Yankees claim that New England Yankees have. He says
that he has suffered from the invasions and that he dislikes the
Spartans as much as the next man; but at the same time he does
not think they are altogether at fault for what has happened. There
has been some right and wrong on both sides. Emotions have been
allowed to interfere with sound thinking. The war is a result of misunderstanding and continued fighting is not likely to resolve the
matter. Aristophanes oversimplifies the problem, but significantly in
a dark hour he is telling the Athenians that their enemies are not
all bad and that they should try to appreciate *their* point of view.
Such sentiments could hardly have been comforting to those who
had lost sons in the war. The Athenians may not have welcomed
Aristophanes' point of view, but they did hear it. However, if the
rest of the play had not been very funny, Aristophanes might have
found himself back in the dock.

## The War in the West and in the North

The Peloponnesian War had many fronts and the most distant
was Sicily. The rivalries of the various Sicilian cities led to almost
constant warfare. Because the centuries-old ties with the homeland
were still intact, Doric colonies received support from their Doric
mother cities and Ionic colonies from the Ionians. In this circumstance, the war was easily expanded. However, in the light of what
had happened to the Delian League, the Ionian cities were faced
with the question whether they had more to fear from their aggressive neighbors or from the helpful Athenians.

In the late summer of 427 an Athenian fleet arrived to aid Leontini in that city's struggle with Syracuse. During the following two
years, additional Athenian forces were sent out and the Syracusans
were prevented from winning control of the strategic Strait of Mes-
sina. In 424, however, a general conference of Sicilian cities was held
at Gela on the southern coast of the island. The various factions
decided to forego their differences and restore peace to the island.
In effect, sentiment ran against the Athenians and by common con-
sent they were invited out of Sicily.

At home, the three Athenian commanders received a hostile reception. The Assembly had not ruled out the possibility of conquering Sicily. Two of the commanders were sent into exile and the third
was fined for failing to share this grandiose dream. It was charged

that bribes had made them shortsighted. At this point in his story Thucydides observes that the Athenian citizens were at times unable to distinguish between what they wanted to do and what was possible, given their resources.

Thucydides spoke from experience. In the same year, 424, when on active service at Thasos in the northern Aegean, he became involved in a chain of events which led to his own disgrace at Athens. It was his subsequent exile which afforded him the time and opportunity to visit many places, receive first hand reports on both sides, and so devote his full time to writing his history of the war.

Hostilities in the northern Aegean had commenced with the Potidaean affair in 432. After that city fell to the Athenians in 429, activity died down until 424. The tempo was then raised by the Spartans who sought to relieve the pressure on the Peloponnesus by distracting the Athenians with a campaign in a more distant region. They also wanted to block the flow of tribute to Athens from her allies in the area. Whether these allied cities wished it or not, the Spartans intended to liberate them. Some of the cities were reluctant for fear that in return for all their trouble they might only be trading one master for another. Others wondered if Sparta was willing to supply the continued support necessary to protect them from Athenian revenge.

In the ensuing struggle, the Spartan commander Brasidas made a decided difference. He was the very opposite of the stereotype which Spartan commanders were expected to be. Unlike the ill-famed Pausanias who had typified the customary tactlessness and insensitivity of Spartan officers, Brasidas had learned that as much was to be won by fair and reasonable dealings as by bullish dictation. He accomplished what he could by diplomacy and was careful to keep his promises. On the other hand, if he found force to be necessary after fair warning and ample chance for negotiation, he knew how to win that way too.

Brasidas did not confine himself to liberating Athenian allies. He also led an attack on Amphipolis, the colony which the Athenians had finally managed to establish on the Strymon River in 437. It is during his report of this engagement that Thucydides introduces himself in the third person and records his part in the episode with a cool detachment. The same technique would be used effectively by Julius Caesar four centuries later in his *Commentaries*. Unfortunately, Thucydides had none of Caesar's good fortune. Before he could reach Amphipolis with reinforcements, Brasidas had offered the residents such lenient terms that they surrendered at once. Thucydides managed to save Eion, the coastal city three miles down river, but the loss of Amphipolis was too serious to go unpunished. From what Thucydides writes, it seems apparent that he was not really at fault. Yet he does not discuss the matter any more than he would if it had happened to somebody else.

The following spring, in 423, the Athenians and Spartans signed an armistice to last for a year. Presumably it was to allow each side a chance to work for a just peace. Actually the Athenians were anxious to recruit their resources in the face of Brasidas' continued success in the north. On the other side, the Spartans were still worried about the fate of the Sphacterian captives and had actually been holding back on reinforcements to the ambitious Brasidas. They were genuinely interested in coming to terms and getting their men back. Brasidas may have convinced the northern cities that Sparta was sacrificing herself for their good. His problem was that he had never completely sold the Spartans on the idea.

The armistice was kept in a technical sense. At least, no one admitted to not keeping it. Still, there was trouble here and there, and on each side the opponents of a general settlement had an articulate leader. Neither Brasidas nor Cleon had any intention of accepting a peace without victory. In 422, after the truce ended, these two warhawks and their armies met at Amphipolis. The top general of militarist Sparta faced the popular leader of the Athenian democracy and in a climactic battle both were killed. Peace was finally possible. Sparta and Athens, two old friends, the major powers in Greece, suspicious of their own alliances and weary of war, turned to each other at last. During the winter, negotiations were carried back and forth. In the spring of 421 the signing of a treaty was a foregone conclusion.

### The Peace

Before the formal ceremonies introductory to the so-called Peace of Nicias, Aristophanes celebrated the event in the *Peace*. This play was as lively as his earlier productions, but not as pungent. The straw man Cleon was dead and Aristophanes had the peace he wanted.

The story tells how, during the war, an adventuresome Attican farmer, Trygaios, saddled up a gigantic beetle and flew off to visit Zeus. Something had to be done before the Greeks demolished each other. Besides the farmer's daughters were hungry. Aristophanes could not forego mentioning his old wartime complaint about a shortage of food. Trygaios finds that Zeus and the other gods have abandoned their usual abode and forsaken contact with men. Only Hermes remains. He reminds Trygaios how time and again the gods have tried to secure peace on earth. First, the Spartans refused when they had the advantage (the plague at Athens) and then the Athenians refused when they had the upper hand (Pylos). Nothing could be done for such foolish mortals. War, appropriately depicted as a greedy giant, has been allowed to bury the frail goddess Peace in a pit. Trygaios calls upon all decent folk in Greece to help him pull her out.

Midst the heaving and hauling it is apparent that some citizens are pulling more of their share than others. The Spartans, with men imprisoned in Athens, are trying hard. The Argives, enjoying a profitable neutrality selling helmets and spears to both sides, are not pulling at all. The poor Megarians, starving because of the Athenian blockade, have hardly any strength left with which to help. As for the Athenians, they cannot take their minds off their lawsuits long enough to be of much assistance.

The first attempts to retrieve Peace are not successful. It is the farmers who finally succeed, unhindered by the mixed efforts of the city folk. When Peace is freed at last from her entrapment, she is accompanied by Plenty and Holiday.

After Trygaios returns to earth, there is much singing, jesting and feasting. Amid the festivities, however, a sour note is injected. A soothsayer, while trying to push his way to a table, raises doubts about the possibilities for peace. Trygaios, Aristophanes' favorite farmer, has no use for prophets of gloom whose brooding over ill omens prevents peaceful folk from joining their hearts in happy song. Yet the soothsayer manages to sneak in a few remarks before being beaten and driven off. He insists that nothing can change the way a crab walks or the roughness on a hedgehog's back. A disturbing thought is planted. The Spartans have a poor record when it comes to keeping their word. How could the Athenians trust them? As it turned out, he was at least half right. The Spartans could not trust the Athenians either.

## The Third Generation:
## The Defeat of Athens

**XIII**

The Peace of Nicias was possible because both in Sparta and Athens those who favored cooperation had for the moment an upper hand; it did not mean that in either city there was unanimity of support for the accord.

The treaty was to guarantee peace for fifty years. Both parties recognized the right of free access to the common shrines of Greece. They also agreed to respect the ties of each to their separate allies. Territories captured in the war were to be given back and there was to be an exchange of prisoners.

The two major powers considered the agreement to be binding on their allies. But this did not mean that it was. Sparta felt unable to coerce her former friends into accepting it and some of them never did. What had Corinth to gain by such a treaty? In return for her losses she saw Athens restored to pre-war strength. The Athenian Empire was intact. Sparta had actually handed part of it back. Other cities were equally resentful toward both Sparta and Athens who had made themselves the sole arbiters of the peace. The Boeotians held Panactum, one of the places which the Spartans had promised to return to Athens. How could it be returned unless the Boeotians agreed to the treaty?

There were Athenians who suspected that certain Spartans found such uncooperativeness a convenience. They were right. The following winter, the new board of ephors included men who were opposed to the treaty with Athens. They foresaw the renewal of hostilities in the near future and were determined to be prepared for it. Specifically, they entered into a separate agreement with Boeotia without first consulting the Athenians.

At Athens, the Spartan duplicity was embarrassing to Nicias who had been the foremost advocate of the peace and the man who gave it his name. On the other hand, the ill-wind brought an opportunity which a young man in the wings had been waiting for.

Alcibiades (*circa* 450-404) was in some respects the most dramatic figure in Greek history save for Alexander the Great. He was about thirty years old in 420 and already a prominent figure in the public eye. He was a nephew of Pericles and had been raised in the great statesman's household. His own father Clinias was killed at the battle of Coronea in 447. Alcibiades was wealthy and by his own estimate, as well as others', the handsomest man in Athens. That he was intelligent besides made him dangerous, for it was well said that he had everything except character. The first time Thucydides mentions him is to cite an example of his dishonesty. The incident was indicative of this young man's lifelong dedication to his own ends, regardless of the laws of gods or men.

Alcibiades recognized that so long as the peace with Sparta was maintained, Nicias, who sponsored it, would hold the first place in Athens. It was to be the younger man's advantage to do what he could to break down confidence in the Spartans. As part of his scheme he approached a group of Spartan envoys in Athens and convinced them that he would use his influence to settle all issues at stake between his city and theirs. The Spartans were delighted by his proposal, for they were hoodwinked into thinking that he only sought to take credit for having brought about a *rapprochement.* They underestimated him. So would others who trusted him during his amazing career. By neglecting to pursue their own purposes and leaving everything to Alcibiades, they left themselves open to the charge of intriguing behind the back of the citizenry. Alcibiades so informed the Assembly.

In spite of this clever trick, Nicias was still able to persuade the Athenians to bide their time while he went in person to Sparta

with an ultimatum. He informed the Spartans they must either renounce their alliance with Boeotia or force the Boeotians to obey
the terms of the treaty which ended the Ten Year War. At Sparta,
the ephors who opposed the treaty were able to prevent such a concession. Their intransigence was all that Alcibiades needed to rush
through the Assembly an alliance with an anti-Spartan coalition including the Argives, Mantineans and Eleans. It was another mutual
assistance pact and followed the usual formula for these treaties
which the Greeks were so fond of contracting. Ironically, the longer
the term such pacts were written to cover, the shorter they lasted.
The present one was for a hundred years. It lasted two. Even so,
when it went into effect it did not interfere with the Athenian fifty-
year pact with Sparta.

Thus, in 420 the states of the Peloponnesus had divided into two
camps. Argos, Mantinea and Elis stood on one side and Sparta with
her loyal friends on the other. Athens had a mutual assistance agreement with both sides. It was a rare kind of insurance.

Nevertheless, at Athens a decision would soon have to be made.
Major trouble was brewing in the Peloponnesus over a small matter
concerning Tegea. Alcibiades, riding one of the crests of his on-again,
off-again popularity, talked the Athenians into fighting with the coalition against Sparta. The crucial battle was fought at Mantinea in
418 and Thucydides says that it was one of the largest engagements
in years.

At Mantinea the real strength of Sparta was shown once more.
Spartan diplomats had made many false moves, but the fighters in
the line restored Sparta to her old glory. Marching steadily with
measured steps to the cadence of their pipers, they brought a determination to the field which was more than a match for the skillful
maneuvering of the enemy.

Although Athenians and Spartans lay dead, neither city admitted
that their treaty had been broken. The smashing victory for Sparta,
however, had revived her confidence. She was again the foremost
power in the Peloponnesus and again able to force the Argives to
sign a fifty-year alliance. It was, to be sure, a shaky bargain. At
Argos, the aristocratic party favored Sparta but the democratic faction stayed in communication with Athens. As in Spain in the 1930's,
each of the local forces was aided and abetted by outsiders. It was
under such circumstances that the uneasy Peace of Nicias continued
into its fifth year.

## The Melian Debate

It has often been said that Thucydides' history was a tragedy in which Athens, the hero, so wonderful in the arts, so daring in her democracy, fell prey to *hybris,* a fatal weakness—the same even as had infected Xerxes—the conviction that men could be the masters of their own fate and needed no help from any higher power. Thucydides did not spell out this idea, yet his report of the so-called Melian Debate in 416 presented Athens in the role of an arrogant and ruthless power. Since the incident came just before Athens plunged into her fatal Sicilian debacle it had a dramatic impact.

Melos, a small island in the southern Aegean, is known best for a renowned Aphrodite, popularly called the *Venus de Milo,* found there in the early nineteenth century. This famous work, however, was created long after the events at hand. In the late fifth century, Melos was a small neutral state which preferred to remain uncommitted. The Athenians pressed them to join their maritime empire.

Customarily, Thucydides is inclined to grant that a little light and reason are to be found on both sides of any argument. However, in his account of the confrontation between the generals sent to Melos and the leaders of that state, the Athenians are portrayed as offering nothing more than the argument that "might makes right." They did not bother to make up excuses for their harsh treatment of Melos. On the contrary they admitted that the Melians had never offended them. That was beside the point. The way of the world demanded that the strong give orders and the weak obey them. What was the advantage of strength if not to command obedience?

Such was the sentiment of Darius, the Great King who had come in 490 to punish the insignificant Athenians for interfering in a corner of his mighty empire. Could the descendants of those who had fought for freedom deny freedom to others? According to Thucydides they did worse than that. The overbearing Athenians were claiming that the victory at Marathon gave them the right to dictate to others. It was a curious reading of their own history but the Athenian generals believed it, and right or wrong that was what mattered.

The Melians insisted that the gods would help them. The gods, the Athenians replied, struggled amongst themselves. Moreover, in heaven as on earth, the strong ruled the weak. Why look to the gods for justice? The Athenians laid siege and after a time with the help of traitors took the city. All the grown men were slain and the women and children sold into slavery.

Athenian generals had nonchalantly dismissed the gods as caring no more for justice than men did. It was not the attitude that the devout Hesiod had taken when abused by ruthless aristocrats. In this brief episode, Thucydides gives Hesiod's role to the Melians. They appear simple and trusting whereas the Athenian spokesmen sound sophisticated and overly confident in their own powers. In the years of trouble ahead, devout Athenians had not far to seek for those responsible for the city's ill fortune. Skeptical and irreligious men had brought down upon all their heads the wrath of heaven.

## The Sicilian Venture

Clearly the gods abandoned the Athenians during the two-year campaign (415–413) in Sicily. Thucydides holds that this venture was the most important event of the Peloponnesian War. Even though hostilities lasted another decade, the catastrophe which Athens suffered in the Battle of Syracuse was the beginning of the end for her.

In 424 the accord reached by the Sicilian representatives at Gela had ended Athenian intervention in the island for the time being. After the Athenians left, the Sicilians returned to their old pattern of strife. In 416, the citizens of Segesta had become embroiled with their neighbor Selinus and asked the Athenians to return. A treaty still in effect with Segesta supplied the Athenians with an excellent reason for intervention. Back of this technicality was the fact that Syracuse supported Selinus, and if allowed to extend her power might one day send assistance to her fellow Dorians in the Peloponnesus. The Syracusans as always were the people to watch, so the Athenians would prevent them from taking over the island by conquering it for themselves. On the other hand the Segesteans were interested in Athenian help only because of their local problem. To keep the Athenians interested they exaggerated the size of their resources and even fooled the envoys sent from Athens to check on the matter. In short, the Athenian-Segestean alliance was a bargain between thieves.

In Athens, Nicias warned the citizenry not to be duped into believing they could win such a gamble. He had every reason to voice his opposition to the campaign because he was one of the three generals chosen to conduct it. The citizenry may not have liked his opinions, but they did admire his abilities. The other generals were

Alcibiades, the chief promoter of the scheme, and Lamachus who, according to Thucydides, had little to say.

Nicias opposed the Sicilian campaign because it was a bad risk for Athens to take. How would they handle affairs at such a distance if they had difficulty managing what was close at hand? He went on to warn the Assembly about the overly ambitious Alcibiades. This young man, he insisted, was motivated only by his own appetite for wealth and fame. In solemn words Nicias asked the Athenians to consider what a serious undertaking this was. He begged them not to be swayed in so important a matter by Alcibiades, whose reckless private life gave ample evidence of his poor judgment.

Alcibiades was a spendthrift and kept more horses than even he could afford. He was also an egotistical schemer. But he had great charm and was in the public eye a picture of youth and daring. Such qualities were strong competition for age and experience. Alcibiades made the most of them.

After downgrading the capabilities of the enemies of Athens in Sicily and exaggerating the amount of help which could be expected from their friends, Alcibiades proceeded to set a familiar trap for willing minds. If the power of Athens did not grow, then it must necessarily decline. That was all the choice there was. To go ahead or to go back. There was no middle ground. According to Thucydides, when Alcibiades had finished speaking the Assembly was more enthusiastic than ever. Nicias rose again and attempted to dampen this spirit laying stress on the money and materiel that would be required, but the citizens voted for everything the generals thought they might need. The excitement was so great that even those who still agreed with Nicias kept silent lest they make themselves unpopular.

Never had a single Greek city sent so many men and ships so far away on such an ambitious mission. A great armada set out in 415, full religious rites having been performed at the seaside. Those leaving caught last glimpses of their friends and relatives who, with the usual mingled feelings of hope and sadness, had come to wish them well. The departing men were facing an uncertain future. Uncertain for everybody except Alcibiades.

Alcibiades had recently been placed on the defensive about his personal conduct. Just prior to the departure of the fleet, those busy with the preparations very naturally sought release from their labors and joined in farewell celebrations. Presumably after such a party a group of carousing young men went through the streets one night and damaged many of the busts of Hermes which by custom stood before Athenian houses. To their contemporaries, this was a more serious matter than vandalism. It was sacrilege. Defacing such statuary reflected a lapse in piety which even drunkenness could not excuse. Other wanton behavior had been attributed to Alcibiades as well as this. Stories were circulated about wild parties in which even the ceremonials of the Eleusinian mysteries were parodied.

Nothing could have been more offensive to a pious Athenian; the rites of the Eleusian Temple were too sacred even to be mentioned. In fact, the ceremonies were the best kept secret in the ancient world. Although attended for centuries by men and women in all walks of life, the literature of the ancient world contains no explanation of what went on. That any one should parody these rites was an abominable and shocking act. Alcibiades was only implicated by rumor, but for those who disliked his swagger rumor was enough. The eve of the fleet's departure, however, was not the time to bring charges. Furthermore, at the moment he was too popular with the citizenry, and so he was allowed to sail as planned. It was decided that more serious accusations would be raised against him later.

Alcibiades' enemies were determined on one thing. If the venture in Sicily should prove a success, he must not receive any credit for it. They suspected that he aimed at the establishment of a tyranny whereupon, like Peisistratus, he would order the affairs of the state. They believed that Alcibiades' catering to the Assembly and his flattery of the citizens were only a blind for his true anti-democratic sentiments. He was in the eyes of his enemies a demagogue with all the sincerity of a successful charlatan.

The departure of the Sicilian expedition did not abate the public furor over the recent acts of sacrilege in the community, for such behavior was risking the public welfare by giving offence to the gods. An outsider might call this superstition. The fact remains that the overwhelming majority of the Athenians believed that the gods existed and that they had power. There was a genuine fear of the consequences of sacrilege, and the public outrage served the political purposes of Alcibiades' enemies. They claimed that the recent disturbances were part of his plan to create dissension as a cover for the overthrow of the democracy and the establishment of a tyranny. His friends in other cities were probably intended to be useful in the plot. With the evidence mounting and Alcibiades not present to defend himself, the Assembly voted that he and certain of his companions be ordered home to stand trial on these charges. When Alcibiades heard the news, he decided that the situation was too dangerous for even his silver tongue. So, at Thurii in southern Italy, he slipped away from the men who had been sent to escort him home and made his way to Sparta where his knowledge of Athenian plans and his own abilities would do him the most good. The Assembly at Athens condemned him to death *in absentia*.

The Athenian reception in Sicily had on the whole been disappointing. They soon learned that the Segesteans had deceived them about the support they could offer. With Alcibiades gone, Nicias and Lamachus were eager to get on with the matter and press for a decision. Diplomatic and military preparations on both sides made it evident that Athens and Syracuse were the real contestants; nothing could prevent a clash between them. It came before the year was out. This struggle began in 415 and lasted two years. The Athenians were victorious in the initial encounter which occurred in the vicinity of Syracuse, but they were weak in cavalry and unable to press their advantage. The Syracusans were aware that their own lack of discipline, especially the excessive quarreling among their commanders, had cost them the day.

Both sides continued their quest for support. The Athenians posed as the protectors of the neighbors of Syracuse. The Syracusans asked the local citizens why the Athenians had come so far to assist these colonies whose mother cities were enslaved by them at home? Thucydides was fond of such questions. He had a special knack for singling out instances where self-interest led to opposing positions in different places.

## Alcibiades at Sparta

At Sparta the scene was a familiar one. Corinthian envoys were again urging the Spartans to take up arms against the Athenians. Now, however, Syracusans were also present asking that Spartan aid be sent a great distance. This was a move which the Spartans were always reluctant to make. How could they be persuaded? Alcibiades, at home everywhere, stepped forward. Like a fallen angel, he raged against the Athenians. His own past actions were explained as having been due in part to the ridiculous demands of a democratic majority. He would tell the Spartans how much they had to fear from these Athenians who had treated him so treacherously. They intended to

conquer first Sicily, then Italy and finally Carthage and her possessions. The full weight of these conquered peoples and their resources
would be used to crush the Peloponnesian League. Athens would
rule the Greek world. On this occasion at least, Alcibiades was willing to give the Athenian citizenry full credit for his own imaginative
plans.

Alcibiades gave the Spartans excellent advice and they made
good use of it. He told them that the most pressing need at Syracuse
was for a commander who could quickly establish discipline. They
therefore sent one of their ablest generals, Gylippus, with instructions
to do what he could. Next, Alcibiades suggested that the most damaging action which could be taken against Athens would be to seize
a place like Decelea in Attica and fortify it as a base for operations.
This site was about mid-way between Athens and the Boeotian border. By holding such a position the Spartans could harass the Athenians the year round instead of invading Attica only on a seasonal
basis. This, Alcibiades added, was something which the Athenians
had always feared. If they were prevented from using their silver
mines at Laurium, it would be a special hardship. The following
spring, in 413, the Spartans followed Alcibiades' advice.

## Disaster at Syracuse

Time was against the Athenians in Sicily. They had settled
down to invest Syracuse by land and by sea, but their line was too
long and the whole of their resources was unable to prevent men
and supplies from reaching the city. In addition, they were harassed
constantly by counter-attacks and the Syracusan cavalry prevented
them from making closer contact with the interior. The besiegers
were themselves placed on the defensive.

Lamachus was killed in one of the numerous skirmishes, and,
as fortune would have it, Nicias—the man who had most strongly
opposed the venture—was left alone in command. He had kidney
trouble and every day increased his physical and mental anguish.
He wanted to resign. In a letter to the Athenian Assembly he reviewed
the situation. It was impossible to win unless some larger force be
sent to cut off the city effectively from outside aid. Nicias told the
Athenians plainly that both his materiel and morale were deteriorating. In sum, the Athenians must either abandon the Sicilian venture altogether or send out forces as large as those which had come
with him. He also asked for a commander to take his place.

The men in the Assembly were willing to admit neither their original mistake nor the present odds against them. They decided to double the stakes. Another large expeditionary force was sent. Although unwilling to let Nicias retire, the Assembly did elect Eurymedon and Demosthenes as replacements for Lamachus and Alcibiades. If this daring show of determination had succeeded, their descendants would have praised them for their courage; because it failed it was called folly and the decision became an indictment of democracy.

Yet a disastrous outcome was still unthinkable in 414. Even Aristophanes' comedy the *Birds,* which took second prize in the city Dionysia that year, reflected the high hopes of the citizenry. The play was a utopian fantasy. It diverted the anxiety-ridden Athenians from their present problems by presenting a never-never land, a city in the sky. Aristophanes could not resist the temptation to parody the Sicilian venture and the *Birds* can be read as a subtle satire on Athenian greediness in reaching out for yet more empire. Still, the audience had too much at stake for the author to have risked an unhappy ending. All was finally glorious, except for persons Aristophanes disliked who were, as usual, lampooned along the way.

In Sicily, the general Demosthenes, famed for his service at Pylos, brought a fresh approach to the Athenian effort. His ingenuity, however, did not pay off. He led a surprise night attack on the Syracusan defenses, but the darkness caused the attackers more confusion than their enemies. The failure of this offensive was a severe setback to an already discouraged army.

Demosthenes now became convinced that the Athenians should withdraw from Sicily altogether without waiting for approval from the Assembly which, in any event, might be difficult to obtain. They should get out while they still had the means to do so. He was concerned, moreover, about conserving Athenian resources for an all-out effort to evict the Spartans from Decelea. He said exactly what Nicias might have been expected to say, yet, strangely enough, Nicias refused to leave. He said he was fearful of returning to Athens lest the Assembly blame him for the Sicilian calamity. Thucydides had previously depicted Nicias as a sensible and sober thinker, yet now, he shows him in defiance of the opinion of his fellow commanders and determined to run a very bad risk. Aside from the suggestion that Nicias may have had secret information about plans for a revolt in Syracuse, Thucydides offers no explanation of this contradiction in the general's behavior. This was how Nicias acted and Thucydides reports it that way. Here again is that true-to-life quality which characterizes so much of Greek literature. Men were not depicted as either all wise or utterly stupid, all strong or completely weak.

A little later the Athenians learned of the arrival of yet more help for Syracuse from the Sicilian cities and from the Peloponnesus. Nicias, faced with the growing discontent of the soldiers, many of whom were as sick as he was, now changed his mind and agreed to the proposal of an escape by sea. Yet at the last minute came another reason for delay. An eclipse of the moon occurred. It was an omen. Nicias refused to carry out the evacuation until the necessary waiting period of twenty-seven days had passed. Such was the popular belief about such matters and he was supported by the soldiery. In reporting this event Thucydides does not openly criticize the decision to remain, yet he does not disguise his feeling that it was a lucky break for the enemy.

During the interim the Syracusans attacked the Athenian fleet and scored an impressive victory in which Eurymedon was killed. The added time also gave them an opportunity to block the mouth of the Great Harbor by linking various kinds of ships together in a chain. The Athenians were faced with the prospect of trying to escape while the enemy was attacking them from all sides. Nor would their remaining superiority in ships avail them much in the close quarters of the bay.

When the waiting period was over and the day for the attempted escape was at hand, Nicias in a speech to his officers was prophetically apprehensive. The balance shifted back and forth as the day wore on but the trapped ships did not get through. The stakes for the Athenians were enormously high. The result was disastrous.

The battle, incidentally, is still in the news. The success of recent work in underwater archaeology, especially along the coasts of Italy and Turkey, has lead to speculation about the possibility of recovering the ships that went down in the bay of Syracuse on that momentous September day. The silver piece issued by the Syracusans in commemoration of their victory is today considered one of the most beautiful of ancient coins. Although a large number of these silver coins were struck, their unusual attractiveness has helped to make them worth over a thousand dollars apiece in the current collector's market.

Although badly beaten, Demosthenes and Nicias favored another attempt by sea. Their men would not agree to it. They insisted on a retreat by land. It was now every man for himself. The Athenians departed in an atmosphere of panic. The dead were left unburied; the unattended sick and wounded were left to watch one another die. The bodies of those who tried to follow marked the course of a death march. On the way inland, the Athenians faced roadblocks and harassments on all sides. One night, during a sudden attempt to change course, the army was split in two. Demosthenes was unable to keep his disorderly ranks marching at the same pace as those under Nicias. Gylippus surrounded this remnant and forced an unconditional surrender. He caught Nicias' troops while they were attempting to cross the Assinarus River.

Nicias had always been a friend of Sparta and Gylippus would have spared him but the Syracusans and Corinthians demanded that both he and Demosthenes be executed. All the other captives were enslaved in Sicilian rock quarries, there to die amid hunger, filth, thirst and disease, a weary long way from the glories of Athens.

## Athens Facing Defeat

Athens was stunned by the news. However, the warning by Nicias that a loss in Sicily would mean the collapse of resistance at home was not borne out. The citizens turned against those men whose advice had prompted them to pursue such a disastrous course, but they did not abandon themselves to regret and recrimination. They were determined to build another fleet and willing to exercise the strictest economies in order to make it possible. A committee of respected elders, including Sophocles, was elected to supply the citizens with sober and steady counsel—the kind of counsel which they seemed often unwilling to take when matters were going more smoothly. The citizenry continued to enjoy Aristophanes' comedies and to ignore his pleas for peace. In his *Lysistrata*, produced in 411, the women of the city seize the Acropolis and refuse to have anything more to do with their husbands until peace is achieved. It is a comic conception, but there is nothing imaginative or comic in the complaints of these women about the suffering which the war has brought to Athens.

The outcome of the war in Sicily had an impact everywhere. Neutral cities, hitherto wary of Athenian power, felt that the time had come for choosing sides. Even the members of the Athenian alliance finally dared to raise the banner of revolt in their own behalf. They were encouraged by the vigor of the Spartans. Alcibiades urged the ephors at Sparta to take advantage of the situation and their response inspired revolts at Chios, Erythrae and Clazomenae. Later, even Athens' long-time friend Miletus joined the enemy.

The Athenians were resolved to force these cities back into the fold, but, no matter what the immediate objective might be, the major aim of their policy was the same as it had always been— the protection of the import of grain from the Black Sea area to Athens.

Taken as a whole these developments were not unexpected. However, that Sparta would now ally herself with Persia may strike the modern reader as an amazing turn of events. Yet the move was not only a measure of the ill-will among the Greeks, but a clue to how near the Spartans sensed their victory to be. They only needed additional ships and money. The Persians had both. Furthermore, the Persians could aid in an uprising against Athens in the Ionian cities of the eastern Aegean. At the moment the point was to win and to win fast, by any means possible.

Tissaphernes, Darius II's satrap in the region that the Persians still held in southwest Asia Minor, was anxious to profit by the new state of affairs in Greece, but he needed good advice on how to proceed. Enter, Alcibiades!

At Sparta, the former Athenian commander had at first proved very useful. Eventually, however, it dawned on the Spartans that this man could only be loyal to himself and was no more to be trusted by them than by the Athenians. There was also a tale, repeated by Plutarch, that Alcibiades had seduced the wife of King Agis. According to this story, Alcibiades intended to introduce his own blood into the royal line by having his child accepted as a legitimate heir. However, a son was born after the king had been absent from Sparta for ten months. This event prompted Alcibiades to join the Persians.

No matter what anyone might think of Alcibiades personally, there was no gainsaying the excellence of his advice. He told Tissaphernes to help the Spartans regardless of their terms. He should not, however, help them enough so that they could win. In brief, he should keep promising them the Phoenician fleet, but never deliver it. The continuation of the war would exhaust both the Athenians and the Spartans and leave Persia in a far stronger position than either of them.

Tissaphernes was greatly impressed by Alcibiades and his reasoning. Since scheming and subtle Greeks had been outwitted by this clever man of many faces, a Persian satrap could hardly be blamed for failing to see how Alcibiades was in fact putting himself back on the road to Athens. Persian aid to Sparta was too crucial a matter for the Athenians to ignore. Now they were informed that Alcibiades had the ear of Tissaphernes. The outlawed leader sent word to the army commanders at Samos that if the democracy at Athens could be replaced by a friendlier oligarchy, he would return home and bring the friendship of Persia with him. In light of his fantastic luck, who could doubt that he would? A majority of the Athenians saw the plan as the only hope. An envoy was sent to parley with Alcibiades and the Persians.

A few years earlier, any concession by the Assembly over altering the constitution would have been unthinkable. Yet the Syracusan disaster had brought home the lesson that defeat was possible. If a *rapprochement* with Persia would save them, they would go along with it. Behind the excuse of expediency there lurked a subtle disillusionment. The decisions about Sicily which had proved so utterly wrong were, after all, choices that citizens had made themselves. Complain as they would about being deceived by their leaders, the fact remained that Nicias had warned them plainly and that they had not listened. A loss of confidence by the rank-and-file was precisely what the enemies of the popular democracy had long been waiting for. While the citizens' faith had remained strong, they were unshakable. Now doubts allowed for confusion and indecision. In such an hour those who favored rule by a "few" made their way to the front. In any democracy there are always such men, obsessed with their own sense of right and the desire for power. In times of fear and anxiety there seem to be more than usual. The strength of this minority was owing to the fact that they came primarily from the well-to-do classes with the best education. During the war, these people were expected to make sacrifices in money and property, yet their interests were ignored by a government sensitive to the more populous and less prosperous. Anti-democratic feeling was also strong among the military officials, to whom the disorderly actions and fickle attitudes of the popular majority were not only disconcerting but dangerous.

In modern terminology, there was in fifth century Athens a "right of center" and a "far right." As usual, the farther to the right, the fewer the true believers. Most of those who opposed the popular democracy were only anxious to take the vote away from the poorest class, but they did not want to narrow the electorate much more than that. These were the supporters of what came to be called "The Five Thousand." This government would stabilize power in the hands of men over thirty years of age who were members of the top three property classes. In the writings of both Thucydides and Aristotle, approval is given this idea as a reasonable compromise. Such a limitation of the franchise would exclude the uneducated who were most easily swayed by unscrupulous orators. On the other hand, the electorate would be broad enough to keep the state from falling into the hands of an equally unscrupulous clique.

There were, however, extremists—particularly the members of the aristocratic clubs who considered four hundred a safer number to trust than five thousand. They sought a highly restricted oligarchy. These men were especially anxious to come to terms with Sparta and to end the war which, they contended, was the result of democratic mismanagement.

In April of 411, Androcles and certain other prominent democrats were assassinated. The willingness of the Assembly to compromise the democracy had been a sign of weakness and the would-be oligarchs knew it. The long-time enemies of democracy decided not to await the outcome of diplomatic dealings with Alcibiades and the Persians; they saw a better chance in intimidating the citizenry by instituting a reign of terror. In an atmosphere of suspicion, a confused citizenry was shocked into silence. No one in Athens wore a badge to indicate which shade of opinion he supported and the Athenians suffered through troubled days when to be safe was to be quiet. Given this advantage, a militant band of eager men was able to take control.

The leader of the inner circle was Antiphon, a lawyer with a talent for organization. With armed followers, he and his closest friends intimidated the Council of 500 and caused its members to abandon their duties. The conspirators then produced a list of one hundred "safe" associates. Each of the hundred men chosen in turn picked three others and the resulting group of "Four Hundred" assumed control. They made appointments, established policy and decided which "enemies" of the state were to be executed or exiled. In theory the electorate was henceforth to be limited to five thousand citizens. However, the moderates did not have a strong voice in the operation of the new government. From May until September in 411, Athens was ruled by an oligarchy of the "far right."

The Four Hundred sought to win the support of the armed forces based at Samos and also to come to terms with Sparta. They were not successful on these counts, or any others. News of their repressive tactics reached Samos before their official envoys did. The rank-and-file on military duty, ever the mainstay of the democracy, were enraged, and under the leadership of their own generals, particularly Thrasybulus, they set up a government in exile.

The beleaguered Athenians were now faced with civil war. Who could prevent a clash between these antagonistic factions? Alcibiades arrived in Samos, full of promise and good advice. He was elected a general and successfully prevented a clash between the rival Athenian governments. Thucydides says it was the best deed he ever performed for Athens. For once, the welfare of his native city coincided with his own.

Aware of the rising tide against them, the ruling oligarchs turned openly to Sparta for help and left no doubt about their intention to betray the city to save themselves. The moderate forces, with all the shortcomings of a "home guard," were soundly defeated when they sailed out to attack the Peloponnesian ships coming to aid the Four Hundred. Yet the Spartans, in another of their inexplicable decisions which baffled even the urbane Thucydides, decided not to press their advantage. Those within the city who had depended on outside help were forced to flee for their lives. The moderates, led by Theramenes, then established the *de facto* rule of the Five Thousand by which the city was governed from September, 411, until June, 410. By rescinding all charges outstanding against Alcibiades and by showing good faith in carrying on the war, the new government showed itself to be more compatible with the democracy at Samos.

## The Last Years of the War

Meantime, the Spartans were having their own kind of trouble. Their failure to act decisively at critical moments wore heavily on their allies. They were also bewildered by Tissaphernes, who kept them on a string with promises but withheld money and ships at crucial moments. The Spartans finally rotated their high command in the eastern Aegean in an effort to get more decisive action. The result was an all-out effort to win control of the Hellespont. It was here that the Athenians had to hold in defense of their lifeline. And hold they did. Their victory in a sea battle near the promontory of Cynossema during the summer of 411 was the best news Athens had had since the victory at Pylos in 425.

Thucydides' history breaks off at this point. While he lived until possibly 397, he did not finish his work on the war. The continuous account of the period after 411 which is extant is the prosaic *Hellenica* by Xenophon. Like Thucydides, he was an Athenian general. Generals possessing the literary talents of a Thucydides or a Julius Caesar are rare indeed, and by comparison Xenophon was an also-ran. Be that as it may, his work remains the major source of information for the years 411 to 362.

The victory at Cynossema in 411 revived all the old dreams at Athens, especially among the commoners. Although the moderates in command were willing to cooperate with the democratic leaders in charge of the fleet, they were also in favor of finding an honorable basis for ending the war. Yet they had respect for democratic procedures and so had abandoned the repressive features of the Four Hundred. This meant that a man like Cleophon, a kindred spirit to Cleon and his successor Hyperbolus, could advocate a return to popular democracy. The moderates may well have realized that such an event could not be forestalled in the face of continued successes by the democratic armed forces. A major victory at Cyzicus, in May 410, did in fact raise the hopes of the populace to such heights that in June the government of the Five Thousand passed from the scene and the full democracy was restored.

If the moderates had hoped that they might be able to direct the policies of the restored democracy *à la* Pericles, they were mistaken. The Spartans made a respectable bid for peace after Cyzicus, but the democratic leader Cleophon thwarted any effort for a settlement. The citizenry were again convinced that they could win a triumphant victory and so rejected the offer. Historians have readily agreed that this was Athens' last chance to save herself before the final disaster. That she missed such an obvious opportunity made her final demise seem fated. In a sense it was. The revival of the popular democracy again placed ultimate decisions directly in the hands of the citizens themselves. In the past this had not proved to be the best way to handle foreign policy.

The Athenians never worked out a representative system. They did not establish a body of legislators each responsive to his constituency. Such a congress could have acted with more consistency and deliberateness than the whole citizenry gathered together. Students of American history will be familiar with James Madison's *Federalist Papers* in which he discusses the usefulness of "representation" in avoiding the shortcomings of "pure democracy."

In Athens in 410, the citizens expressed a renewed determination to fight the war to a victorious conclusion. They also reinstituted the old payments for jury service which the Four Hundred had abolished and added to these a special assistance allowance for the poor. These expenditures were by no means a sign of solvency. On the contrary, the Athenian commanders were squeezing every town—friend and foe alike—for funds.

As might be expected, Alcibiades proved himself a master pirate. The memory of his past misdeeds caused some uneasiness at Athens. It was hardly possible that he had abandoned all thoughts of tyranny and yet the Assembly continued year after year to elect him a general, as the democracy in exile had done. He was perhaps the best commander they had; certainly he was the most daring. In 407 he dared to come home. Since his ships were carrying rich treasures it was hardly much of a personal risk. On the day he arrived, as on that day in 415 when he had sailed away to Sicily, there were crowds at Piraeus. Among those at the quayside were young boys of seven, long familiar with exciting tales about this man who had left before they were born. They stood by their elders who pointed out the dramatic figure standing in the bow of the main galley as it moved slowly toward the shore. Alcibiades looked at first apprehensive and then jubilant as the crowds pressed forward and shouted their welcome. The Athenians received their prodigal son with open arms. In the days which followed, Alcibiades regaled the citizenry with his talk of re-establishing the Athenian empire in all its glory. The Assembly made him commander-in-chief. How could so many men have forgotten his treachery so soon? Aristophanes once wrote, "they love, and hate, and cannot do without him." When Alcibiades sailed away again in command of a hundred ships, the highest hopes for another great triumph went with him.

It was not to be. Early in 406, Athenian forces suffered a severe defeat at Notium. Their hopes were turned into the bitterest disappointment. At Notium, before leaving his fleet in search of supplies, Alcibiades had given strict orders that there was to be no engagement with the enemy in his absence. His subordinate Antiochus disobeyed. He provoked a fight and lost many ships, as well as his own life. When Alcibiades returned, he attempted to re-engage the enemy, but Lysander, the Spartan general, refused the challenge.

The citizenry whose hopes for an immediate recovery of Chios and the Ionian coast had been dashed were ready to believe anything. The enemies of Alcibiades claimed that he had left the fleet in charge of his drinking companions rather than able men who would have followed orders. Alcibiades was himself accused of neglecting his duties in riotous living. He was not re-elected as one of the ten generals in the spring of 406 and the last days of his life were spent in exile.

Six of the generals who were elected that year suffered a less honorable fate. In August of 406, another sea battle was fought near to the Arginusae Islands and while the Athenians suffered heavy losses they managed to drive the Spartans from the scene. The generals then made the mistake of deciding to give chase rather than devote their full energies to rescuing the Athenian survivors still in the water. Many men were lost who might have been saved and the anger of the Athenians was compounded by the fact that the enemy escaped anyway. The fifty-man prytany in charge of affairs at Athens during this period were compelled by an aroused citizenry to break with precedent and to try the six generals in charge at Arginusae as a group rather than as individuals. The philosopher Socrates, as he was later proud of saying, was one member of that prytany who voted against allowing this illegal procedure. Yet the angry citizens would have their way. The six were condemned to death and immediately executed. Among them was the son of Pericles and Aspasia.

The Assembly had behaved like a mob and with this event, if not earlier, Socrates' estrangement from his fellow citizens had begun its fatal course.

After Arginusae the Spartans again proposed a peace based on the *status quo*, but the Athenian Assembly still felt that they would be giving up too much if each side were allowed to keep what it now held. Unaware of the lateness of the hour and the growing odds against them, the Athenians refused. The hour was late indeed. The Persian king had now decided that the Spartans must win. He dispatched to the scene his son Cyrus "the younger," so-called to distinguish him from the founder of the Persian Empire, Cyrus the Great. The cooperation between this able prince and the brilliant Lysander, Sparta's leading commander, finally brought the war to a close.

The last battle of the war was scarcely a battle at all. One hundred and eighty ships, the last fleet the Athenians could afford, were stationed at Aegospotami in August of 405. On successive days they challenged the enemy at Lampsacus on the opposite shore. On each occasion when Lysander refused to fight, the Athenians under their admiral Conon returned to their own side, disembarked, and went searching for food.

Lysander observed the Athenian routine. On the fifth day he waited until the Athenians were busy inland and then gave the order to attack. The unattended ships and the unprepared camp were easily and decisively overcome. Only eight Athenian ships managed to escape. Aboard one of them was the commander Conon. In view of the recent mass execution of six victorious, yet negligent generals, it was not surprising that he did not return to Athens. The flagship *Paralus* did return, however, and the news of the loss of their last naval force was passed from man to man. Xenophon remarks that it was a night when no Athenian slept. They now were trapped within the walls which had been erected to guarantee their freedom. Lysander and his fleet stood off Piraeus and the Spartan kings Agis and Pausanias commanded the land forces which surrounded the city.

During the agonizing winter of 405-404, food and tempers grew short within Athens as the citizenry argued about the terms for their surrender. Theramenes, a leader in the former government of the Five Thousand, was sent to bargain with Lysander and the Spartans. During his three months' absence, as the food supply dwindled so did the Athenian price for surrender. Finally, the hungry city was ready for any kind of terms Theramenes could obtain. As it happened, they were fortunate to be dealing with the Spartans. Among the Peloponnesian allies were those who thought that Athens should receive the same punishment she had meted out to the Melians. The Corinthians and the Thebans were willing to have all the adult Athenian males killed and the women and children sold into slavery. The Spartans would not allow this. Again and again, the Athenians had reminded the other Greeks that something was owed them for the saving victory at Marathon. The Spartans believed it. So the Athenians were left with their lives but that was about all. Their empire was gone and they were committed to follow the dictates of Sparta in foreign affairs. In April 404, the Spartans came and destroyed the fortifications of Piraeus and tore down the Long Walls. Left with only twelve ships, Athens was helpless.

The Peloponnesian War was over. It had been longer, bloodier and more destructive than any previous war in Greek history. Yet in one respect it was like all the others. It sowed the seeds of the war to follow.

## The Unscrupulous Hero

The first generation of the fifth century led by the courageous Cimon had built the Athenian Empire. The second generation, living in the Age of Pericles, had managed this inheritance and enjoyed its best fruits. The third generation lost everything. What went wrong was a puzzle of many parts, not the least of them Alcibiades.

The life of Alcibiades was sensational enough without embroidery. His reputation for erratic behavior won willing listeners for the tales told by his enemies. Brilliant and daring, egocentric and amoral, he was a curious mixture of talent and self-indulgence. That such a unique personality became the foremost general of Athens during the Peloponnesian War was significant. That he also served Sparta and Persia during the war seems fantastic. Yet in one way he was typical. His self-centeredness and his cynical attitude reflected a new kind of individualism, particularly rife among the well-born and well-bred. He was not the only gilded youth of his time, nor was he the only man to put his own welfare before that of the *polis.*

Alcibiades could not escape the burden of vanity. As a man of stunning handsomeness and disarming charm, he found it impossible ever to accept second place gracefully. Plutarch makes it plain that from his childhood on he was flattered, even fawned on. An appetite so encouraged became insatiable. As a youth he found a variety of ways to attract attention. They included cutting off the fulsome tail of his beautiful dog, wearing unusual garments which trailed after him as he walked, and hurling insults at those who begged for his company. People talked about Alcibiades. That was what mattered to him. When he himself talked, his lisp was a characteristic affectation.

Alcibiades came of age at a time when sophistic reasoning and cosmopolitan airs were in vogue. Smart conversation in Athens took nothing for granted. The most cherished beliefs and traditions were open to debate. If questions of right and wrong eluded even his elders, Alcibiades was content to let his ends justify his means. Pericles and his friends may have enjoyed speculative arguments but they were aware at the same time of the necessity for standards of morality by which to judge public conduct. Alcibiades and others of his generation, including the high-handed generals at Melos, presumably did not realize this distinction. They were motivated by the appearances of life. The familiar goals of material success were all that really existed or were worth striving for.

Through his remarkable friendship with Socrates, Alcibiades was exposed to a totally different outlook. He was one of Socrates' most celebrated students and certainly his most celebrated failure. Socrates taught that virtue alone was worth possessing. It was obtainable through a patient search for knowledge and not by the insatiable and wearisome pursuit of material ends, bought and sold, won and lost. Listening to Socrates talk, Alcibiades could be moved to tears. Yet not for long. He was too much of a sensualist, too fascinated by his own attractions, to appreciate truly what Socrates tried to teach him. On one occasion, the young student boasted of his own beauty and the sturdy Socrates reproached him for shallowness. Beauty, Socrates said, was not a quality to be found expressed in a transient body. It was only to be found in the permanence of the soul.

When Socrates later stood accused of having taught sophistry and thereby corrupting the minds of Athenian youths, Alcibiades was given as a notorious example. The truth was that Socrates had accounted for those rare moments when Alcibiades felt ashamed. That so few of this young gallant's well-spoken and well-read companions found anything to be ashamed about was a sign of the times.

To a busy man in search of success, friendship with a philosopher could only be a corner of life. Alcibiades was such a man. Moreover, he could adjust himself to the particular habits of people wherever he lived. During his sojourn in Sparta, he gave up perfumes and purple robes and adopted the regimen of his hosts. His hair was cut shorter, he exercised strenuously, and he ate simple foods. In brief, as might be expected, he was the model Spartan. Only his attentions to the Queen Timaea betrayed his other self.

When Alcibiades moved on to join the Persians, his gift for ceremonial opulence and colorful dress amazed and delighted the hard-to-please Tissaphernes. Alcibiades, Plutarch says, could drink with the Thracians or ride with the Thessalians. He was popular everywhere except in his own home. His wife seems not to have appreciated him. Hipparete was a well-bred girl who in time grew weary of the kind of guests, male and female, whom Alcibiades invited for his own company. Eventually she went to seek a divorce, but, according to Plutarch, Alcibiades seized her and carried her back to his house. This was not an unusual procedure. A wife was required to appear in public so that her husband might remonstrate with her and triumphantly display his manliness by carrying her through the marketplace. There is no reason to think that Alcibiades would have missed the chance.

Alcibiades, a man of many moods, was an enigma to the end. When the sad news of the humiliation of Athens reached him, he again set out to win help from the Persians. He went to live in Phrygia and there sought to reach the king's ear through the satrap Pharnabazus. Dared the Athenians hope to see him sail home again to save them? The Spartans thought not. Lysander prevailed upon Pharnabazus to have Alcibiades assassinated. Those who were sent to kill him hesitated to attack him even as a group. They set his house afire. Then when he emerged alone, sword in hand, they stood at some distance and shot him through with a volley of arrows. Had Alcibiades died a hero, cruelly slain by those who feared what he might yet accomplish for his native Athens? Plutarch wondered. He added that there was another story told about the death. The second version was not political. The men who killed Alcibiades were the outraged brothers of a local girl whom he had misused. Such conflicting accounts were the measure of the man. Nothing was impossible in his case.

## The Unpopular Immortals:
## Euripides and Socrates

**XIV**

Herodotus had found the peoples of the Near East living in mute backwardness, hampered by a rigid class system and dominated by an omnipotent king. He had discovered among them no literary or artistic expressions of individual self-consciousness or of a habit of thought. In all the world, the Greeks alone had produced tragedies and comedies and devised contradictory philosophical systems. Especially did he praise the Athenians for their love of freedom and their democracy, yet by the end of the fifth century these same literate and progressive Greeks had dealt their own future a crippling blow. The war had left thousands of their sons slain and much of their land in ruin. The Persian Empire, a monolithic despotism, was stronger than ever. The Great King had regained possession of Ionia. Even more humiliating, he had actually become an arbiter of Greek affairs.

In the Persian Empire, political speculation was outlawed and criticism was severely repressed. Ironically, the aspects of Persian rule which Herodotus found least attractive were sources of its strength and unity. On the other hand, the Greeks, restless, and independent, anxious to excel and always in competition, brought themselves to ruin by the very habits which had produced a unique civilization. The men at Athens who watched their Long Walls being demolished might well ask themselves why they had failed.

Aeschylus and Sophocles had sought to reconcile their fellow Greeks to the inexplicable ironies of existence through acceptance of fate and the often curious intervention of the gods. Euripides (478–406), the third of the three great Athenian tragedians, had a different answer, a more familiar one. He said that men must try to understand themselves. Their suffering was the difference between what they hoped to be and what they really were (Pl. 72).

Euripides was a humanist. Like other humanists from Homer to Herodotus he was preoccupied with studying man, what he thinks, how he acts, what he creates. Yet there was a difference. Most of the Greek writers were like the Christian humanists of the sixteenth century—Erasmus, for instance. Interested in all the many sides of man, they never moved him beyond the reach of divine power. Aeschylus, Pindar, Sophocles and Herodotus each acknowledged the omnipotence of the gods and the punishment which awaited men who would not bend their will to the will of Zeus. Euripides attributed to man a greater degree of power over his own destiny. For

*Pl. 72 Head of Euripides*

better or for worse, he adopted a secular view. Aristophanes, his fellow playwright, thought he might be even an atheist.

Euripides' choruses, as if from force of habit, hailed the rule of the gods but these pronouncements were like the sonorous messages tagged on to present-day Biblical movies wherein orgies abound until the final reel. Euripides was not concerned with providence. He was preoccupied with the realities of everyday existence. His dramas, therefore, had a common touch and his characters exhibited strengths and weaknesses identical with those of the audience.

Aeschylus and Sophocles retold the tale of the House of Atreus the way men had learned it. Their versions showed the intervention of the gods and the working-out of fate. Orestes was acting under orders from Apollo and had been urged to do his duty by his high-minded sister Electra. Clytemnestra and her lover must be punished for having committed murder and adultery. In Aeschylus' *Oresteia*, the trilogy was concluded on a hopeful note. Athena founded the Areopagus which acquitted Orestes and supplanted private vengeance with public justice. In Sophocles' *Electra*, Orestes never stood trial. His "execution" of Clytemnestra and Aegisthus ended the ancient curse on the House of Atreus. Harmony was restored.

Euripides was not distracted by grand excuses. In his *Electra*, produced in 413, he stripped away the religious aura and left bare the devious and transparent motives of the men and women involved. When Orestes stabbed his mother to death, it was a vicious act, no different from any other crime. Moreover, it seems clear that his sister bullied him into it.

Sophocles had shown Electra tormented with the pain of memory. She could not erase the thought of her mother and a secret lover plotting in an adulterous bed to slay her beloved father. In disgust and horror at this vileness, she lived only to see the guilty pair punished. Euripides' Electra lived for other things. Like the rich who have lost their money, she was obsessed with how it happened. Her mind was more filled with what she had once possessed and hoped to win again than with the punishment of a crime. She had been born a princess and her life should have been beautiful, but her mother had cheated her out of it. In Euripides' play she finds refuge with a simple peasant who respects her royal blood and never dares to suggest they consummate their marriage. Within his lowly hovel, the very symbol of her misery, she would have her revenge.

Clytemnestra is tricked into making a visit by a message that her daughter is pregnant. Electra welcomes her with the warning to be careful lest she soil her gown by touching the walls. It is left to the audience to imagine Orestes standing in the shadows, sword in hand.

Euripides' *Orestes,* a sequel to the *Electra,* was produced five years later in 408. The action in this play takes place six days after the murder. In the prologue, Electra retells the course of events in the House of Atreus which had led to her brother's act of vengeance. She eagerly claims that it was Apollo's fault. He had talked Orestes into the deed. Yet she also admits that she had aided the act. Both she and her brother were to be judged this day in Argos. In sharp contrast to the Aeschylean version, Euripides had placed the murder of Clytemnestra at a time after the institution of courts of law. Thus, Orestes and Electra could have taken their accusation against their mother through legal channels if they had chosen to do so.

When Menelaus, the king of Sparta, arrives from Troy accompanied by his errant wife Helen and their daughter Hermione, he already knows about the murder of his brother Agamemnon. It might have been expected that he would help those who had avenged this crime, but he refuses to become involved. Whereupon Orestes resolves to kill the much-hated Helen in the hope of winning sympathy from the Argives. Electra has a better plan. She suggests that in addition to killing Helen they seize Hermione and threaten to kill her too unless Menelaus agrees to intercede on their behalf. Everything goes as planned, except that with Helen dead and a knife at Hermione's throat, Menelaus refuses to yield. Instead, he sounds an alarm calling the Argives to witness this further outrage. Amid the ensuing uproar it might be imagined that Hermione would be killed and the palace set afire to become the funeral pyre for the plotters. It was not to be. Apollo, heretofore insulted by all, arrives to provide a happy ending. Orestes is to marry Hermione and his friend Pylades to marry Electra as previously planned. Orestes will be reconciled to the Argives and reign in peace. Menelaus will do the same in Sparta. Most astounding sequel of all, Helen is to serve in Heaven. Apollo has ushered this vain woman in among the stars to shine as a guide for sailors.

The use of the *deus ex machina* was totally out of character with the rest of the play. For that reason it had its usefulness. Euripides was able to say what he wanted to say without really saying it. He attached to his hard-hitting drama a completely unrealistic, if orthodox, ending. It was like appending *Genesis* to a biology textbook. A clever device perhaps, but not one to endear him to those who realized what he was up to.

Euripides did not openly disavow the gods, although it could be argued that at times he wanted to. What he did was to raise embarrassing questions about their behavior. There were aspects of accepted myths which when blended with the whole religious picture could be easily overlooked. It was precisely these somewhat embarrassing elements which Euripides chose to emphasize. Spotlighted, they seemed less palatable. Both he and his contemporary Socrates were honest with themselves about what they found to be contradictory in current beliefs. Unlike other men, who kept quiet out of respect for others or in search of popular favor, Euripides and Socrates openly expressed their doubts. As intellectuals are often wont to do, they took the position that they were doing their fellow men a favor. Most of their fellow men did not appreciate it.

Never in any society has there been more than a small number who have devoted themselves to the re-evaluation and criticism of currently held beliefs. Like most of the Athenians, the vast majority of men have always been too busy with manual labor or professional duties to afford any leisure time for contemplation. Neither, as a rule, do they choose to spend what leisure time they have in contemplation. Nor is there any reason why they should.

This is not to say that men of all sorts do not from time to time have their private thoughts and doubts. The difference is that mostly everybody assents in the general willingness to accept inherited beliefs and standards rather than pursue inconsistencies in the arguments which support them. Since the late nineteenth century, for example, modernist Christians have retained their church affiliation regardless of any misgivings they might have about a man walking on the water. They simply do not talk about it very much. There are also those who if not actually churchgoers are nevertheless friendly. When asked if her husband was a member, Mrs. Wiggs of the Cabbage Patch replied that ". . . he was what you might say a well-wisher." Fundamentalist, modernist, or well-wisher, most men have never been skeptics.

## The Embarrassed God

Euripides' play *Ion* was of little comfort to the pious. Apollo, a shining light of prophecy, the god of youth, is presented as a seducer of a young girl. When she becomes pregnant he refuses to help her lest he be implicated.

Ion is the child eventually born to Creusa, daughter of Erechtheus, a mythical king of Attica. In lonely despair she exposes her baby and later presumes him to be dead. Apollo, however, has secretly arranged for the child to be taken to Delphi and there raised as a ward of the shrine. Creusa later marries a stalwart friend of Athens, Xuthus, who has helped the Athenians conquer Euboea. After many childless years the couple take their problem to the oracle of Delphi. Apollo seizes the opportunity to pass off Ion as Xuthus' own son. Xuthus because of a youthful escapade is willing to accept Apollo's word that Ion is his. Again, Apollo dares not say that Ion belongs to Creusa for fear he will be exposed. What kind of god do we have here?

Later in the play the priestess of Delphi shows Creusa the cradle in which Ion was brought to Delphi. A recognition scene follows. Mother and son are united. But Ion is troubled. Why had the revered Apollo lied the way he did? His mother insists that it was for Ion's own good. When Ion seeks some further explanation from Apollo, Athena says that the god is too embarrassed to see him. The youth is disturbed. Well might the audience be too.

The Athenians knew that the gods misbehaved even as anyone who has read the books of *Samuel* might gain the uneasy impression that Yahweh had a vicious streak. Still, Sophocles had rarely talked about the gods that way, any more than Aeschylus did. It was shocking for Euripides to do so but he did so repeatedly. His plays lent support to the nagging proposition that the gods were actually created in man's image. This subtlety has been the hallmark of the skeptic from his day to ours.

## Sympathy

It was not only in religious matters that Euripides offered a minority opinion. A very obvious reason for his unpopularity in Athens was his tendency to criticize the pet foibles and prejudices of the Athenians themselves. Time and again in his plays, he asked his audiences to sympathize with persons about whom by custom they were disinclined to be concerned. In Athenian society the feelings of women were not especially important yet Euripides showed his sympathy for women in a number of plays, notably the *Andromache, Hecuba* and, of course, the *Trojan Women* and *Medea*.

Sophocles had given women prominent roles in his plays to be sure, yet his Antigone and Electra each suffered because of a special circumstance or decision of their own. Euripides was more interested in a social question. He depicted women abused in a man's world simply because they were women.

Unlike Aeschylus and Sophocles whose tragic figures stand in heroic defiance or muted resignation, there is an ordinariness about Euripides' characters. In the *Trojan Women,* shocked widows and mothers of the dead commiserate with one another and call to mind memories of other days. To a tragic circumstance, unrelieved by any hope, Euripides has here added pity.

The play is a mood piece—a series of episodes strung together which stress the humiliation and despondency of women who must submit to their most hated enemies. Cassandra is assigned to Agamemnon. Andromache is given to Neoptolemus, the son of the man who slew her husband. This proud wife of Homer's valiant Hector is no more than a piece of property loaded into a cart with other booty. Euripides asks his audience to share his pity for the shocking treatment of these sad creatures. To the men in his audience who were themselves soldiers, this was a novel way to look at war, or women. Yet Euripides' concern was not mere feminism. He expressed sympathy toward all underdogs in a callous society, including neglected beggars and cripples.

The *Medea* (produced in 431) has a special significance. It has always been the most celebrated example of Euripides' concern with the pain that women must suffer from thoughtless men. Yet Medea is also a barbarian. Male or female, the feelings of barbarians were discounted at Athens, if indeed it was allowed that they had any.

Euripides' play tells how Jason, the much-heralded commander of the Argonauts, treated the woman who helped him obtain the Golden Fleece.

Back of the play is the story how Medea, the daughter of the king of Colchis, had betrayed her father, delivered the fleece into her lover's hands, and then killed her brother so that she and Jason could escape together. When they return to Jason's homeland, his uncle Pelias still refuses to relinquish the throne and Medea again serves her beloved Jason. She persuades the daughters of old Pelias that she can rejuvenate their father by magic if they will follow her orders. So, they kill the king, cut him into pieces, and await the work of Medea's mysterious powers to revive him, whole and young. It never happens. This latest service, however, brings Jason ill-will. He and Medea, along with their two children, are forced to go into exile. In Corinth, Jason fares better on his own. There he is offered the daughter of the king in marriage if he will put aside his foreign wife, indeed if he will allow Medea and the children to be driven out of Corinthia altogether. He agrees. This is the point at which Euripides begins his play.

The *Medea* is a story of revenge. Crazed with hatred at being cast aside, Medea cannot bear to think how she has betrayed and slain her own kin for this man who has deserted her. Now, if ever, she needs her sorcerer's art. Feigning regret for her earlier outbursts, she sends her children with a gift for the new bride by which it is supposed they will win mercy. The garment has been rubbed with a potion which will poison the body of the wearer. Medea does not know that it will kill two instead of one. When Jason's bride falls dead, her unsuspecting father takes her in his arms, but cannot then tear himself away; the garment clasps his flesh to hers.

Jason fears that his children will suffer for this terrible deed. He comes to Medea to ask that he be allowed to take them out of the land. She has already murdered them and stands triumphant with their dead bodies in her arms. The blood of these innocents is an irretrievably disastrous conclusion. When Medea flees to Athens in a chariot drawn by dragons it is a decorative touch. Euripides has artfully supplied a mystical frame. The story itself reads like a police blotter and is totally depressing.

It is Medea's realization of how she has been "used" by Jason which causes her to behave like a caged animal, murdering her young. Euripides was not concerned with the gods, nor with the question of how this "family trouble" might have been avoided. His play describes an unquestionably selfish act by a husband which results in the murderous rage of his wife. What happens is part of the human complexion. Yet only part of it. Euripides' play does not describe how human beings must behave, only how some of them do. It is a simple, common sense distinction. Many who are obsessed with "realism" often let it escape them.

There are lines in *Medea* which unhappy wives and husbands of any era might be tempted to underline. Medea in the midst of a long lament points to the easier freedom of a man. If he gets tired of life at home, he can go out and end his boredom quickly. Later, however, she admits that if the disadvantages of women expose them to their husbands' cruelty, they also have the keenest sense of evil devices by which to get even.

Neither Medea nor Jason was a tragic figure in the traditional sense. They were not heroic characters brought low by some "dram of evil" or an unalterable fate; they were both doomed by their own consuming passions. Was it right for Medea to betray her father and murder her brother out of love for Jason? Was it right for him to abandon her after she had made such a sacrifice? In the end, was it right that a mother murder her children to get even with their father? Euripides makes it plain that it was their own natures which set these ill-starred lovers on the course of their destruction.

In the tragedies of Aeschylus and Sophocles, reconciliation came when man submitted to powers beyond himself. With Euripides, there was the chilling horror of knowing that the destructive power was inside a man and could destroy him sometime. Little wonder that Euripides has been called the "most modern" and the "most tragic" of the Greek playwrights. His exposition of the self-destructive power of the irrational had everything except the present-day terminology.

Euripides was interested in equalizing more than the sexes. He did not apply one standard for a Greek and another for a barbarian. In all times, it has been possible for men to excuse, or at least condone, the abuse of inferiors because they are inferior. What was startling in Euripides' play was that he treated this man and this woman, hero and sorcerer, Greek and barbarian, as equals. He suggested that there was a degree of indignity and degradation which no human being should suffer. That was his message. In extending his compassion to slaves, he provided them with one of the very few voices in the ancient world raised in their behalf.

## From Patriotism to Pacifism

During the early years of the Peloponnesian War, Euripides exhibited a proper patriotic attitude. It has been suggested that he wrote the *Andromache* to express his revulsion at the behavior of the enemy at Plataea in 427. The pro-Athenian defenders of the town had surrendered and asked for mercy but they were murdered to the last man. In the *Andromache,* Euripides tells a tale which allows him to show his contempt for the Spartans who had let this happen.

At the outset of the war, Euripides also helped to maintain the reputation of Athens as a citadel of freedom and a defender of holy causes. Athens was, in fact, a kind of haven for those ill-treated elsewhere. Thus, the *Heraclidae* (*circa* 429), the *Suppliants* (*circa* 423) and *Heracles* (*circa* 420) all picture Athens as a refuge or willing helpmeet for the afflicted. Even the ill-starred Medea had found protection there.

Later, when the Athenians began to commit atrocities of their own, the sensitive and conscientious Euripides was forced to admit that "we" were no better than "they." In the spring of 415, his *Trojan Women* was an indictment of war itself, not just the enemy. Was it not obvious that war made men on all sides treacherous and brutish? During the previous winter, Athenian commanders had ordered the adult men of Melos massacred and their women and children sold as slaves.

By the end of the Peloponnesian War many "patriots" had become disillusioned; for Euripides, disillusionment had come much sooner. Unlike Aristophanes, he harbored no special interest. Rather, he condemned the war with the fervor of a pacifist. It was cruel and meaningless savagery. To the despair of his audiences, men did die in vain.

## The Bacchae

It is a commonplace that intellectuals are often too busy criticizing the opinions of others to take a critical look at their own. Toward the end of his life Euripides redeemed himself from this charge. In the *Bacchae,* a play written a year or so before he died and produced after he was gone, Euripides re-examined his own view of religion. He found that it was not the only one possible.

The studies of a man's youth are not easily shaken. Euripides had listened to the materialistic teachings of philosophers like Democritus who had ruled out the existence of the non-material. He had also grown up amid the uncompromising relativism of the Sophists. These influences had prompted him to dismiss romantic and mystical notions which he felt beclouded the true picture of man. In the *Bacchae,* he admitted that his former single-mindedness had denied him the true picture after all. It was not that he had given up his old position, for in this play he reaffirmed his suspicion that religion may be used to shield the devious motives of gods and men. Yet now he openly agreed that it was more than that. His choruses sang of the joys and wonder which were known in the worship of Dionysus. Euripides had not joined hands in the circle, but he had concluded that for those who did, the song was real.

The *Bacchae* takes its name from the chorus of devotees to Dionysus, who was also called Bacchus. In the prologue, Dionysus says that he has come to Thebes to vindicate his mother, Semele. Her sisters, the daughters of Cadmus, king of Thebes, had claimed that

Dionysus was not fathered by Zeus as Semele said, but by some ordinary mortal. Dionysus will show them how much of a god he is.

Disguised as one of his own devotees, he answers to the Greek description of a typical effete easterner. He has long golden curls, a ruddy face, and is dressed in a decorative fawn skin. Immediately upon his arrival, he puts his magic charms to work among the Theban women. Under his spell, they abandon their looms to pursue his rites in the countryside.

Prior to the arrival of the disguised Dionysus, the aged Cadmus had abdicated the throne in favor of his grandson Pentheus. This athletic youth now marches on the scene with heavy strides to deal with the mincing magician. Pentheus is all good sense. He is impatient with anyone who entices women from their tasks and undermines the routine of the state. Yet even his mother, Agave, has succumbed to this witchery and has joined in the rapture of the dance by which worshippers of this foreign god happily return to the bosom of nature. Pentheus also discovers that the blind seer Tiresias and Cadmus, his grandfather, have joined in the hysteria. When Pentheus takes Tiresias to task, Euripides' familiar "anticlericalism" reveals itself. The soothsayer lives off the superstitious needs of the pious. Any new god means more sacrifices, more oracles and more profit. Cadmus reveals that he too has a private reason for joining the worshippers. If Dionysus be accepted as a god, whether he actually is one or not, then Cadmus' daughter Semele must have mothered him by Zeus and that brings credit to the family.

Pentheus will have none of it, even if Dionysus is his cousin. When he imprisons the magician, unaware that he is the very god himself, the contest is joined. Dionysus promptly escapes mid thunder and lightning. He deceives Pentheus completely. The eager young king first wrestles with a bull which he imagines to be Dionysus; he then exhausts himself attacking the god's ghostly vision with his sword. These are strange happenings and not to be found in man's philosophy. There are others. A messenger brings news that the women who worship Dionysus have wrought many wonders. One struck a rock and a fountain gushed forth. Another brought milk from the earth. The messenger urges Pentheus to accept a god who can perform such miracles. Pentheus remains adamant. He declares war against these wild women. Those who die, he defiantly states, will be a fitting sacrifice to their false god.

Suddenly there is a revelation. It appears in Pentheus himself. He is not governed by reason alone any more than any other man and his curiosity tempts him to see the revels for himself. To keep from being recognized he accepts Dionysus' suggestion that he dress as a woman. So with a wig of golden curls, wearing a fawn skin and carrying a wand, he abandons his manliness and common sense in order to spy out the secrets of the worshippers. The trap is sprung. Word is sent to the women that a man disguised as one of them is coming to spy. In an hypnotic trance the women set upon Pentheus and tear his body to shreds. His own mother thinks that the head she carries to Dionysus belongs to a mountain lion. She cries out that her unbelieving son should see what she has won. At her father's gentle prompting, her vision clears and she sees the truth. The price for Agave has been too dear and she abandons the god to other Bacchae to come. There will be other Bacchae of course and another Cadmus, another Tiresias, another Pentheus, another Agave—all to act out the same drama prompted by the powers within man which never change.

In one respect Euripides had remained true to sophism in this drama. He was still offering choices. The wide spectrum of opinion among critics of the *Bacchae* is evidence that it can mean to any man what he wants it to mean. Man remains the measure. For those who would warn the faithless to beware of the mysterious workings of divine power, there is the sight of Pentheus' dismembered body. For others who see this same power as nothing more than the hysterical imaginings of neurotic women, there is Agave holding the head of her son.

Euripides was not lacking in admiration for the wonders of nature which the god had urged his worshippers to adore. He, too, could find God in a garden. Yet the playwright never abandoned his contempt for the superstitions and fears of the faithful. He also found distasteful the smirking hypocrites who for political reasons gave lip service to the worship of the Olympian gods while scoffing at the morality and justice which these gods upheld.

The *Bacchae* gives rise to speculation and imagination at every twist and turn because it presents different experiences, side by side, often in conflict. Unlike the typical Sophist, Euripides no longer said that any of these experiences might be true. He said they were all true. They were all a part of reality. He abandoned the habit of most men, even tragedians, of selecting certain experiences as guides to truth and excluding all others. The *Bacchae* is pantheistic. It has the mood of the East, especially of Zen which finds a final peace and pleasure with the reality of "what is." Euripides was still accept-

ing human experiences as his only guide. Now he included the contradictions. His play reveals religion as a powerful force in human
life, one which brings out the best and the worst in man. Do the
histories of Judaism, Christianity and Islam prove him wrong?

There were moments of deep religious feeling in Euripides' writings. Although he would have been a skeptic toward the gods and
dogmas of any age, he sensed the need for spiritual strength. The
answer he found in a sympathy for all humankind—a sympathy
unattended by ceremonial or creed. In the Western world this has
remained the religion of humanism, without Scriptures, church, or
promise of eternal life.

Euripides wrote nearly one hundred tragedies, of which nineteen
have been preserved. That is to say nineteen counting *Rhesus,* about
which some serious doubts have been raised. This is more than the
combined total of the surviving works of Aeschylus and Sophocles,
yet Euripides was never as popular as they were, and he won fewer
prizes. It was in the fourth century and in later Hellenistic times
that his forthrightness and candor were greatly admired and his
plays read, produced and preserved. However, his estrangement from
his contemporaries seems to have developed gradually. As time
passed, he became ever more disenchanted with the long civil war
and the post-Periclean democracy. It seems apparent that as the
troubles and disappointments of his fellow citizens increased, so did
their impatience with his unpopular opinions.

As with any playwright determined to wean smug audiences
away from their happy illusions, he placed heavy emphasis on the
darker side. Euripides offered the Athenians a mirror in which they
could see themselves as part passion and part charity. Man's tragedy
was not that he was irrevocably subject to fate and the gods; it was
that he could not escape from himself. His nature doomed him to
an exhausting inner conflict.

The late Gilbert Murray, a noted authority on Euripides, once
commented that some men may have agreed with Euripides at the
theater, but he doubted that many took his ideas home with them.
This was very likely true. St. Paul stated the problem four centuries
later: "For the good that I would, I do not: but the evil which I
would not, that I do." (*Romans* 7, xix). Those who ponder the mystery of man inevitably restate that conclusion. No one ever excelled
Euripides at presenting it in the theater. The average Athenian,
however, found his message more depressing than enlightening.

Euripides left Athens in 408 at the age of seventy and went to live in Pella, the capital city of Macedon. King Archelaus who reigned from 413 to 399 was a patron of Greek culture who sought to advance his court by inviting noted artists and poets to live there. Euripides, unhappy and aging, found a congenial refuge for his last years at Pella where he died in 406. Sophocles died at Athens in the same year. All at once, nearly coincident with the finish of Athens, the era of the great tragic poets was over.

## Athens After the War

Between 406 and 399 when the philosopher Socrates was executed, Athens suffered through the painful aftermath of her defeat. Again, the city followed the tortuous route from democracy through an oppressive oligarchy and back to democracy again.

After the Peloponnesian War, the Spartans dictated a peace which put the shoe on the other foot but it did not stand the Greeks on their feet. The Spartan victory set the clock back. The Athenian Empire was broken up and expropriated territories were returned to their rightful owners. Wherever the political enemies of Athens had been driven into exile they were allowed to come home. In various cities these returning oligarchs, protected by Spartan garrisons, wreaked vengeance on the democrats who had driven them out. There was no magic means for ending the persistent inter-party strife which plagued the Greek states. As in the past, a temporary stability was achieved by an outside power supporting one side against the other. The Athenians had favored the democrats. Under Sparta the oligarchs had their turn.

In defeated Athens the pattern was the same as elsewhere. The capitulation in the spring of 404 meant another eclipse for the popular democracy. The city was defenseless at the moment and totally dependent on Spartan sufferance. The circumstances called for a more conservative government. The thirty men chosen to establish a new constitution delayed carrying out their instructions and instead ruled in their own name. These "Thirty Tyrants" were willing to serve Spartan interests and Lysander, in keeping with his general policy, sent troops to enforce their orders.

During the winter of 404–403, the Thirty ruled with a bloody rod; by their wanton confiscation of property and illegal executions they exceeded the limits of fear beyond which there was only reckless hatred. Finally, men who despaired of their lives in any event chose rebellion. The partisans of democracy, who had been living in exile at Thebes, returned to Attica under the leadership of Thrasybulus. In the ensuing battle, Critias, the leader of the Thirty, and one other member were killed. The remaining oligarchs were no longer safe at Athens and fled to Eleusis which had been previously selected as a place of refuge.

The moderates in Athens now elected a Committee of Ten who attempted to chart a course between the extreme oligarchs at Eleusis and the adherents of democracy entrenched at Piraeus. In the summer of 403, there were three governments on Attic soil. In such a predicament the role of the Spartans would be decisive. At first Lysander was sent to help the Thirty, which was the *de facto* government recognized by Sparta. However, for the Athenian democrats and moderates there were some fortuitous circumstances. Lysander's recent successes and rumored ambitions had evoked second thoughts at Sparta. Among those who had them were the kings, Agis and Pausanias. Whether out of jealousy or for whatever reason, the two kings persuaded at least three of the five ephors that Lysander was accomplishing more for himself than for Sparta. Furthermore, it was now apparent that Lysander's partiality toward extreme oligarchs had encouraged vengeful and corrupt governments. The disorders created by these governments at Athens and elsewhere were not winning the Spartans any friends. When Pausanias marched into Attica, Lysander was outranked and his ambitions outflanked. The king was determined to achieve a negotiated solution of the civil strife.

Pausanias showed enough force to make all parties appreciate his seriousness and then, with secret and skillful diplomacy, arranged for an accommodation between the "reasonable" conservatives in the city and the "reasonable" democrats at Piraeus. Moreover, he sought to end the cycle of revenge by insisting that the Thirty be left alone at Eleusis, a vine to wither in its own time.

The government at Athens was a coalition under a new Committee of Ten selected to guard the interests of the two factions. This was not difficult, for there existed broad areas of agreement between them. Both abhorred the suspension of justice and the confiscations of property under the Thirty. The rash acts by individuals in their own parties during the recent troubles were to be forgotten. In a spirit of good will, moderates and democrats sought to restore a stability to the political life of the city which would in turn enable her economy to revive.

As in 410, the leaders of the moderates competed with the democrats for public support. Inevitably this meant acceptance of citizen demands. As a result, the democratic practices which had been abandoned for the second time in 404 were gradually reinstated one by one. By the spring of 402, the franchise was as inclusive as it had been under Pericles.

As might be expected, the leaders of the restored democracy were under heavy popular pressure to rid Attica of its "government in exile." At the first hint of trouble, they suggested that the oligarchic leaders at Eleusis come to a parley. It was a massacre instead. Although a truce had been declared, the democrats had decided to save several lives by sacrificing a few. They then awarded the leaderless faction at Eleusis full rights, agreed that bygones would be bygones, and made Attica a united state once more.

In the years to follow, "unity" in Athens had a special meaning. Again, as during the war, anxiety about the favor of the gods and the tensions of the times created an air of suspicion toward the Sophists or any man who sounded like one.

The trial of Socrates, a scant three years after the restoration of the democracy, meant that even a full-fledged native citizen, who had fought courageously in the war, could no longer speak his mind if his views ran counter to the fixed opinions of the majority. The Athenians had lost confidence in themselves and could no longer bear the criticism which true freedom allows. The execution of Socrates, in 399, cast a long shadow over the fourth century.

## Socrates

Socrates has a good name with people today who might not have liked him in person. He readily admitted that he was unpopular with his fellow citizens. It was one of the reasons why he was brought to trial. Nor was his misfortune only because men did not like his ideas. It was his attitude that bothered them. The wise Socrates did not suffer fools gladly. Lazy or careless thinkers were his special target. In the course of a conversation he might ask a man what he actually meant by a certain word. This can be an annoying habit (Pl. 73).

Ordinarily, men accept each other's vague terminology with a gentleman's agreement not to press for definitions. If someone says a vase is beautiful, then it is beautiful to him. Asking what he means by "beautiful" is not necessarily helpful. "Justice" is another term

*Pl. 73 Bronze head
of Socrates*

usually employed without challenge. Nobody likes to be embarrassed. Socrates went out of his way to make sure that some people were. In the *agora*, if he encountered an orator who gave an outward show of being well-informed, he would ask a series of pointed questions ostensibly seeking information. Gradually, it would be revealed that the man who had so much to say in fact knew very little. The trap was sprung many times, and a victim left stammering and ashamed might be especially angry if his son was among those listening to the encounter. How could a youth respect a father whose inflated image had been punctured by this street corner philosopher?

The Delphic Oracle had informed Socrates that he was the wisest man in Greece precisely because he was willing to admit his ignorance, or, as he phrased it later, because he did not think that he knew what he did not know. Thereafter, Socrates deemed it a service to show others how little they knew. He was obsessed with the idea that his fellow citizens were ignorant, and worse, not aware of it. He would help them dispose of a hoard of misinformation including sheer superstition. Then, beginning right, they could find some more substantial ground for truth.

According to tradition, Socrates' father was a stonecutter. Very likely Socrates had been apprenticed to this trade as a youth. His mother had a reputation as a skilled midwife which meant that she was a good neighbor, not necessarily a working woman. The family seems to have been comfortable but not wealthy; apparently, there was money enough to provide the young Socrates with leisure time for an excellent education. True to the old tradition which emphasized athletics, he always maintained himself in rugged physical condition. As a soldier, he was noted for a Spartan-like disregard for the discomforts of bad weather. In sophisticated Athens, his penchant for going barefoot and wearing one cloak the year round symbolized the disdain of the true thinker for the petty concerns of workaday men. In subsequent times, including our own, men possessing Socrates' mental and physical stamina have ever been rarer than pretenders to distinction who affect a disregard for social amenities as the badge of intellectual stature.

The men who wrote about Socrates' life actually knew him only during his later years. Socrates was seventy at the time of his trial in 399; Aristophanes was forty-seven, Plato about twenty-nine and Xenophon only about twenty-seven. Anything these writers included about the philosopher's youth and early middle age would have been received secondhand. There seems little reason to doubt, however, that Socrates' engaging intellect had early attracted attention in the best Athenian circles and that he was a personality much sought after for salons and at dinner parties. In fact, Socrates may have been one of the great free-loaders of all time. He had a reputation for outlasting other guests and was noted for his good wind at dawn.

Very little is known about Socrates' personal life, but it appears certain that he did not marry until he was about fifty. Even less is known about his wife. By one means or another she seems to have supported their children. Her reputation as a nagging spouse may be traced to the report that she found Socrates' preoccupation with philosophy no more practical than did those fathers whose sons pursued truth instead of the family business.

If university professors allowed themselves such a thought, surely Socrates would be their patron saint. He was a teacher all his life, on his own time and at his own expense. His career has a special fascination for anyone who has observed the changes which take place in good teachers as the years go by. They begin as Socrates seems to have begun, with a careful attention to subject matter. He was eager to acquire all the knowledge available in the fledgling sciences and to keep abreast of the latest speculation and debate. To the young men who listened to him in his earlier days before the Peloponnesian War, most of the knowledge he transmitted had been acquired from others. Then, as the years passed, he paid less and less attention to routine material and concentrated on those few ideas which interested him the most. It was a distillation process in which the final product was uniquely his own. Like the modern professor who stops carrying notes to class, he was finally content to be a sage.

To many young men of the third generation Socrates was an idol. There were also men for whom Socrates' courage, self-confidence and independence of mind were unhappy reminders of their own failings. Unquestionably, he was a model nonconformist, enjoying all the advantages and suffering all the penalties.

To a majority of Athenians, Socrates need not have offered any personal challenge at all. They took him as they saw him characterized in Aristophanes' the *Clouds*—as a fuzzy-minded teacher who put curious notions in his students' heads, raised doubts about the gods, and inspired insubordination of young men toward their fathers.

Aristophanes attacked the Sophists by poking fun at them. Socrates, the best known of the Athenian "eggheads," was used as the chief target. He was presented as a teacher in a school which offered two kinds of logic—Right Logic and Wrong Logic. For a price, a student could have his choice. And there were other things to learn too. The busy thinkers in this school carried on experiments to determine how far a flea could jump. Socrates makes his first appearance in a basket hanging in the air. From this vantage point he can better contemplate the sun. He answers questions in a typically sophistical way by asking questions of his own. When asked if it was not Zeus who strikes perjurers with lightning, he inquires why the notorious Cleonymus has never been hit? Then he names two other known perjurers who have escaped. Why too, he wants to know, does lightning strike Zeus' own shrines and sacred oaks? These were hard questions. Are not men who ignore such arguments happier than those who confuse themselves with contradictions? Certainly Socrates was a disturber of peaceful minds.

Aristophanes' imaginary school offered an ideal setting for the customary debate which the playwright included in his comedies. The contest was between Right Logic and Wrong Logic. Here was an opportunity for Aristophanes to contrast the sturdier values of the "Marathon" generation with the debilitating skepticism and unmanly self-indulgence which infected his own. Right Logic argues that youths should be taught to revere the ways of their ancestors, to be active and strong and not dawdle in warm baths all day. To which Wrong Logic replies that the baths of bold Heracles were warm, an allusion to the warm spring at Thermopylae which had refreshed the hero after his labors. It was a clever reply, or so it would seem to youths who no longer found time for strenuous exercise.

Among the characters in the *Clouds* are Strepsiades and his son Pheidippides, who seek to learn the practical arts. For example, they want to discover how by any logic a man can get out of paying his debts. Wrong Logic can manage it. Says a creditor to a debtor: "You swore by the gods to pay me." Replies the debtor: "Well, now I swear by the gods I will not." Creditor: "Then you defy the gods?" Debtor: "What gods?"

Socrates was properly resentful at having been involved in this parody on the Sophists. It was absurd to represent him as teaching men to profit by trickery. In truth he had no concern at all for material ends. Thus, the *Clouds* says less about Socrates than it does about the popular misconceptions concerning him. Curiously, that has remained the real value of Aristophanes' play; it inadvertently stresses the paradox of knowledge. In *Ecclesiastes* there appears the provocative statement: "For in much wisdom is much grief; and he that increaseth knowledge increaseth sorrow." (*Eccl.* 1, 12–18). The *Clouds* shows how men may protect themselves against the harmful effects of knowledge by refusing to understand those who teach it.

Socrates did not teach under formal conditions; he held discussions wherever he happened to be, probably in the *agora* for the most part. His favorites gathered around him and the regular attendants became a sort of "school." Plato was in the last class, and after the execution of Socrates this talented admirer wrote accounts of the way his teacher had behaved and what he had said during his trial and his last days. The *Apology,* and pertinent references in the *Crito, Phaedo,* and *Euthyphro* (as these accounts are entitled), were undoubtedly authentic. Although Plato was an avowed partisan of Socrates, he could scarcely have risked presenting a fabricated account of the trial and execution, for his contemporaries were as well-informed about these events as he was.

As far as we know, Socrates never wrote down any of his own ideas. His teachings have been learned from the writings of others, especially from Plato whose major writings were a series of dialogues in which Socrates was the principal speaker. In these artistic pieces, the master's teachings on a variety of subjects including democracy, education, courage, piety, and love were expounded. The question has naturally been raised whether Plato's own ideas may not have crept in here and there. The matter has been deliberated at great length by a long list of authors who afford the interested reader ample material to form an opinion of his own. During the last years of his life, Plato wrote certain works—the *Laws* for example—which are free of this kind of controversy. They seem to express only his own ideas. Socrates does not even appear as a speaker.

In the dialogues, Plato preserves the form of the Socratic method of teaching in which the master engaged one or several persons in a question-and-answer session. Using this dialectical technique, a discussion might start with a relatively broad definition of a certain term. Then by examining each part of the definition, it would be whittled down by a process of elimination. During the proceedings Socrates would explain why wrong answers were wrong and provide his listeners with experience in logical thinking.

If Aristophanes' comic burlesque of Socrates is unfair, Plato's idealized concept is perhaps too generous. The younger Xenophon, whose valuable *Hellenica* has already been mentioned, also wrote an *Apology* and a *Memorabilia*. His Socrates appears somewhat prosaic in these works—certainly not too good to be true. Although Xenophon lacks imagination, his report is helpful for Aristophanes and Plato may have had too much.

## The Trial of Socrates

Socrates lived too long. The democracy had been restored in form, but not in spirit. The temper of the times was overly serious and self-conscious. There was a determination by the citizenry to root out those who proposed to teach young men how to think instead of teaching them what to think.

The new mood could be noted in the civic theater where potent satire and strong invective were out of fashion. Aristophanes bent with the prevailing wind and toned down his comedies. His *Assembly of Women* (*circa* 392) and *God of Wealth* (388) lack the old punch. The master of the Old Comedy had become the founder of the Middle Comedy. Henceforth, the theater would provide an escape from crucial problems—not a confrontation of them. In brief, the history of comedy in Athens charted the shift from the rough-and-tumble days of the democracy in its confident heyday to the post-war period of unconfidence and despair.

Socrates was unwilling to change. He would not stop talking and he would not suppress his opinions. The issue, so far as he was concerned, was not whether he had said anything contrary to the public interest, but simply whether or not all ideas should be heard. For this, he has been considered a hero of democracy. At the same time he did not try to explain his doctrines to the jury at his trial, for it seemed plain that he did not think many of the jurors had the capacity to understand them.

Socrates had been charged on two counts. First, he was accused of being an unbeliever. While he had never refused to cooperate in the rites of the official religion, he had from time to time made remarks akin to those which had made Euripides unpopular and had caused Anaxagoras to be sent into exile at an earlier time. It is true that Greek religion was not dogmatic in the sense that the myths were Holy Writ; nevertheless, if the overwhelming majority of the citizenry felt it necessary to offer gifts and festivals in honor of the gods, it was scarcely fitting for a few to insult these deities with clever remarks and embarrassing questions. The second charge was that Socrates had corrupted the young men who associated with him. Certain of his aristocratic students had been discredited in the recent overthrow of the oligarchy, and no one needed to be reminded that the infamous Alcibiades had been one of the defendant's dearest young friends. Ironically, Socrates who had sought to offer an antidote to the poisonous side of sophism was denounced as one of its most vicious agents.

Today, Socrates' name is a household word. The names of his accusers, Meletus, Anytus and Lycon, are found only in reference books. Meletus was the actual prosecutor who delivered the speech for the prosecution. He was apparently much agitated over the current irreligion in Athens; in fact, he was probably also the prosecutor of Andocides, another man charged with impiety in the same year. Anytus had a personal reason for thinking that Socrates was a corrupter of young men. His son had been advised by Socrates that he was worthier of a better life than that to be found in his father's tannery. The third plaintiff of record, Lycon, seems to have been a hanger-on, a butt for some of the comedians. The comic poet Cratinus said he was effeminate. Socrates never mentioned him. He was very likely beneath contempt.

The course of the trial before 501 jurors followed the customary procedure. Meletus spoke first on behalf of those who brought the charges. Then Socrates offered his own defense. Next the jury cast a vote and found Socrates guilty. Since it was the prerogative of the jury to set the penalty, the prosecution stated briefly what they thought the punishment should be. Socrates offered his own proposal. The jury agreed with the accusers that he should be executed. Whereupon Socrates made a final statement. Plato's *Apology* reports only what Socrates said: First, his long defense; then his short statement about the penalty; and finally his valedictory.

From the beginning, Socrates fought the charge that he was a Sophist. It is not that he thinks it is a crime to be one, but simply that it is a false accusation. He says his defense will be one of plain spoken honesty unadorned by sophistical phrasing. Then, without airs for the occasion, speaking only as he was used to speak in the *agora*, he strikes at popular misconceptions about himself. It is wrong, he argues, to say that any man who investigates or studies a variety of theories about the nature of man and the universe is, for that reason alone, a dangerous and heretical person. He reminds his listeners that at seventy he is being charged in court for the first time in his life. Even so, many men had long been poisoning even children's minds against him with false stories and unfair caricatures. He cites as an example Aristophanes' the *Clouds*. It is highly doubtful that Aristophanes had intended any harm to Socrates. Yet the playwright had planted the seed which produced ugly fruit. In 423, this play had been entertaining; in the darker days after the war the residue it left in men's minds was one of suspicion.

Socrates emphatically denies that he has ever taken money for his teaching. This in itself disassociates him from the Sophists, for they accept fees. At the time, such practice was considered the equivalent of a present-day doctor's advertising in the newspapers. Knowledge was not a commodity to be bought and sold. It was imparted by a father to his son or a friend to a friend. Those who peddled it were suspected of selling trickery. There was no need to argue whether Socrates took money or not. His poverty was obvious. Nor did he behave like a typical Sophist. His blunt manners and simple dress evidenced a humble naturalness. It is easier to read into his words a willingness to trust to the common sense of an illiterate farmer than to the theories of a pretentious book-fed intellectual who has a ready panacea for every ill; yet he is equally scornful of simple folk who carry an ingrained prejudice against any form of speculation. Such persons were easily victimized by a man like Mele-

tus, who had accused Socrates of saying that the sun was a stone
and not a god. Was not this charge an insult to the jury? Any man
knew that this theory was actually to be found in Anaxagoras' book
now on sale in the marketplace. Meletus' ignorance was patent. He
did not know what Socrates was teaching his young friends, nor had
he ever bothered to find out. Like many another self-appointed reformer of education, Meletus had failed to educate himself.

Socrates offered a strong defense. Yet, ironically, he was a wise
man trapped by the very ignorance he deplored. The average citizen
knew the Sophists only by reputation. They were clever arguers who
could prove anything good or bad. Might not then a Sophist use
deceit to prove he was not a Sophist? By the time the jury began
to listen to Socrates' case, the prosecution was already winning.

It was like Socrates to perform before the jury according to his
own wishes and to refuse the best advice on how to win votes. For
all of his plain speaking, much of what he says sounds less like a
plea than a lecture. He reminds the jurors how in the *Iliad* Achilles
had been offered his life if he would forsake honor and go home.
The threat of death had not mattered to Achilles nor would it to
Socrates. Even if they were to bargain with him and tell him he can
go free if he will stop talking, he will refuse. The philosopher's quest
is for truth and without this search life has no meaning. Again and
again, Socrates avows that *to live* is not of itself important. *To live
rightly* is all that matters. The true purpose of education is to learn
how to live, not how to earn a living. Socrates was dedicated to the
idea that learning was an end in itself. A man should pursue knowledge for the good it will avail him personally. He repeats an admonition he has often given to his students. Money does not guarantee
goodness, yet goodness is the real wealth of life.

Socrates had obeyed his commanders at Potidaea, Amphipolis
and Delium. So would he continue to obey the gods. He would fulfill his destiny to awaken the city to the slothful thinking of its citizens. His statement to the jury shows him in full sail. The most
famous passage of the *Apology* is the analogy in which Socrates com-
pares Athens to a large and lazy horse and himself to a gadfly which
stings the horse to arouse it into activity. Like a gadfly, he can be
slapped down so that the horse can go on sleeping, but then again
perhaps other gadflies will be sent to do the job.

Socrates' description of his mission prompted him to make one
of the most curious statements of his speech. He says that all his
life a "voice" has spoken to him and told him what to do. It is not

known whether he was referring to a "still, small voice" of conscience or whether he thought he had his own special "little god" or daemon. In any event, this statement from a man whose religious views were already suspect was hard on the jurors' ears. To the charge that he did not believe in the gods, it could be added that he had invented them.

Socrates says that his "voice" warned him about politics. He had not sought public office, but as a citizen he was bound to do his duty. And so he did, but only as he saw fit. The jurors are reminded about the incident of the generals who had lost the four thousand men at Arginusae. Although the other members of the pyrtany had been coerced into accepting the illegal procedure of trying the commanders as a group, he had refused. Threatened with arrest, he had stood firm and defied even the majority of the citizenry. Later it was admitted that he was right, but by then the generals had been executed.

He had also resisted the Thirty Tyrants. On one occasion they summoned him and four others and ordered them to go and arrest a man whom they planned to execute summarily. The other four had obeyed, but Socrates went home. Only the subsequent fall of the Thirty saved his life. Was not this courage a proper example for young men? And Socrates offers the names of several fathers who would be willing to testify to the good influence he has had on their sons.

Throughout his speech Socrates avoids any appeal to sentiment and refuses to beg for mercy. He has three sons, one nearly grown, the other two small children, but he excuses himself from bringing his family into court as others had done. He says he would not insult the jurors. They were bound by their oaths to Zeus to judge this case on its merits and not to follow the fickle dictates of emotion. Socrates' attitude was clearly in violation of all the usual rules for flattering the jury and wringing an acquittal from them. His friends had cautioned him about the risk. It was as though he dared the jury to find him guilty by exhibiting the very contempt for mass opinion that had invited his present trouble. To some he seemed extraordinarily courageous and to others merely foolhardy. In either case, he had the credentials of a martyr.

The vote was 280 to 221 in favor of conviction. Although thirty votes would have reversed the verdict, Meletus asked for the death penalty. Socrates, still insistent that he has actually been serving the Athenians, suggests they give him what he really deserves, free maintenance by the state. It is obvious that he had no intention of trying to make amends for his outspoken position. He had no plans for changing his ways. Yet neither imprisonment nor exile appealed to him. If his habits were so vexing to his fellow citizens, could he expect a better reception among strangers? A life without debate and speculation would be impossible for him. Toward the end of his brief statement, however, he says that he will pay a fine. Four friends, including Plato, have agreed to put up the money. The jury rejects it. In fact, Socrates' refusal to go into exile, which would have been a good compromise, did not sit well with the jurors. They voted that he be put to death, 361 to 140.

Socrates begins his final remarks to the jury by wondering about their eagerness to kill him. Surely, he says, they will bring ill-repute both to themselves and to the city for having done so. Plato, who reports his statement, was himself one of the severest critics of the Athenian democracy in the years to follow. Socrates reiterates that he would no more have sought to escape the wrath of the jury by cowardly means than he would have run away from battle. The problem is not how to avoid death. No one can do that. It is rather how to escape the temptation to do evil. In this he has been successful, but they have been ensnared. A teacher to the end, he adds that his enemies could not stop criticism of themselves by putting their critics to death. The only sure way is to become better men themselves.

Turning from the jurors who have condemned him, Socrates addresses those who have considered him innocent. He offers the comforting thought that death is not to be feared. It may be, he says, an endless unconsciousness in which eternity is like a single night of sound sleep. If not that, then death is a threshold to another place where men can meet the worthies of the past, Homer and Hesiod among them. And lesser men too presumably, for Socrates says he would be as busy there as on earth, asking questions in order to find out who is truly wise and who is not.

Socrates was completely at ease. He had an abiding faith that no harm could come to a good man either here or in the hereafter. He does not condemn his accusers and the jurymen who voted against him. Yet, he adds, it is true that certain men had *wanted* to do him harm and for their motive they should be censured. No one can really hurt him, except himself. That would happen only if he should cease to follow his own best conception of right. This he has refused to do.

Socrates was the master of his own destiny, his own happiness. Like Solon he wanted only to possess those qualities of mind he already owned. Other men had not given them to him, nor could other men take them from him. This was his strength. He sought power over no one except himself. This gave him freedom from every other power on earth.

## Socrates in Prison

The execution was delayed for a month. At Athens there was an annual festival in honor of Theseus. As part of this rite a ship was sent to Delos, where one of the largest shrines to Apollo was located. It was forbidden to put anyone to death during the time it took for the ship to go and return. In this interim, Socrates was visited in prison by his friends who urged him to escape. Among his most frequent callers was Crito, a man about Socrates' age. Plato recreated one of these occasions in a dialogue entitled *Crito*.

Crito remonstrates with Socrates on behalf of his friends. They will suffer an incalculable loss in his death, and will surely be thought to have let him die without doing all they could to save him. There are also his children and their education to consider. Furthermore, there is no reason for Socrates to doubt that his escape can easily be managed. His well-to-do and influential friends, both in Athens and abroad, will make all the arrangements, including bribes.

Socrates was not moved by these considerations. He again insists that there is never a good reason or excuse for doing wrong. To the usual arguments of "what will other people think" or "what would other people do," Socrates replies that he makes up his own mind and lives by his own dictates. Moreover, he obviously considers his decisions superior to those of average men. Socrates may have been a hero in the fight for freedom, a stalwart of the democracy, but he did not have a very high opinion of humankind. He was a staunch upholder of the idea that good laws strictly enforced were the best guidance for men to follow. This was in fact the reason he refused to leave the prison, even if his escape could be arranged.

Socrates believed in the ideal of the *polis*. He was born and raised in the community and had enjoyed a good life there. It was his home. He was beholden in return not to connive at breaking its laws. What kind of example would Socrates, the teacher, offer, if he ran away? Would it not then appear to others that each man had the right to pass judgment on his own sentence? Who would accept a penalty, if every man was to be his own judge? Socrates would not disobey the law, even though he felt certain that the jury had abused the law by finding him guilty. If he did not like the laws in Athens, he had had a long life in which to have chosen to go elsewhere. He would not at seventy disobey.

There is perhaps something missing here. Under certain conditions, might not a man feel compelled to resist injustice even though it be cloaked by law? Was not the contract between Socrates and the *polis* only valid if both sides faithfully upheld the law? If wicked men pervert the established laws for their own purposes, do not righteous men have recourse to revolution? Socrates' silence on these vital questions was due to his overriding interest in a philosophical attitude toward life, rather than a political response to a particular question. His refusal to consider the context in which the laws were being administered was no more out of character than was Jesus' admonition to the complaining Jews, burdened by taxes, to render unto Caesar the things which were Caesar's. As it happened, Socrates' kingdom was not of this world either.

Socrates was preoccupied with that life which transcends the petty concerns of any moment in history. It was obvious that he was not interested in day-to-day matters which blinded other men to the problem of eternity. He stressed an old idea which has been restated countless times. Virtue is its own reward. He was not doing right because it would save him, or win him friends, or help him succeed. He was doing right for its own sake and insisting that there was no other reason.

This doctrine would become the cornerstone of Stoicism. The giver of a gift received his reward in the giving, not by receiving anything in return. Or as Cicero would long afterwards insist in his *Laws,* the good man loves goodness for its own sake, and not because he fears a witness or a judge. Socrates would not break the laws because others had, even though the laws had been used against him. He was the spiritual father of all those who have gone peaceably to the stake, falsely accused, tried and sentenced. Many of these men, particularly the Christian martyrs, had the prospect of an immediate blessed vision in heaven. So too did Socrates envisage a far, far better world, the real world of ideas.

## Socrates' Last Day

The *Phaedo* is a Platonic dialogue named for another of Socrates' friends. It is a companion piece to the *Crito.* In this work Phaedo recounts to others who had not been present what happened during Socrates' last day on earth, especially what he said to his friends who had assembled from Athens and from abroad for his final hours. Death was not the awesome end which his companions pleaded with him to avoid. Socrates welcomed it as the fulfillment of his philosophical search.

The dialogue presents Socrates in a happy state of mind and, as usual, in command of himself and the conversation. The advice he receives, that his talk would heat him up and so require extra dosages of hemlock, must be one of the most renowned examples of uncalled-for counsel in history. He would not stop talking before he had made plain to his companions the reasons why a true philosopher welcomes death.

Socrates' preoccupation with his other life, a spiritual existence unknown to the senses, was a landmark in Greek thought. A concept, previously suggested by Orphism and the teachings of Pythagoras and Parmenides, became an established doctrine. Socrates talked constantly of the necessity to guard the welfare of the soul. This idea has been a commonplace in Western literature since the time of Plato and his contemporaries in the fourth century. They heard it first from Socrates.

In the *Phaedo* Socrates tells his followers that death means the separation of the soul from the body. Such a state is to be sought by anyone who would have true knowledge. The bodily senses are an impairment to spiritual sight. His elaboration of this notion provides one of the most devastating attacks on the body to be found anywhere in the literature of the Western world. Gone is the "whole man," mind and body, as celebrated in the odes of Pindar and seen in the statues of Myron and Polycleitus. Rather the body is now depicted as the deceitful source of all human ills in constant antagonism with the soul which alone can know the good, the true and the beautiful. The body distracts men from their proper goals by consuming them with all manner of physical desires which are in turn the cause of human warfare. The same bodily wants constantly interrupt the thoughts of those who would study or contemplate. Man must therefore be absent from the body if he is to gain any true knowledge. Socrates concludes that only those who are still ensnared by the love of the senses will want to live. He who seeks pure wisdom will seek to rid himself of the body. For this reason Socrates has actually been seeking death throughout his career as a philosopher. This final day is for him happy, not mournful. The hemlock will not kill him; it will set him free.

Socrates was not entirely successful in lifting the minds of his companions above their attachment to mundane things. Crito asked how they should bury him. Socrates was indifferent. After death *he* would be gone from them. What difference did it make how they disposed of the body which he had left behind?

The circumstances surrounding the trial and execution of Socrates were not unlike those which have attended other periods of anxiety in history. In Athens, the law against sacrilege was a convenience. It was rarely applied under fair skies, but always available should darker days require the expulsion or even execution of men who seemed to undermine "unity" and "faith." On a technical basis, Socrates was apparently guilty. The law specifically forbade the dissemination of unorthodox views. Since Socrates did not pick and choose his remarks about the gods, he was, in the strict sense, an offender. At the same time, the trial of an aging philosopher, a loyal son of Athens for seventy years, allows the conclusion that he was being used to satisfy the need of the moment for a sacrificial offering by a worried people.

The fate of Socrates at the hands of the masses cannot, therefore, be read as a condemnation of democracy without considering the hard conditions under which this democracy was operating. He was killed by jealousy, ignorance, and fear, qualities which are not partial to any form of government.

Socrates' uncompromising stand was admirable, but it would not have damaged his position if he had been humble enough to recognize that most men do not arrive at their answers the way he did. There remains the danger that intellectuals will take the position that their views are absolutely best, instead of just better for them. Such an attitude lacks magnanimity. At the same time, the jurors who voted to condemn Socrates failed to have the patience and tolerance which men in a free society must have if they are to enjoy the fruits of diversity. Here was a fatal misunderstanding for Socrates, the Athenians, and others since.

# PART THREE

*After the Fifth Century B.C.*

## Sparta and Thebes

**XV** The survivors of the Peloponnesian War included the usual types of misfortune—sorrowful widows, ruined farmers, indigent refugees and experienced, idle soldiers. During the unsettling aftermath, the veterans fared the best. Beginning in the closing years of the fifth century, they began to earn their way as mercenaries, both at home and abroad. Cyrus the Younger, the Persian prince who had helped Sparta win the war, was their first major employer.

The inordinate concentration of power in the person of the Persian king was a reason for stability while he lived and for competition when he died. With the passing of Darius II in 404, his elder son came to the throne as Artaxerxes II. He was the rightful heir, but neither time nor custom had changed his mother's mind about him; she favored her younger son, the brilliant and resourceful Cyrus. With her encouragement and his own ambition, he needed only an army. He was in luck. Sparta was willing to let him recruit mercenaries from all parts of Greece. At the very least, it was a means of draining off restless men from the home scene. More importantly, Sparta hoped that her helpfulness would redeem a regrettable pledge made in the closing years of the war. She had agreed to recognize Persian control over the Greek cities of Asia Minor in return for assistance against Athens. If Cyrus should be successful in his bid for the throne, he would surely not press the matter.

The young prince managed to amass a Persian-style army, composed of various native contingents; even so, when he headed east in the summer of 401, his real hope rested with his 14,000 Greek mercenaries. Nor did they fail him. The crucial battle with his brother's forces was fought at Cunaxa, located eighty-seven miles northwest of Babylon, about where the Euphrates River curves toward the Tigris. It was a triumph for Greek arms. The Spartans might have foreseen such a result, but not that Cyrus would be killed. Their gamble on behalf of the Greek cities had failed. Artaxerxes would hold the Spartans to the agreement of 412. He would be even less likely to forget their help to Cyrus.

The Greeks at Cunaxa were stranded. Worse, during a parley with the Persians their commanders were treacherously murdered. Among the new ones elected to lead them home was Xenophon whose *Anabasis* (meaning to go inland or "upcountry") described both the march to Cunaxa and one of history's notable retreats. His work recaptured the agony and the heroism of the famous Ten Thousand who roughed it in strange country and fought hostile tribes all the way back to Trapezus on the Black Sea coast. From there they sailed to Thrace.

The *Anabasis* was Xenophon's own story. As an account of real life adventure, it has always had more appeal than either his *Hellenica*, which continued Thucydides' work, or his *Memorabilia* about Socrates.

## Sparta Triumphant and in Trouble

Eighty years had passed since Sparta had abandoned the initiative against Persia to the Athenians. Now, for the first time dominant on the sea as well as the land, the Spartans lived up to their new obligations and made preparations to meet the Persians head on. As usual, they asked for help from other Greek cities and as usual, because of local issues, the response was mixed. The Athenians, having been protected by the Spartans from Theban revenge, felt obliged to send at least a token force. The angry Thebans refused to contribute at all. Their decision was not a crippling blow. The joint expeditionary force was better than doubled when it was joined by

6,000 veterans who had survived the perilous trip home from Cunaxa.

Manpower and supplies were not the real Spartan problem; it was, as usual, management. During the first three years of the war (400 to 397), the ephors jealously guarded their power by placing land and sea operations under separate commands. Furthermore, the lack of coordination at the top was matched by poor discipline in the ranks. Thibron, the commander of the army, allowed his men to loot the countryside and so made more enemies than he defeated. Even without this careless dissipation of their energies, the Spartans' hope for a crucial decision by land was due to be frustrated. The Persians had plans of their own. They were reluctant to challenge the veterans of Cunaxa in a set battle and actually hoped to win the decision against the Spartans at sea. This would take time. Meanwhile, the initial skirmishing and maneuvering proved inconclusive and a truce was concluded in 397 on the basis of neutralizing the cities in dispute. As so often happened, the armistice was actually spent in further preparations.

In 396, Sparta showed a renewed determination by sending King Agesilaus to Asia Minor. In the following year he was given command of both land and sea forces. The Greeks fared better under his command but their daring attacks were not the means by which to conclude the issue. At the same time, Artaxerxes had begun his vast naval rebuilding program. The man he chose to mold his navy into a first-class fighting force was an able and experienced admiral, and also, strange to say, an Athenian. The command was given to Conon who, wary of the Assembly's temper, had thought better of returning to Athens after the defeat at Aegospotami in 405.

Despite the usual Persian reluctance to meet payrolls which precipitated trouble amongst already quarreling mercenaries, Conon had whipped these diverse units by 394 into a fighting force which he considered capable of driving the Spartans from the Aegean waters.

A worse threat to Sparta than the resurgence of Persian sea power came from her fellow Greeks whose growing animosity toward Spartan hegemony would eventually bring Agesilaus' campaign in Asia Minor to an abrupt end.

Again, as had happened after the Persian Wars, the heavy-handedness of a martial Sparta aroused dissension in Greece more quickly than the subtle machinations of a diplomatic Athens. After the Peloponnesian War, when Sparta replaced Athens as the dominant power in the Aegean, she acted almost exclusively for military reasons and without the economic motivations and considerations which the Athenians had used to justify the maintenance of their maritime empire. In any event, the trouble which came to Sparta was the same. The former Athenian allies no more enjoyed sending tribute to Sparta than they had to Athens. The presence of Spartan forces on their soil, under the command of a resident harmost, was a constant reminder of how hollow the promises of a "liberator" could be. Furthermore, as with Athens, Sparta's growing power was matched by the apprehension of old friends as to what might be in store for them. In a small war against Elis (399-397), Sparta gave them a clue. As part of her policy of paring down other states while building up her own, she had ordered the Eleans to give up certain bordering towns which they had incorporated during the Peloponnesian War. Defiance led to a one-sided contest in which the recalcitrant Elis managed to lose more than she might have bargained for. Under the circumstances, the major cities of Greece—Corinth, Thebes, and Megara—so long worried about Athens, and so long trusting in Sparta, found it necessary even as modern nations do to assess a new set of factors. Year by year, hostility toward Sparta mounted. According to Xenophon, the Greek leaders in the forefront of the anti-Spartan movement were by 395 receiving incentive pay. The Persians had sent an agent into Greece with gold to be dispensed to key officials, who were in return to instigate a second front against Sparta. Xenophon says that the bribes were taken at Thebes, Corinth and Argos, but not at Athens. The Athenians hardly needed them. Nearly ten years had passed since the end of the war. The democratic leaders at Athens did not require foreign encouragement to begin thinking again of the glories lost and of a better day to come.

The time was not far off, however, when even Athenian leaders would succumb to the subtle trap which the Persians had baited with their money. In the fourth century, the charge that one faction or another was accepting foreign money became a familiar one. To be sure, with or without the temptation of bribes, the Greeks seemed unable to live agreeably with one another. Yet the readiness with which prominent men took foreign gold and served causes other than their own made the later history of the Greek states not only suicidal, but pathetic.

### The Corinthian War

The Thebans knew how and where to stir up trouble. Separate calls for help by the Locrians and Phocians, two jittery neighbors in central Greece, usually brought larger powers to their side. An incident was arranged. The Thebans rushed to the aid of Locris and, as expected, the Spartans answered the Phocian appeal. The Spartans were already at odds with the Thebans over their stubborn refusal to help solve the confused political situation in Attica after the war, not to mention their failure to lend any aid in Asia Minor. So the Spartans, eager to punish Theban insolence, were drawn into a war at home precisely as the Persians had hoped they would be.

The Thebans sent word to the Athenians that if they hoped to recover their former position, now was the time to begin. The Athenians agreed. Although their walls had not yet been rebuilt, they again took up arms against Sparta.

The adverse turn of events, plus the knowledge that Persian money was at work in Greece, prompted the Spartans to recall Agesilaus. The Persian investment had paid off. Although Agesilaus left 4,000 men behind to guard the Ionian cities, his feelings were apparent in the terse remark, "A thousand coins have defeated me."

While the king led his army home through Thrace and Macedonia, the Spartans won a victory over the coalition which now included the Corinthians. When Agesilaus arrived at the border of Boeotia, however, he received bad news from Cnidus. The Spartan fleet had been soundly defeated by the combined Persian forces under Conon. The victory gave the Persians control of the Aegean and the last of the Spartan garrisons were forced to return home from the islands and the coastal cities of Asia Minor. The twists and turns of history do indeed take the edge off surprises. The former subject states of the Athenian Empire had been freed from their Spartan "liberators" by a Persian fleet under the direction of an Athenian admiral.

The hostilities first instigated by Thebes in 395 continued sporadically until 387. Because Corinth became the base of operations for the coalition against Sparta, the series of battles in this period has been called the Corinthian War. To find Corinth on the same side as Athens, and both opposed to Sparta, was a sign of how times had changed. On the other hand, the Spartan decision to attack her neighbor Argos was an old story. The Spartans could never turn their backs on the Argives. Nor, according to Xenophon, could they trust them to be honest about sacred matters. His story offers an aside on the perfunctory attitude which ceremonial religions may sometimes encourage. The Spartans complained to the oracles at both Olympia and Delphi that the Argives scheduled religious festivals whenever they were about to be invaded—not according to a proper sequence. By this device, they were ever ready with a truce of the gods. According to the oracles, Zeus and Apollo were not amused by such arrangements. With their support, the Spartan king Agesipolis proceeded with his invasion. His appeal to the gods and their encouragement for his mission were surprising to the Argives, as well as costly.

While the Spartans were thus repairing their position at home, Conon continued his service to the Persians by advising them how best to harass their enemy. To begin with, they could win over the island and coastal cities of the Aegean by foregoing the building of any military installations and by leaving each place independent. Gratitude would insure friendship; and, better, it would detach these states from the Spartans on whom they had recently perforce felt dependent. In Greece, the Great King could best revenge the Spartan betrayal by helping Athens which was again showing vigorous signs of life. Consequently, Conon was allowed to take the Persian-owned fleet to Athens and put the crews of eighty ships to work rebuilding the Long Walls. Later, a statue was erected to Conon. He deserved it. To have rebuilt Athenian defenses with Persian money was no mean accomplishment.

It was the Great King's satrap Pharnabazus who directed these developments, and the Spartans made haste to inform Artaxerxes II how such a policy would have the very opposite effect of the one intended. They pointed out that Conon, a native Athenian, was interested only in restoring the power of his city so that he might be the hero of a revived empire. This report was substantiated by news from Athens that the leaders of the restored democracy, Thrasybulus in particular, were promoting a return to the old aggressive policies which best served the interest of their popular supporters. The Spartan argument made sense and when the unsuspecting Conon went on a mission to the Great King in 392, he was seized and thrown into prison. Although later released, he died in Cyprus.

Second thoughts about the past history of Greece had also prompted the Great King to review his policy. Because of Sparta's stable economy, rooted in the land, she had never been as interested in the Aegean as had the commercially minded Athenians. That fact, plus Conon's recent duplicity, made Artaxerxes wary of any further dealings with the Athenians.

On the other hand, Agesilaus, faced with the drawn out Corinthian War, was willing to come to terms with Persia as early as 392. Sparta would renounce any interest in Asia Minor in return for a

Persian promise not to interfere further in Greek affairs on the main-land. At the time, the Persian king was not ready to forget the trouble the Spartans had caused him. The continued resurgence of Athens in the years following helped to change his mind.

One reason for a revival of Athenian power was their willingness to abandon the concept of a citizen army and make use of available soldiers-for-hire. Outstanding among the professional commanders of these mercenaries was Iphicrates, an innovator who adopted new styles in armor and training. His peltasts, men armed with very light shields, *peltae*, were extraordinarily effective against the heavily armed, old style *hoplites* of tradition-bound Sparta.

On the diplomatic front, Athens began sending delegations to old friends looking for new alliances. All in all, as time passed, it became increasingly apparent to the Persians that support for Sparta would serve their own interest best. Yet so significant a shift in Persian policy could not take place overnight.

It must be remembered that contact with the Greeks was made only in one corner of a vast empire. The Great King's attention was largely taken up with other matters and his relations with the Greeks were left to his military and political agents in that part of the world. Since the competence of these men varied and as they were often at odds with one another, the history of this period is beclouded with their dealings and cross-purposes. Ultimately, major decisions were made by the Great King, but much could happen while delegations were making the long journey east to visit him. Well did the Persians know this. They had often found it necessary in their dealings with the Greeks to switch back and forth, and it would be a gross under-statement to say that they found the politicians on both sides untrust-worthy. To have conquered these busy people a century beforehand would have saved time and trouble. Two centuries later, after similarly baffling experiences, the Romans reached the same conclusion and rather than continue to listen to one side and then the other, incor-porated the Greeks into their Empire.

## The King's Peace of 386

The most that Artaxerxes accomplished was to become the arbiter of Greek affairs, albeit less by his own strength than by Greek weak-ness. The Corinthian War reached a crippling impasse. Each state was too proud to compromise. Any combination of states was too weak to impose its will on the others. Finally, the Spartans appealed to the

Great King for help in establishing a permanent peace, a move which gave him the power to dictate the terms. There was no better proof of political ineptness on the part of the Greeks than the King's Peace of 386. For his part, Artaxerxes must at least be credited with having successfully exploited his advantage. The skillful distribution of bribes and the hiring of some Greeks to fight others had succeeded where Xerxes, for all his time and trouble, had failed.

For the Athenians to accept dictation from the Great King was unfortunate but expedient. Despite recent promising military and diplomatic successes, the combined might of Sparta and Persia could mean another humiliating defeat such as they had suffered less than twenty years before. Athens had to accept an imposed peace or risk losing the gains she had made.

Artaxerxes declared that there could only be peace if the Greek cities were each left free. He would call to account any state which broke this agreement. The Persian plan was fair on paper, but it favored the Spartans who wanted it most. Their own Peloponnesian League was left intact since theoretically all of its members were free and independent states, voluntarily cooperating with Sparta. The Spartans had good reason, however, to be concerned about the future of their alliance. The Mantineans had sent excuses for not cooperating in the Corinthian War; and worse, they had sent food to the other side. Since they could not be trusted, the Spartans ordered them to tear down their walls. When they refused, a river which passed through Mantinea was dammed up. The ensuing flood not only endangered the Mantineans' homes but the walls too. With their walls likely to be razed either way, they surrendered and agreed to live in small villages instead of a united city. Thus, did the Spartans violate the independence of Mantinea. For all its show of fine words, the King's Peace had restored Sparta as the first power in Greece and she acted like it. Was there a lesson to be learned from this? Xenophon suggested that in the future men might avoid letting a river run between their walls.

In any age, the seat of power is a magnet for lesser states seeking help, often against each other. So, now the petitioners came to Sparta. Among them were exiles wishing to return to their native lands, and the Spartans proceeded to interfere on behalf of those individuals and parties which had supported their own cause in the past. Moreover, because their alliance was to be the only one allowed, they became the champion of autonomy. It served the Spartan interest to interfere wherever there were power groups which might become allied with either Athens or Thebes.

In the decade following the King's Peace, Sparta was at the pinnacle of her power. Curiously, only a few years later she would suffer the most crippling defeat in her history.

By the end of 379, the pro-Spartan oligarchs at Thebes had been slain in a revolution led by democrats eager to renew hostilities. Moreover, by an unusual sequence of events, the Thebans were again joined by the Athenians. A Spartan general had led an abortive attempt to seize the Athenian port of Piraeus. Whether he was acting on his own or had been paid by the Thebans to create an incident was never cleared up. However, the Spartan refusal to satisfy the Athenian demand that he be punished prompted Athens to renew their old antagonism.

Traditionally, Thebes and Athens were uneasy partners, but the Athenians did not have far to look for other friends. Posing as the keepers of the King's Peace, the Spartans had offered only a thin disguise for their own hegemony. Smaller states were wary of generous guardianship. Larger rival states were not fooled at all. But how could Sparta be challenged without violating the King's Peace? Why not form an organization for the sole purpose of promoting the independence and integrity of all Greek states? A crusade launched by Athens against Spartan power would be a means to attain power for herself.

## The Second Athenian Confederacy

In 377, a century after the founding of the Delian League, the Athenians formed the Second Athenian Confederacy. Once more the rallying cry was freedom. The new alliance specifically declared itself bound by the oaths given to Persia in 386. There was no intention of challenging Sparta and Persia at once. On the contrary, the aim was to divide them, if possible.

Clearly, the Athenians had no more intention of maintaining the spirit of the King's Peace than had the Spartans, but every effort was made to abide by its letter. Care was taken to make it evident that each of the members of the new alliance was autonomous and independent of Athenian authority. All decisions were to be made by joint agreement of two groups acting separately. One was an assembly of representatives from all the member states except Athens, each state large or small having one vote. The other would be the regular Athenian Assembly. Action by the confederation could only be taken when both assemblies were in agreement. A majority of small Aegean and Hellespontine cities could not commit the Athenian citizenry to unwise policies, nor could Athens compel these allied states to accept her will.

Athens was explicit that tribute should be outlawed and so offered a guarantee against one of the major abuses of the ill-famed Delian League. The assessments of dues in money or ships or both were to be made by the Allied Council, which also controlled expenditures. Jurisdiction over claims and disputes among members belonged to the representatives of all the states and Athens specifically promised that she would not attempt to place garrisons on any property belonging to a member state. In short, Athens did everything possible to make the new alliance attractive and to blot out her former image as a predatory power.

The prestige of the new alliance was much enhanced in 376 by a smashing victory over the Spartan fleet near Naxos. As time passed, hesitant cities were slowly convinced that the Athenians had indeed dedicated themselves to the practical and published goals of the alliance, including the offer to protect all states endangered by Sparta. In 375, Timotheus, the son of Conon, effectively blocked Spartan interference in the affairs of Corcyra.

The success of the confederacy was helpful to Thebes, for the Spartans found themselves beset by land and sea. On the other hand, Athens was increasingly preoccupied with her own ambitions and, by the same token, disenchanted with Theban ruthlessness—particularly, in 373, their destruction of Plataea for the second time in a little over fifty years.

## The Failure of Sparta

In 371, the Spartan efforts to have a new peace proclaimed by the Persian king ran afoul of the familiar insistence by Thebes that they be the sole signer for all the Boeotian states. The Theban stand on this point angered both the Spartans and the Athenians, but the Theban stubbornness was prophetic. In the mid-summer of 371, they won a momentous victory over the Spartans near Leuctra, a Boeotian village about ten miles southwest of Thebes.

The refusal of the Thebans to disband their army or renounce their claims over Boeotia had prompted the Spartan King Cleombrotus to march into Boeotia for a showdown. There had been talk

that Cleombrotus had let the Thebans off lightly in previous encounters, and he was eager to prove these rumors false.

The battle was given major significance by the number of
oracular stories attached to it. It was reported, for instance, that at
Thebes the priestesses saw omens which forecast a great Theban
victory. Xenophon acknowledges that such announcements were often
used to inspire morale, but adds that so far as the battle went, they
were true. The Spartans most certainly had the worst of it.

The first contact was made between the horsemen. The inferi-
ority of the Spartan cavalry caused a retreat which created disorder
among the *hoplites* behind them. Then the Spartan left wing, massed
only twelve deep, was swamped by a Theban phalanx fifty deep which
sought a quick decision by capturing Cleombrotus. Their strategy
worked as planned. The king was struck and mortally wounded, and
many of his high aides were killed on the spot as they sought to
guard the retreat of those carrying his body. The reversal prompted
a general retreat, and the whole army fell back on its camp. Losses
had been extremely heavy owing to the concentration of the Theban
attack; of the 700 full Spartan citizens present, about 400 had been
struck down. This was one-third of the estimated 1200 Spartiates
then of military age.

The news of this catastrophe arrived at Sparta in the midst of
a happy gymnastic festival. The ephors ordered the singers and
dancers to continue. Next day, those who had lost their kinfolk went
about the streets heads-up and proud, while the relations of the living
did not show themselves, or, if they did so, appeared downcast. The
Spartans proved that they could still muster the stolid strength of
time gone by. They would need it. The city could never recover
those four hundred of her finest warriors who had fallen at Leuctra.

The sharp reversal of Spartan fortune was not all due to the
happenstance of one hot summer day. Xenophon's praise of Spartan
morale does not allay the impression that something had gone wrong
in the previous decades. Unfortunately, the city never produced a
Thucydides to write the story with the same dramatic impact as the
fall of Athens was described.

Xenophon's *Hellenica* makes it plain that changes were taking
place at Sparta, even though change was what the Lycurgan laws
were intended to forestall. Centuries earlier, the introduction of a
money economy (as opposed to one based almost exclusively on land)
had led to significant innovations in the lives of other Greeks. Now,
in a sense, this happened to the Spartans. When they took over the

Athenian domain after the Peloponnesian War, the influx of tribute money led inevitably to alterations in policy. From the time of the wealthy Gyges, king of Lydia, coins had proved useful for paying mercenaries. So now, the money paid to Sparta made possible a shift to the use of mercenaries for certain police actions wherever necessary in Greece. As a matter of record, the Spartans were not as fortunate in the use of mercenaries as the Athenians had been. The Athenians had always had a more flexible society. For the Spartans to hire soldiers was a sharp break with the military tradition which had been the chief bulwark of Spartan society in the past and had sustained them because it had never been broken. To be sure, one of Sparta's most serious weaknesses was the fact that the Spartiate class had always remained a closed community. Unlike Athens during the prosperous times of Peisistratus, Sparta had never undergone an "urban revolution." She had not expanded her class of full citizenship to include immigrants from the countryside. The Spartiates had remained a small exclusive group, jealous of their privileges and their land. Yet one war followed another and Sparta was in them all. Inevitably, the attrition of her Spartiate class began to tell. Since no new blood was introduced, a sufficient rate of reproduction became a big problem for this aristocratic warrior group.

The consequences of Sparta's new "international" role were added to her other difficulties. Her unusual social system, based on rigid home-bound discipline, was adversely affected by the greater incidence of overseas travel and experience. In short, the peculiarities of her isolated way of life, long a source of strength and stability, began to crumble from exposure to outside influences. In later times, the irascible old Cato (234–149 B.C.) would warn his fellow senators at Rome of the dangers in exposing well-disciplined young Romans to the luxurious arts of people less rugged than themselves. While Sparta was content to rule the Peloponnesus, she remained strong. The temptation to rule Greece was her undoing. Lycurgan Sparta, like Cato's noble Rome, was in part ruined by its own success.

### Now Thebes

With Sparta faltering, Athens stepped into the breach. She invited the signatory powers of the aborted King's Peace of 371 to come to Athens and pledge themselves to preserve the independence of the Greek states. By so doing, it was hoped that Sparta would be restrained from any further interference in the affairs of her neighbors. This meant that the Mantineans would be able to unite again and build a wall around their city. Yet when they were so bold as to attack Tegea, the Spartans did interfere. The incident provided the Thebans with an excuse for invading the Peloponnesus on behalf of the Mantineans, but the campaign expanded into much more than that. The Thebans knew that the Spartans were shorthanded. Furthermore, their second-class citizens, the *perioikoi*, needed only the appearance of the Thebans to encourage them to revolt. The bordering peoples—Eleans, Arcadians and Argives—joined in for the kill.

Epaminondas (418–362), the Theban commander who had engineered the momentous victory at Leuctra, also directed the campaign aimed at the heartland of Laconia. Although Sparta was unwalled, she did not suffer a direct attack. However, the surrounding territory was scorched and plundered. Because the Spartans could only guard the land they stood on, they were helpless to prevent the Thebans from freeing the long-enslaved Messenians. Nor would Sparta ever again be able to muster strength enough to recapture them. Stripped of her "empire," Sparta would henceforth be a second-class power. When the Thebans founded Megalopolis as "the great city" of Arcadia, their intention was to shift the focus in the Peloponnesus away from Sparta altogether.

While the Thebans and their allies were effecting these changes in the Peloponnesus, envoys from Sparta and Corinth sought to persuade the Athenians to intervene. Some members of the Assembly felt that the Spartans had brought on their present trouble when they violated their recent oath by moving against Mantinea. Others pointed to Mantinea's guilt in attacking Tegea. To most of the Athenians this was not the point. The real issue in the game of Greek politics was the apparent intention of Thebes to stand on "top of the hill." Spartan envoys reminded the Athenian Assembly that the Thebans had favored the destruction of Athens after the Peloponnesian War but Sparta had prevented it. The Corinthians had a fresher argument. They had not troubled anyone since the taking of the oath, yet the Thebans had marched through their territory destroying houses and trees and helping themselves to cattle. Was this to go unpunished?

The story was familiar, only the names were changed. The Athenians must act or be left alone to face a triumphant Thebes. They finally decided to send Iphicrates at the head of an army into the Peloponnesus. Xenophon in his description of the events which followed does not disguise his disgust with this otherwise much-praised general. With winter approaching and the anxious Thebans homeward bound, Iphicrates' inept decisions made it possible for them to return to Boeotia without suffering any punishment for their recent misdeeds.

By these events, Sparta was replaced by Thebes as the dominant land power in Greece. Athens remained dependent, as she always had been, on the strength she could muster at sea. The smaller powers realized that by helping Sparta in the past they had made that city great; and now by following Thebes they were doing the same service for her. It was time they thought of themselves. Subsequently, the Arcadian League, which the Thebans had helped to set up, defected to the Athenian side.

In 367, the Thebans, enjoying their one great era of political hegemony, sought a King's Peace of their own. Certainly no other people in Greece had a better claim to Artaxerxes' friendship. They had fought on the Persian side as long ago as the battle of Plataea in 479, and had more recently distinguished themselves by refusing to contribute men to the renewed struggle over the Greek cities in Asia Minor (400-394). Surely the Thebans were Greeks whom the Great King could trust. He was willing to proclaim a peace based on the independence of Messenia and the disarmament of the Athenian navy. Nothing came of it. Other considerations aside, the very arguments by which the Thebans had won the king's hand made other Greek states disinclined to accept it.

Epaminondas invaded the Peloponnesus again in 362. He was determined to bring unity and peace to Greece by winning a general acceptance of Theban leadership. The Spartans, Athenians, Arcadians, Achaeans, and Eleans were willing to unite against him. However, when the initial attack came, the badly outnumbered Spartans were on their own. They so decisively repelled the Theban army that Xenophon could only attribute the reversal to divine intervention. A skirmish with Athenian cavalry at Mantinea was also unexpectedly disappointing for Epaminondas. Yet the final battle for the control of the Peloponnesus was still to be fought and the morale of the Thebans and their allies was extraordinarily high despite their reverses and short supplies. Xenophon does not hesitate to attribute this condition to Epaminondas whose remarkable qualities of leadership made his name the second best known in the annals of Thebes. No one ever displaced the poet Pindar.

The crucial battle was fought at Mantinea. As at Leuctra, Epaminondas depended on a decisive blow at one point calculated to capture or kill the Spartan king and thereby disrupt the enemy's line. The assault, made by cavalry mixed with foot soldiers, was successful. Yet, ironically, with victory in their grasp, the Thebans lost Epaminondas. Their attack stopped where he fell, as if they could go no farther without him. Only those who had not heard of his death rushed on. Left alone, they were annihilated. Nor indeed did Thebes flourish beyond the day that Epaminondas died.

Under the circumstances, each side claimed victory but, as when Pericles died at Athens, the Theban loss was incalculable. More humane and enlightened than his narrowly partisan followers, Epaminondas has been credited with having envisioned a better use of Theban power than the examples set by Athens and Sparta. He insisted on mutual respect between the various territorial leagues of Greek cities and at the height of his power had talked of magnanimity. Whether his ideal would have succeeded cannot be known. It can be doubted, however, for his talk of victory without spoils was not the prize that other Thebans had waited so long to win.

## An Old Story

After the Theban heyday had passed, open revolt in the Second Athenian Confederacy was not long in coming. From the beginning, it had been difficult for Athens to forget her own ambitions. In 367, when she sought to recover Amphipolis, the cities of the Chalcidic peninsula withdrew from her alliance for the same reason that Thasos had left the Delian League a century earlier. Nor were the anxieties of these northern cities unfounded. By 364, the Athenians had broken their pledge and were again establishing bases (cleruchies) in the vicinity of their allies. The fact that Potidaea, which they seized, was not a member of the confederacy was beside the point. Athens was again pursuing a policy of aggressive imperialism. Friend and foe alike had cause for alarm. The old mistakes by which the Delian League had been transformed into an unhappy empire were repeated again. Ceos, which had withdrawn, was forced to rejoin with a status inferior to the "loyal" members; allied states with anti-democratic or anti-Athenian officials were subjected to pressure; contributions were forcefully collected from recalcitrant members; and Athenian courts again took precedence in cases where an Athenian and one hundred drachmae or more were involved. It was the second time around, and all the more disappointing for what had happened previously; yet even if it all seemed the same as a century before, there was a crucial difference. Athens had never completely recovered her former wealth or power, whereas the maritime states, Chios, Rhodes and Cos, which challenged her authority had grown in size and might.

The Second Athenian Confederacy ended in the Social War (357–355), so called from the Latin *socii* which means "allies." The Athenians and their friends in Euboea and the Cyclades could not patrol the entire Aegean for long against sizeable rebel fleets. In order to obtain money, they backed a rebellious Persian satrap but the gamble backfired. Artaxerxes III, whose ascent to the throne in 358 had prompted this rebellion in the western provinces, responded to the Athenian blackmail by threatening to send his Phoenician fleet into the Aegean. The over-extended Athenians were forced to recall their mercenaries from Asia Minor and to recognize the independence of their former allies.

The collapse of the Second Athenian Confederacy meant that Athens had failed for the second time in her bid for leadership. In the fifty years since the Peloponnesian War, both Sparta and Thebes had learned what Athens had discovered twice—that any attempt by one *polis* to impose its will on the others, regardless of the good intentions which might be urged, was doomed to failure.

There are periods in history which are marked by a wearisome repetitiousness. The same mistakes are repeated time and again, and endless recriminations are exchanged amongst men with undying memories of old wrongs. There was no event in the first half of the fourth century which gave rise to a confident and hopeful spirit akin to that of the Battle of Marathon, now already a part of the hallowed past. Instead of victory over the despised barbarians, the Greeks seemed intent on defeating themselves.

# The Intellectual Mood
## of the Fourth Century

**XVI**

Time has a way with champions. At Athens, during her best days, stresses and strains began to appear which foreshadowed the coming of unhappier times. Sophistry was the undertow in Periclean society. The assault on tradition played havoc with the old fraternal spirit, especially among the educated classes. And at the end of the fifth century came the shattering impact of the Peloponnesian War.

For the Athenians, who had known only success for the better part of a century, the occupation of Attica, the plague, the debacle at Syracuse, and finally the destruction of their walls had been humiliating and bitter experiences. The Athenians had lost too much self-esteem to recover the spirit which they had known in pre-war days. The departure of Euripides and the execution of Socrates were signs of the times. A pervasive nervelessness and insecurity had replaced the earlier daring of an open society.

If the Athenians were ill-prepared to face the future, who could hope to be well prepared? Amid frustration and confusion the Greeks seemed to have lost their sense of a common destiny.

Despite the usefulness of this kind of resumé in which the story of a people is told in a sequence of "rise, peak, and decline," any historian who announces that "the Greeks" were rising during the eighth century and declining during the fourth century has baited his own trap. He must squeeze his story into these limits and there are pieces which do not fit. By ignoring them or forcing them into place, he perpetuates an unrealistic view of history and misguides those who seek to understand the present better by reading about the past. In ancient Greece, as today, the "rising" and the "declining" depended to some extent on who you were, and where you happened to be.

In the fourth century, the fortunes of the major cities declined most noticeably. Before the century was over, these former "powers" had become the pawns of Macedonian kings. The wars of the future would be fought by the giant Hellenistic kingdoms which ringed the eastern Mediterranean. As the proud principalities of Europe in the later Middle Ages were caught up amid the roaring struggles of the emerging nation-states, similarly the Greek cities kept their identity, but lost their place.

Away from these cities, however, life went on as before. Farmers and herders lived as they always had, and as some of their present-day descendants still do. The smaller communities of Greece had little to lose because of the new developments. They had never been allowed any more freedom by the major cities than they could expect from Macedon. In fact, the federal leagues of small towns and villages, like the Aetolian League in central Greece and the Achaean League in the northern Peloponnesus, provided a brighter era for these regions than they had ever known before. Certainly the Messenians, freed by Epaminondas after more than two centuries of Spartan enslavement, felt themselves better off.

The sequence of "rise, peak and decline" seems a useful formula for giving an account of individual cities, yet reactions to events were never all alike, even in Athens. In the wondrous years of the Periclean Age, the members of the aristocratic clubs had complained that the flourishing democracy was a decided comedown from those better days when only the "best" people had political power. In the fourth century not all Athenians would have agreed that their best years were behind them. After the shock of the war subsided and the democracy had been restored, the resiliency of shipbuilders, merchants, and mine operators soon provided Athens with a new era of prosperity. Those who were making large fortunes could hardly have been depressed by the times.

Scattered remarks in the writings of Plato and Aristotle and in the speeches of Demosthenes and Aeschines confirm the impression that a fortunate few were indeed accumulating great wealth. Plato mentions that rich men of his time employed at least fifty slaves in a single household. Such ostentatiousness was bound to bring complaints. But the complainers were waging a losing war against the attractiveness of oriental rugs and tapestries, which supplied new backdrops for the sculpture now gracing private mansions.

Pity the rich! At Athens, the moralists jibed at them for their display of wealth and tax-hungry politicians accused them of trying to hide it. Many of the well-to-do bid for a little praise by giving their money away. Nevertheless, the liturgical system, whereby wealthy men paid for the chorus of a play or outfitted a warship, was less voluntary than it had been. After the loss of the empire with its tribute, the Athenians had to depend on local sources for the support of state obligations, including the gratuities which kept the poorest citizens from starvation. During the fourth century, additional social welfare programs on behalf of the elderly and sick were instituted. Public revenues, obtained from abundant court fines, and levies ranging from a two percent tax on transient cargoes to a four percent tax on silver mined at Laurium, were not sufficient to support these added costs. Frequently, the expense of mercenaries was met by not paying them anything. Because occasional peacetime surpluses were immediately doled out by order of the Assembly, rather than saved for an emergency, default on wartime payments became the customary means of staving off bankruptcy.

Any special tax, such as an assessment based on the number of slaves a man owned, met vociferous opposition by those who condemned the Assembly for its "soak the rich" solutions. Even so, graduated taxes served as a safety valve in the popular democracy. The numerous poor caught between rising prices and stable wages were a miserable lot. Without collective bargaining, much less a cost of living index, the average laborer in Athens was worse off in good times than he would have been in a period of normalcy.

The internal tension caused by the disparity of wealth in Athens was not assuaged as it once was by a real sense of common interest. The disintegration of the *polis* ideal had been accelerated by the breakdown of the old community ties. Increasingly, a man was identified with his own special interest, be it soldiering, athletics, politics or poetry. What did mercenaries in the service of a foreign power have in common with philosophers, merchants or politicians? To be sure, not all men in the Periclean Age had joined in all the varied aspects of life. Differences in class, education and wealth had prevented that. But then there had been an important bond, now missing. It was a feeling of being a part of a very special city, somehow different from any other in the world. Such illusions of invincibility and a special destiny have as much importance to a whole people as do hopes and dreams to one man. Nor should such props ever be taken lightly, for, once gone, there are no substitutes. Athenian citizenship remained a matter of pride, but in comparison with former times, less a cause for rejoicing. The greatness of the Athenians was in the past. Like a man living after his dream, so too a people may cling to memories and go on. But looking backward has never been the same as looking ahead.

## *Introspection*

Intellectuals do not as a rule celebrate the material prosperity of their times. They are more sensitive to the impact which changes have had on the spirit of a people. In the later years of the fifth century, the futility and frustrations of recent experiences had fostered self-searching. Socrates and Euripides established the directions. Socrates emphasized the possibilities of man's rational capacities, while Euripides stressed the problems of his irrational propensities. Amid a narrowing of spirit at the end of the fifth century, their views reflected the individualism and introspection which would be the predominant characteristics of the intellectual life of the fourth century.

In Periclean times, the leading intellectuals had been the confidants of statesmen. In the years ahead, their counterparts would be aloof critics of the democracy. Only in this special role, however, was there a change. The towering reputations of the fourth century philosophers, Plato and Aristotle, would be a credit to any age. Yet their careers, spent in semi-isolation in their respective schools, typified a new day. These men studied and taught, examined and criticized. They were not involved in the military, political or athletic life of the *polis*. Rather they were looking at society and wondering what was wrong. In the Socratic tradition, the search for improvement was to be conducted through a thorough study of human capacities, beliefs and institutions. The works of the fourth century philosophers were the culmination of this emphasis on self-examination.

Among those who speculate about the basic worth of their fellow men, there are some who ask if the human species, like any other, can only learn so much and no more. What are man's ultimate possibilities? Democracy, with its faith in majority rule, has seemed to many minds the best way to find out. To others it is a blind alley. It was a majority which voted to kill Socrates.

There has been a further division of opinion among those critical of democracy. Some judge the majority of men to be petty and brutish, self-seeking and cowardly, murderers even of the high-minded who would serve them. If this be true, then an orderly society may only be maintained by repression. The masses must be indoctrinated with passive habits and demoralized by the unnerving fear of secret eyes or, failing these devices, beaten into submission.

There have been other critics whose reservations about the worthiness of most men have not led them to advocate such tactics of despair. They see in men the capacity for good and useful lives if only they are properly assigned to tasks for which they are best suited. The failures of the past have not been caused by bad men, but by bad planning. With guidance, every man would be pleased with his contribution and the state would function harmoniously without overt coercion. At Athens, in the fourth century, Plato was an eloquent spokesman for this point of view.

In the *Republic,* one of Plato's best known dialogues, Socrates is the principal speaker in a lengthy discussion about justice. A brief but provocative section of this work includes Plato's description of an ideal state. Unfortunately, this passage which accounts for the fame of the whole piece has often been used out of context and the impression given that Plato was proposing an ancient Brook Farm or New Harmony. He was not. His remarks about a "good state" were only an incidental extension of his thesis. He simply sought to show how his definition of justice, "each part playing a proper role," might be useful in arranging a better social order. It has frequently been said, for the sake of brevity, that Plato proposed a division of society into thinkers, soldiers, and workers. The term workers has been misleading. The main body of his society included traders, artisans, farmers and city laborers. Obviously, a group which included bankers and goldsmiths was more than a class of workers in the modern sense of that term.

Plato would subtract from this body politic two minorities: a small circle of intellectuals who showed a capacity for "philosophical" living, and a larger company of soldiers who would serve as the enforcing arm of the decision-making executives. Both groups would be trained to be duty-conscious and concerned for the welfare of the state as a whole. Even as today an educated clergy might prepare itself for guidance of the faithful, so too, highmindedness among Plato's guardians would be a concomitant of philosophical study. So far as the military was concerned, Sparta had long ago shown what could be accomplished when soldiers were occupied with soldiering and relieved of any concern about money or property.

In effect, there would be three classes, but not castes. Plato was famous for his interest in eugenics, especially as a means of perpetuating desirable qualities among the guardians. He believed that physical and mental attractiveness was very largely inherited, yet he also admitted that mobility between classes was possible. As a teacher, Plato was aware that certain noble sons were unworthy of their noble fathers, and he must have observed too that among the less well-born it was possible to touch the coal "where the corn is green." Therefore demotions and promotions would be desirable. What really mattered was to see that talent was properly placed.

When Plato wrote the *Republic* he appears to have thought that men would accept this point of view for its reasonableness. In the course of his career he seems to have reached the conclusion that they might have to be forced to accept it for their own good.

## The Life of Plato

Plato's devoted students preserved a remarkably high proportion of his writings but have left us surprisingly little about his personal life. The extant biographies of him were fabricated by later writers who embellished their accounts with apocryphal stories. In his own writings, Plato made only two references to himself. In the *Apology*, he is named among those willing to pay Socrates' fine, and in the *Phaedo* it is mentioned that because of illness he was unable to be present on Socrates' last day. There are, in addition, a group of letters attributed to him, but these are rarely mentioned without reservation. It is not possible to be sure that Plato wrote them, yet many scholars have accepted them as authentic and used them, particularly for his later years.

A sketch of Plato's life must be written with caution therefore. Only a few facts can be reasonably ascertained. The year of his birth is not one of them. Nevertheless, it is customary to accept 428, the year after Pericles died. His father's lineage was said to go back to the early Attic kings and his mother's was traced back at least to Solon. Plato took great pride in his good birth and had a strong

sense of family in the aristocratic meaning of the word. On the surface at least, this predilection helps to explain why he was ever on
the side of the "best" in opposition to all that was common. Nor
did his attachment to Socrates discourage that attitude. His affable
teacher may have been a better mixer, but on one occasion he point-
edly told Crito he cared little for what "most people" thought. His
behavior in court bore him out.

Plato was twenty-four when the Peloponnesian War ended. At
that point he was undoubtedly sympathetic toward the oligarchical
rule of the Thirty. His uncle Charmides and his second cousin Critias
were both active in this élite government. These oligarchs were,
however, no more tolerant of the disobedient Socrates than the later
leaders of the restored democracy. The dual experience seems to
have disenchanted Plato with Athenian politics altogether.

When Socrates was executed, Plato left Athens along with other
members of the master's circle. For the time being, the atmosphere
of the city was unpleasant, perhaps even dangerous. In any event,
the moment was auspicious for visiting old friends. Plato stayed for
a time with Euclides in Megara and then began to travel from place
to place, probably first to Egypt, and then on to Italy and Sicily.
During his sojourn in Syracuse he met Dion, the son-in-law of the
tyrant Dionysius, and began the friendship which accounted for his
later involvement in the political life of Syracuse.

While in his early forties, Plato returned to Athens from his
travels and began his career as a teacher. About 387, he gathered
around him a select group of young men who became the first generation of students at the Academy. This school, named for the old
*gymnasion* nearby, was to have a continuous history until the sixth
century A.D., when the Emperor Justinian announced his decision
to suppress all pagan learning.

The Academy has been called the "first university," but the
members were more like a company of scholars at work in a museum
or an institute for advanced study than what would be considered
a university today. To be sure, Plato gave lectures occasionally and
so did the mathematician Eudoxus of Cnidus who came with his
students from Cyzicus to join him. The actual learning process, however, was in the Socratic fashion of conversations between teacher
and students and the joint study of proposed problems.

Astronomy and mathematics were the major areas of study, although a student did not pursue one subject to the exclusion of any
other, as is the custom now. Moreover, although the emphasis was

on "science," this term must be understood in the light of Plato's metaphysical interests. He was a theorist, not an inventor. Mathematics (especially geometry) and astronomy were preferred because these disciplines led to an orderliness of mind. Plato had little use for the romanticism of poets. Their meandering thoughts and ridiculous stories would not teach young men to think sensibly and to make wise decisions. That was Plato's primary purpose.

In the popular democracy of the fourth century, having the best education was not the same thing as knowing how to get elected to the highest offices. So, although some of Plato's students entered public life, their teacher never became a guiding light in Athens. As it happened, his one opportunity to educate a "guardian" was with a young man already in power.

In 367, Plato went to Syracuse at the invitation of Dion and became the tutor of Dionysius the Younger who had inherited his aggressive father's domain. It was proposed that Plato teach this young man how to govern wisely and provide for a stable government. In the letters which have been ascribed to Plato, he elevated this assignment to a mission of the greatest consequence. Specifically, Syracuse had to remain strong as a defense against the Carthaginians who were considered a threat to Greek civilization.

The youthful tyrant could share in the high hopes with which the experiment began. That was easy. Geometry, however, was not. Furthermore, Dionysius lacked the staying power for the studious regimen which Plato sought to impose on him, nor was he immune to the less idealistic influences of court politicians who eventually succeeded in turning his mind against his brother-in-law. When Dion was exiled, Plato's plans went with him and the philosopher returned to Athens. Six years later he was back in Syracuse for the third time. Dionysius, in spite of his shortcomings as a student, had greatly admired his teacher and kept up a correspondence with him. It appeared, therefore, that Plato might be able to help Dion regain his former place. But the break between the king and his brother-in-law was beyond repair. In fact, Dion's enemies at the court seem actually to have posed a threat to Plato himself. Nevertheless, Dionysius persuaded him to stay on for a time as a kind of court philosopher.

## Plato's Laws

In 360, Plato went home to Athens and spent the remainder of his life teaching and writing, still laboring at the projection of better cities than any he had ever seen. The *Laws,* written during the last decade of his life, was his final vision of the good life, to be lived in the good state, and to be achieved by the right kind of education. It was in this work rather than the *Republic* that Plato actually detailed his plans for a never-to-be-realized but unforgettable city.

The *Laws* was not a work inspired merely by wishful thinking. A lawgiver was a familiar figure in the ancient world. The founding of new cities enabled men to start over fresh with the knowledge of past mistakes to guide them. Although in this work (the longest Plato ever wrote) there was not much story line, the founding of an imaginary city gave Plato a chance to expound his views. Three elderly persons, an Athenian, a Spartan and a Cretan, are presented as advisors to a commission making plans for a new city to rise at a site where an ancient Cretan town had fallen into ruins and been abandoned. The Athenian does almost all of the talking with the other two asking him appropriate questions and attending his every word. The listeners were called Megillus and Clinias. The wise Athenian was modestly left unnamed.

Plato was used to giving advice. Although his three trips to Syracuse had not been successful, they had undoubtedly prompted him to consider what he would do if not thwarted by selfish politicians. The theory of the *Republic* was not forgotten, but his approach in the *Laws* was more historical and practical. He returned to Solon's idea that the best system of government was one in which every party received enough power to keep any other party from assuming full control. The secret was balance. The fault of the Persian system was the absence of a counter-balancing power to check an obsessive despotism. In the Athenian democracy of the fourth century, Plato decried the lack of enlightened leadership and the triumph of politicians who served themselves best by following the "uneducated" whims of the populace.

In the *Republic,* Plato had said that a state would be managed best if most men left the important thinking to be done by those few men who were better equipped to think. The lives of these men were of course to be regulated in order to rule out self-interest. In the *Laws,* he insists that ordinary men must also be given proper moral and religious training, lest their weaknesses destroy the state. In fact by the time he wrote the *Laws,* Plato was determined that all aspects of human activity, including religious beliefs, must be vigorously controlled and recalcitrant citizens severely punished. It was not enough for a state to win wars and rule others. A people must first learn to control themselves, since the strength of a community depends on harmony among its various classes. Each faction must be taught to make correct, even self-sacrificing choices, rather than foolish, merely pleasurable ones. This could not be accomplished by the Spartan system as Sparta's experience had proved. At Sparta, men were presumably made virtuous by denying them any opportunity for temptation. Living without luxury they obviously could not become luxury-ridden. But Plato observes that that was not the same thing as teaching them to resist it. Time and again, away from home, the Spartans had succumbed to the temptations which they had never been allowed to face. A correct education, Plato insists, teaches men how to choose what is right in the face of temptation. It should begin with the young. Children are often moved to scream at the top of their lungs and to jump up and down. Their education should begin with singing and dancing—orderly singing and orderly dancing. By giving children from the earliest age an acquaintance with the best music, they would retain throughout their lives a standard by which to recognize what was bad. The proposal agreed with Plato's complaint that in the Athens of his day men with neither intelligence nor taste were being allowed to exercise their own opinions in music and art. In this circumstance the determining influence in Athenian culture was no longer intellectual, but glandular. Obviously, in our egalitarian society Plato is a worry. He is certainly of the opinion that gentlemen are born, not made.

Once a majority of citizens held that every man's opinion in music, drama, and politics was as valid as any other's, could the trend be reversed? Perhaps not. Plato obviously preferred to start over with a new city.

A sound educational system could not be the whole answer. Circumstances might ruin the best plans for success. In order for a city to maintain moral soundness under wise laws, it must avoid overseas entanglements by being self-sufficient and semi-isolated. In Plato's *Laws,* the location of his proposed city provides for ideal conditions. There is enough pasturage, farm land and woods to provide for local needs, yet not for a surplus which would lead to overseas trade. The site is at a distance from the sea or even from other cities. Here, away from the world, men of common interest and common purpose could work out a special destiny without the taint of foreign influence or the meddlesomeness of neighbors. Special planners have ever thought so, from the time of the Lycurgan laws in Sparta to Brigham Young's selection of a site in Utah.

Still, whether in the Old World or the New, the idyllic life of the "better place" has inevitably been challenged by change. Change was what Plato sought to avoid. To that extent he was in league with the idealists in all ages who have sought heaven too soon. At the same time, his proposals for the new city reflected his own interpretation of why Athens had failed.

In the seventh century the Atticans lived a semi-isolated almost exclusively agrarian life. Early in the sixth century, this economy was altered by a shift to a lighter coinage and a new policy of balancing overseas exports with the imports of grain. Under the tyrants, Athens flourished. Yet by her very success and the rivalry it entailed, she found it necessary to build more and more ships. The conversion of the Delian League into an overseas empire was a consequence of this trend. Finally, it was her own treacherous imperialism which had brought on the Peloponnesian War by which she was ruined.

At the height of the Periclean prosperity, any criticism of Athenian commercialism and sea power would have had to explain away the new buildings, a vigorous political life, and the ingathering of talent from all parts of the Greek world. In the fourth century, with Athenian power fading, the democracy floundering, and sensationalism blotting out taste, Plato was not alone in dreaming of a bucolic othertime when there was peace and decency and good manners.

In the *Laws,* Plato sought to rule out the inequities which usually resulted when men were left free to operate on their own. This included keeping the population as constant as possible. Overpopulation caused hardships and underpopulation was bad for defense. Every family should be about the same size, with one or two children.

While some disparity in wealth was inevitable, the state could be sure that it was limited by regulating the economy. There would not be much to regulate. A flat prohibition of both usury and credit eliminated capitalism with its encouragement to initiative. Plato sought to forestall any changes, up or down. Generation after generation, the incomes and expenditures of each family were to remain as stable as possible. Any excess of wealth which a man might acquire under these circumstances would be taken by the state—not because the state was all important, but because it would save men from themselves. It is a familiar antidote against man's predilection for mammon. The medieval philosopher St. Thomas Aquinas condemned usury as a means by which men damaged their souls and suggested that any excess wealth be given to the Church.

Unlike the *Republic,* where the guardians were to be a self-perpetuating class of philosophers, the caretaker council of the *Laws* was to be elected, albeit with the care which might be taken in choosing an assembly of bishops. They were to be men of proven morals and intelligence between the ages of fifty and seventy, selected by a multiple-stage process akin to the manner in which archons were chosen at Athens. Like the members of the old Areopagus, these thirty-seven men would have a general supervision of all public activities. They would also concern themselves with private matters, including a careful supervision of family life. Men were to marry between the ages of thirty and thirty-five and girls by the time they were twenty. Even after marriage, childlessness or any irregularities in behavior were open to investigation. Homosexuality was explicitly forbidden. Plato viewed such behavior as incontinence and along with overeating and overdrinking a bane to civilized life.

## A Nocturnal Council

It is ironical that Plato who began his career in defense of Socrates should have ended it with the *Laws* wherein he advocates the use of a Nocturnal Council. The name of this committee was derived from the fact that it was to meet early in the morning before dawn. If it also suggests "a knock on the door in the middle of the night" that was not far from its spirit. The rationale of the Council would be paralleled by the later Medieval Inquisition or the trials for heresy in Calvin's Geneva. In each instance, men were asked to think right for their own good.

Plato was not the first author of oppression in the long tradition of curious encounters between truth and freedom of conscience. If his letters are an accurate guide, he went to Italy in the early fourth century to study the Pythagorean communities. The Pythagoreans had often made themselves unpopular by seeking to impose their strict discipline on others. Because of their mathematical interests and their emphasis on a special educational system, they have usually been credited with at least helping to orient Plato's thinking.

In the *Laws*, Plato contends that men who did not believe in God, or who thought God was indifferent, or that He could be bribed with gifts, were a threat to the well-being of the community. He wrote down the arguments which should be used by the Nocturnal Council to win back the minds of these dissemblers. Any who persisted and would not be convinced must be punished. In fact, a man convicted twice of impiety would be put to death as incorrigible.

Plato considered his theology to be "scientific" for it was based on astronomical and mathematical studies of nature. In brief, it was the argument from design. The regular movement of the stars and the routine from seed to blossom to seed were evidences of planning by an intelligence which Plato called the perfect Soul or Mind. Those actions which were sudden and destructive, volcanic eruptions and the like, he did not claim to be acts of this God, but of other lesser souls. Clearly, Plato's theism was neither polytheistic nor monotheistic. It was, however, exactly what he intended it to be, a reflection of nature as it is. The permanent orderliness of nature argued for a wise and good God; the temporary disruptions for some other beings, possibly evil. He left it at that. And he expected others to accept it, since the evidence of nature supported his thesis. His argument against those who said that the Supreme God was indifferent or could be bribed was that by definition God would not be guilty of such short-comings. The Best Soul was neither likely to ignore details nor to succumb to the wishes of lesser beings whose desires would be ruinous to the divine order. Could even an earthly architect ignore the details of his project? Would a shepherd make a compact with a wolf? With this homiletical approach Plato offered parallels to the Biblical question: "Are not five sparrows sold for two farthings, and not one of them is forgotten before God?" (*Luke:* 12, vi).

Plato's Nocturnal Council was a further example of how his ideas were perhaps not so much wrong, as that they were carried too far. It is a familiar problem. In the *Phaedo*, his attitude toward the body resulted from the observation that physical appetites do distract from the contemplative life. If such a life be the goal, it follows that to deny the body a little would be a positive good. Would it not be better to deny it more, or best to deny it altogether? Monks, east or west, practicing an extreme asceticism, have on occasion thought so. Again, in Plato's concept of the ideal state, if it is profitable for the good of society to arrange some matters, would it not be best to arrange them all?

From a predilection for the contemplative life on the one hand and orderliness on the other, his teachings about the "good life" and "good state" followed. His presumption to know what was best for men, whether they liked it or not, has caused him to be included among those dogmatic manipulators of human destiny who would have eliminated his beloved Socrates faster than the jury could have voted. It is a pity. Plato's teachings had a different tone from that of activists in totalitarian states wherein philosophers are employed to "window dress" naked power. Because his rulers were to be true philosophers whose values ruled out selfish motives, they had more in common with men whose moral and theological training was designed to make them better shepherds of their flocks. It therefore follows that Plato has been taken too seriously by his enemies.

On the other hand, he has not been taken seriously enough by his friends. For it is also true that whether among good guardians or bad fascists, controls rule out democratic choices. Allowing a minority to assume a managerial role may achieve unity and stability, but it does so at the expense of plebiscite, petition and recall. Assuming that men favor the sacrifice of these democratic procedures to achieve other goals, then Plato makes sense. He knew how to do it. Where men are left free to behave as they please, they will often act selfishly toward one another. There will be trouble.

Trouble itself is a symptom of a free society. Those seeking a better society by more controls must face this awful irony, which has so often plagued men of good intentions. The idea that cruel masters who suppress all incentive have a deadening effect on creativity is a commonplace. It is more difficult for men to realize that other leaders who seek to do so much good in one area may do so much harm in another. Greek history, any history, teaches man that he cannot achieve opposite goals simultaneously. For whatever good purpose, whether higher standards of living or a greater justice, whenever human propensities have been restrained, whether the methods be hard or soft, the result has been a lessening of excitement and a dampening of creativity. Can men have strength without being tested in adversity, spirit without the inspiration of a struggle?

Today, state subsidies for the purpose of advancing able young people toward careers in government, science and industry are considered necessary for the survival of an egalitarian society which the ancients had not envisioned. It is part of the preparation for the future. Yet when the tests are given by which a few are chosen and the brain power of a nation is harnessed for the good of all, who can help looking back and remembering Plato? As a matter of fact a great many people know nothing about his teachings, if indeed they have ever heard of him. His works are rarely encountered before the college level and nowadays a college degree is by no means a guarantee even of that. So too, in his own day, Plato spoke to a select group. Important as the history of philosophy may be, there has always been the challenging question: "Who was listening?"

## Religious Trends

In every age, far more men have been attuned to religion than philosophy. Nowadays of course a man has his own religion. In Greece the state cult belonged to everybody, for, generally speaking, the welfare of the average man was bound up in the fortunes of his *polis*. Public ceremonials, including processions, poetry contests, and athletic games, were conducted by official priests who sought to win the favor of the gods for the community as a whole. Yet the goal of this religious activity was sought only for the needs of the city, not the souls of its citizens. The state religion was therefore perfunctory, not evangelical. Missing was the satisfaction of the hope for immortality. Nor were Homer's writings, the literary prop of the Olympian deities, much help.

Concerning the after-life, Homer had the courage to be vague in his references to a shadowy nether world. In popular belief the dead reached this place by boat, and anyone who received a proper burial complete with coins for Charon, the ferryman, could presumably join his ancestors. For Achilles this was no happy end. In the *Odyssey,* he told Odysseus he would rather be the hired hand of a poor man on earth than reign among all those who had departed. If the heroic Achilles could not take a brighter view of the after-life, who could? Homer allowed that a choice few did reside in the Elysian fields, but this comfortable meadow was apparently a special place reserved for Zeus' relatives.

Hesiod wrote about the islands of the blest as a haven for heroes. Pindar gave Achilles a better rest by assigning him to this favored place in a story which told how his mother Thetis had interceded with Zeus. However, according to Pindar, intercession was presumably not necessary for those who had passed through three lives without fault. In any event, by the early fifth century the notion of one place for the good and another for the wicked was a familiar one. Aeschylus in his *Suppliants* spoke of evil-doers being judged in Hades. It cannot be known what the majority of men in Greece thought about these poetic passages, if indeed they ever heard them. For personal comfort many of them turned elsewhere.

A more definite answer was offered by the cult of Orphism, named after Orpheus, a poet who was said to have lived in Thrace sometime in the remote past. At a time when legend passed for history, he was considered an historical figure. He may have been one, but all that we know about him now is in the realm of myth. He was a talented musician who had inspired Jason and his crew on the Argo and had saved them from the seductive and fatal strains of the Sirens whom he overpowered with his lyre. The beauty of his music, however, was in sharp contrast to the miseries of his life. His beloved Eurydice was lost to the underworld when he disobediently looked back at her while they were coming to the upper world. Afterwards, he lived a solitary and lonely existence which ended with a horrible death. He was torn to pieces by Thracian Maenads (*mainades,* "the frenzied ones"). These women were celebrants of Dionysus and according to myth had come upon Orpheus in his wooded retreat, as others had encountered Pentheus in the *Bacchae.*

The Orphics believed that before his death Orpheus had taught certain ideas about the future life of which their religion was the continuing tradition. In contrast with the Homeric view of man, and more in line with oriental ideas and certainly with Egyptian practice, the poet was said to have believed that the soul must be purified of its contamination of the flesh. For this purpose he prescribed ritual cleansing exercises and other familiar self-denying practices, including fasting.

Although tales about Orpheus were already hoary with age by the sixth century, it was about that time when his teachings began to have a definite impact at both the philosophical level and at the level of popular religion. The Pythagoreans, seeking a perfect order for men akin to the harmony which mathematical proportions gave to music, accepted the Orphic emphasis on purity as a means to a better life. Consequently, the ascetic practices of the Pythagorean brotherhoods were akin to those of the Jewish Essenes and the later Christian monks. Both the Orphics and the Pythagoreans, however, believed in the transmigration of souls. Many lives must be lived before perfection could be attained. Entrapment in the body was an impediment for the soul, but denial of the flesh meant freedom. In the Platonic dialogues, especially the *Phaedo,* these same ideas were given another setting and supported with rational arguments.

During the sixth century, a variety of hymns, liturgies and magical treatises appeared by which Orphism was brought to a more popular audience. Initiates were told that they need not wait to pass into some dreary region where it mattered not how they had lived. They could and should participate in sacramental "experiences" here and now to insure the well-being of their souls after death. At about this time the Orphics attached their doctrines to Dionysus, the deity who apparently from time immemorial had been worshipped in Thrace. The Mycenaean tablets show his early arrival in Greece. Because myths arose from different places and often incorporated the same deities, Dionysus was the central figure in a variety of stories. One story told of his birth to Persephone, the daughter of Demeter. His father was Zeus and the Persephone myth told how Hera in anger and jealousy had driven the Titans to tear Dionysus to pieces. Significantly, however, Dionysus was restored to life whole. It was this sequence of events which his worshippers celebrated in frenzied rituals during the longest night of the year. The sadness of Dionysus' death was not one ceremonial to be followed by the joyful celebration of his rebirth; rather the two were mixed together in a single, confusing, even maddening rite. His worshippers tore to pieces sacrificial goats or fawns or any animals they could lay their hands on, even as Dionysus had been killed by the Titans. Presumably Orpheus himself had been sacrificed and the parts of his body scattered.

To the psychological eye of twentieth century man, these rites appear cathartic. Civilization may repress certain human tendencies but does not cure them. The dignified Apollo, serene and self-confident, was a sufficient god for men whose education and status called for restraint. Dionysus was anybody's god who wanted him. Hardworking peasants and especially slaves welcomed the chance to escape from humdrum lives and temporarily "be themselves." The strange conjunction of grief and ecstasy which accompanied these rites appears to have been a naive expression of the paradoxes of life. Dionysus beguiled his worshippers into returning to the uncomplicated joys of nature. Yet, at the same time, they despoiled the beauty of the wood and purity of the brook with savagery. He was the god of wine. What else may at once make men both joyful and disgusting?

The release of pent-up emotions through hysteria has occurred in other ages under varying auspices. In ancient times, whether as the Greek Dionysus or the Roman Liber, a youth with long, luxuriant, curly hair, a slightly effeminate stance, a cup in his hand and satyrs and nymphs beside him was a symbol of the unrestrained side of life. And maybe still is, or so it would seem.

Although Homer had not included Dionysus among the august company on Mt. Olympus, this peasant deity was as widely worshipped as the Olympians and was certainly received in a more personal sense. The Orphics sought to cure his undisciplined worship by adding a theology. They taught that the Titans, before they were destroyed by Zeus, had eaten the limbs of Dionysus. When man was made from the Titan ashes, he possessed both their evil habits and the divine element of Dionysus. Here was justification for the Orphic teachings concerning the necessity for the soul to overcome the body.

On the other hand, the attempt to purify the Dionysiac orgies could not be entirely successful, for obviously the motivations behind these rites were not altogether religious. Yet the Orphics did seek to supplant sheer excitement with more regular ceremonials. The most significant of these was an initiatory rite intended to be cleansing in character. There is no way of knowing what actually took place. The Orphic-Dionysiac cult was one of the so-called mystery religions which took their name from *mystes*, meaning one who had been initiated. Literally, the word means "closemouthed," and the devotees were supposed to remain silent about what happened. They did.

The most respected of the mystery rites in Greece were celebrated in the great temple of Demeter at Eleusis in northwest Attica. They were attended even by the better educated who shunned the Dionysiac revels or the orgiastic cults imported from the East which were led by priests who practiced flagellation and self-mutilation. At Eleusis, men and women of all classes took part in a secret initiation and presumably, as in Orphism, were the better for it. Although more refined, Demeter was nonetheless the Greek expression of the Eastern Mother Goddess who represented the fertility of the earth. Demeter's ceremonials were also fixed on the cycle of the seasons. Her celebrants too would die and be born anew.

The religious trends of the fourth century were another concomitant of the age. As the old close-knit ties within the *polis* weakened, the individual was forced to search for his own sense of security and emotional satisfaction. In the future, larger and larger kingdoms would finally culminate in the ecumenism of the Roman Empire. As the state grew in size and complexity, men grew lonelier. Philosophy comforted only a few. The mystery religions with their personal gods and their emotional outlets were the popular panaceas of the ancient world prior to the triumph of Christianity.

In the stories which clustered around Dionysus, as well as the Egyptian Osiris, the coincidence that in each case a god had at one time been brutally slain and at a later date restored whole cannot be ignored. Nor can the usual inference that the worshippers of these deities expected to share in their death and rebirth. Here is an expression of hope by humans that they might find immortality and be aided in doing so by a divine agency. Any mention of the obvious parallels to the later Christian experience, for one purpose or another, should also consider that a yearning for immortality may be detected as early as Neanderthal man, whose burials included things he might need in a future life. So too, in the mystery cults, the correlation between human life and nature's cycle of birth, death and rebirth was to be expected. However, each religious unfoldment to man must be judged by its own manifestations. The worshippers of Dionysus and Osiris were busy with exotic festivities. In *Amos* there is a different mood: "Though ye offer me burnt offerings and your meat offerings, I will not accept them: neither will I regard the peace offerings of your fat beasts. Take thou away from me the noise of thy songs; for I will not hear the melody of thy viols. But let judgment run down as waters and righteousness as a mighty stream." (*Amos* 5, xxii–xxiv). In this tradition over three centuries later came the Sermon on the Mount without flutes or drums.

## The New Mood in Sculpture

To talk about "fourth century art" befits the mentality of an historian, not that of an artist. A sculptor in the fourth century did not intend to make a "fourth century" work. Within the limits of his patron's patience or the place and occasion for which a statue was to be used, he did as he pleased. It is the historian who gathers together the sculptures and paintings of a given era and then observes that the artists were reflecting the temper of their times. And he is almost right. By eliminating the experimental pieces which placed certain artists ahead of their day or those works which represent a conscious effort to revive past styles, there is left a group of pieces which when considered collectively do have a different tone or emphasis from a corresponding selection from another period. Surely Constable's serene *Dedham Mill* looks more comfortable at the Victoria and Albert Museum than it might among the anxious works of the Museum of Modern Art.

A comparison of samples from the fifth and fourth centuries of the Classical Age does not, however, offer so sharp a contrast as one between the romantic landscapes of the nineteenth century and the Freudian perceptions of our own time does. The obvious reason for this was the continuing preoccupation of Greek sculptors with a single subject, the human body. If more Greek paintings were known, this apparent one-sidedness would probably not seem so real, but given what is available in Greek art, the body is the center of interest. Consequently, in comparing fifth century works to those of the fourth century it is the mood which is different, not the subject. Myron, Phidias, and Polycleitus, the major figures of the earlier period, idealized the body. They gave men god-like forms. In the fourth century, there was a shift toward greater naturalism. Bodies and faces were no longer "heroically" all alike, but became individualized as men are. Akin to the philosophical and religious trends of the period, the arts appear to have taken a more introspective and personal direction.

Among the outstanding sculptors of the fourth century, interest centers on Praxiteles and for a good reason. His marble *Hermes* (found by German excavators at Olympia in 1877) is one of the few original works of any of the known Greek masters. It has, therefore, received a disproportionate amount of attention and unexpectedly so in view of the fact that except for Pausanias, ancient authors never mentioned it. However, copies of the works they considered superior to this statue show that the other artists of the time had much in common with Praxiteles (Pl. 74).

*Pl. 74* Hermes
*with infant Dionysus*
*by Praxiteles*

*Pl. 75* Aphrodite of Cnidus,
*Roman copy of*
*Praxiteles' original*

In contrast to the sturdier fifth century *Discus Thrower* or the *Spearbearer,* the *Hermes* appears languid. The body has more grace, but not as much strength. This work has therefore encouraged the view that the fourth century artists tended to give their male bodies a soft, sensuous, even effeminate appearance. The prettiness of the face accentuated Praxiteles' preoccupation with the flesh. Moreover, the deep furrowed locks of the hair helped by contrast to emphasize the smoothness of the skin. In the fifth century, the poise and confidence of the athletic figures had expressed the mood of the Marathon generation. They had an heroic idealism which moderns might acquaint with recruitment posters. The *Hermes* has lost that mood. He appears self-conscious and dreamy. The "ideal" of the whole man which Myron and Polycleitus portrayed has given way to the acceptance that in any man the balance is not perfect.

Copies of works by Praxiteles, particularly his *Eros of Parion,* the *Lizard Slayer* and the *Satyr,* show an even greater affection of posture than the *Hermes.* It has been argued that these later copies corrupted Praxiteles' style by making his figures seem softer than they were intended to be. According to this point of view, these works better represent a later over-ripening trend toward sweetness rather than

Praxiteles' dignified grace. Maybe so. There can be no doubt, however, that Praxiteles did consciously stress grace for its own sake. In
his own day his beautiful female nudes were the mainstay of his
reputation and in fact his *Aphrodite of Cnidus* (now known from copies)
was then far more celebrated than the *Hermes* (Pl. 75).

The most famous of Praxiteles' older contemporaries was Scopas
of Paros who was resident in Athens from about 377. Again, what is
known about his work reinforces the traditional view that artists of
the time were interested in capturing an emotional expression and
showing an individual as he might appear in a moment of surprise,
or perhaps of contemplation. Among the broken pieces of figures
which once belonged to the pediments of the temple of Athena Alea
at Tegea are two male heads which are typical of Scopas' style. The
eyes are deep set and turned slightly upward giving the face a look
of intenseness and affectation. Other means which Scopas employed
to achieve vividness were to tilt a head at an unusual angle or to
show a mouth slightly open (Pl. 76).

The abandonment of Polycleitus' canon of measurements for the
male nude is best illustrated by the *Agias,* attributed to Lysippus of

*Pl. 76 "Scopaic" head of* Hermes *on sculptured drum from a column of temple of
Artemis at Ephesus*

Pl. 77 Agias. *Marble copy
of Lysippus' bronze original*

Sicyon, a younger contemporary of Scopas and Praxiteles. Modern
excavators at Delphi found a marble copy of it which apparently was
made about the same time as the bronze original. Lysippus did not
choose to make his figure a composite of anatomical perfection. The
head is smaller and the torso and legs longer than the earlier canon.
The result is a superb statue of a particular athlete, not The Athlete.
In the other works attributed to him, Lysippus also exhibits the characteristic interest of his times in reproducing a body the way it might
be, rather than the way it should be (Pl. 77).

The emphasis was still on beauty. Individuality had been added.
As the unique communal character of the *polis* began to disappear,
so did the idealism which was part of it. Some critics have hailed this
new naturalism as the peak of Greek sculpture, rather than a decline
from the works of the fifth century. All would agree that it was
different.

## Drama: A Loss of Vitality

The Greek "decline" in the fourth century has been treated
equivocally. The creative giants of this period have not been de-

meaned, only the milieu in which they worked. But in the dramatic arts, at least, it must be admitted that there was a very definite decline in quality. As a matter of fact, the Greeks in the fourth century quite consciously recognized the difference by continuing to perform the works of the Old Masters of the fifth century in conjunction with the contests among their would-be successors.

To ask why there was not another Aeschylus, Sophocles or Euripides is the same as asking why there has not been another Shakespeare. It is better to talk about comedy, for in comic writing the reason for a loss of vitality is more apparent. In the fifth century, playwrights had been inspired by a prevailing climate of forebearance to exercise their talents freely in thinking up ever new satirical devices. Their plays were thinly disguised weapons of common sense in a never-ending battle against pomposity, false sentiment, and political hypocrisy.

The lighter fare which followed the Peloponnesian War reflected the less tolerant air in Athens during the restored democracy. The trials for impiety, not to mention the execution of Socrates, made it apparent that a man who spoke too freely could get into trouble. Aristophanes had gotten into difficulties with Cleon much earlier, but that was more of a personal matter. In the fourth century, this most famous of the comic playwrights continued to comment on political and social problems, but the fire was gone, the teeth drawn. The custom of having the chorus speak directly to the audience and issue in effect an editorial was abandoned. Poking fun at poets and philosophers became a safer course than attacking men in official positions.

Gradually, after Aristophanes' time, the comic poets abandoned satire in favor of slapstick versions of everyday life. The emphasis was on *double-entendre*, mistaken identity, wayward sons and impudent servants. This particular brand of comedy which flourished after the middle of the fourth century has been called the New Comedy. Menander (*ca.* 343–*ca.* 291) was the foremost writer of these lively and easily digestible comedies. He was unquestionably a successful crowd-pleaser in the late fourth century—a credit to him perhaps, but not to the drama. Formerly, great artists wrote for their own ears and audiences listened in. Aeschylus' satyr plays, like Shakespeare's interludes of buffoonery, were concessions to a human inclination for relief from serious art. In the fourth century, as in other times and places, the theater became a haven for lesser writers who offered more relief than art, or maybe no art at all.

# The Struggle for Greece:
# Philip and Demosthenes

**XVII**

Different eras in history leave contrasting impressions behind them even as men do. We all know the type of bold, self-confident man who is fearless of mistakes so long as he is forging ahead; we are also familiar with the hesitant, self-analytical man who is worried about himself and his future. The philosophy, art and drama of the fourth century resemble in some respects the mood of the latter kind of man. So do the politics. By the mid-fourth century, the most casual observer of recent events might have concluded that the Greeks were not going to achieve unity and a working peace by their own efforts. A noted teacher who had been studying the problem for forty years had reached the same decision much earlier. Isocrates (436–338) was a teacher of oratory and a prolific writer. The speeches, pamphlets and "open letters" he wrote during an exceptionally long career wisely assayed the past and included some remarkable hints about the future.

Isocrates belonged to an old and honored family of Athens. He grew up during the Peloponnesian War listening to the Sophists and to Socrates who, according to Plato, thought well of him. It was said that Socrates harbored students with strong anti-democratic feelings.

In Isocrates' case, the charge was true. The political traditions in prominent families could be very binding. His attitude was firm. The execution of Socrates under the restored democracy only hardened his view toward popular rule, and throughout his career he stressed the danger of mobocratic tendencies at Athens.

Isocrates favored a reform in the constitution which would permit a more conservative program, or at least a more moderate one. He once wrote that when he was a boy it was not a disgrace to be wealthy. Then Pericles was still alive and the citizenry chose their leader from the best class, a man with good breeding. Nowadays, he said, a man was ashamed to admit that he owned anything and everyone felt compelled to act and talk like a wage earner. His complaint may well have been exaggerated. Yet it might be appreciated today by relatives and friends who must wince occasionally while watching millionaires perform on the political campaign trail.

In the fourth century, Isocrates was also the foremost advocate of pan-Hellenism, the same program favored by aristocrats since Cimon's day. What could have been more humiliating to a man dedicated to all things Greek than the peace dictated by a Persian king in 386? What more self-defeating than the Athenian democrats using their Second Confederacy against Sparta and Thebes?

In 390, Isocrates started a school at Athens for the training of orators and in the ensuing years students traveled from all parts of Greece to study with him. They became the evangels of pan-Hellenism. Isocrates sent them home presumably better speakers and certainly better informed about his opinions on Greek problems. The teacher had a weak voice. His skillfully written orations, however, were widely read. In fact, beginning with a call for Greek unity in his *Panegyricus* presented at the Olympian games in 480, he issued a steady stream of propaganda for over forty years.

Who could forget the unity and determination of the Greeks when they stood together against the Persian invaders in 480? Why not recapture that long lost unity by a counter-invasion against the Persian Empire? There were practical considerations, too. Besides alleviating political strife at home, a war against Persia would offer economic gains. The Greek cities were periodically faced with bankruptcy. Their willingness to hire mercenaries unmatched by any feeling of responsibility to pay taxes was a familiar story and there were other circumstances which made the prospect of booty from abroad appealing all around. Greek soldiers could be the pathfinders for settlers to follow. At home, land was as scarce as it had ever been.

Overpopulation and underemployment continued to create desperate poverty and, as usual, many were willing, if not eager to emigrate.

In view of recent failures, Isocrates' program for successfully invading the Persian Empire and resettling indigent Greeks on Asian lands sounded like a fantastic scheme. After he was gone, when it all came true, the accomplishment was even more astounding.

Isocrates was convinced that nothing would be achieved without a strong leader. By 370, he had already published three pamphlets arguing the merits of a monarchy. In times of trouble, those who know what should be done and must be done often seek a hero—a strong man who will be faithful to their ideals, a dynamic personality, a man with a proven capacity for action. At the time, an obvious choice was Jason, the tyrant of the ancient city of Pherae in southeast Thessaly. By daring feats of arms and diplomacy, this soldier of fortune had managed to win control of a rugged land where independent-minded ranchers and farmers had long resisted a central control. It was there, however, that his brilliant career began and ended. He was assassinated in 370.

Two years later, Isocrates wrote to Dionysius I, the tyrant of Syracuse, and urged him to seize the reins of Greek leadership. Like Jason, by fair means or foul, he had made an impressive record. The length of his rule, thirty-eight years, offered strong evidence of his abilities; during this time he was able to hold the Carthaginians at bay long enough to build a vast empire including most of Sicily and Italy. Yet his hold on areas he claimed was always tenuous and when Isocrates' appeal reached him in 368 he was again at war with Carthage. When he died the following year, Isocrates' imaginary throne was still open.

## Philip

Not until he was ninety did Isocrates find his leader, a man who would come and save Greece. However, by 346 when Isocrates wrote his oration entitled *Philippus,* Philip II, the king of Macedon, was in a manner of speaking already on his way.

At the time that Isocrates made his appeal to Dionysius I of Syracuse, Philip was a youth of fifteen being held as a hostage in Thebes, then enjoying its one decade of glory. He was not an ordinary hostage. His elder brother, Perdiccas, was the king of Macedon and a prince, even though technically a prisoner, would have had entree to the upper circles. Presumably, during his three-year stay,

Philip became better acquainted with Greek accomplishments in the arts, warfare and politics. Whether this firsthand observation of Greek practices persuaded him of the usefulness of bribes in the years ahead, or he came by the habit naturally, is a matter for speculation. Suffice it to say that one day he would buy as well as fight his way to power in Greece.

Early in life he showed that he knew how to get what he wanted. The kings of Macedon were no safer among their relatives in the palace than on the frontier. When Philip's elder brother died in 359 fighting the Illyrians to the west, his son Amyntas, still a child, became a political pawn. Philip, now twenty-three, was the regent, and from that vantage point managed to rid himself of all rivals for the throne including its rightful heir, his unfortunate nephew.

Even if Philip's credentials were false, his qualifications were good. He was a master of men and around him mustered an army which became the nucleus of a united state. His leadership transformed his backward land into the major power of the Aegean world. A man like Philip was not deceived about where his real strength lay. The Macedonians had remained a rough-and-ready people with neither the taste nor the tarnish of Greek civilization. Most Greeks in the fourth century counted them as barbarians. Some still do.

Philip's modernization of war techniques in conjunction with the earthy spirit of these back-country fighters was a winning combination. For expansion he needed gold, and so he reached out in the direction of the mines of Mount Pangaeus. Amphipolis was taken with bribes and Potidaea by force.

A conquest was as a rule a cruel invasion by which a whole people were captured against their will. Not the least of Philip's advantages when he began his "conquest" of Greece was the encouragement he had from articulate supporters among the Greeks themselves. They included some of the most thoughtful men of the time. In addition to Isocrates, two prominent historians, Ephorus and Theopompus, wrote works obviously sympathetic to the king.

Intellectuals, who usually think unkindly of mass opinion, sometimes show a collective predilection for a particular point of view. In fourth century Greece, the intelligentsia favored a united Greece under the aegis of Philip as the best hope for solving the problems of their time. Isocrates set the pattern. His orations showed how history could be used to argue in support of a given policy. The historians of the period took a similar view. Unlike Thucydides who sought to let events speak for themselves, Ephorus and Theopompus arranged their material to suit a conclusion preconceived. Aside from any question of ability or concern for accuracy, their works have emotional and propaganda qualities avoided by Thucydides with his cold and scientific eye.

Thucydides saw the events preceding and during the Peloponnesian War as typical of the way in which wars begin and prolong themselves. He offered his account of them as a meaningful manual for future ages. How meaningful it has been may be arguable, yet it has been preserved and widely read. Ephorus and Theopompus have not enjoyed such longevity. Only fragments of their voluminous works are now extant. They supported particular solutions for current problems and were slanted toward their own times rather than all time. Their obvious catering to Philip was sharply rebuked by ancient critics who thought historians should be more objective.

In Philip's case, this might not have been easy. He was a man of many moods, each usually well-matched to an occasion. If he was uproariously drunk, it was because at the moment he could afford to be and if horribly cruel, it was because he felt he had to be. Duplicity, bribery, blackmail were all means to an end. Yet, he also displayed a disarming charm, tears for fallen comrades, and finally forebearance toward his enemy, Athens, the golden city of Greek culture.

The Greeks who supported Philip, with or without his bribes, gave him an edge on victory. Yet it should not be surprising that the generosity of intellectuals toward the king was countered by an old-fashioned defiance on the part of patriots whose views were less cosmopolitan.

## Demosthenes

Demosthenes (385–322), a young orator whose career at Athens began in the 350's coincident with the early years of Philip's reign, was Philip's most adament opponent. Yet he admitted that the reputed strength of this wily king was not the heart of the matter. It was the lethargy, hesitancy and confusion of the Greeks themselves. Demosthenes was a super-patriot; his gaze was fixed on that wondrous era after Marathon when determined and vigorous citizens were alert to any danger at home or abroad, every man of them. Now that the independence of the Greek cities was threatened again, he urged his contemporaries to bestir themselves and rally again to the cry of freedom. In the Athenian Assembly, he tirelessly extolled the glories of the good old days, especially the former triumphs of Athens.

His position was exactly the opposite of Isocrates and his academic friends who considered the good old days gone beyond recall. They stressed the failure of the city-state system and insisted that Philip was the answer to the need for unity. Only a strong monarchy could end the current suicidal squabblings.

Demosthenes answered these "traitors" with impassioned oratory. The Athenians, not Philip, must save Greece. He recalled the Periclean vision of Athens as the school of Hellas and of the whole civilized world. This city of destiny must lead all the Greeks into a harmonious union in which no single power would seek to dominate the rest. Was it not a noble cause? It was, and had been so since Cimon first advocated the same course more than a century earlier. But Demosthenes chose to ignore the fact that his much-heralded ancestors had rejected the chance.

There was nothing amiss in calling the Athenians to greatness. Their accomplishments at home and abroad had been many and marvelous; however, these wonders had been performed on behalf of a proud city within a jealously guarded border. Most Athenians were obviously more interested in their own welfare than in the welfare of the rest of Greece. The Delian League, founded in 477, and the Second Athenian Confederacy, a century later, had made that clear.

In the rest of Greece there was the same division of opinion about Philip as there was in Athens. Certain states even found it expedient to accept his help against their local enemies. The king could not have hoped for more. There had never been any secret about Philip's own aggressiveness. He made frequent attacks on his neighbors, yet his forays into Thessaly, which bordered Macedonia on the south, could not actually be counted as invasions of Greece. In fact, Philip had no excuse for so bold a move until the Greeks offered him one. This came in 356 when they began another so-called "sacred war," a drawn-out affair which lasted ten years. It was fought over control of the Amphictyony of Delphi, a very old league of states which had originally been organized to provide cooperative care for the oracle, a sacred precinct of Apollo. In recent years the functions of the council had become *pro forma*. The Theban leader Epaminondas then decided to revitalize this body and use its prestige in support of his plans for Greek unity. Whatever his intentions may have been, the Theban control of the Delphic Council was no more than shabby politics after he died. Before long some prominent Phocians were fined for refusing to cooperate with the Thebans. When they refused to pay, each side assumed a pose of righteous indignation and hostilities followed.

The Phocians seized the sacred shrine, which was located in their territory, stole the treasury, and used their new wealth to hire mercenaries with whom to hold off the Thebans. Amid the confused purposes in this struggle, Philip announced that he would be the protector of Delphi. He would restore Apollo's shrine. In 353, he led an army south to stand with Thebes against the Phocian robbers. When he reached Thermopylae, a concerted effort by Phocians and their allies, including the Athenians, caused him to turn back. The defeat did not cost him anything. He had posed as the defender of Delphi and had sought to punish the Phocians for sacrilege. He had also demonstrated his friendship to Thebes. There was nothing in his action to discourage his supporters. They continued to hail him as a true defender of the Greek heritage.

Friend and foe alike could agree that Philip was perceptive. Certainly, he was aware of Athenian self-interest. Time and again, in the years to follow he sought to placate the Athenians and relieve them of any anxiety about their own interests, lest they be moved to cooperate more frequently with his open enemies. Demosthenes was not deceived. Philip's sly tactics made Athenian unpreparedness all the more pitiable. In the *Philippics,* his best known orations, he damned the Macedonian king to the ends of the earth—so much so, that the word philippic has taken on the larger meaning of "any discourse or declamation abounding in acrimonious invective."

## The First Philippic

The *First Philippic* was delivered in 351. At that time, the Athenians were disturbed by a rash of troubles in Thrace and in nearby Euboea. In all ages, such small but infectious irritations have served the interests of aggressive powers seeking to gain their own ends amid an atmosphere of uneasiness. Demosthenes was certain that Philip's agents and sympathizers were to blame. Other Athenian leaders were less positive, and reluctant to react too strongly lest their suspicions prove ungrounded. Philip's maneuvering was artful. He turned the pressure on and off, a little here and a little there. Could anyone prove that these incidents were all a part of a master plan? Demosthenes frankly admitted that Philip was a difficult target. He called him a clever boxer.

When Demosthenes rose to deliver his *First Philippic* he was a relatively young man of thirty-three. His presumption in opening the debate that day required an apology. Ordinarily, the older citizens present in the Assembly spoke first and the junior members waited to comment on what their seniors had said. In previous sessions, long speeches had already been made about Philip's aggression and how it should be met. Today I will speak first, said Demosthenes, for if these elders had any worthwhile ideas we would not still be discussing the matter.

His biting politeness was characteristic of the briskness in Athenian debate. Citizens in attendance at the Assembly or serving on juries expected and enjoyed the dueling between orators who mixed sly innuendo with outrageous accusation. Demosthenes, like the later Roman orator Cicero (106–43 B.C.), was admired as a master of the well-turned insult. Both men were more quoted than loved.

Demosthenes' *First Philippic,* as we read it, has an air of feigned optimism. There is no reason to despair, he says. The problem at hand is caused by Athenian negligence. Hopefully, that can be repaired. Sudden changes of fortune can also provide reason for comfort. In recent times Sparta has been supreme, but has since fallen on evil days. So too, Macedon, now on the rise, would be vulnerable to a well-planned attack. The Macedonians are only seizing opportunities. If the Athenians fail to protect their interests in the north, can they blame Philip for taking advantage of the situation? Demosthenes insists that a weak Athenian foreign policy has produced the present crisis.

Can Athens take a stronger stand while wealthy men hide their money and sturdy youths shirk wartime service? Such men seem to think that if they do nothing others will do their share for them. Such an attitude courts disaster. So does the false hope that some accident will befall Philip and so end the present troubles. What difference would it make? If anything should happen to him your procrastination will invite some other ambitious leader to take his place.

There is a remedy. Demosthenes proposes that the Athenians outfit fifty warships and, if need be, man them themselves. This task force should be sent to the northern Aegean as a check against Philip's moves. Athenian resolve and alertness will act as a deterrent. Let no one doubt that Philip will hear the news of their decision before he sights their ships. Certain of our own people, Demosthenes observes, keep him informed of everything we say or do.

There is an added reason for making arrangements in advance rather than on the spur of the moment. The Etesian winds, which blow from the north during the late summer and early autumn, prevent ships from making any headway up the Aegean Sea at that time of year. Experience has shown that Philip usually launches his attacks under these circumstances. To counteract his advantage, the Athenians must establish bases in the northern islands, such as Lemnos and Thasos, and so be on hand and ready when trouble starts.

More than a show of naval strength is needed. Demosthenes also urges the Assembly to create a special force to consist of two thousand soldiers and five hundred cavalrymen. This small corps should be used to harass Philip wherever possible with hit-and-run raids. Although the use of mercenaries seems unavoidable, at least one-fourth of the total contingent should be native Athenians in order to insure some patriotism in the ranks.

Demosthenes warns his fellow citizens that if they do not fight Philip in the north, they may one day be forced to fight him at home. This counsel has a haunting ring to those of us who remember the Munich Pact.

## Both Right and Self-Righteous

I have told you only what I think is best, Demosthenes says, even though my advice may cause some people to dislike me. This was a familiar theme with him. He protested too much, and there were other reasons why he never became a truly popular figure. His enemies called him a water drinker. Among the wine-loving Greeks there were those who wondered if such a man could be trusted. Demosthenes' abstinence fitted in with other evidence of his austere and overly serious nature. Nothing had been easy for him. He had had to work hard to overcome the ill-fortune of poor health and dishonest relatives. When he was only a boy of seven, his father, a successful sword maker, had left him a modest fortune. In succeeding years his guardians stole some of it and mismanaged the rest. In fact, Demosthenes' first speeches were written against his relatives in an effort to recover his legacy. He won an empty verdict. The money was no longer there to recover. Even so, the experience was not lost on him, for his victory encouraged him to become an orator, an ambition he was said to have acquired as a boy while attending public trials. The success of his first case had misled him however, for his next ventures into public life were disastrous. Neither his style of composition nor his voice was well received, and so he began a long, arduous, often lonely, sometimes discouraging attempt to provide himself with a better speaking voice. He had been sickly as a child and in early manhood his voice was still not strong. Poor breathing caused a distracting catchiness in his speech. He sought to cure this defect by running and trying to speak when out of breath. The famous device of carrying pebbles in his mouth was to help him with his enunciation.

Demosthenes' exercises were accompanied by constant writing and rewriting of his orations. In the course of this self-improvement program, he apparently developed an unremitting impatience with laziness and self-indulgence. Such an attitude is probably to be expected among those who achieve success through practice rather than good fortune. Did Demosthenes' experience also cause him to become a self-centered and ungenerous person? It is said that his fellow orator Demades would often jump up to help him if he seemed to falter in debate or become confused. No one could recall that he had ever returned the favor.

Demosthenes' patriotism was unquestioned. Yet a righteous cause is not always best served by self-righteous men. In the heat of controversy, they often make the mistake of assuming that every other man must either be for them or against them. The *First Philippic* left that impression. Athenians who supported Demosthenes and his all-out opposition to Philip were hailed by him as energetic citizens. The rest were lazy, perhaps even traitors. His attitude was unrealistic. There was a respectable middle position and Eubulus, a politician noted for his reasonableness and caution, was its leading representative. Although an able administrator, he was not an accomplished debater. In consequence, the orator Aeschines (389–314) became the leading spokesman for him and those in his party. In the Assembly, Aeschines answered Demosthenes' charges and contested his judgment.

Eubulus had the mind of a banker and he gave the Athenians a financial reason for supporting his program. From 354 to 350 he was the treasurer of the Theoric Fund, the source of payments allotted to the citizens for various purposes including their seats at the theater. Naturally, the larger the Theoric account, the better the "dole" would be. Under Eubulus' leadership a law was passed assigning all surplus revenue to this fund. The measure was obviously of special interest to the numerous poor. Since expenditures for war would use up any surplus, they were given a practical reason for loving peace. The heavily taxed well-to-do had always loved peace. It was cheaper.

Eubulus' "business" administration was popular for other reasons. His program called for tighter controls in the collection of taxes and greater efficiency in working the silver mines at Mount Laurium. Increased revenues from both sources enabled him to improve the harbor facilities at Piraeus and to increase the city's water supply. In short, greater emphasis was given to domestic needs. This was peacetime normalcy and it was a refreshing change no matter how much the war party might complain. Eubulus and his followers were willing to protect Athenian interests at home and on the seas and so would take steps to stop Philip's encroachments. At the same time, they took a dim view of any overseas commitments which might tax the budget.

So long as Eubulus made ample payments to the citizens, he carried them with him. Demosthenes' campaign for a more aggressive foreign policy was aided only by Philip's own threatening moves, as when he began a campaign in 349 to conquer the Chalcidic peninsula.

## Aggression in the North

If Philip had any serious intentions about conquering Greece, it was apparent he would have to establish his authority firmly in the north before committing his forces too strongly in the south. His chief target was Olynthus, the major city of the Chalcidic penisula.

Demosthenes' three *Olynthiac Orations* delivered in 349 echoed the *First Philippic*. Again, he called for prompt action. In the past, he had often attempted to frighten his fellow citizens by emphasizing Philip's potential danger. Now he reversed himself and sought to cajole them into action by suggesting that their task was easy after all. The Chalcideans had shown stiffer resistance than Philip could have expected. At his back were the recently conquered Thessalians whom Demosthenes happily describes as "born traitors." In addition, the unruly Illyrians would soon give Philip trouble, for he was a hard master and these tribesmen were not easily disciplined. The time was ripe for action.

In his *Second Olynthiac*, Demosthenes continued to argue that the tide was running against Philip. Surely his dishonest dealings had cost him any good reputation he may have had. Who would ever trust him again? Ironically, however, in reviewing the course of Philip's manipulations, it was plain that only the larceny in the hearts of his Greek victims had made his good fortune possible. For instance, when Philip attacked Amphipolis in 357, he concluded a secret treaty with the Athenians whereby he promised to give them that city if they would help him against Pydna, long a thorn in his side. This Thessalian city was their own ally, yet the Athenians were so anxious to possess Amphipolis that they went along with the scheme. Later, when Philip broke his promise, Athens lost both places, along with some of her own reputation. Other cities had been tricked the same way. Such a despicable man, all agreed, must face a day of reckoning.

Perhaps, Demosthenes says, it will come because of the dissatisfaction of Philip's own subjects. They are being driven endlessly by this man for his own glory, not theirs. Nor do they share in the sporting life which characterizes his court, where he surrounds himself with companions who share his limitless capacity for drink and indecent entertainments. Demosthenes was not a man to make concessions. On a later occasion when someone mentioned Philip's good looks and how well he held his drink, Demosthenes replied that the first quality befit a woman and the second a sponge.

The attempt to portray Philip as a dissolute monarch ruling over dissatisfied subjects did not ring true. The Macedonians were not known for their decorous habits and no one expected that Philip's Greek veneer could hide his lusty tastes. He was undeniably a man of action.

Significantly, it is action which Demosthenes is demanding of his fellow citizens at the conclusion of the *Second Olynthiac*. Addressing himself to the largest class of citizens, he asks how they can hope to accomplish anything by voting a heavy war-tax on the wealthy and hiring mercenaries instead of serving in the field themselves. What else do you do besides complain? You should pay your fair share and you should fight. Demosthenes might have paused to wonder if their fathers had done so. In any event, he was touching on a sensitive issue—one which went back to the time when Pericles first paid jurors for public duty. Afterwards, citizens were also paid to attend the theater and even the Assembly. Was it so strange that a generation had grown up believing that the majority in a democracy should serve itself at the expense of everybody else? Demosthenes was alarmed.

The aging Plato, now seventy-nine, would not have sounded so surprised.

There was something else. In comparing the "Marathon" generation with his own, Demosthenes was touching on the contrast between periods in which men seem to "know what is right" and other times when they are more inclined to "discuss the matter." The earlier "knowing" was based on custom and faith which, in the latter half of the fifth century, became twin targets for intellectuals who failed to appreciate the strength of these sustaining influences in society. Demosthenes was faced with the awesome prospect that even ordinary citizens in his day were no longer as sure about the old ideals as they used to be. At Marathon the champions of "right" defeated the slaves of "wrong." The men whom Demosthenes called to arms did not have so clear a vision.

Early in 348, the Athenians began sending a limited amount of help to Olynthus. Throughout the spring, they had been preoccupied with a disastrous uprising in Euboea. By summer all their allies on that island had left them except Carystus. The loss of the island as a defensive base was a serious setback and it meant that carrying the war to the north was all the more important. Unfortunately, the large force which was finally sent during the summer of 348 was delayed by winds friendly to Philip. Meantime, the Macedonians captured and destroyed Olynthus. Those inhabitants who survived were sold into slavery.

The Athenians had been slow to respond to the desperate need in the Chalcidice. Assessing the blame for the disaster was a fruitless task, yet they could not forbear pursuing the question in their Assembly. Philip would not have wasted the time.

## An Uneasy Peace

Amid their recriminations the Athenians could agree on at least one point. They were checked for the time being. Even Demosthenes had to admit it. He was dismayed of course by the outcome of the Olynthian affair, but the present circumstances dictated a breather.

All during the year 347 there was talk of peace. Philip's restraint in not attacking the Thracian Chersonese, so vital to the Athenian sea routes, and his sending of only nominal aid to Thebes against Phocis in the continuing Sacred War, argued that he wanted sincerely to come to terms with Athens. Yet he never said why. Surely there was the danger of another subterfuge. Nevertheless, Demosthenes joined Aeschines and Philocrates, another member of Eubulus' party, on a commission to Pella where they talked to a cordial Philip in the spring of 346. Macedonian envoys had at the same time traveled to Athens. Out of these meetings, and a highly emotional debate in the Athenian Assembly, came a treaty and an alliance. It has been called the Peace of Philocrates because he was the author of the final draft. The *status quo* was recognized, along with mutual interests in suppressing piracy and keeping the seas open to all. By the terms of the treaty Athens acknowledged all of Macedon's gains. Demosthenes did not object. It was obvious that he favored buying time. No one believed that he had decided to trust Philip.

During the summer of 346, Philip asked the cooperation of his new ally in ending the Sacred War and restoring Delphi to its former place of honor. The Athenians had not committed themselves to support his claims as the arbiter of such matters and refused to join him. In July, he won without them and so they faced a further humiliation. Philip claimed as his own the two votes of Phocis on the Amphictyonic Council. Moreover, in the future, Macedon, not Athens, would have the highest privileges at Delphi. Finally, Philip would preside at the Pythian games in 346.

At Athens, an almost inevitable reaction had set in against the treaty with Philip. Demosthenes, steadily rising in public favor, was prepared to make the most of it. He had acquiesced reluctantly in the peace as a necessary evil, but he had never claimed any credit for it as Philocrates and Aeschines had done. He insisted that his own hands were clean and he accused these men of having sold out Athenian interests. They had not only accepted bribes, he charged, but had also profited from their perfidy in receiving estates which Philip had appropriated from Olynthus. As usual, the purpose of such accusations was to inflame public anger; Demosthenes' colorful orations are by no means reliable guides to the truth. Nevertheless, Philocrates fled for his life and Aeschines narrowly escaped having to follow him. After a bitterly contested trial in which he and Demosthenes battered each other with words, he was saved by only thirty votes out of 1501. Despite the acquittal, Demosthenes had succeeded in thoroughly discrediting those who stood by the treaty with Philip. Thereafter, Athens under his leadership took the initiative in an eleventh hour effort to create a new alliance of Greek states.

This move by Demosthenes and his friends was calculated to coincide with an expected reaction against Philip elsewhere. They were right. Appearances in 346 had been misleading. Philip's sensational success against both Athens and Phocis had not melted all resistance; actually it had aroused a fresh determination to prevent him from taking over altogether.

Philip's efforts to sell himself to a majority of the Greeks had obviously not succeeded. In 342, Philip decided to abandon his diplomatic efforts and again use force. His point of attack at the Thracian Chersonese was a carefully calculated move. Domination of this narrow strip of land (modern Gallipoli) could mean control of the Hellespont and the blocking of grain shipments to Athens from the Black Sea ports.

Cardia, one of Philip's allies, had recently been complaining about the misdeeds of a mercenary captain named Diopeithes, currently in the pay of the Athenians. The king chose to exaggerate the problem and sent a message to Athens asking for arbitration. Demosthenes in his speech *On the Chersonese* dismisses the incident at Cardia as a smoke screen. He can hardly restrain himself as the Athenians quibble over the guilt of a single mercenary commander, when the danger to the Hellespont is the real issue at stake. He observes that Philip now talks about settling this issue by peaceful means as if his meddling in the region, even before the incident, was not a provocation to war.

Demosthenes does not deny that Diopeithes was guilty of reckless behavior while conveying colonists to the area. But if the Assembly censures him, how can they be assured that Philip will desist from his undercover efforts to take over? It is a familiar theme. How do the high-minded, who insist that their side play fair, guarantee that the other side is not cheating? Philip denied that he had any intention of warring against Athens or of making territorial claims. Was not that just what he always said before he grabbed something?

In the same year as *On the Chersonese,* Demosthenes delivered his *Third Philippic,* in which he combined with his now familiar fulminations against Philip a slashing attack on those who talked of peace and reconciliation with him. He voices the sense of frustration which seemed to grip his times when he says: "For not without reason, not without just cause, the Greeks of old were as eager for freedom as their descendants today are for slavery. There was something, men of Athens, something which animated the mass of the Greeks but which is lacking now, something which triumphed over the wealth of Persia, which upheld the liberties of Hellas, which never lost a single battle on sea or land, something the decay of which has ruined everything and brought our affairs to a state of chaos. And what was that? It was simply that men who took bribes from those who wished to rule Greece or ruin her were hated by all, and it was the greatest calamity to be convicted of receiving a bribe, and such a man was punished with the utmost severity. At each crisis, therefore, the opportunity for action, with which fortune often equips the careless against the vigilant, could not be bought at a price from our politicians or our generals; no, nor our mutual concord, nor our distrust of tyrants and barbarians, nor, in a word, any such advantage. Now, however, all of these things have been sold in open market, and in place of them we have imported vices which have infected Greece with a mortal sickness. And what are those vices? Envy of the man who has secured his gains; contempt for him who confesses; hatred for him who censures such dealings; and every other vice that goes hand in hand with corruption. War-galleys, men in abundance, money and material without stint, everything by which one might gauge the strength of our cities—these we as a body possess today in number and quantity far beyond the Greeks of former times. But all our resources are rendered useless, powerless, worthless by these traffickers."

Again, as before, Demosthenes insists that the real war the Greeks must fight is with themselves. They must at last listen to him and face the prospect that freedom means sacrifices. And at last they do. In the following year he would be given a gold wreath for his services to the state.

The new resoluteness at Athens was matched by that of cities nearer to the scene of action. Perinthus and Byzantium had long sought to avoid offending Philip, but now they refused to help him against the Athenians and so brought his wrath upon them. In both instances, he failed either to shake the local resolve or to take the city. His usual plan of dividing Greek cities against one another in order to ensnare them all failed completely and he was forced to abandon his campaign against the Chersonese.

Philip was not an invincible conqueror. On the contrary, in the course of his career he had had several setbacks which might have discouraged a different kind of man. Demosthenes was right about Philip. Temperamentally, he was not suited to a settled reign, quietly ruling what he was able to hold; he was always more interested in what might still be won. If blocked in one direction, he would turn to another. He was indeed, as Demosthenes put it, always casting his net.

Although wounded in a skirmish with Triballi tribesmen while on his way home, Philip was no sooner back in Pella than he was plotting his next move. A climax was imminent. As evidence of their awakening, the Athenians at last voted to deny themselves. They would use their extra funds for defense instead of putting them in the Theoric Fund.

## The Last Stand Taken Too Late

To Philip, the Delphic Amphictyony and its troubled affairs provided a lode of opportunity. His friends on the Council voted to give him the command of a punitive mission against the town of Amphissa in Locris whose people had been accused of plowing up sacred ground. It was a small affair, but it provided Philip with the excuse and the cloak of legality he needed. However, it was a poor blind for the size of his forces or the speed with which he moved. When his army arrived at Elatea in Phocis, only his presumed ally Thebes stood between him and an assault against Attica. Ironically, however, his speed and confidence caused the Thebans to pause and ponder their own future. When Demosthenes arrived from Athens with all the haste and generosity of a desperate man, the Thebans were eager listeners.

The Athenians were willing to serve under Theban commanders, to pay most of the expenses and to give their future support to the Boeotian League, if only now the Thebans would at last stand up to Philip. They decided that they would and their decision gave Demosthenes the battle he had always wanted, a united Greek coalition resisting Philip. When the day came, Demosthenes was in the line, side by side with his fellow citizens in a Boeotian plain near Chaeronea, less than a hundred miles from Marathon.

The battle of Chaeronea was fought in 338, early in August. Both sides lined up for a set battle, each in a broad formation extending across the two-mile plain which stretched between the Cephissus River and the high ground around the Acropolis of Chaeronea. They were roughly equal in strength. Each side had between 30,000 to 35,000 infantrymen and an additional 2,000 cavalry, with the Greek allies perhaps having the edge. On this occasion, however, numbers were misleading. Only the Boeotian *hoplites* could be considered equal in experience to the Macedonian regulars. The Athenians were the greenest troops of all since they had only recently decided to fight.

Philip's strategy turned on his ability to trick these inexperienced men into making a mistake which would split the allied line and give his cavalry a chance to break through. It was all too easy. By making contact with the Athenian wing first and then retreating toward the high ground in feigned retreat, he drew a great number of the Athenians into an excited pursuit. As a result, the entire Greek line was drawn to the left and, in so doing, became detached from the famed Theban corps known as the Sacred Band. At that moment, the Macedonian cavalry led by Alexander, Philip's eighteen-year-old son, rushed forward, surrounded this elite force and wiped it out. The Macedonian foot soldiers who followed the cavalry were able to turn the Greek line. By this time too, the forces under Philip had reversed themselves and wreaked havoc on their Athenian "pursuers." A thousand were slain and another two thousand were captured. Demosthenes was among those who fled homeward.

In the aftermath of the battle, Philip treated the Thebans with severity, but the Athenians with such surprising leniency that they might almost have been on his side. He had his own code. The Athenians had been open enemies, opposing him whenever and wherever they could. The Thebans had long ago sought his help and posed as grateful friends. Their betrayal at the last minute, therefore, was not easily overlooked. He dissolved their Boeotian League, put a garrison in their city, and made them buy back their dead. His deference to Athens was obvious. He made no plans to invade Attica, but simply asked the Athenians to ally their city with Macedon. Their dead, even their prisoners of war, were to be freely given back.

Philip's generosity was accepted. His friends and sympathizers felt themselves vindicated. Isocrates sent a congratulatory letter to Philip and urged him to launch a war of retaliation against Persia. Demosthenes was away seeking Persian aid when the peace was concluded.

## Philip, the Hegemon of Greece

The League of Corinth, established at Philip's invitation in the spring of 337, was the instrument by which he intended to control Greece. The organization of this federal union was hopefully designed to prevent the domination of any single Greek city, yet as each state's representation was proportional to its military potential, the major powers had a stronger voice. The Spartans were conspicuous by their absence. Although unable to prevent Philip from settling the affairs of the Peloponnesus to suit himself, they felt secure enough to remain aloof from the newly formed League. Actually, it was a measure of Philip's power and Spartan weakness that he could safely ignore them.

The League entered into partnership with Macedon and Philip became the commander-in-chief of this grand alliance. With unity thus achieved, a war of retaliation against Persia was now possible. As Isocrates was wont to recall, there was an unsettled account which went back to the desecration of Greek shrines by Xerxes in 480. Philip's memory was fresher. The Persians had sent aid to Byzantium during his abortive attempt to take that city in 340—and this was only one instance of their efforts to forestall the unity he might bring to Greece.

Philip's plan for the attack on Persia had proceeded so far by the spring of 336 that an advance force had already been sent to Asia Minor. Encouraged by this development, the Greek cities and other Persian dependencies in the area revolted against Persian rule. They confidently expected the determined Philip, now at the height of his career, to arrive in the autumn with a mighty army. What power on earth could prevent it? One man with a dagger did. While Philip was attending festivities at his daughter's wedding, a Macedonian nobleman stepped out of the crowd and stabbed him to death.

Although the young assassin belonged to the aristocracy, he was not otherwise distinguished. Nor has it ever been satisfactorily explained why he acted as he did. It was said that Philip's first wife, Olympias, was responsible for the murder. By all reports theirs was a stormy marriage. For dynastic or diplomatic reasons, Macedonian kings might have more than one wife. The first marriage to a woman of royal blood established the queenship. Philip's father, Amyntas, had six sons by two wives. Philip, forever pursuing his duty, reversed the process and had two sons (one of them retarded) by six wives. His last alliance with the young niece of an ambitious Macedonian nobleman alarmed Olympias, lest the new union produce a rival to her son Alexander. These were the circumstances when the family gathered for the marriage of a daughter to Alexander of Molossia.

If Philip's death were not an affair of the palace, could it have been a result of Persian intrigue? Surely no power had more to fear from him. His avowed intention was an invasion of the Persian domain and obviously he was not easily to be sidetracked.

There was never any proof that Philip had, in fact, been murdered for either of these reasons. Nevertheless, the conspiratorial stories survived and would have, even if an impartial panel of judges had sifted the evidence. Without such an investigation, the rumors passed triumphant into the literature. They count for very little now. Philip was killed by a Macedonian named Pausanias. That is actually all we know.

That Philip's victory at Chaeronea was a triumph for Isocrates and a disaster for Demosthenes, both of whom were loyal Athenians, marks it as the crucial event that it was in Greek history. The Greek states were at last united under a single rule. Demosthenes feared that the absorption of these states into some larger political complex would end their uniqueness, and that they would never be the same. He was right; they never were.

# New Directions: Alexander, Aristotle and Diogenes

**XVIII**

Few sons have managed to escape from the shadow of a father so notable as Philip. Alexander has been the most renowned exception. During his life, he was sometimes intemperate, not a little self-satisfied, and on one occasion a murderer, but history has called him "the great" and by the standards of his time he was.

The accolade of greatness has been bestowed by history on some men for their varied accomplishments throughout a long life. Alexander's career was remarkable for its brevity and for a single conquest. He did not live long enough to face the long-range problems of a statesman, nor, like Caesar, did he leave his own commentaries on what he had won. Nevertheless, in his short lifetime he inspired more elaborate legends in Europe, Africa and Asia than a man might have hoped for on a single continent. A thousand years later, Islam found a place for him on the roll of prophets (Pl. 78).

Alexander was acclaimed king by the Macedonian army after his father's death in 336. In some respects Philip had left a copy of himself. Alexander was a man of action and he had the scars to prove it. Plutarch recounts the young king's mishaps in a youthful essay which glorifies the conqueror even more than the favorable

*Pl. 78 Head of youthful Alexander; found on the Acropolis of Athens in 1889*

biography which was written later. While fighting in Illyria, he was hit in the head with a stone and in the neck with a club. His head was cut with a knife at the Granicus and his thigh with a sword at Issus. When an arrow struck him in the ankle at Gaza, he fell and dislocated his shoulder. On various occasions in India he was pierced by arrows in the shoulder, leg and breast. In brief, Alexander was not a man to await the news of a battle, he was the first over the wall.

Yet the young king was also moody and given to brooding, like Achilles whom he so greatly admired. In this respect he was Olympias' son, and like her more temperamental than Philip. Although he married twice (some say three times) for political reasons, it has been claimed that he was careful not to overindulge himself in sexual enjoyments lest he dissipate his energies. Plutarch says that Alexander thought it more kingly to conquer himself than others. W.W. Tarn, the best known of Alexander's modern biographers, accepts this explanation of the young king's much discussed continence. If the interpretation is correct, the son was in this respect very different from his father.

How many men might have been "great" if they had had the chance to prove it? Surely some outstanding figures benefited from the coincidence of a matching crisis in which they could display their mettle. Alexander was doubly remarkable. He created his own challenge and responded to it so well that he left a lasting impression. Rarely has the history of an age been so determined by the personal decisions of one man. When he led his army eastward to India he fashioned a destiny for himself and with it the world to come.

Philip had planned a war of retaliation against Persia. Yet, at the time, he was already a man of middle age and had a career of many triumphs behind him. It seems doubtful that he would have considered going beyond the Halys River in eastern Asia Minor. Alexander was only twenty when he succeeded his father. At twenty-two, he left his homeland and headed toward the east never to return. When he died in Babylon in his thirty-third year, he left as his legacy a claim to the largest land area ever held by a single authority. That it was his alone was proved by the fact that no other man held it after him.

According to tradition, Alexander began his invasion of the Persian Empire by sailing to Troy and hurling his spear ashore. Was this to prove to the Greeks that he was their champion? More likely, his homage at that famous plain was a dramatic expression of his personal sense of destiny by which lesser men were convinced that he must win. And with their help he did. However, his success must not be attributed only to his extraordinary *élan* and charismatic leadership. This young chieftain was an ingenious planner with an iron nerve. His campaign to free the Ionian cities was a smashing success. From late in May 334, when he won his first major victory near the Granicus River until the end of the summer when Halicarnassus was besieged, he swept all before him. But only on the land. He lacked the ships with which to challenge the fleet of Darius III. The shortage was solved by eliminating the need. He marched down the Mediterranean coast and closed the ports of Tyre and Sidon. The Persian fleet was trapped at sea.

In the course of this venture he inflicted another crushing defeat on the forces of Darius III at Issus in October 333. The Persian king fled eastward in such haste that his mother, wife and daughters were left behind and captured. These hostages would have been valuable bargaining points if Alexander had been a bargainer, but he was not. He stuck to his plan. Envoys of the Great King brought an offer of a cession of all land west of the Euphrates, plus an alliance to include a daughter in marriage and a great sum of money, if Alexander would return the royal family and make peace. There is a story that Parmenio, a close friend and confidant, said that he would accept the offer if he were Alexander. The king replied that he would too if he were Parmenio. And with that he turned it down. Alexander did not seek to hide his own personal sense of superiority to less talented men.

Parmenio's ready willingness to accept such a generous offer showed the limited war aims of the men who had served with Philip in contrast to the greater expectations of the young Alexander, now inspired by his early successes. When he marched into Egypt late in 332, he had already more than fulfilled the mission his father had left to him and he celebrated the liberation of this ancient land from Persian rule by having himself crowned Pharaoh at Memphis. Next, he visited the famed oracle at Siwah in the western desert. When he arrived, the chief priest of the shrine hailed him as the son of Ammon. This was to be expected. In Egyptian belief a Pharaoh was an incarnate god. It was reasonable that Alexander become a god in Egypt, or anywhere else when people expected this role of their rulers.

By his triumphs to date and those to follow, he might well convince other men that he was indeed receiving the special favors of the gods reserved for one of their own. Did he convince himself? It is a moot question. He never said so. Yet some of his later actions suggest that he thought about it.

The establishment of authority among peoples of different languages, customs and history by the claim to be a god or to be an agent of a god has been one of the continuing power motifs in Western society. It was already an ancient idea in the Near East when Alexander was born. Later, when the Romans sought to unite diverse peoples within their Empire, they established the state cult of the deified emperors. The "divine right" concept of monarchy lasted until modern times.

The line between the human and the divine was shaded in the mind of the average man in the ancient world. Gods who were conceived in human forms and with human traits mixed in the affairs of earth and at times cohabited with humans for both good and bad purposes. Heracles, from whom the Macedonian kings claimed descent, was once a man who had become a god after completing superhuman tasks. Here was the clue. A man who showed the capacity or inner power to perform great deeds might well be considered a god, and by being so considered he achieved supreme external power over those awed by his accomplishments. His power, thereafter, was proportional to the number of his believers. *Soter,* the Greek word for savior, meant to save a people from physical calamity like famine, flood or cruel treatment. In our own time, newspaper reports have told how illiterate country folk in India considered President Eisenhower to be a god. Who else could give away so much wheat? Similarly, Alexander was a god to the illiterate natives of the Middle East who witnessed the destruction of the mighty Persian Empire.

At home, the reaction to Alexander's mounting power and wealth had an air of expedient toleration. "Of course, he can be a god," said a wag at sophisticated Athens, "and his horse can be one too."

Before leaving Egypt in the spring of 331, Alexander founded Alexandria which was destined to replace Athens as the queen city of Greek culture in the succeeding Hellenistic Age. As the conqueror marched eastward, he would found or substantially rebuild over sixty cities including another fifteen named after himself. Many of the new settlements remained little more than military bases, but others became full-fledged cities equipped with *agora,* theater and gymnasium. As Isocrates had hopefully predicted, the Greek and Macedonian migrants who "followed the flag" were to help alleviate the ever-pressing problem of land shortage and overpopulation at home. However, as always, side-by-side with the practical considerations of war and prosperity was the need for some higher meaning. The Greeks claimed that they were also carrying their superior civilization to the backward peoples of the East. As early as 380, Isocrates had said, "The name Greek is no longer a mark of race but of outlook, and is accorded to those who share our culture rather than our blood." Could it be that as the Hellenic Age drew to a close at least a few Greeks caught a glimpse of the ideal of "one world," in which the enlightenment of all mankind would replace the advantages of any single race or people? Perhaps, but it was only in the regions adjacent to the coast of the Mediterranean that the Hellenization process was successful. It was in this area too that the clearest record has been left of resistance to the Greek customs. The Jews in Palestine, faithful to the Law, saw nothing superior in the inquiring mentality of sophism or the nudity of athleticism.

Even so, the Jews did not escape the influence of the Greek style altogether, and the decoration of their temples in the succeeding

Hellenistic Age actually incorporated Hellenic forms. The term Hellenistic, therefore, properly refers to an amalgam of Greek and oriental customs and motifs which contrasts with the earlier native Hellenism of the fifth century.

## Conquest and Mutiny

In October 331, Alexander won another decisive victory over the Persians in the vicinity of Gaugamela, a village eighteen miles northeast of the ancient Assyrian capital of Nineveh. He would soon be rid of his rival to the title "Lord of Asia." The commanders around Darius III had long considered their king to be a major liability in any attempt to save the empire. He was murdered as he fled northward in the summer of 330.

Meantime, Alexander had reached Persepolis, the major capital of the Persian Empire. The city offered great treasure and also the chance for revenge. Persepolis was burned as Xerxes had once burned Athens. Today, the ruins of a magnificent palace still remain at this obscure site to remind us how far the centers of power have shifted in the past and are likely to shift again.

During the following two years Alexander pursued Bessus, the pretender to the Persian throne, into an area now known as Afghanistan and from there into the territories which are today the Soviet Republics of Uzbek and Kirgiz. At Khojend (modern Leninabad), Bessus was finally captured and killed.

Most of the Macedonians and Greeks wondered why they had come so far. Very few shared Alexander's desire to go further and at the Hyphasis River (modern Beas) in India he was faced with an uncheckable mutiny. His weary, long-suffering followers had no wish to conquer all of Asia. They wanted to go home. Only some of them made it. The first leg of the trip was the easiest. They built ships which carried them to the Indian Ocean. These ships were then placed under the command of Nearchus who explored the Indian Ocean and the Persian Gulf. The main body of the army spent the year 325 journeying by foot through southern Persia over land as cruel as the treacherous natives.

Alexander spent the last year of his life at Babylon making plans he never lived to fulfill. In June 323, at the age of thirty-two, he died. Plutarch simply says that he suffered "a fever" and discounts the rumors that he was poisoned. Undoubtedly his strength had been sapped by the long and strenuous campaign and by his numerous wounds.

Alexander's first wife Roxane, the daughter of a rich Sogdian baron, gave birth to a son, Alexander IV, after the conqueror died. As the heir, he posed a threat to the ambitions of Alexander's generals and was later murdered as was also Olympias, Alexander's mother, and Philip III, her mentally defective step-son. Even in death Alexander was exceptional. Apparently, he was the only notable member of his family who died of natural causes.

Alexander's generals were the actual heirs of his empire. Those who came out on top in the scramble for power after his death were the founders of the dynasties which ruled the Hellenistic kingdoms. The Antigonid dynasty claimed control over Macedonia and Greece; the Seleucid dynasty secured Syria, Mesopotamia, and all the territory farther east which they could manage to hold. The Ptolemies ruled Egypt until Cleopatra, the last of their line, committed suicide in 30 B.C. Even as the Greek *poleis* had weakened themselves by their constant struggles, so too, in the course of time, these kingdoms fell prey to Rome.

Historians have always agreed that Alexander was an extraordinary general. Some like to stress his vision in explanation of this, and others his luck. Without denying either possibility, it seems apparent that Alexander developed with his experiences. Each episode in his life prepared him for some new venture ahead. Everything he did was on a grand scale: the distances he covered, the wealth he collected, and the number of people he ruled and planned for. No matter who he thought he was, or what he dreamed about, the significance of his career was that he had changed the scale by which events were to be measured.

His teacher Aristotle, the foremost mind of the age, insisted that man's happiest condition was to stay at home in a *polis* where every citizen could know every other. In Alexander's wide new world, such advice was the equivalent of being told today that the small town is still our best hope.

## Aristotle

The careers of Alexander and Aristotle were linked together. These two men were the major precursors of the epoch which followed their own. Alexander's conquest of the Persian Empire inau-

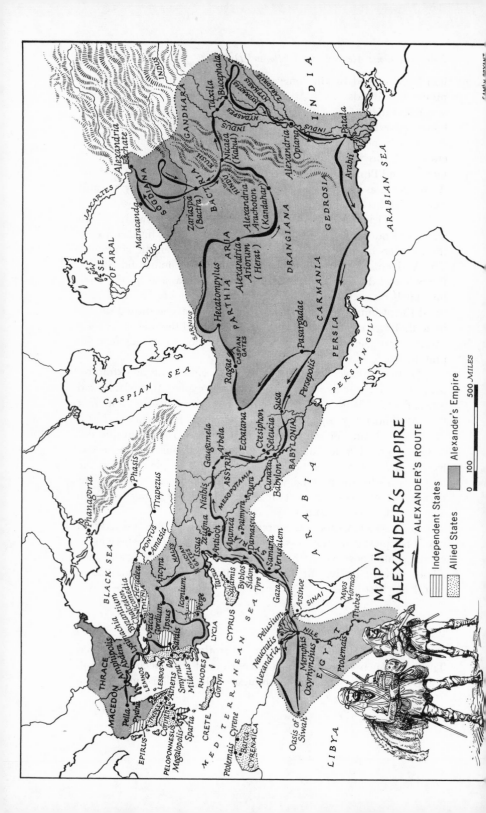

MAP IV

# ALEXANDER'S EMPIRE

→ ALEXANDER'S ROUTE

⬚ Independent States

⬚ Allied States

⬚ Alexander's Empire

0    100                    500 MILES

INDUS

GANDHARA

Bucephala

Taxila

Hydaspes

Hydraotes

Zaradros

INDIA

Nicaea (Kabul)

Alexandria Opiana

Indus

Patala

ARIA

BACTRIA

SOGDIANA

Alexandria Eschate

JAXARTES

Maracanda

OXUS

SEA OF ARAL

Zariaspa (Bactra)

HINDU

Alexandria Arachoton (Kandahar)

Alexandria Ariorum (Herat)

Arabii

ARABIAN SEA

DRANGIANA

GEDROSIA

CARMANIA

PERSIA

Pasargadae

Persepolis

PERSIAN GULF

Hecatompylus

PARTHIA

Ragae

CASPIAN GATES

Susa

Ecbatana

BABYLONIA

SARNIUS

CASPIAN SEA

Phanagoria

Phasis

Trapezus

Amasia

PONTUS

BLACK SEA

Gaugamela

Arbela

ASSYRIA

Ctesiphon

Seleucia

Cunaxa

Babylon

Dura

MESOPOTAMIA

Nisibis

Zeugma

Palmyra

Apamea

Antioch

Damascus

ARABIA

Samaria

Jerusalem

Gaza

Pelusium

SINAI

Myos Hormos

Arsinoe

NILE

Memphis

Oxyrhynchus

EGYPT

Thebes

Alexandria

Naucratis

Ptolemais

Oasis of Siwah

LIBYA

Ptolemais

Barca

Cyrene

CYRENAICA

MEDITERRANEAN SEA

CRETE

Gortyn

RHODES

Cnidus

CYPRUS

Salamis

Byblos

Sidon

Tyre

Tarsus

CILICIA

Issus

CILICIAN GATES

Cyrrhus

Perge

LYCIA

Iconium

Gordium

Miletus

Smyrna

Sardis

Ipsus

Cyzicus

BITHYNIA

Nicomedia

Chalcedon

Byzantium

Lysimachia

Heraclea

Abdera

Amphipolis

THRACE

MACEDON

Pella

Pydna

Thessaly

Thebes

Athens

Corinth

Megalopolis

Sparta

PELOPONNESUS

EPIRUS

Lemnos

Lesbos

Chios

Samos

G. EDEN RYANT

gurated the Hellenistic Age, a period marked by political change, and also noted for the most remarkable scientific advances prior to the seventeenth century of our era. It was Aristotle's compromise between Plato's otherworldliness and the world of the senses, plus his influence on a generation of students at the Lyceum, which channeled Greek thought in the direction of scientific research.

Aristotle needs no specific identification now, but he was once called "the Stagirite" after his birthplace Stagira (modern Stavro), a colony in the Chalcidic peninsula settled by emigrants from Andros and Chalcis. When he was a boy, his father was appointed a physician in the Macedonian court of Amyntas II, the father of Philip. So, in all probability Aristotle spent part of his childhood at Pella, where he was to return in his forties to serve as a tutor to Alexander, Amyntas' grandson. Most of his time in between was spent in Athens. He went there in 367, when he was seventeen, to study at the Academy and remained until after Plato's death in 347. Some say that he was disappointed at not having been chosen Plato's successor, but he nowhere admits it.

A year or two after Philip's death, while Alexander was preparing for the invasion of Asia, Aristotle established his own school at Athens—the Lyceum. He was popular as a teacher, but not well-liked by the average Athenian citizen who saw him as an outsider and friend of the reigning conqueror. When Alexander died in 323, Aristotle was forced to flee to Chalcis. In view of the high feelings of the anti-Macedonian party, the charge of impiety which was lodged against him seemed almost a courtesy. In any event, the times were again too political for philosophy. A year later in 322, Aristotle died in the city whence his mother's ancestors had gone to Stagira.

## Aristotelianism

Plato had neither denied nor ignored the existence of the material world. On the contrary, it bothered him. Yet, he was committed to a proposition which he considered irrefutable. If the non-material world of Ideas was real, then the material world of the senses could not be real. In his mind this statement was logical, and he followed Parmenides' dictum that what was logical was true. That was as far as Plato went. As the son of a physician, Aristotle was not so easily satisfied. It seems reasonable that before he joined the Academy he had served as an apprentice to his father. In that capacity he would have been impressed with how much men had learned about the treatment of wounds and diseases through observation and even trial and error. So, while he may have at first accepted the restrictions of Platonism, his earlier experiences had predisposed him toward a compromise with the world of the senses. His eventual conclusion that reality consisted of both the Idea and its material expression meant that there was truth in nature after all.

Aristotle's new concept of reality, however, carried with it at least one implication which he was unprepared to accept. If the non-material element, the Idea or Form, did not exist apart from matter, then the soul must be one with the body and not merely imprisoned in it, as Plato had said. Did that mean that there was no immortality? Aristotle felt unable to break with Platonism to that extent. In order to save himself, he allowed that in so far as the soul concentrated on the eternal forms it too was eternal. This note of mysticism saved him, and his soul, from the total commitment which materialism had imposed on Democritus and his followers. Nevertheless, for Aristotle, the straight thinker, it had been an embarrassing moment.

To the Platonists, Aristotle's acceptance of matter seemed a step backward. And so it was. Two centuries earlier at the beginning of the Greek philosophical tradition, the Ionians had said that there was an order in nature which the senses did not at first perceive, but investigation would reveal. To Thales that meant walking around and looking at the earth, the sea and the sky and not just sitting down with students and thinking about them. Aristotle agreed. While still a member of the Academy, apparently he did not make any overt moves toward the study of nature yet he was moving gradually and cautiously in that direction. Certainly he admired and respected Plato too much to have disturbed the aging teacher's last years with contentious debate. At the same time, he had not tried to hide from his teacher the fact that he was having some independent ideas. The dialogues he wrote during his twenty years at the Academy have been lost but certain comments in his later writings reveal that, even while his teacher was alive, he had begun the revision of Platonism which would be known as Aristotelianism. Aristotle's later encouragement to students to gather specimens of animal and plant life and to examine, study, and catalogue them cannot be underestimated in its importance to Greek science. When the spell of Platonism was broken, the way was open for crucial discoveries, particularly in biology.

In the last years of his life, the years at the Lyceum, Aristotle produced his *History of Animals, On the Parts of Animals,* and *On the Generation of Animals.* About 500 different animals were mentioned, but the reports were uneven, depending on the source of Aristotle's knowledge. The information he received from hunters and fishermen was bound to be sketchy. Even so, their descriptions were superior to the accounts in old stories where the imagination of travelers produced some strange animals indeed. Nevertheless, because material of doubtful origin was allowed to stand side-by-side with the best work which Aristotle produced, his authority perpetuated for centuries some of the fantastic lore of the ancient world.

Aristotle's descriptions were obviously most reliable when he was speaking from firsthand knowledge, as was the case with the fifty types of animals he dissected himself. His observations about various reproductive processes and the development of embryos were amazingly accurate in certain details. On the other hand, his efforts at classification were not altogether successful. However, his discussion of the problems encountered and his attempts to resolve them brought the study of biology to the level at which it remained until modern times.

In the years ahead, the same spirit of inquiry was to lead to new discoveries in chemistry and physics with resulting advances in both medicine and warfare. The prospects for science in the ancient world went only that far, however, and no farther. Neither Aristotle nor his successors sought to harness the forces of nature or to invent labor-saving machines by which to improve the standard of living and make everybody happy. That turn of events had to await the eighteenth century Enlightenment, and the idea then propounded that every man had a right to be happy.

## The Good State

Aristotle's decision to search for truth in things as well as in thought was his most significant break from Plato's influence. He never strayed far from the master's teachings in politics and morality. He saw society as an orderly arrangement of parts and considered it "unnatural" that men of unequal mentality should have an equal share in the state. Looking at humankind with the eye of a scientist, untempered by humanistic or theological predilections, he found that some men were more intelligent than others and concluded that the superior must rule the inferior, lest the same disorders result as happen when the body overrules the soul. Moreover, he contended that certain human beings had a slave mentality which made it natural for them to receive orders rather than to give them.

Typically, Aristotle sought to support his conclusions about man and society by observation of real conditions rather than depend on Plato's abstract discussion of justice. He put his students to work compiling histories of one hundred and fifty-eight constitutions which had evolved in Greece. Unfortunately, out of all these studies only the *Constitution of Athens* has survived; its unevenness has raised some questions about its authorship. For the present purposes, the available papyri edition is assumed to be a copy of a draft which Aristotle had not found time to prepare adequately for publication before he died. Because it represented a report on data gathered from several sources, this historical account of democracy at Athens was probably intended to be as objective as possible. That may in fact be the answer to those who think that the document shows too much sympathy for democracy to suit Aristotle's temper. Actually, here and there, certain of the opinions expressed agree with his known views. For instance, there is the statement that the loss of Pericles to "guide" the Assembly was a crucial turn of events. Aristotle certainly believed that without this better mind to manage for them, the citizenry, unable to think for themselves, fell prey to men of lesser capacity. Further along in the work, there is praise for the government of the Five Thousand which limited the franchise to the upper three classes. Obviously, Aristotle favored a restriction which eliminated the "emotional" voters at the lower end of the scale.

In his *Politics,* Aristotle elaborates on his reasons for placing democracy—as he observes it in his own time—among the bad forms of government. He classifies all constitutions according to whether the power devolves to one man, a few men, or many men. He then distinguishes theory from practice by observing that if the power in each of these three categories is used in an enlightened manner for the welfare of all citizens, then the government is good—but if the rulers serve only their own interests the government is bad. Accordingly, by his definition, a monarchy is better than a tyranny, an aristocracy preferable to an oligarchy, and a polity more desirable than a democracy. In theory, Aristotle, like Plato, preferred a monarch of god-like qualities or an aristocracy of "guardians" as the best of the good forms of government. As a realist, he chose to talk about polity.

The distinction between polity and democracy was one based on wealth. Aristotle would not have objected to a maximum number of participants in a government, for this was beneficial to both the individual and the state. Yet he felt that, for one reason or another, there were those who were unable to assume the responsibilities of citizenship and he found such men to be mainly among the ignorant and the poor. He was not optimistic, however, about the prospects of any state left in the hands of either the few who were rich or the many who were poor. He acutely observes that those who are better off do often think that they are better absolutely, and arrange all affairs, therefore, to suit their own best interests; furthermore, they think the rest of the population neither worthy nor deserving of consideration. On the other hand, the poor who insist on equality before the law tend also to think themselves equal in all matters; in consequence, they insist that even though a majority of those voting in a given election be ignorant of the issues they have the right to determine policy. Aristotle's solution was characteristic of him. He would assign the power in any state to the middle class. Such citizens are neither so rich that they must live in fear lest any change be a move to take their money, nor are they so poor as to be always grasping for what does not belong to them. A constitution which extended the franchise well beyond the very rich but did not include the very poor was what Aristotle called a polity. He favored it because it combined numbers with wealth. His praise for the government of the Five Thousand at Athens was therefore predictable, since it was intended to be a government of the arms-bearing middle class.

As the mean between the selfish rich and the grasping poor, the middle class offered the state stability. The present troubles of nations (particularly in South America) which lack a large middle class lend familiar evidence to support Aristotle's observation. He looked for his own evidence in Athenian history and recalled that Solon, a man of middling means, was the best legislator the city had ever known. This, indeed, is only one example of the mass of historical material which Aristotle presented in the *Politics*. Again, it was his interest in "how things really happened" which distinguished him from Plato and the preoccupation with "what should be."

Aristotle had observed from his study of history that where men are allowed to subvert the law in matters of small importance, they soon lose respect for law altogether. He was also aware that among those who press for revolution there are a few who would destroy all law in order to live as they please. They obviously have failed to observe that animals live as they please and yet cannot escape the harsher law that might makes right. Why do young men forget this? Could it be because their education has served to make them egotistical rather than virtuous? Aristotle thought so. His longing for a return to the ideals of former times was based on his conclusion that the disintegration of the city had led to the decline in education. He considered the natural habitat of man to be a small community in which all the citizens could know one another. The good life is lost to the hermit shut off from other voices, to the rootless wanderer, or to the lonely man adrift among the multitudes of a great kingdom. Moral virtue is attained in the give-and-take of community life and intellectual growth comes from listening to and pondering over what close friends and neighbors have to say. The outsider cannot achieve these goals anymore than a spectator can acquire the valued traits of sportsmanship by watching other men in competition.

Aristotle argues that the *polis* is the last step in the fulfillment of man's unique capacities. In the beginning was the family. Male and female united for the reproduction of their kind. Then several families joined together to form a village for mutual protection. So far, the instincts for self-preservation, sex and food were served. But did not packs of animals achieve the same ends? The *polis* helps to make man a man. It goes beyond his need to live and serves his higher need to live well. Thus did Aristotle root his defense of the *polis* in a natural development. This was his answer to those who would call the city a "convenience." Yet that is what it had become in Aristotle's day when men were finding other ways of living well and finding them on their own. "What is your religion?" Major Barbara asks her father. "I am a millionaire," he replies.

In his *Politics*, Aristotle shows the same contempt for usury that Plato does in the *Laws*. He condemns the acquisition of any wealth beyond proper needs. If profit becomes the end of living, a man is distracted from the pursuit of moral and intellectual goals. Worse, the accumulation of money undermines the good life, for one man may be tempted to take advantage of another. How could that contribute to his own well-being? Aristotle was talking values, not economics. He was not interested in what commercialism could do for society in the way of the transfer of goods for a greater abundance. Nor had Socrates been interested in such matters when he preached in the *agora* that learning how to make a better living was not the same as learning how to live. Plato had retreated with this credo to the Academy and it still finds a more congenial home in universities than anywhere else.

Aristotle's proposal for a good state based on academic ideals shows to what extent he always remained a child of the Academy. Like Plato, he believed that the state must have restrictive laws which prevent men from harming one another. Such an experience would educate or "condition" men for morality. It is important to recall again that the state religion in Greece was perfunctory rather than moral. These fourth century philosophers were repeating at greater length what Aeschylus suggests in his *Oresteia*. The *polis* was the civilizing experience for the Greeks, as the Law was for the Jews. It followed that a breakdown of the *polis* would presage a collapse of morality.

It is the conservative view of society which holds that for men to have justice they must have guidance. Otherwise, left to their own resources, they will seek only selfish interests. The notion that laws must be enacted to coerce men into the habit of being just toward one another, and thereby in time learning how to be just, has enjoyed a renaissance in the United States in our own time. Of course, many of those who favor such legislation today do not think of themselves as conservatives. Yet they are, for, like Edmund Burke whose works enshrined custom as necessary for the welfare of society, they have abandoned the eighteenth century notion of every man's reason as his own best guide. Again, they are only optimistic about the chance for justice if men are "educated" by laws which command obedience to principle, whether a citizen like it or not. Principles in the ancient world did not, to be sure, apply to as many people as they do now, but the overall idea was the same.

## The Good Life

For Aristotle, laws which prescribed how men should behave toward one another were not the whole answer to the "good life." Socrates had made the question of how a man was to achieve such a life the central problem in philosophy. As could be expected, Aristotle's answer was a practical one. It was not that he abandoned Plato's concern for "what was best," but rather that he kept adding on "what was possible."

Two treatises, the *Nicomachean Ethics* and the *Eudemian Ethics,* are assumed to have been summaries of Aristotle's teachings, the first by his son and the second by a student. According to these works, Aristotle stated that the ultimate good in life must be self-sufficing, an end in itself, not merely a means to some other end.

He calls it *eudaimonia,* a word which has usually been translated as happiness. It might be said that the pursuit of happiness is the final aim even of life and liberty. Yet it is not in such a sense that Aristotle uses the term. His discussion makes it apparent that his "end of all living" means a form of activity, not a state of pleasure or satisfaction. This activity, which some have preferred to call "well-being," is in fact the exercise of man's reasoning by which he enjoys an excellence, or virtue, not known to animals. In brief, the more man thinks and acts according to the highest human capacities, the closer he comes to the ideal life. The intellectual virtues attained through study and reflection introduce philosophers to the contemplative life which is the best of all. So be it, but all men cannot be sages. Therefore, Aristotle distinguishes between the kinds of virtue to which men can aspire. For those living in the workaday world, the moral virtues are possible of attainment by the acquisition of good habits.

A man becomes a musician or a carpenter by practice; so too, by practice, he can become a virtuous man. A man does not acquire honesty by suddenly deciding to tell the truth, but by being honest over the course of many years. Magnanimity, temperance, and modesty are also traits of character to be achieved by habit—*ethos.* They are not endowed by nature. They become "second nature" through training. Aristotle arrives at a familiar conclusion. The manner in which a child is raised does not make just a little difference. It makes all the difference in the world. Aristotle's emphasis on discipline does not have Plato's rigidity, however, and noticeably missing is that refrain of abstinence which keeps repeating itself in his teacher's work.

Aristotle preferred to talk about a proper balance between two extremes. Courage is the middle way between foolhardiness and cowardice. So too, in talking about one's self, truthfulness is the mean between an exaggerated boastfulness and self-depreciation. Wittiness is the mean between buffoonery and boorishness. The body is also to be met half-way. Too little exercise, food or drink is as bad as too much. And since the right amount for one person might be wrong for another, each individual must consider his own capacity. In short, the mean is golden and relative.

With a generosity of spirit which Plato's temperament did not allow, Aristotle readily admits that such a target is hard to hit. It was said that as a young man he had been wide of the mark himself. The stories told about him were perhaps exaggerated or maybe even made up by his enemies; still, his reflections do seem ill-suited to an ascetic man and more like those of one who may have taken a few chances.

Aristotle accepts human desires as neither right nor wrong in themselves. The man who pursues only his desires, however, and avoids the painful responsibilities dictated by reason, cannot possibly know the virtue of the balanced life which makes room for both. Aristotle is careful to limit his meaning. He states that he is not dealing here with an exact science such as mathematics, but only with certain observations which should be attended by common sense. In suggesting, therefore, that human desires can be properly proportioned, he is careful to exclude inclinations toward stealing and murder. Such acts are bad in themselves. There is no such thing as a moderate amount of murder. Nor is there the right person or time for adultery.

One of the rewards of the balanced and self-ordered life prescribed by Aristotle would be the self-confidence which would allow a man to like himself and, therefore, to enjoy his own company. It follows that those who lack such control and are forever alternating between extremes or endlessly seeking sensation show their distaste for themselves by being unable to bear solitude.

## A Spirit of Inquiry

There have been many lively debates about the genuineness and dating of Aristotle's works. One complication has resulted from his habit of giving different kinds of instruction. His regular students, already conversant with his general ideas, were able to understand the allusions and nuances of rather technical lectures. He also spoke to outsiders, however, and gave them popular lectures. In these afternoon sessions, his remarks on a given subject would be more general. They might even be attuned to the public ear by confirming notions which were popular but not necessarily in agreement with what he had said in his more precise lectures given in the morning. Some of both kinds of these lectures were published, even if only as notes recast in essay form. This circumstance explains in part why there appear to be contradictions in his teachings. Similar contradictions appear today between a scholar's remarks during an hour's lecture on television and what he would say to his students in a graduate seminar.

About two-thirds of the forty-six treatises ascribed to Aristotle can safely be said to be his. The rest, including the *Constitution of Athens,* leave room for argument. Furthermore, although his writings have been convincingly arranged in rough chronological order according to the theory: "the less Platonism, the later the work," this guide-rule is only a working hypothesis. Scholars quarrel about such issues but they are united in awe of Aristotle's learning.

Dante (A.D. 1265-1321) calls Aristotle "the master of those who know." With the amount of knowledge available today, no one could hope to write so well about physics, astronomy, biology, physiology, psychology, metaphysics, ethics, politics, rhetoric and poetics. That Aristotle was a pioneer, especially in logic, makes his accomplishment all the more impressive.

During the Middle Ages, the Muslim Averroës (*circa* A.D. 1126-1198), the noted Jewish scholar Maimonides (A.D. 1135-1204) and St. Thomas Aquinas (*circa* A.D. 1225-1274) each, in turn, grappled with the problem of reconciling the remarkable erudition and wisdom of this fourth century philosopher with the truth they had received from revelation. Wherever there were contradictions, faith was triumphant, yet if the three major religions of the Western world could use a scaffolding erected by reason, Aristotle had supplied one. What could be more useful than his arguments for the existence of God? In all of his varied interests he had placed a conspicuous emphasis on gradation, whether between lower and higher animals, moral and intellectual virtues, or poor constitutions and good ones. In his *On Philosophy,* he expresses the view that among all existing things there must be a gradation toward the "best." So too in his *Metaphysics,* that which moves without being moved governs those objects which move and are moved. When Aquinas, in his *Whether God Exists,* adds that everybody knows that "the best" and the "unmoved mover" are God, he uses Aristotle's arguments to support a Judaic-Christian doctrine of a theistic divinity who in *Genesis* had created all things. Aristotle did not know *Genesis.* On the contrary, he says that matter is not created, it is eternal.

One of the difficulties, albeit a natural one, in interpreting Aristotle's views is that they may at times be contradictory, for, as mentioned earlier, they represent his ideas at various times when he was seeking to emphasize different points. When he is talking about order in the universe, he ascribes it to God and there are other passages in his works which have overtones of a providential deity who directs the affairs of a household.

The role which Aristotle played in the Middle Ages differed from his place in his own time. In the later period, a spirit of conciliation existed in which faith and reason were used to fortify a single and known truth. In the fourth century B.C., Aristotle contradicted Plato precisely because he was willing to accept other evidence and to reorder his concept of reality to suit new knowledge. In brief, his approach inspired a spirit of inquiry. He began with cosmological observations and from these arrived at the conclusion that there must be a divine being; he did not seek an accommodation with reason of a primary faith in such a being.

Aristotle's break with Platonism was made, to be sure, in the interest of inquiry for which he deserves and has received full credit. Yet it would be a mistake to think that he had no preconceived notions of his own. His approach to knowledge was uncompromisingly teleological, which means that he insisted that every creature and every happening had a purpose. When he postulated his reality as consisting of Ideas combined with matter, he did not believe that this process was random or "in vain." Aristotle's study of astronomy and mathematics in the Academy had made the precise impression which Plato hoped they would make on him. Aristotle always accepted the orderliness of the universe as a basic premise. So, while he may have turned away from Plato's spiritual world and looked to nature itself for truth, his classification of animals was to him what he expected to find.

## The Divorce of Metaphysics and Science

Aristotle's notable pupil Theophrastus looked at his master's work with a critical eye, much as Aristotle had examined Plato's conclusions. And, as Aristotle never divorced himself entirely from Platonism, so Theophrastus accepted his teacher's teleological principle up to a point. Yet it was for him only part of the truth, not the whole truth. If all happenings had a purpose, then he wanted to know the purpose of disastrous floods and droughts. Since he knew of none, he concluded that if examples of planning existed in nature, as his own *History of Plants* and *Causes of Plants* suggested, then to that extent nature might be said to have a purpose—*but* this evidence did not permit a scientist to assume that all of nature was free from mere chance. Aristotle, of course, knew that criticism of his teleological system was possible, yet he had not pursued the matter. Significantly, it was Theophrastus who insisted on absolute scientific evidence. If the evidence was contradictory, that was still an answer in the absence of other knowledge.

Perhaps a student is never truly worthy of his teacher unless he is in some way critical of him and even in some way excels him. Theophrastus was a credit to Aristotle, and when his teacher died he took his place at the head of the Lyceum. Like Aristotle, Theophrastus had begun his studies at the Academy but later became a member of the Lyceum. He was actually only twelve years younger than Aristotle, but he lived thirty-five years longer. During the years 322–287, he carried on Aristotle's interest in observation with such zeal that he began to overturn certain of Aristotle's pronouncements. For instance, he came to the conclusion that fire was not an element as Aristotle thought, but a compound. In a fragment of his work *On Fire* he explains that it is obvious fire cannot be a First Principle, because it needs material to burn. Moreover, while air, earth and water cannot be generated, fire can. He mentions the rubbing together of sticks and striking flint on metal. These are simple acts, yet, as he cites them, they are experiments. It was a prophetic development. His successor Strato, who headed the Lyceum from 287 to 269, was anxious to demonstrate the advantages of experimental science. How may it be proved that air consists of minute particles of matter? Turn a vessel upside-down and thrust it into water. The water cannot rise in the vessel because it is "occupied" with air. Bore a hole in the bottom of the vessel and the air will escape and water will rush in to its own level, for water does not travel upward. Can it be made to do so? Take a vessel and suck the air out, then invert it and watch the "void" draw the liquid up to fill the empty space.

These exercises serve to indicate the new emphasis which Strato gave to learning through the senses, as he shifted the search for knowledge from observation to experimentation. Aristotle had "observed" that earth and water have a natural downward motion and fire and air an upward motion. Strato's research caused him to disagree and inclined him toward Democritus' view that lighter matter was simply resting on heavier, since all four elements were subject to gravity.

Strato was not the first man to begin testing his ideas. The Pythagoreans and pupils of Hippocrates had carried on experiments as adjuncts to the knowledge they received from other sources, but Strato made experimentation the central task and his dependency on physical evidence led him to equate God with nature. Moreover, he turned away from Socrates' interest in ethics and concentrated on natural phenomena. The age-old marriage between metaphysics and science was coming to an end and Aristotle was the last philosopher to attempt the mastery of all knowledge. Strato's career fell wholly in the Hellenistic Age which boasted, on the one hand, of philosophers like his contemporary Zeno, the founder of Stoicism, and, on the other hand, of mathematicians and physicists like the renowned Euclid and Archimedes.

Although, in the last analysis, Aristotle's own discoveries became victims of imaginative inquiry, it was not "what he thought" so much as "how he thought" which contributed to the reputation of the Greeks. When the Western observer looks at India, he finds that a certain "kind of thinking" has perpetuated for thousands of years modes of living—the caste system in particular—which to his eye are passive and unprogressive. By contrast, the dynamism and invention of the West have been due to a willingness to re-examine inherited knowledge and to use all of man's capacities to find new ways to know.

## The Road Ahead

In 322, the same year in which Aristotle died, the end also came (and a bitter one) for Demosthenes. With the death of Alexander, his regents everywhere began to solidify their positions in anticipation of the unsettled years ahead. Antipater, who had been left in charge of Macedon and commissioned to maintain peace in Greece, was determined to hold the allegiance of the Greek states. After a brief period of inconclusive warfare for which most of the Greek states showed no real heart, he agreed not to invade Attica if the Athenians would accept his terms. The Assembly, recognizing their weakness by land and sea, agreed. They were willing to set up an oligarchic government sympathetic to Antipater with the franchise limited to 9,000. They also agreed to turn over to him those orators who had urged resistance. Among them, of course, was Demosthenes who had again fled from Athens. He was finally hunted down at the temple of Poseidon in Calauria (modern Poros), an island in the Saronic Gulf off the coast of the Peloponnesus, opposite to Troezen. According to the story of his last hour, he took his own life by poison.

The sorry scene of this great Athenian patriot committing suicide in his hiding place might seem a convenient setting in which to end this history. Yet to leave off at that ancient altar where Demosthenes fell would turn the mind backward to the memory of better times. History is better served by a road which leads ahead.

And so it is that this story ends, not with Alexander, Aristotle or Demosthenes, but with Diogenes (*circa* 412–*circa* 323). These men all died at about the same time, yet no one could better symbolize the break with the fraternal traditions of the *polis* and the disintegration of the fabric of a passing age than Diogenes whose life had in part quite literally been spent on the open road. Amid the unsettling times of the fourth century, Plato and Aristotle had argued for the greater application of human reason in order to make man's life more civilized. Diogenes, in a startling disavowal of the Hellenic tradition, taught that civilization was actually the cause of most of man's problems.

Pythagoras, Plato and Aristotle found orderliness in musical tones, the stars, and the classification of animals. Diogenes renounced the quest for truth in books or in research or in any of the trappings of academia. Men could find the answers within themselves, if only they could be free from the artificiality of society. Where could the troubled mind find peace and freedom? Diogenes pointed out and led the way through the scenic countryside to the serenity found in a hushed wood or by a quiet stream.

What created strife amongst men? Was it not Plato's valued citizenship narrowly restricted to exclude troublesome foreigners? Could his isolated city of the *Laws* really foster peace? Or in refusing to have trade or cultural contacts with others, did it not harbor a sense of superiority which bred ill-will? What of Aristotle's contention that the Greeks were superior to their neighbors? Such were the barriers set up by civilized men. Diogenes did not find such exclusiveness in nature. But before it be assumed that Diogenes preached the brotherhood of man and sought universal love, it should be observed that his real concern was that men should leave one another alone. He was not actually as much interested in the welfare of his fellow man as he was in escaping from his control.

Characteristically, Diogenes is reported to have said, "I am a citizen of the world." In a sense he was. Although little is known about his life, the tradition says that he fled from his native Sinope in Pontus after his father had been jailed for malfeasance in office. Although positive details are lacking, it was believed that Diogenes felt that his father had been betrayed by men whom he had assumed to be his friends. The story is agreeable to a strain of misanthropy in Diogenes' teachings, yet it need not be used to account for it. The emphasis in his doctrine was not one of ill-will toward others; it was simply a belief in individual self-sufficiency. A man should not hope for any happiness beyond what he could obtain by himself. The refugee, unable to go home and a stranger everywhere else, learns to trust to what he has at the moment. As an outsider, he takes a hard look at the comfortable convictions of those in better circumstances. Diogenes did not find the old customs of the *polis* to be means to virtue and the good life, rather they were ramparts of selfishness and hypocrisy.

In the fourth century, the chronic warfare between states and the class struggles within cities took a heavy toll. Refugees and exiles, like the numerous mercenaries, were estranged from familiar surroundings and family shrines. Yet even at home, particularly with the decline of civic loyalty and the increase in skepticism about the old gods, men felt disoriented, insecure, anxious. They too sought an inner peace amid times of change and turbulence.

The members of the Academy and Lyceum might preoccupy themselves with their masters' teachings about the revitalization of the *polis,* but to the more realistically minded, the scope and complexities of the fourth century ruled out a return to the happy contentment of Periclean Athens. For some men, the answer to their personal hopes was to be found in the mystery religions. The gift of faith, however, is not for everybody. Diogenes urged men to turn to themselves; if the world was noisy and complex, they should find a quiet haven of natural simplicity. At the same time that Alexander was conquering the Persian Empire and marching farther and farther to the East, as Aristotle was writing his *Politics* and Demosthenes continuing his anti-Macedonian crusade, Diogenes was leading his followers down the long road to Walden Pond.

The philosophy of life which Diogenes preached was called Cynicism; he and his followers were known as Cynics. The honor of founding Cynicism has not been given to Diogenes, however, but to a lesser known figure, Antisthenes (*circa* 455–360) who was a student of Socrates. He is well remembered for a remark which expressed the Cynic's attitude toward the popular mystery gods of the day. When asked for a contribution to the mother-goddess Cybele, he is reported to have replied: "Let the gods support their own mother."

Whether in fact Diogenes was ever a disciple of Antisthenes or not has been disputed, but certainly the views of the two men were similar. Tradition has it that there was one significant difference

between them. The older man was a talker. His younger contemporary, a doer. Because actions attract more attention, Diogenes was
made famous by the stories which told how he had lived in a tub
and at noonday carried a lantern about in his search for an honest
man. There seems little doubt that he and his followers felt free to
behave as they pleased, and may at times have dramatized their
contention that the politenesses of society were hypocritical forms of
false modesty. It has been assumed therefore that they scratched
when and where they felt like scratching, and perhaps in other ways
behaved like dogs in public. Since the Greek word *kynikos* means
"like a dog," this has generally been accepted as the reason for the
appellation Cynic, as applied to Diogenes and those who imitated
him.

The Cynics considered all customary habits and particularly the
polite amenities of society to be pretentious. Worse, since conventions
often hid true human motives, they were actually dishonest. There
had been a touch of this in Socrates. He said in the *Apology* that he
had not cared about the things which most men cared about. This
included steady employment, an impressive house, or in fact any
comfort above the minimum required to lead his life of the mind.
An emphasis on escaping the domination of "things" in order to be
free in the "spirit" was a recurring theme in Diogenes' teachings.
"I threw away my cup," he says, "when I saw a child drinking with
his hands." He describes a man who was having a great amount of
furniture moved: What a pity, Diogenes thought, he governs all that
furniture, but not himself. Or did the furniture govern him? It is all
summed up in one of Diogenes' aphorisms: "It is a mark of God to
need nothing, and of those who are like God to need little."

Cynicism was called a "short cut to virtue." Instead of seeking
the golden mean, as Aristotle suggested, the Cynics refused to risk
temptation. To avoid materialism, they gave up all material things.
The Biblical admonition that not money alone, but the love of it,
is the root of all evil would not have satisfied them. They did not
trust human nature that much. If a man had money, he would love it.

In subsequent ages, including our own, social movements with a
similar emphasis on "honesty" have been initiated. Their partisans
have launched assaults upon the pious hypocrisy and smug pretense
of custom, the Establishment, or a variety of sacred cows. This kind
of social protest, no matter how sincere, has ever tended to develop
certain side effects which negate the original purpose. Diogenes,
who criticized the wealthy for their pretentious dress, observed a

group of Spartans wearing spare and dirty clothing in order to stress their disdain for the tidy customs of other men. There goes another kind of pride, he said.

Diogenes would also have been quick to censure any disciple who was looking for a lazy, self-indulgent existence. His reason for abandoning the softness of civilization was to develop a discipline over both his body and soul. His escape from convention was not a search for license. Moreover, he was completely orthodox in his agreement with Socrates, Plato and Aristotle that the soul must not succumb to the body. So that the Cynics were not actually "immoral," although their general behavior certainly ran counter to accepted standards. The true Cynic did control himself. Nevertheless, in assuming that a similar course was safe for more than a few, he wore the blinders of an anarchist.

A familiar story about Diogenes illustrates the power of a man who asks nothing of this world except to be left alone, and who wants to control no one except himself. According to tradition, Alexander once passed Diogenes sitting on the ground sunning himself. The powerful young ruler asked the philosopher if he could do something for him. "Yes," Diogenes replied, "you can stand from between me and the sun." True or not, the story shows how Diogenes sought to reduce every man to the common denominator of what he was really worth. It is a good, old question: Who has the more power, the man who has everything or the man who does not ask for anything?

Another anecdote told about Diogenes is one which combines sly wit with his usual blunt honesty. While attending a lecture, he observed the speaker coming to a page which was only partially filled. Diogenes nudged his companion. "Courage," he said, "I see land."

### The Greek Realities

The study of the Greeks can never be a closed account. The wide variety of critical and descriptive works written about them, both foolish and profound, bear witness to man's continuing preoccupation with himself. Other ages might talk of God or machines; the Greeks, from Homer to Diogenes, were fascinated with man. Plato's emphasis on the spiritual world and Diogenes' unheroic retreat may seem to be departures from the Greek way. But that would be true only if there were a single Greek way. Obviously, there was not. It is the variety of the Greek ideas about man, who he is and who he hopes to be, which is the real Greek legacy.

For this reason the Greeks remain at the center of all humanistic training. Their story may help to save an individual from being engulfed by the passing events of the moment, to encourage a sense of forebearance with the incidents of "now," and to allow for a calmer deliberation than is sometimes shown by those whose actions bespeak an ignorance of ages past or a failure to be reconciled to the fact that the human complexion will remain the same in the years ahead.

This book began with the rich tombs of Mycenaean kings who tried desperately to preserve what they had won. It ends with Diogenes and his fellow Cynics who say that it is better to let it all go. In between are the heroes, the art, the history which belong to the ancient Greeks. The questions they raised and the answers they offered are still the concern of us all.

*Bibliography:*
*Books of Interest*

# Bibliography:
# Books of Interest

Paperbound editions are indicated by a dagger (†) following the date of publication.

## Literature

The works of the Greek poets, historians, philosophers, and orators from Homer to Demosthenes are available in the Loeb Classical Library published by the Harvard University Press, Cambridge, Massachusetts. The original and the translation are offered on opposite pages. The following is a selection of other translations.

Aristophanes. *The Complete Plays of Aristophanes.* Translated by B. B. Rogers, R. H. Webb, Moses Hadas, and Jack Lindsay. New York: Bantam, 1962†.

Grene, David, and Lattimore, Richmond, eds. *The Complete Greek Tragedies.* 9 vols. Chicago: University of Chicago Press, 1959–60†.

Herodotus. *The Persian Wars.* Translated by George Rawlinson. New York: Modern Library, 1947.

Homer. *Iliad.* Translated by Andrew Lang and others. New York: Modern Library, 1959†.

———. *Iliad.* Translated by Emil V. Rieu. New York: Penguin, 1950†.

———. *Odyssey.* Translated by S. H. Butcher and Andrew Lang. New York: Macmillan, 1947†.

———. *Odyssey.* Translated by Emil V. Rieu. New York: Penguin, 1950†.

Pindar. *The Odes of Pindar.* Translated by Richmond Lattimore. 2d edition. Chicago: University of Chicago Press, 1976†.

Plutarch. *The Lives of the Noble Grecians and Romans.* Translated by John Dryden. New York: Modern Library, 1932.

Thucydides. *The Complete Writings of Thucydides.* Translated by Richard Crawley. New York: Modern Library, 1951†.

———. *The Peloponnesian War.* Translated by Rex Warner. New York: Penguin, 1954†.

## SOME USEFUL ANTHOLOGIES

Finley, M. I., ed. *Portable Greek Historians: The Essence of Herodotus, Thucydides, Xenophon, Polybius.* New York: Viking, 1959†.

Higham, T. F., and Bowra, C. M., eds. *The Oxford Book of Greek Verse in Translation.* Oxford: Oxford University Press, 1938.

Lattimore, Richmond, translator. *Greek Lyrics.* 2d edition. Chicago: University of Chicago Press, 1960†.

## Reference Works

Cary, Max. *The Documentary Sources of Greek History.* Oxford: Basil Blackwell, 1927; reprinted, Westport, Conn.: Greenwood, 1969.

Fornara, Charles W., and Badian, E., eds. *Translated Documents of Greece and Rome: Archaic Times to the End of the Peloponnesian War.* Vol. I. Baltimore: Johns Hopkins University Press, 1977†.

Hammond, N. G. L., and Scullard, H. H., eds. *Oxford Classical Dictionary.* 2d edition. Oxford: Oxford University Press, 1970.

Lewis, Naphtali. *Greek Historical Documents: The Fifth Century B.C.* Greek Historical Documents Series. Sarasota, Fla.: Samuel Stevens Hakkert, 1970†.

Radice, Betty. *Who's Who in the Ancient World: A Handbook to the Survivors of the Greek and Roman Classics.* New York: Penguin, 1973†.

Rose, Herbert J. *A Handbook of Greek Literature from Homer to the Age of Lucian.* 4th edition. London: Methuen, 1956.

Seyffert, Oskar. *A Dictionary of Classical Antiquities.* Revised and edited by Henry Nettleship and J. E. Sandys. New York: Meridian, 1956†.

## General Works

Bury, J. B., and Meiggs, Russell. *A History of Greece.* 4th edition. New York: St. Martin's, 1975.

Edwards, I. E. S., and others, eds. *The Cambridge Ancient History.* Vol. II, 3d edition; Vols. III–VI, 2d edition. Cambridge: Cambridge University Press, 1925–75.

Hammond, N. G. L. *A History of Greece to 322 B.C.* Oxford: Oxford University Press, 1959.

———. *Studies in Greek History: A Companion Volume to A History of Greece to 322 B.C.* New York: Oxford University Press, 1973.

Kagan, Donald. *Botsford and Robinson's Hellenic History.* 5th edition. New York: Macmillan, 1969.

## Brief Histories

Finley, M. I. *The Ancient Greeks: An Introduction to Their Life and Thought.* New York: Viking, 1963; reprinted, New York: Penguin, 1977†.

Frost, Frank. *Greek Society.* New York: Heath, 1971†.

Kitto, H. D. F. *The Greeks.* Revised edition. New York: Penguin, 1957†.
Lloyd-Jones, Hugh, ed. *The Greeks.* Cleveland: World Publishing Co., 1962; re-
    printed with the title *The Greek World,* New York: Penguin, 1965†.
Robinson, C. E. *Hellas: A Short History of Ancient Greece.* New York: Pantheon,
    1948; reprinted, Boston: Beacon, 1955†.
Rostovtzeff, Mikhail. *Greece.* Sections from Vol. I of *A History of the Ancient
    World, The Orient and Greece.* 2d edition. Translated by J. D. Duff. Oxford:
    Oxford University Press, 1930; reprinted, New York: Galaxy, 1963†.
Smith, Morton. *Ancient Greeks.* Ithaca: Cornell University Press, 1960†.
Starr, Chester G. *The Ancient Greeks.* New York: Oxford University Press, 1971†.

## Works with an Emphasis on Cultural Developments

Barr, Stringfellow. *The Will of Zeus: A History of Greece from the Origins of Hellenic
    Culture to the Death of Alexander.* New York: Lippincott, 1961.
Bowra, C. M. *The Greek Experience.* London: Weidenfeld & Nicolson, 1957; re-
    printed, New York: Mentor, 1960†.
Dickinson, G. Lowes. *The Greek View of Life.* 7th edition. New York: Doubleday,
    1925; reprinted, Ann Arbor: University of Michigan Press, 1958†.
Hamilton, Edith. *The Greek Way.* New York: Norton, 1930; reprinted, New
    York: Avon, 1973†.
Jaeger, Werner. *Paideia: The Ideals of Greek Culture.* 3 vols. 2d edition. Translated
    by Gilbert Highet. Oxford: Oxford University Press, 1939–44, Vol. I,
    *Archaic Greece: The Mind of Athens,* New York: Galaxy, 1965†.
Payne, Robert. *Ancient Greece: The Triumph of a Culture.* New York: Norton,
    1964.

## Art

Beazley, J. D. *The Development of Attic Black-Figure Vases.* Sather Classical Lec-
    tures, Vol. 24. Berkeley: University of California Press, 1964.
Boardman, John. *Greek Art.* Revised edition. New York: Praeger, 1973†.
Carpenter, Rhys. *Greek Sculpture.* Chicago: University of Chicago Press, 1960.
Cook, R. M. *Greek Painted Pottery.* 2d edition. New York: Barnes & Noble, 1972.
Lawrence, A. W. *Greek Architecture.* Revised edition. New York: Penguin, 1975†.
McLeish, Kenneth. *Greek Art and Architecture.* New York: Longman, 1975†.
Pausanias. *Description of Greece.* 5 vols. Translated by W. H. S. Jones. Loeb Classi-
    cal Library. Cambridge, Mass.: Harvard University Press, 1935.
Pollitt, J. J. *Art and Experience in Classical Greece.* New York: Cambridge Univer-
    sity Press, 1972†.
Richter, Gisela M. A. *Attic Red-Figured Vases: A Survey.* Revised edition. New
    Haven: Yale University Press, 1958.
———. *A Handbook of Greek Art.* London: Phaidon, 1959.
———. *Kouroi: Archaic Greek Youths.* 3d edition. London: Phaidon, 1970.
———. *The Sculpture and Sculptors of the Greeks.* 4th edition. New Haven: Yale
    University Press, 1970.
Robertson, C. M. *A History of Greek Art.* 2 vols. Cambridge: Cambridge Univer-
    sity Press, 1976.
Schoder, Raymond V., S.J. *Masterpieces of Greek Art.* Greenwich, Conn.: New
    York Graphic Society, 1960; reprinted, Chicago: Ares, 1975†.
Swindler, Mary H. *Ancient Painting, from the Earliest Times to the Period of Christian
    Art.* New Haven: Yale University Press, 1929; reprinted, New York: AMS
    Press, 1976.

Wycherly, R. E. *How the Greeks Built Cities.* 2d edition. London: Macmillan, 1962; reprinted, New York: Norton, 1976†.

## Studies in Greek Literature

Bowra, C. M. *Greek Lyric Poetry from Alcman to Simonides.* 2d edition. Oxford: Oxford University Press, 1961.

Burn, A. R. *The Lyric Age of Greece.* New York: St. Martin's, 1960.

Bury, John B. *The Ancient Greek Historians.* New York: Macmillan, 1909; reprinted, New York: Dover, 1957†.

Dobson, J. F. *The Greek Orators.* London: Methuen, 1919.

Dover, K. J. *Aristophanic Comedy.* Berkeley: University of California Press, 1972†.

Ehrenberg, Victor. *The People of Aristophanes: A Society of Old Attic Comedy.* 3d edition. New York: Schocken, 1962; reprinted, New York: Barnes & Noble, 1974.

————. *Sophocles and Pericles.* New York: Humanities Press, 1954.

Else, Gerald. *The Origin and Early Form of Greek Tragedy.* Cambridge, Mass.: Harvard University Press, 1965.

Ferguson, John. *A Companion to Greek Tragedy.* Austin: University of Texas Press, 1972.

Fornara, Charles W. *Herodotus: An Interpretative Essay.* New York: Oxford University Press, 1971.

Gomme, A. W., et al. *A Historical Commentary on Thucydides.* 4 vols. New York: Oxford University Press, 1945–70.

Hadas, Moses. *A History of Greek Literature.* New York: Columbia University Press, 1950†.

Kirk, G. S. *The Songs of Homer.* Cambridge: Cambridge University Press, 1962.

Kitto, H. D. F. *Greek Tragedy: A Literary Study.* 3d edition. New York: Doubleday, 1950; reprinted, New York: Barnes & Noble, 1966†.

Lattimore, Richmond. *The Poetry of Greek Tragedy.* Baltimore: Johns Hopkins University Press, 1958.

Lefkowitz, Mary R. *The Victory Ode: An Introduction.* Park Ridge, N.J.: Noyes Press, 1977.

Page, Denys L. *History and the Homeric Iliad.* Sather Classical Lectures, Vol. 31. Berkeley: University of California Press, 1959†.

Pearson, Lionel. *Early Ionian Historians.* Oxford: Oxford University Press, 1939; reprinted, Westport, Conn.: Greenwood, 1975.

Sandbach, F. H. *The Comic Theatre of Greece and Rome.* New York: Norton, 1977.

Scott, John A. *Homer and His Influence.* Boston: Marshall Jones, 1925; reprinted, New York: Cooper Square, 1963.

Sheppard, J. T. *Aeschylus and Sophocles: Their Work and Influence.* New York: Longmans, Green, 1927; reprinted, New York: Cooper Square, 1963.

Wace, Alan J. B., and Stubbings, Frank H., eds. *A Companion to Homer.* New York: Macmillan, 1963.

## Philosophy and Science

Cohen, Morris R., and Drabkin, Israel E., eds. *A Source Book in Greek Science.* Cambridge, Mass.: Harvard University Press, 1948.

Diogenes Laertius. *Lives of the Eminent Philosophers.* 2 vols. Translated by R. D. Hicks. Loeb Classical Library. Cambridge, Mass.: Harvard University Press, 1925.

Dudley, Donald R. *A History of Cynicism from Diogenes to the Sixth Century A.D.* London: Methuen, 1937.

Guthrie, W. K. C. *The Greek Philosophers from Thales to Aristotle.* London: Methuen, 1950; reprinted, New York: Harper, 1960†.

———. *A History of Greek Philosophy.* 4 vols. New York: Cambridge University Press, 1962–75.

Kirk, G. S. and Raven, J. E. *The Presocratic Philosophers: A Critical History with a Selection of Texts.* New York: Cambridge University Press, 1957†.

Lloyd, G. E. R. *Aristotle: The Growth and Structure of His Thought.* Cambridge: Cambridge University Press, 1968.

———. *Early Greek Science: Thales to Aristotle.* New York: Norton, 1974†.

Ross, W. D. *Aristotle.* 5th edition. London: Methuen, 1955; reprinted, New York: Meridian, 1959†.

Sarton, George. *A History of Science.* Vol. I: *Ancient Science through the Golden Age of Greece.* Cambridge, Mass.: Harvard University Press, 1952; reprinted, New York: Norton, 1970†.

Smith, T. V., ed. *Philosophers Speak for Themselves: From Thales to Plato.* 2d edition. Chicago: University of Chicago Press, 1956†.

Taylor, A. E. *The Mind of Plato.* Ann Arbor: University of Michigan Press, 1960.

———. *Socrates.* New York: Appleton, 1933; reprinted, Westport, Conn.: Greenwood, 1975.

## Religion

Cumont, Franz. *Astrology and Religion Among the Greeks and Romans.* New York and London: G.P. Putnam's Sons, 1912; reprinted, New York: Dover, 1960†.

Dodds, Eric R. *The Greeks and the Irrational.* Berkeley: University of California Press, 1951†.

Flaceliere, R. *Greek Oracles.* Translated by Douglas Garman. London: Elek Books, 1965.

Graves, Robert. *The Greek Myths.* 2 vols. New York: Penguin, 1955†.

Guthrie, W. K. C. *The Greeks and Their Gods.* Boston: Beacon, 1950†.

Hamilton, Edith. *Mythology.* Boston: Little, Brown, 1942; reprinted, New York: New American Library, 1971†.

Murray, Gilbert. *Five Stages of Greek Religion.* 3d edition. New York: Beacon, 1951; reprinted (1925 edition), Westport, Conn.: Greenwood, 1976.

Nilsson, Martin P. *Greek Folk Religion.* First published as *Greek Popular Religion.* New York: Columbia University Press, 1940; reprinted, Philadelphia: University of Pennsylvania Press, 1972†.

———. *Greek Piety.* Translated by H. J. Rose. Oxford: Oxford University Press, 1948; reprinted, New York: Norton, 1969†.

———. *A History of Greek Religion.* 2d edition. Translated by F. J. Fielden. Oxford: Oxford University Press, 1949; reprinted, New York: Norton, 1964†.

Parke, Herbert W. *Festivals of the Athenians.* Ithaca: Cornell University Press, 1977.

———. *Greek Oracles.* Atlantic Highlands, N.J.: Humanities Press, 1967†.

Reinhold, Meyer. *Past and Present: The Continuity of Classical Myth.* Sarasota, Fla.: Samuel Stevens Hakkert, 1972†.

Rose, H. J. *Gods and Heroes of the Greeks.* New York: New American Library, 1958†.

———. *A Handbook of Greek Mythology, Including its Extension to Rome.* 6th edition. New York: Dutton, 1958†.

## Special Periods and Places

### BEFORE THE GOLDEN AGE

Alsop, Joseph. *From the Silent Earth: A Report on the Greek Bronze Age*. New York: Harper & Row, 1964.

Blegen, Carl W. *Troy and the Trojans*. New York: Praeger, 1963.

Chadwick, John. *The Decipherment of Linear B*. New York: Cambridge University Press, 1970†.

————. *The Mycenean World*. New York: Cambridge University Press, 1976†.

Coldstream, J. N. *Geometric Greece*. New York: St. Martin's, 1977.

Finley, M. I. *The World of Odysseus*. Revised edition. New York: Penguin, 1956†.

Graham, James W. *The Palaces of Crete*. Princeton: Princeton University Press, 1962†.

Hammond, N. G. L. *A History of Macedonia*. Vol. I: *Historical Geography and Prehistory*. Oxford: Oxford University Press, 1972.

Hood, Sinclair. *The Minoans: The Story of Bronze Age Crete*. New York: Praeger, 1971.

Jeffery, L. H. *Archaic Greece*. New York: St. Martin's, 1976.

Pendlebury, J. D. S. *The Archaeology of Crete: An Introduction*. London: Methuen, 1939; reprinted, New York: Norton, 1965†.

Perowne, Stewart. *The Archaeology of Greece and the Aegean*. New York: Viking, 1974.

Starr, Chester G. *The Origins of Greek Civilization, 1100–650 B.C.* New York: Knopf, 1961.

————. *The Economic and Social Growth of Early Greece, 800–500 B.C.* New York: Oxford University Press, 1977.

Stubbings, Frank H. *Prehistoric Greece*. New York: John Day, 1973.

Ventris, Michael, and Chadwick, John, eds. *Documents in Mycenaean Greek*. 2d edition. Cambridge: Cambridge University Press, 1973.

Vermeule, Emily. *Greece in the Bronze Age*. Chicago: University of Chicago Press, 1964†.

Wace, Alan J. B. *Mycenae: An Archaeological History and Guide*. Princeton: Princeton University Press, 1949.


### COLONIZATION AND TYRANNY

Andrewes, Antony. *The Greek Tyrants*. New York: Hillary, 1956; reprinted New York: Harper, 1963†.

Burn, A. R. *The World of Hesiod: A Study of the Greek Middle Ages, ca. 900–700 B.C.* New York: Dutton, 1936; reprinted, New York: Arno, 1966.

Dunbabin, T. J. *The Western Greeks: The History of Sicily and South Italy from the Foundation of the Greek Colonies to 480 B.C.* Oxford: Oxford University Press, 1948.

Ure, P. N. *The Origin of Tyranny*. Cambridge: Cambridge University Press, 1922; reprinted, New York: Russell & Russell, 1962.

Woodhead, A. G. *The Greeks in the West*. New York: Praeger, 1962.


### CITY-STATES

Burn, A. R. *Persia and the Greeks: The Defence of the West, ca. 546–478 B.C.* New York: St. Martin's, 1962.

Ehrenberg, Victor. *The Greek State*. New York: Barnes & Noble, 1960; reprinted, New York: Norton, 1964†.

Freeman, Kathleen. *Greek City-States.* New York: Norton, 1950†.
Sealey, Raphael. *A History of the Greek City States, ca. 700–338 B.C.* Berkeley: University of California Press, 1976.


ATHENS

Aristotle. *Constitution of Athens and Related Texts.* Translated and edited by Kurt von Fritz and Ernst Kapp. Hafner Library of Classics, No. 13. New York: Hafner, 1950†.
Bowra, C. M. *Periclean Athens.* New York: Dial Press, 1971.
Burn, A. R. *Pericles and Athens.* New York: Macmillan, 1948; reprinted, Mystic, Conn.: Verry, 1973.
Hignett, Charles. *History of the Athenian Constitution to the End of the Fifth Century B.C.* Oxford: Oxford University Press, 1952.
Jones, A. H. M. *Athenian Democracy.* New York: Praeger, 1958.
———. *The Athens of Demosthenes.* Cambridge: Cambridge University Press, 1952.
Meiggs, Russell. *The Athenian Empire.* New York: Oxford University Press, 1972.
Pickard-Cambridge, Sir Arthur W. *The Dramatic Festivals of Athens.* 2d edition. Oxford: Oxford University Press, 1968.
Robinson, Charles A., Jr. *Athens in the Age of Pericles.* Norman: University of Oklahoma Press, 1949†.
Seltman, Charles. *Athens: Its History and Coinage Before the Persian Invasion.* Chicago: Ares, 1974.
Zimmern, Alfred. *Greek Commonwealth: Politics and Economics in Fifth-Century Athens.* 5th edition. Oxford: Oxford University Press, 1931†.


SPARTA

Chrimes, K. M. T. *Ancient Sparta: A Re-examination of the Evidence.* Manchester: Manchester University Press, 1944.
Forrest, W. G. *History of Sparta, 950–192 B.C.* New York: Norton, 1969†.
Michell, Humphrey. *Sparta.* Cambridge: Cambridge University Press, 1952.

## Special Topics

Adcock, Sir Frank E. *The Greek and Macedonian Art of War.* Sather Classical Lectures, Vol. 30. Berkeley: University of California Press, 1957†.
Barker, Sir Ernest. *Greek Political Theory: Plato and His Predecessors.* Revised edition. London: Methuen, 1918; reprinted New York: Barnes & Noble, 1960†.
Bieber, Margarete. *The History of the Greek and Roman Theater.* 2d edition. Princeton: Princeton University Press, 1961.
Bonner, Robert J., and Smith, Gertrude E. *The Administration of Justice from Homer to Aristotle.* 2 vols. Chicago: University of Chicago Press, 1930–38; reprinted, Westport, Conn.: Greenwood, 1969.
Cary, Max. *The Geographic Background of Greek and Roman History.* Oxford: Oxford University Press, 1949.
Cary, Max, and Warmington, E. H. *The Ancient Explorers.* New York: Dodd, Mead, 1929.
Casson, Lionel. *The Ancient Mariners, Seafarers and Sea Fighters in the Mediterranean in Ancient Times.* New York: Macmillan, 1959.
———. *Ships and Seamanship in the Ancient World.* Princeton: Princeton University Press, 1971.

Daube, David. *Civil Disobedience in Antiquity*. Edinburgh: Edinburgh University Press, 1972.

De Ste. Croix, Geoffrey E. *The Origins of the Peloponnesian War*. Ithaca: Cornell University Press, 1972.

Ehrenberg, Victor. *From Solon to Socrates: Greek History and Civilization during the Sixth and Fifth Centuries B.C.* 2d edition. New York: Barnes & Noble, 1973†.

Finley, M. I., ed. *Slavery in Classical Antiquity: Views and Controversies*. Cambridge: Heffer, 1960.

Finley, M. I., and Picket, H. W. *The Olympic Games: The First Thousand Years*. Revised edition. New York: Viking, 1976.

Forrest, William G. *The Emergence of Greek Democracy, 800–400 B.C.* New York: McGraw, 1967†.

Freeman, Kathleen. *The Murder of Herodes and Other Trials from the Athenian Law Courts*. London: MacDonald, 1946; reprinted, New York: Norton, 1963†.

Gardiner, Edward N. *Athletics of the Ancient World*. Oxford: Oxford University Press, 1930.

Hill, George F. *Ancient Greek and Roman Coins: A Handbook*. Revised edition. Chicago: Argonaut, 1964.

Johnson, Marie, ed. *Ancient Greek Dress*. Including *Greek Dress* by Ethel Abrahams. Chicago: Argonaut, 1964.

Jordan, Boromir. *The Athenian Navy in the Classical Period*. Berkeley: University of California Press, 1974†.

Kagan, Donald. *The Archidamian War*. Ithaca: Cornell University Press, 1974.

Kurtz, Donna C., and Boardman, John. *Greek Burial Customs*. Ithaca: Cornell University Press, 1971.

Larsen, J. A. O. *Representative Government in Greek and Roman History*. Berkeley: University of California Press, 1976†.

Lawler, Lillian B. *The Dance in Ancient Greece*. Middletown, Conn.: Wesleyan University Press, 1965; reprinted, Seattle: University of Washington Press, 1967†.

Lefkowitz, Mary R., and Fant, Maureen. *Women in Greece and Rome*. Sarasota, Fla.: Samuel Stevens Hakkert, 1977†.

Littman, Robert J. *The Greek Experiment: Imperialism and Social Conflict, 500–400 B.C.* New York: Harcourt Brace, 1974†.

Marrou, H. I. *A History of Education in Antiquity*. New York: Sheed & Ward, 1956.

Marsden, E. W. *Greek and Roman Artillery: Historical Development*. Oxford: Oxford University Press, 1969.

Myres, John L. *Geographical History in Greek Lands*. Oxford: Oxford University Press, 1953; reprinted, Westport, Conn.: Greenwood, 1974.

Pomeroy, Sarah B. *Goddesses, Whores, Wives and Slaves: Women in Classical Antiquity*. New York: Schocken Books, 1975†.

Pritchett, W. Kenrick. *The Greek States at War*. 2 vols. Berkeley: University of California Press, 1975.

Seltman, Charles. *Women in Antiquity*. New York: St. Martin's, 1956.

Slater, Philip E. *The Glory of Hera: Greek Mythology and the Greek Family*. Boston: Beacon, 1968†.

Tarn, W. W. *Alexander the Great*. Vol. I, *Narrative;* Vol. II, *Sources and Studies*. Cambridge: Cambridge University Press, 1948; reprinted, Boston: Beacon, 1956.

Webster, Thomas B. L. *Greek Theatre Production*. New York: Hillary, 1956.

Woodhead, A. Geoffrey. *Thucydides on the Nature of Power*. Cambridge, Mass.: Harvard University Press, 1970†.

# Index